Preface to Philosophy:

TEXTBOOK

THE MACMILLAN COMPANY
NEW YORK · BOSTON · CHICAGO · DALLAS
ATLANTA · SAN FRANCISCO

MACMILLAN AND CO., Limited
LONDON · BOMBAY · CALCUTTA · MADRAS
MELBOURNE

THE MACMILLAN COMPANY
OF CANADA, Limited
TORONTO

Preface to Philosophy:
TEXTBOOK

William Ernest Hocking
Brand Blanshard
Charles William Hendel
John Herman Randall, Jr.

New York   THE MACMILLAN COMPANY   1947

PREFACE

Every man is a philosopher. Every man has his own philosophy of life and his special view of the universe. Moreover, his philosophy is important, more important perhaps than he himself knows. It determines his treatment of friends and enemies, his conduct when alone and in society, his attitude towards his home, his work, and his country, his religious beliefs, his ethical standards, his social adjustment, and his personal happiness.

Nations, too, through the political or military party in power, have their philosophies of thought and action. Wars are waged and revolutions incited because of the clash of ideologies, the conflict of philosophies. It has always been so. World War II is but the latest and most dramatic illustration of the combustible nature of differences in social and political philosophy.

Philosophy, says Plato, begins with wonder. We wonder about the destructive fury of earthquakes, floods, storms, drought, pestilence, famine, and fire, the mysteries of birth and death, pleasure and pain, change and permanence, cruelty and kindness, instincts and ideals, mind and body, the size of the universe and man's place in it. Our questions are endless. What is man? What is nature? What is justice? What is duty? What is happiness? What is God? Alone among the animals man is concerned about his origin and end, about his purposes and goals, about the meaning of life and the nature of reality. He alone distinguishes between beauty and ugliness, good and evil, the better and the worse. He may be a member of the animal kingdom, but he is also a citizen of the world of ideas and values.

Some of man's questions have been answered. Where the answer is clear, we call it science or art and move on to higher ground and a new vista of the world. Many of our questions, however, will never have final answers. Men will always discuss the nature of justice and right, the significance of evil, the art of government, the relation of mind and matter, the search for truth, the quest for happiness, the idea of God, and the meaning of reality.

The human race has reflected so long and often on these problems that the same patterns of thought recur in almost every age. We should know what these thoughts are. We should know what answers have been suggested by those who have most influenced ancient and modern thought. We shall want to do our own thinking and find our own answers. It is, however, neither necessary nor advisable to travel alone. Others have helped dispel the darkness, and the light they have kindled may also illumine our way.

This *Preface to Philosophy* does not pretend to be a complete introduction to philosophic thought. We say little here of logic (the science of accurate thinking), aesthetics (the study of ideal form or beauty), or epistemology (the theory of knowledge). Significant as they are, they can be put aside until we have first made our acquaintance with more immediate problems. Because of the critical importance of the ethical issues growing out of the present crisis of civilization, it has seemed wise to focus attention primarily on ethics and religion.

The four authors who have written this volume have worked closely together. They owe much to each other and much also to others. Professor Theodore M. Greene of Princeton University, Professor Ross Earle Hoople and Professor Raymond F. Piper of Syracuse University, Professor Mary Shaw and Dean Thomas R. McConnell of the University of Minnesota made many useful suggestions in the preparation of the original outline; and Professor Russell M. Cooper of the University of Minnesota and Professor Robert F. Davidson of Stephens College are among those who have been particularly helpful in the revision of the manuscript.

The *Book of Readings*, which is a companion volume, is also the outgrowth of cooperative action. The two volumes should be read and studied together.

Much of the confusion of contemporary life is due to the conflict of values and ends. A careful study of the text and readings should help to resolve that conflict. For here an attempt is made to promote clear and ordered thought about man and his progress, the individual and the good life, society and its problems, the significance of religion, and the nature of reality. The practice of critical reflection on these questions should be a major contribution to enlightened and effective citizenship in the postwar world.

WILLIAM PEARSON TOLLEY, EDITOR

TABLE OF CONTENTS

Part I. What Is Man?

Part II. Personal Ethics

Part III. Social and Political Philosophy

Part IV. The Meaning of Religion for Man

Part V. A World-View

PART I. WHAT IS MAN?

William Ernest Hocking

Harvard University

A. MAN AND ANIMAL

1. Man's Unique Interest in Himself

There is no sure way of telling what animals think about. But it seems safe to say that the human being gives more thought than any other animal *to himself*. He alone keeps diaries, uses mirrors, writes histories, makes innumerable comments on human nature, and develops such sciences as psychology and sociology. He alone speculates on the origin of his species on the earth, on what happens to the individual soul after death, and on what is to be the destiny of the race in the long future of the planet.

This interest of man in himself is a justified interest. Purely as a biological study, the human body is the most complex and interesting of all organic forms. There are animals that live longer; but there are none that live so much during their lifetime, and none which are capable of so great variety in behavior. No other creature has found ways of living in all climates, from equator to arctic zones. No other fits himself out with clothing, varying from season to season, place to place, and fashion to fashion. No other uses his sense organs to improve on his sense organs until he can hear his own whispers around the world and bring both the incredibly minute and the incredibly remote into his field of sight. No other land animal projects himself for long journeys under water and through the air. All this variety is a result of one asset — the human mind, with its inner resources of imagination. Is there any limit to these resources?

Some are ready to say that there is no limit, that the human mind is "infinite." This sounds more enthusiastic than instructive. Yet in one sense it is literally true. An individual may come to the end of his inventiveness. But the race never gives up. It keeps returning to old problems and getting new ideas for solving them.

Some old Greek thinker gave his people a bit of advice in two words, "Know thyself," a precept which they cherished among

the Seven Great Sayings.[1] Why did this seem to them so important? Partly because the natural trend of human curiosity is
outward: man begins his more systematic inquiries with the
objects of nature and contents himself, at first, with rather casual
self-observation, embodied in proverbs and folklore. Partly, however, because self-knowledge, taken seriously, proves to be difficult. On the face of it, nothing should be easier to know than
ourselves, and certainly nothing is more accessible. Everyone
has a sample of human nature in his own person, body and mind;
and surely every man knows his own mind: no one else can
tell him how *he* feels and thinks. In another sense, every man
is a puzzle to himself: there are things about him which his
friends may know better than he does. He may be overconfident,
and they can point out the dangers of conceit; he may be over-
diffident, and they can give him self-assurance. And there are
other riddles of human nature to which no one yet knows the
final answer: why human beings feel as they do, entertain wishes,
take likings or aversions, become excited or hold steady, remember some things and forget others, have nagging anxieties or
queer private superstitions or hunches about this or that or
strange bursts of confidence. For that matter, our simplest
mental operations — attending, learning, forming habits, imagining, deciding — are still not fully explained by any science.

The simplest of all tasks connected with self-knowledge ought
to be, one would think, to report what is in the mind at any
moment, since what we mean by the mind is simply the activity
of knowing, feeling, deciding, and so on, which makes up the
"stream of consciousness." It might be worth trying, to make
up a swift inventory of what is "in your mind" just now, under
such heads as:

Sensations, clear and obscure	Expectations
Feelings, agreeable and disagreeable	Thoughts
Tendencies to action	Imaginations
Memories	Beliefs

You will come on a number of difficulties. How much of what
you remember is in your mind? How much of what you know?
How much of what you think and believe? If these things are

[1] Book of Readings (hereafter abbreviated BR), No. 5, Plato, "Socrates' Defence of Himself."

not in mind at the moment, where are they? Perhaps we could use the idea of "subconsciousness" to include what we very well know but are not always thinking of? The word "mind" must cover both the conscious and the subconscious.

But the chief puzzle of human nature is its doubleness. It is both *mind and body*. These two are fused into one being so closely that it is impossible to say where the joint is! And yet the words "mind" and "body" do not mean the same thing.[1]

The body can be seen; no one will claim that he can see the mind. The body can be handled, weighed, measured, but not the mind. If anyone is under the momentary illusion that the brain and the mind are the same, let him consider whether he is prepared to take the chemical analysis of the mind, as he can of the brain.

But if we are not to think of the mind as a measurable object in space, how are we to think of it? A great deal of your philosophy will depend on how you answer this question.

There is a certain awkwardness in thinking *about* the mind, because the mind is usually occupied in thinking about other things, such as physical shapes. To think about the mind would therefore be *to think about the thinking*. Or, to complete the phrase, it would be to think about the thinking about other things. It is not surprising, then, that when men first began to think seriously about the mind, they conceived of it as a fine substance, like vapor or breath, spread through the body or concentrated in the heart. And we, on the same principle, are likely to think of the mind as having at least the physical attribute of location and consider it as being within the skull, as a functional activity of the brain. These conceptions trip over the fact that the mind is not the physical object thought about, but simply the *thinking* of that object. The difficulty is that the mind is so near to us, so identical with ourselves; and even here we are using the spatial metaphor of "near" to express the intimacy of mental process!

It is enough at present to see (a) that mind and body are not the same; (b) that they are inseparably joined in the living person; (c) that, to think truly of our own mind, we must manage

---

[1] BR, No. 16, Antoine de Saint-Exupéry, "A Flyer's Reflections in the Face of Death."

to think of thinking; (d) that since we cannot directly perceive the thinking of other people, we have to get at their minds by way of their bodies, their gestures, expressions of emotion, language. In the same way, we interpret the minds of animals.

2. Resemblances between Man and Animal

Men have always been interested in the resemblances between themselves and animals. In ancient times, they were inclined to read the likeness backward: animals are surprisingly like men. In modern times, they have been more inclined to read it forward: men are surprisingly like animals. The animal stories of India, Aesop's fables, the Uncle Remus stories use animals as exaggerating some trait in human nature; lion and fox become universal symbols of courage and cunning. So far as animals are like ourselves in mentality we can understand them, tame them, use them, and occasionally feel flattered when we win the confidence of a wild or timorous beast. As the bodily shape of the animal diverges from our own, the sense of understanding weakens. We feel remote from the psychology of the lobster, whereas the ape is almost too much like us for comfort, one reason no doubt why he is given a semidivine status by some Hindus.

During the last century, science has been interested in reading the continuities between animals and men, emphasizing everything in man that could be regarded as inherited from an animal ancestry.[1] Instead of holding to the traditional contrast, that man is governed by reason and animals by instinct, science has been busy showing traces of reason in animals and remnants of instinct in man. The word "instinct" needs watching. If the scientist uses it at all, he does not mean by it a mysterious and infallible guide to successful action. He means a complex series of actions (like the nest-building processes of birds or the stalking behavior of cats and hounds), which is hereditary in the sense that it is carried through, with little or no instruction, very much in the same way by all members of the species, to a result important for the life history of the animal.

Using the word "instinct" in this way, we find that the instinctive "round of life" in most higher animals strongly resembles

[1] Cf. BR, No. 6, James Harvey Robinson, "Characteristics of Early Man."

the broad outlines and motives of human life. There are at least three main elements in such a round: *nutrition*, including all the animal arts of getting food; *reproduction*, including the preliminary arts of wooing and preparing the shelter; and the *parental impulse*, directed to the care and rearing of offspring. It seems evident that all three of these impulses ought to be present, together with strong cravings and emotional satisfactions, if a species of animals is not to lose out in the struggle for survival. The human species would be no exception to this rule.

Accordingly, if we ask the question "What is it that human beings most care about?" we find that nature has already taken care of a good part of the answer. There is no need to instruct a boy, during the years when he is burning to grow up to man's powers and estate, that he has a "nutritive instinct" as an aid to getting command of his own capacities. There is no need to tell him, later on, that he wants to make a living (as a further stage of this same nutritive instinct). Or, still later, to find a mate, to beget children, care for them, and educate them. So far, the shape of human life corresponds fairly well with the animal program.

The picture is, of course, incomplete. In both man and animal there are two powerful auxiliary instincts, commonly referred to as fear and anger, leading respectively to flight or combat. Neither of these belongs to the regular routine of life (except in the case of beasts of prey); but when they are needed, they can use all the reserves of energy that nature is prepared to pour into their operation. There is also an instinct of curiosity, strong in animals that live more by their wits than by their physical powers, especially the ruminants (deer, cattle), apes, and man. And there is an important group of social instincts for social animals, including the simple gregariousness whereby birds of a feather and beasts of a stripe find their own sort, certain impulses to dominate or to follow leaders, and (especially strong in man) an impulse to achieve standing in one's community, for the benefit of his family as of himself.[1] This last-named impulse tends to grow in relative influence toward the latter end of life, when the nutritive instinct (with its development into "acquisitiveness") and the reproductive and parental instincts

[1] Cf. BR, No. 7, E. G. Conklin, "The Question of Racial Differences."

have achieved their ends.[1] All of these impulses have roots in
the animal kingdom, including (I suspect) the social concern for
community standing, if one can judge by the occasional behavior
of swagger cocks or champion bucks.

If we take all these facts together, the biological view of human
nature based on resemblances between man and animal does
throw much light on why we are as we are. For the nineteenth
century, it was the great source of illumination.

But it leaves many questions unanswered.

For example, human interests do not limit themselves to what
aids survival. No doubt hunger aids survival; but this does not
explain why eating and cookery develop into fine arts. The
human eye is an aid to survival, but who limits his interest in
what he sees to what aids survival? Or in what he hears? How
does music aid survival? So with curiosity. It is through knowledge, as Bacon said, that we master nature; but when has curiosity stopped at that point? It is hard to tell how the added
reach of the 200-inch reflector at Mount Palomar will aid human
survival. We shall be able to investigate with that telescope
ten times the volume of space hitherto accessible to our instruments. Someday, some of this knowledge may be useful; but
that is not why we take the trouble. It is because we want to
know what is there, and how the new data will affect our ideas
of the laws of the astro-physical universe. Human interest out-
runs any biological concern.

Again, no man feels bound to stick to the biological pattern.
Many deliberately break away from it. In some, scientific curiosity or ambition or some special lifework displaces all family
attachments. Others turn down the whole biological invitation,
taking the vows of poverty, chastity, and obedience, as devotees
of a religious life. There are some failures in these ambitious
efforts to spurn ambition; but there are some remarkable successes which show that the thing is possible. Biology does not
tell us how it is possible; there are no voluntary ascetics among
the animals.

The truth seems to be that the human mind is interested in
survival rather as an afterthought. A man eats because he
likes food; survival happens as an incidental result. The mind's

[1] Cf. BR, No. 11, Otto Klineberg, "The Original Drives of Human Nature."

interests are its own, not nature's; they tear away from every biological limitation. It may devote itself to ends which are clearly at odds with its biological welfare. In the interest of a friendship, a social loyalty, the fulfillment of an agreement, the testing of a medical theory, a man may deliberately risk his life. Here the biological explanation gives out.

In truth, the whole plausibility of this explanation vanishes if we ask the question whose answer has been taken for granted: why should any one want to survive? As a fact, we usually do want to survive; but that fact does not answer the question. If the only value of human existence is to take one's part in a round of life which repeats itself forever, the outlook may even become repellent. Unless the whole series of biological generations moves toward something, the sense drops out of the picture, and the sum of it is an incessant and profitless treadmill. The animal never asks this question; he makes no mental picture of the species, still less of any goal for the species. But the human being is definitely not content with the animal round: he insists in seeing some sense in the total trend of things.

For all these reasons, any real understanding of the human being and his interests must go on to consider the differences between man and the animals. Man can understand the animals; the animal can but dimly understand man, for whatever is most characteristic of the human being passes him completely by.

3. Differences between Man and Animal

Most definitions of man begin with the words "Man is an animal." They then proceed to mention what they regard as the most important difference which separates him from the other animals. Thus, Aristotle defined man as the animal that *reasons*. He also proposed that man is the "political animal," [1] i.e., the animal that builds societies going beyond the family to the more impersonal groupings of the village and the state. He added the remark that man is political because he has language. This seems to run afoul of the fact that all social animals — bees, ants, birds, ruminants — have some form of speech or communication. But Aristotle goes on to explain that human lan-

[1] Cf. BR, No. 49, sec. a, Aristotle, "Politics."

guage contains signs for general ideas, such as "justice"; and that without such ideas the kind of political society human beings build would be impossible. Animal societies often have a remarkable organization, and the conduct of their members is "lawful" in the sense of following definite lines of instinct; but we have no reason to suppose that any of them think out rules and change them from time to time, still less that they try to think out an idea of justice. On second thought, we can agree that Aristotle has lighted on an important point of difference.

Many other definitions have been proposed, more or less seriously. Man is the animal that laughs. Man is the animal that draws pictures. Man is the self-conscious animal. Man is the animal capable of shame, since no other animal shows signs of apology for its natural processes. Another definition comes nearer the center of the target: man is the animal with a moral sense; he is therefore capable of remorse and indeed of so much moral suffering that we occasionally fancy that a return to the animal condition would be a relief.[1]

But however man may overdo his moral anxieties, he would not willingly part with his capacity for being discontented with himself; for it is only through this characteristic discontent that his long history is distinguished from that of every other animal species by its progressiveness. Man's compunction is part of the secret of his growth. This brings us close to a definition of long standing — that man is the *animal with a soul*. This is an important proposal, but difficult until we know what is meant by the soul. We shall return to it.

Meantime, having before us numerous mental differences between man and animal, let us inquire more systematically, beginning with the main physiological differences.

4. Physiological Differences between Man and Animal

(a) *Man Is Mediocre, Nondescript, and Unfinished.* In physique, man is a mediocre animal. He has no great strength, no great

---

[1] See BR, No. 23, Walt Whitman, "Song of Myself":

> "I think I could turn and live with animals,
>   They're so placid and self-contained;
>   I stand and look at them long and long.
>   They do not sweat and whine about their condition;
>   They do not lie awake in the dark and weep for their sins.
>   Not one is respectable or unhappy over the whole earth."

speed of motion, no great keenness of eye, ear, or smell. He has no impressive organs of offense (as tusks, horns, claws) nor of defense (as tough hide or carapace). Nor has he special organic tools, such as the elephant's trunk or the beaver's tail.

He is nondescript in the sense that he is not marked out by nature for any distinctive way of life or habitat. The hippopotamus is designed for a river beast; man is only in a broad sense terrestrial. And he is unfinished at birth; his instincts do not carry him at once into successful techniques. A newborn calf will find its legs within a few minutes; the human infant struggles for months with the problem of locomotion.

This very unfinishedness is an advantage: it is man's opportunity for free adaptation to various and changing circumstances. Not having a fixed biological chart of living, he puts his own finishing touches on native impulse by shaping habits to the situation at hand. He can neither spin a web nor build a nest, but his shelters can be igloos, tepees, or thatch-huts as occasion requires.

(b) *Man Is Balanced*. The muscles of his front and back work opposite each other to hold him upright. This allows him not only a free pair of arms and a quick change of direction, but also an easy all-around survey. This is a physical symbol of his mental trait of "looking before and after" — using his memory of the past to anticipate the future.

In a similar way, some of his major instinctive impulses are balanced by counterimpulses, conferring a certain poise in place of animal impetuosity. Unless his impulses of acquisition, mating, and pugnacity had some kind of inner brake, it is hard to see how a stable social order on any large scale could have been started. In the case of pugnacity, there is an evident check even when the prudential element of fear is in abeyance. There is a restraint to be overcome before one passes from the exchange of words to the exchange of blows, a reluctance to break in on the habitual bodily inviolability of another individual. For the sex impulse also there is a well-marked sex-reticence, which not only makes necessary the universal arts of approach but leaves normal men and women for the greater part of the time sex-quiescent. For sex also, as for pugnacity, a certain set toward bodily isolation has to be overcome.

This kind of balance does not limit the energy of action, once action is started. It simply interposes a moment of hesitation; and hesitation gives a chance for the question: What on the whole do I prefer to do? Thus balance confers an element of freedom from the insistence of any one of the competing impulses.

(c) *Man Is Unified*. These numerous instinctive drives of which we have been speaking give the impression that the human self is rather a collection than a single being. Each instinct-name indicates a natural interest, and we get the idea that each of these has to be satisfied in due turn if we are to have a happy normal existence. On this showing, the human self appears more or less passive, being controlled now by hunger, now by fear, now by the ambition for social standing, as if each instinct were a self-operating force, an impression deepened by the word "drive." Animal life bears out this picture: each impulse has its place in the daily routine. There is a time for foraging, for domesticity, for sleep, and some time left to do nothing at all. No beast is oppressed by a crowded program.

But in truth the human being is neither so passive a creature nor so multiple. Take him in the midst of a day's work, with a crowd of impulses and interests competing for attention, and the illusion vanishes. Play impulses, love-making, food-getting are shunted off; nothing gets a hearing unless it belongs to the job in hand. It is not the impulses that fight it out among themselves; it is the man who decides. If there is any drive in the case, it is the man's own drive. It has a singleness and steadiness to which we give the name "purpose." Purpose is something of which the animal is incapable; man's capacity for it is recorded in unity of the organization of his nervous system.

For the high development of the human brain signifies, among other things, that whatever excitements serve as "stimuli" to the reflexes which enter into instinctive behavior *report themselves to that center*, submitting themselves to the consent, modification, or veto of that center. They do not run through wholly separate tracts either of nerve or muscle. They can gain their go-signal only as they combine with, or enhance, the going central-process, which corresponds physiologically to the purposive drive of the man.

This does not mean that purpose rides over instinct and pushes it out of the way. It means rather that purpose *uses* instinct. All the native impulses are a sort of raw material which can contribute to purpose. For in spite of their separate names, they are not wholly separate, even in their satisfactions. For example, curiosity is one impulse, and sociability is another. A man who shuts himself up in his laboratory to finish an experiment appears to be turning his back on sociability in order to satisfy his own curiosity. But is he? If his experiment brings out a new piece of truth which becomes common property, is he not satisfying his social interest also? But this matter is so fundamental for our understanding of human nature that we must give it separate attention.

5. The Several Impulses as Branches of One Impulse

Within the last two centuries, it has been frequently asserted, notably by Schopenhauer, Nietzsche, and Freud, that all impulses (or desires) are forms of one impulse (or desire). Schopenhauer included animals in his theory and held that all instincts are forms of the "will to live." Thus hunger is (consciously or unconsciously) a craving for bodily life and vigor. Pugnacity and fear are positive and negative ways of asserting the will to live in the presence of danger. Sex love carries a promise of adding to individual life but overshoots its mark and leads the individual to spend himself in contributing to the life of the race — in Schopenhauer's view a radical mistake! [1]

There was a deep insight here. But long before Schopenhauer, a Greek thinker had seen that all impulses are forms of one, and had given it a better interpretation. Plato saw that man is not satisfied with living; he asks the further question, Life *for what?* Plato's answer is, for creating or reproducing what we love. [2] All desires, he teaches in the most profound psychological analysis of ancient and of most modern times, are forms of love; and all love is an impulse to create, stirred by a vision of beauty, whether of persons or of ideas. There is something ineffably humble about love, for it confesses poverty, a want of something; and yet there is also something ineffably proud about it, for it

[1] Cf. BR, Nos. 10 and 17, W. MacNeile Dixon, "The Will to Live," and Paul Grabbe, "Psychoanalysis."

[2] Cf. BR, No. 45, Rabindranath Tagore, "Love or the Fulfilment of Life."

feels in itself the same capacity as that of the artist to give du-·
rable form to his vision or that of the legislator to coin into law
his idea of a better social order. Plato's belief was that this kind
of creation is what all desire really wants.

Now strangely enough, the man who in recent times has most
nearly caught this platonic idea is Nietzsche. He saw, as Plato
did, that the "will to live" is not enough to satisfy a man; living
must be *for* something. His idea was that our deepest impulse
is the need to have and exercise power; he therefore proposed
to substitute the "will to power" for the "will to live." Unfortunately he was not so clear as to what he meant by it: sometimes he seems to mean vehement self-assertion; sometimes vehement self-sacrifice for bringing about a better human type;
sometimes he touches the edge of Plato's perception of the creative power that lurks in love.

We can learn from all of these thinkers; but we must put
things in our own way. That which men most care about is to
count for something; what they most dread is to be futile, to be
a cipher, to be wasted. There is no universal will to power in
the sense of a craving to dominate others. But there *is* a universal will to power in the sense of a craving to achieve, to give
scope to one's ability, to contribute to the human scene through
one's ideas or work. The distinction is between power *over* and
power *for*. With this understanding we need not shun the phrase,
"the will to power."

Now our thesis is that when we see what the man is driving
at, we see what all the several instincts are driving at. Their
drives merge in the central stream of his will. Take "fear."
Nothing could look less like a will to power! Yet the whole business of fear is to get a man out of a place where he is powerless
into one where his powers can count. Take "curiosity"; it
makes for knowledge, and knowledge, for a being who can exert
power through ideas, is itself a form of power. Sex love is in
part what Plato thought it was — a premonition of creative
power; but he thought it was a preliminary and imperfect stage
of creativity through ideas; it is more than that. It is the discovery of a present power to assume charge of another life and
with that life to bring forth others, establishing a small society
in which all those ideas can be put to work. Love is the most

concrete form of the will to power *for others*. Thus all the major impulses work toward a common end. And in so far as that end is achieved, all those separate impulses are by that fact satisfied, and none of them requires a separate satisfaction.

To put it in a nutshell, an animal can be satisfied if it lives through the usual round of momentary activities and successes; a man can be satisfied only if he can create. And conversely, he can make out a satisfactory life if he has one adequate region of effectiveness, one full-sized outlet for his will to power. He can get on with a minimum of the success of special drives provided he can accomplish something, leave an effect in the world which is *his* effect. And if he has no such efficiency, no amount of side-long satisfactions can make him content.

This is why man is at once so vulnerable to social approval or disapproval and at the same time so able to stand by himself and to sacrifice almost anything to promote an idea which he believes needs his support or championship. This is the great thing about human nature, so easily overlooked by those who take their cues from animal impulse — its capacity for fanaticism. It is this sort of fanaticism which gave this country its first occupants. It was this force in them which, when we look at the fields they cleared, the miles of stone wall they built, the deep wells they drove into glacial till, the granite rocks they shaped and built into cellar walls and even pigpens, leads us to say, "They were men," and feel anything but sorry for them. Any set of values or satisfactions falls short of being human unless it is built around a self-respecting purpose that calls out the peculiar powers of the individual.

6. Whether Man Can Be Defined as the Animal with a Soul

We are now ready to pick up the question raised a little way back about the "soul." The soul, we thought, has something to do with the human capacity for self-criticism; it has also something to do with the sort of fanaticism we have been speaking of. We wish to consider what is meant by the soul. Let us approach this question by way of a trivial trait of human nature — man's capacity to be bored.

In the Near East one often sees donkeys following a circular path all day long as they work the shaft of a water-wheel. Their attitude expresses patience but not boredom. To a man, this type of work would be provocative first of tedium, then of rebellion, then of insanity. Why? Because the man's imagination would be busy with the things he was *not* doing. Again, animals, if they know they are going to die — which is doubtful — are not bothered by that fact. They make no will; they take out no insurance; they accept each day as so much time in hand and quite literally take no thought for the morrow. Man takes careful account of how much time he has and has *not*.

This means that man's mind sees things on their negative as well as on their positive side. And this is a result of seeing them as *parts of wholes;* for in the light of a totality, every partial fact has two reckonings — what it is and what it is not, what it lacks of being complete. Oftentimes the negative reckoning is the more important side of the truth. No animal is worried by its ignorance; for man, the knowledge of how much he does not know is his perpetual incentive to learn. He grows because on all sides he is aware of the unachieved. When we have a creature whose thought takes account of wholes, we have a radical step, perhaps the most radical step, in mental history.

If so, man can be defined as *the animal who thinks in terms of totalities.* Some word for "all" and some word for "the world" are found in all languages. There are also words for the negatives "not all," "absence," "emptiness," "silence," "nothing," "not enough." These terms separate human from all animal language. Man's early ideas of the whole of things, the universe, provide it with an imaginary rim, a limit of space, a beginning and an end in time. But as his restless thought experiments with this rim, he keeps moving it outward and finally faces the notion of "endlessness," of "infinitude."

Now the term "soul" has been used to indicate that there is an important gap between the animal and the human mind. And this gap has commonly been placed in man's moral nature, his capacity for self-judgment, and for "hitching his wagon to a star." I suggest that these qualities depend on the power we have now observed — the capacity to think of things and of himself in the frame of the whole in which they are placed, the infinite universe. With this understanding we may literally define man as the animal with a soul.

Sometimes the soul has been regarded as separate from the "mind," a sort of duplicate personality, with powers of a higher order than those of the ordinary self of the day's work. Such a separate and separable soul psychology has not been able to find; and some psychologists have hastened to conclude that there is no such thing as a soul, that the idea is at once useless and superstitious. This anti-soul temper has been useful in reminding us that no soul could be of any use to us which was not identical with our self. It is not something else than the mind; it is the mind reaching out to its limit. It is not a different person; it can only be a different mode of activity.[1] *The soul is the self of man engaged in getting its bearings in the total universe.*

Once we see this, as the defining difference of the human mind, we understand many of the other attempted definitions. We understand why man is the animal that writes biographies and histories; for when a group of creatures begins to accumulate what it learns in the form of a tradition, that is a sign of a need to build up a total of knowledge adequate to a total world. And if it is said that man is the animal that laughs, we understand that while many an animal shows signs of glee, it is only man who can feel the sometimes ludicrous contrast between his limited powers and the infinite reach of his thought. And if man is said to be the animal capable of fanaticism in the service of an idea, we can understand that it is only the life of an idea that can give scope to a will to power reaching beyond one's own life into the vistas of the time ahead.[2]

B. THE CULTURAL ACHIEVEMENTS OF MAN AND THEIR PERILS

7. Man as the Maker of Culture

Seeking to extend his control through the future, man has a vested interest in whatever is permanent. He takes a peculiar

[1] BR, No. 15, Thomas Aquinas, "The Nature of the Soul." "The soul by its very essence is act." It may be noted that St. Thomas, following Aristotle, uses the word "soul" for the total self, the equivalent of the Latin *anima*, which, of course, is St. Thomas' word.

[2] BR, No. 19, W. MacNeile Dixon, "The Wonders of the Human Self."

pleasure in any product of his own which he thinks will last. Some of his earliest works are durable simply because they are hard, like his flint implements. But for some of them the materials were chosen because he considered them durable — his stone monuments, tombs, and architecture, his metallic tablets, ornaments, and sacred vessels. Even his paper he may have thought a permanent material; some of his papyri, in the easy climate of Egypt, have lasted upwards of four thousand years. One of the oldest, the Papyrus Prisse, dates from about 2500 B.C.

But the products which have proved most durable are of a much more fragile fabric, namely, his ideas. When an idea "takes hold" in a social group, is remembered and transmitted, especially when it modifies the habits of the group, it may become practically imperishable. No one knows just how the domestication of animals began, but at one time, many thousands of years ago, it was a new idea which revolutionized human economy; and all the subsequent arts of taming and breeding beasts, however altered in technique, continue the life of that notion.

What we call culture is that working of ideas into the patterns of social life so that the freer human interests are not only maintained but developed continuously — the sciences, the technical arts, the fine arts, the customs and laws, the history and the religion.

It is not the purpose of a study of philosophy to tell the fascinating story of human culture; that is for the growing science of anthropology and for the special histories of the several arts and sciences. The business of philosophy is with the judgment of culture, as a part of our knowledge of man: What does it mean? How much have we achieved? How much is left to do? Have we run into mistakes? Are we in danger?

During the past century, there was very little disposition to ask the last two questions about our so-called western civilization. We had come a long way, and we were doing well. We looked ahead with self-confidence. Science was carrying on a successful campaign against the remaining mysteries of the universe and the remaining ills of human life. It knew how to proceed, and the goal was not too far beyond sight. The political situation seemed to confirm this complacency. The Orient

continued to accept the leadership of the West. It is true that
China had its periods of fitful and futile revolt against foreigners
in general. It is true, also, that there were disturbances in Russia, and that Tolstoi was little satisfied with anything in the
established order around him, not even with politics or religion.
But Japan was well-disposed to learn of the West and to enter
quietly the avenues of trade. India was presenting no problem.
No one appeared to realize that revolutionary forces were gathering throughout the East which in a dozen years would unseat
the Manchus in China and mark the beginning of a critical
challenge by the Orient, not only of its own old ways but also
of the ways of the West.

The war of 1914 confirmed in the mind of many a thoughtful
observer, both in the Orient and in the West, the view that
western culture was in some way unsound. Oriental scholars
began to bethink themselves that their own cultures, though they
had been long stagnant, had nevertheless shown stability superior
to anything else in the world. Indian civilization had been continuous since 1500 B.C. and Chinese civilization since perhaps
3000 B.C. Some argued that western individualism was wrong,
some that industrialism was wrong, some that the faith in science
was wrong, some that the whole spirit of material strength was
wrong, some that western religion was wrong. On November 11,
1931, a new Buddhist temple was opened at Sarnath, near
Benares in India. At the ceremony a Hindu pundit, head of the
Sanskrit College in Calcutta, made an address in which he said
that while Christianity professed to be a religion of good will
among men, the late war had shown its lack of conviction; only
Buddhism had succeeded in actually spreading that spirit. But
already Japan, a Buddhist-Shintoist power, had begun in Man-
churia to tear down the old fabric of Asiatic peace.

We can therefore not approach the study of the meaning of
human culture in a spirit of self-congratulation nor in the belief
that something called "evolution" or "progress" is bound to
take place. Neither shall we assume, with Spengler, that our
civilization is necessarily in for disaster. Our problem is to examine its factors for the good they promise and to praise where
praise is due. But we must also recognize the general rule of
experience, that every advance brings new problems and new

dangers. If we wish our best achievements to be secure, we must know what is permanently valid in them, what is subject to error, and where vigilance is required.

8. Language

The oldest of the permanent magazines of human thought is language itself. Before writing was invented, men had to trust their ideas, however memorable, to vocal speech. They did so with extraordinary confidence. Even after writing was invented, some of the greatest thinkers of the race contented themselves with talking to a few young men. Buddha, Socrates, Jesus, Epictetus did no writing out of their own thoughts; neither did Confucius, though he edited the ancient classics of China. Yet today we know, or think we know, what those men thought, in spite of the fact that words change their meanings from century to century. For when language changes, language records the change, and we can make our dictionaries of dead tongues — ancient Sanskrit, early Egyptian — with reasonable confidence.

Thus it is through language that human societies can preserve and accumulate the stuff of thought, the raw material of all we call culture. No one person can create a language or even a word. For while every new word is likely to be the invention of some individual, it only becomes a part of language when it is accepted and used by his social group. A word is of no use if it is only understood by one person; it must express a meaning which is common to many. The English language is the creation of the English people; it reveals the experiences and thoughts which have become the common property of that people. A language is rich or poor as the culture of a people is rich or poor.

As an instrument, language is a two-way affair: it is a means whereby we make our own ideas known; it is also a means whereby we become acquainted with the ideas of others. These others need not be present, if language is written; nor need they be living. The language record is a repository of thought, unlimited in space and time, far exceeding the capacity of any single human being to explore; and through it he in turn may address persons not yet living.

How a newcomer, a human infant, works his way into the use and understanding of language is a process which it is easier to take for granted than to explain. If minds were directly open to one another, language would be unnecessary. Since they are not, there is never any way of directly comparing what one person means by a word with what anyone else means by it. It remains to the end uncertain whether what I call blue corresponds to what you call blue, even if we agree in applying the word to the same object. The learner is in a far more difficult position. No one can explain to him, in the first place, the difference between sounds which are voluntarily used as signs for something else and sounds which are simply sounds. No one can explain to him the scope of a word—whether "cat" means this individual animal or any four-footed beast or some smaller group. The whole affair of learning language is a series of unguaranteed risks. As we analyze it, our respect for the mental prowess of the human infant goes up.

Once the idea of language is gained, there is no difficulty in adding to the vocabulary. Nor is there any difficulty for the group in finding new signs for new customs, new ideas, new equipment. There are plenty of available sounds. Among all the languages, there are astonishingly few accidental duplications of word sounds; and there are thousands of unused tonal possibilities. But words are seldom coined by arbitrary choices among left-over sounds; they are lighted on for some real or fancied fitness. The word "cough" somehow fails to fit a sneeze; it would hardly do to speak of the "cackle" of a lion or the "roar" of a hen. Even in scientific nomenclature, where language has to keep pace with discovery, some trace of suggestion is sought: radium, radio, helium, electron, neutron. . . .

But besides the new objects, there are new ideas. How do these get their words?

Part of the answer comes from the fact that new ideas are never unrelated to old ones: the new words correspondingly branch out from the old words. Not so long ago "liberalism" was a new word, begotten when liberal thought became a political tendency; "totalitarian" is newer, a self-made word; "science" is an ancient word used in a modern way for a part of its ancient self; "profiteers" and "boondogglers" represent new abusers of old functions.

Another part of the answer comes from the fact that sound

shapes, and the sort of vocal effort required to make them, seem to resemble the unique qualities of the new experience. Every region develops local tempers and needs local words. New England had to develop "spunk" and "gumption"; its kitchens had a place for "chankings." The word "slang" is an American invention made to cover a brood of American inventions, now achieving dictionaries of its own.

Before the new words arrive, the idea must have been there, struggling for expression in misfit clothing. Existing thought is always a stage ahead of existing language. Shelters for homeless ideas are needed: slang and poetry provide these, in different ways. Slang is a sort of refugee camp of temporary shelter, for in no field is there so much novelty or so much passing out. Poetry does it by the shape into which it assembles words and the effect of the united *sound* of the chosen words on the *sense* of the picture — what Robert Frost calls "the sound of sense." The form and music of the poem touch each word with a new quality, so that the whole poem amounts to a single word of a higher order, saying something never said before and, if it is a good poem, saying it for all time.

There is no one word for waning-moon-in-the-morning-sky, but this by Father Tabb says it:

> Behold, whatever winds prevail,
> Slow westering, a phantom sail,
> The lonely ghost of yesterday,
> Unpiloted, pursues its way.

9. The Perils of Language

A perfect instrument is one whose use can become unconscious. So long as one has to think of the tool and of how he is handling it, neither is he master of it nor the tool a good servant. On this scale of perfection, human speech stands high. The dangers of language arise chiefly from the fact that it has become so nearly perfect that we expect it to be entirely so. We tend, for example, to take it for granted (a) that when a person speaks, he speaks his mind; (b) that for every word there is an idea; (c) that for every idea there is a word.[1]

(a) The natural effort of language is to speak what is in the mind. But, since language is a voluntary deed, the speaker or

[1] Cf. BR, No. 14, Susanne K. Langer, "The Power and Peril of Language."

writer may use it to misrepresent or divert or conceal. It is because of language that man is able to lie. Political democracy is peculiarly dependent on the meeting of minds between governors and governed; peculiarly sensitive, therefore, to any disposition of governing persons to reserve truth while professing candor.

(b) The presumption is that for every word there is an idea. The learners of language often take on words in the hope that the appropriate idea will arrive in due time, as when they repeat the formulas of politeness, piety, and patriotism. Usually this hope is fulfilled; sometimes the word continues to represent rather the vague aspiration for an idea than its possession. We have painfully to learn that the grasp of meanings runs through a wide gamut of degree, and that a vain show of ability to use in grammatical sentences the words "quantum," "unconscious," "the inscrutable," or professional Latin, or the names of national ideals does not ensure that there are ideas behind the utterance. It is not only in mediaeval times that "potent" words, whether understood or not, had charms, or were charms, to sway the minds of men and spirits.

(c) Most dangerous is the assumption that for every idea there is a word. It lies in the nature of language that it can convey only common ideas; whatever is peculiar to oneself cannot be put into words. There is an ultimate loneliness of the mind only mocked by the necessities of speech, which, using the common coin, must misrepresent what is unique to any person.

In a somewhat similar way, it is probable that the most important truth about the world is something for which we have as yet neither words nor syntax. Philosophical thought, as an effort to get closer to the ultimate truth of things, has to be constantly on its guard against the pitfalls of current speech.[1] We have already seen the strong tendency to think of the mind in terms of matter. Language aids this tendency, for most of the words expressing mental "states" and qualities — the keen intellect, the broad mind, the foursquare character — are metaphors taken from the physical world; the word "spirit" itself at first meant breath.

[1] Cf. BR, No. 13, Stuart Chase, "Semantics: How Language May Deceive Us."

10. Language of Emotion

We have been speaking of language as expressing ideas; but language also expresses feelings. All the epithets of praise and blame, all the words of quality, esteem, dislike, repulsion, all the words of reproach and punishment with which language can sting, or the words of appeal with which it can incite — these are fundamental, perhaps *the* fundamental part of language. The language of emotion is spontaneous and aboriginal; it waits for no mental grasp of the language set-up. It is not separate from ideas, though it needs to be separately mentioned. It is not separate because there are no feelings without ideas, and no ideas without feelings. It is impossible to maintain a perfectly feelingless language as some reformers of speech would have us do.

What the reformer is trying to get rid of is prejudice. Prejudice is the fixed association of an emotional quality with a factual term. Factually, a "native" is a man born in the region; but when a colonizer refers to "the natives," a badge of inferiority sticks to the word. The "accused" is not condemned until he is proved guilty; but the "accused" and the "prisoner at the bar" are already tainted in the public mind. After a time, there is a strong motive to get new terms to escape prejudice. But the retreat is seldom successful for more than a short time. The undertaker only temporarily escapes by calling himself a "mortician"; or the loan-shark by offering "private personal accommodation"; or the scavenger by becoming a "department of public sanitation." The cure cannot be found in mere change of language; it has to begin with the feelings themselves.

As for language, we do not want a language devoid of emotional color: a desiccated language would be empty of the most important burden of speech. Poetry, oratory, exhortation, ritual — all require the increasingly perfect fitting of language to the justice of feeling. It showed deep insight when Confucius said that the right ordering of human societies must begin by "giving things their right names," which means attaching to them the right feelings. If we call "graft" the "intelligent use of opportunity," the chance of honest politics in our community grows dim.

11. Science and Technology

Any creature that learns from experience is assuming that nature follows laws. For if any creature, once burned, thereafter avoids getting into fire, it is because of the belief that what has burned once will burn again. Animals and men can build habits solely because they act on the assumption that nature has ways that can be depended on.

Only man attempts to formulate this reliable behavior of nature and store it up in language. Much of it runs immediately into his practical arts — that copper can be beaten and melted, that corn paste can be cooked into bread, that ash wood makes a good bow — and gets no separate place as "science," though it *is* science. But there are also freer notions of nature's ways, especially of stars and seasons, and strange conjectures about "secrets of nature" — recipes, philters, and cures — known only to those who can penetrate the magical center of things. There is nothing wrong about the main belief on which "magic" was founded — that nature is deep and intricate and that the human mind is called on to fathom the mystery. Its chief error was in its guess as to the kind of power which nature was using. Magic, too, is a sort of science, and if this is granted, we can say that there is no such thing as an unscientific tribe of men.

The interest in mathematics is at first quite independent of the interest in laws of nature. It has more to do with trade, war, and booty. But it also has a free field of its own — the first form of science which, because it is wholly the work of the mind, we call "abstract." Some animal minds can apparently "count" a limited number of objects, seeming to know whether the eggs or the cubs are all there. But man reaches the point of separating the numbers from the objects numbered, and later on shapes from the objects which have shape; and playing with these ideas he sets up the sciences of arithmetic and geometry. Putting numbers and shapes through their possible variations and running them to their limits, he discovers types of order and beauty endless in interest. Mathematics is the progressive discovery of the meaning of what man himself has done when he coins the notions of number, boundary, line. It is the oldest scientific interest which has been effectively universal on the planet; for contributions to it had been made by China, India, Persia, and Egypt before the brilliant Greek period began. And then the Arabs gave us an algebra without which modern mathematics would be unthinkable.

It was in modern times that these two branches of science, the concrete and the abstract, came into a full working partnership; and "modern times" are largely made by the consequences of that merger. For it was this which gave science its methods and got rid of cumbersome rubbish. When the laws of nature were conceived to operate with a perfect exactitude, so that everything truly scientific must be measurable, *everything not measurable had to be cleared out.* Science is interested in vibrations and vibration numbers, not in the sounds and colors that may appear to ear and eye. These qualities concern the mind, but they are not "in nature." Ellipses may be handsome curves; but the planetary orbits are elliptical not on account of their beauty, but because this is what the mathematics of the laws of motion requires. Science specializes in quantity and leaves the qualities of things to human likes and dislikes. The wishes and preferences of men have to be set aside; likewise all spiritual or purposive agencies in nature; and therewith magic has to go, and miracle, from the scientific contemplation of nature.

The rule for mastering nature, said Francis Bacon, is to "obey her," that is, to observe events and their connections with an absolutely disinterested care. Easy as this may sound, it was for its day a high achievement, and not more a mental achievement than a moral achievement. It meant keeping man's self-interest and self-importance rigorously out of his study of nature's ways. Modern science, we may say, is founded upon a methodical unselfishness.

It is indeed an unselfishness which has paid huge dividends in the applications of science. We are today likely to look to science for the cure of every inconvenience. Fortified by this great instrument of human self-help, man has often been ready to dismiss the gods as superfluous in a world of natural law and order.

12. Perils of Science

Science may fairly be called the most brilliant, substantial, and complete of human successes in the field of culture. If pov-

erty and disease are not yet mastered, the principles for their
mastery appear to be in hand. It is not to be wondered at that
some scientists in a justified enthusiasm should say, in effect,
"Trust everything to us." Yet to claim omnipotence for science
is grossly unscientific. Wiser scientists are hesitant about accepting a responsibility which might leave science credited not only
with advancement but also with a possible collapse. Are there
perhaps some things which science in its nature is not fitted to
do or to understand? Two questions, in particular, are raised:

(a) Granted that science deals only with quantity, with energies, distances, velocities, which can be measured, what then
becomes of the qualities of the world, which are there *for us*, if
not in the physical facts? In disregarding them, does science
confess itself incomplete as an account of the world we live in?

If we keep human preferences out of the picture, disease is as
good a scientific fact as health, ugliness is there as much as
beauty, and there is no scientific difference between a wrong
situation and a right one. Nature produces the underlying facts
with the same precision and indifference in either case. In order
to master disease, the physician must, as Bacon advised, take the
disease precisely as nature does: he must forget his squeamish-
ness and plunge into the facts, with no eye for anything but
cause and effect. A foul condition may be a magnificent scientific specimen.

But after he has done his "objective" inquiry, then as a physician his preferences must come back: he must become a fighter
of disease. Science must be carried on in a spirit of detachment;
life cannot be. It is for a purpose that man sets purpose aside.
Then scientific inquiry can only be an interlude in the war
against the qualities we call evil and for the qualities we call
good: science cannot be the primary guide of life.

(b) Can science explain the scientist? The scientist is a self-
forgetful being, especially when he is occupied with the behavior
of the physical world. But when he becomes a psychologist, can
he continue to forget his purposes and preferences? Is he to
explain them, too, as matters of cause and effect, and is all
mankind to be so explained? Does this mean that all our wishes
are what they have to be, as well as all our thoughts, and that
nature, which produces them all with complete indifference,

whether they are right or wrong, true or false, produces them
with the same necessity in either case? Are a man's mistakes,
mental and moral, as inevitable as his going right?

If the answer to these questions is affirmative, two results
follow: (a) Human life is, in the long run, devoid of meaning,
for physical nature will eventually swallow up the whole of
man's work and achievement and with complete unawareness
that anything of value has come or gone.

(b) Human purpose has no real effect on the course of events,
for it is physical nature which produces the purpose and the
thoughts which guide the purpose, be they right or wrong.
Hence it is, in the end, nature which does all "our" doings.
The feeling that *we* are doing something has as much validity
as the feeling of a small boy pedalling a velocipede which is
being pulled along by parental horsepower. Praise and blame
addressed to men are impertinent; addressed to nature, nonsense.

These are serious consequences. It is not unimportant how
a man has to think of the effectiveness of his own choice and
purpose. Nor is it unimportant whether the moral judgments
of justice and injustice, which have had so much to do with the
progress of mankind, are all fallacious, since all praise and
blame are footless. We shall have to meet these issues on their
own ground.[1]

But meanwhile we may remind ourselves of what we know.
We know that man is, in essence, a doer. As a doer, he works
towards ends. Whether or not nature has ends, man must set
up his own. Once he has done so, nothing in the universe
remains indifferent. It is this view of the universe as charged
with quality and meaning which must include the view of science, not the view of science which must include — and dena-
ture — the view of purpose.

13. The Practical Arts: Technology

In working toward his ends, man receives from his inheritance
of instinct an initial push-off; but instinct does very little toward
shaping the actual processes of human behavior. In one respect,
however, nature has made man a shaper of his own instinctive

[1] Cf. Part V of this book, "A World-View."

life. Man's free arms and the shape of his hand, with its opposable thumb, not only enable but invite him to manipulate objects to eke out his own limited physical powers.

Tools and weapons are transportable extensions of the body. A projectile is an extension of the reach of the arm; and, like the hammer, it needs a hardness which the hand lacks. Hence these early tools of flint — mauls, arrows, spearheads. But, like language, a tool is born of an idea; it is, as we say, an "invention."

Behind all the special ideas which devise special tools, there is one master-idea: it is that sequences of cause-and-effect found in nature can be deflected (like sluiceways for waterpower) or lifted out of their context to serve human purposes. Let us call this the idea of *displaceable causality*. For example, a heavy falling body will strike a powerful blow, but not, in general, where we want it. But let us tie this heavy body to the end of a stick, and we can place its causality where we will — we have the hammer. Simple as this notion is, it is all but absent among the animals. With man it becomes a systematic program for using nature against nature, making a running stream lift its own water into an aqueduct, making the heat of a fire harden a clay vessel to stand between the fire and food. It is this idea which makes man, in the end, the maker of machines and of machines for making machines, until, as some think, it is this tool-making capacity which most marks out the human type of intelligence.

Since man keeps reshaping the ways in which he reaches his ends, his actual work habits are products of human device rather than of natural suggestion. Hence we refer to them collectively as "the arts."

Now a large part of what we call the triumph of science consists in the improvement of the practical arts. It seems a truism that we cannot have too much of such increased mastery of physical nature. Its extent is one of the obvious measures of civilization.[1] Lack of such mastery is the most available definition of "backwardness." And these advances, which we call "material," are never merely material. If they give the average man longer life, greater leisure, better health, a roomier period of education, higher standards of living, these are so many addi-

[1] Cf. BR, No. 8, Baker Brownell, "Man's Alliance with Nature."

tions to his freedom. It is not political advance alone, it is technology, that is setting man free. As he is free from disease, drudgery, and fatigue, he is free for other things. For what things?

It is here that we have to speak of the perils of this aspect of our culture; for it may well be that the advance of technology has exceeded the advance of character and imagination.

14. Perils of Technology

We have greater freedom, but what are we prepared to do with it? What are the wealthy doing with their wealth and the leisured with their leisure? These matters, we say, are a man's own business. We talk about the right to "the pursuit of happiness" as one of the inalienable rights of man. True enough; but what is our conception of happiness? If a man has anything in his head or his soul to do with his added freedom, he now has the means to do it. If he has not, he can make himself more vulgar than the beasts. Without freedom there can be no good life. But freedom does not insure that the good life will be lived.

Unless there is an inner critic of the quality of happiness, there is no assurance that the use of freedom will turn civilization upward rather than downward. This being the case, how men do actually use the fruits of technology, including their new freedom, ceases to be purely private business and begins to concern society.[1]

Now a part of the suggestion of what the quality of happiness may be comes from a neighboring aspect of culture known as "the fine arts." These arts begin (as in decoration and architecture) by adding a touch of unnecessary perfection to something useful for other ends. They lead to such activities as music, painting, sculpture, poetry, which appear to exist solely because they are enjoyed for their own sakes. They are a part of the end for which life exists rather than means to any further purpose.

If we look back on older civilizations, we are more apt to judge their degree of advancement by the level of their fine arts than by their technology. If in our own case we reverse this order, this may be because we have to some extent lost our grip on

[1] Cf. BR, No. 18, John Ruskin, "Tools or Men."

what the fine arts have to do for the life of a community. We must give that point some attention.

15. The Fine Arts

Fine art is a language of the feelings. Feeling itself is transitory: whether commonplace or significant, feeling passes. Significant feeling is not separable from thought. It is significant because it is aroused by moments of especially clear perception or insight. The business of fine art is to capture and perpetuate moments of significant feeling.

To do this, it attempts to embody them in some kind of medium that will last, though the effort itself seems a sort of contradiction in terms: the feeling-and-insight together must be set into stone, wood, paint-on-wall, paint-on-canvas, recorded sound, repeatable drama. Music moves most directly with feeling and, being itself a passage through time, comes to an end. But it can be remembered, and, like folksong, be carried through generations; or, if it is written in score, can be renewed, as long as it has something to say to its hearers. The interest of such records, whether of music or painting or other art, is not that they reproduce past feeling, but that they reveal the *possibilities of feeling* and lift the human mind, at least for the time, out of its besetting drag toward the level of commonplace, dullness, apathy, animality.[1]

Fine art has something in common with play (they usually go together in our devices for amusement), music with everything. Both stand in some contrast to work. In work, you have a special result to accomplish; you are up against a real resistance; when that resistance is overcome you have no reason and no wish to repeat the process. In play, you are not aiming to create a result; you have a resistance to meet which is artificially tempered to your powers, so that you have a fair chance to overcome it; and when you have thus tried yourself, you can enjoy the idea of doing it again.

Now fine art also is concerned with the resistances which the world offers to human wishes. Like work, it accepts the resistance as experience offers it; like play, it shows the resistance as overcome or as understood. Dance, which may be play and

[1] Cf. BR, No. 20, Helen H. Parkhurst, "Art as Man's Image."

fine art at once, does not seek to escape the pull of gravity which restrains motion, but through rhythm seeks to accord with it, so that gravity becomes an aid to grace. Art interprets the meaning of hampering conditions and thus foreshadows the human future.

Fine art begins as a purely private experience, a stirring of the artist's imagination, very likely about some theme no one else has ever been stirred by — a broken old woman, a few frenzied fiddlers, a drenching fog at Battersea. What makes him an artist is not the oddity of his subject: it is his ability to see, and his responsibility to show, an element of the mind's mastery in that accidental context. He has to exhibit the possible glory of the imperfect, the touch of the universal, which lights up the odd and local. Hence his product is, or ought to be, an invitation to largeness and a prophecy.

That is why art is one of the treasures men accumulate. It is full of the flavor of particular regions — Chinese or Indian, Persian or Mexican, Dutch or Scottish; yet it belongs to all men, as something which war itself ought not to destroy. For wherever it originates, it keeps for all men the heroic moments of human feeling.

Now if art does its job, it works against the tendency of amusement and the conception of happiness to run downhill. Its danger is simply stated, but deep-going: that it will itself fuse with recreation, without insight and without purpose. If it has nothing to say, it may become nothing more than a vain parade of the subjective fantasies of the artist, a public psychoanalysis of a twisted subconsciousness. If a people's artists see nothing beneath the surface of things, if they have nothing to report but the gay colors of human driftwood, they contribute more than their share to the general sense of meaninglessness which accompanies social decay. Because art, as the one language everyone understands without barrier of tongue, is that to which men instinctively look for their wider and uniting horizons.[1]

16. Religion

The soul we have defined as the mind of man engaged in getting its bearings in the total universe. Religion is an encour-

[1] Cf. BR, No. 21, Maxwell Anderson, "Whatever Hope We Have."

agement and aid in defining those bearings. It is a practical relation established between man and the totality with which, in some way, he is destined to deal.

That totality, taken in its physical aspect, is not reassuring. To become aware, as man does, of an endless stretch of space and time beyond what is within his corporate control is a disturbing thought. It is just because of his intelligence and responsibility that he cannot banish his awareness of the unexplored and uncontrolled margin. It is to the credit of the human mind that it is beset by a fear which does not haunt the animals; man alone is capable of cosmic anxiety.

Now this trouble is not religion: it is philosophy. Religion is the cure of the trouble, or at least its relief. For religion thinks of the universe not in terms of "It," but in terms of "Thou." It exists when man apprehends, beyond or within the dark reaches of his environment, a controlling power or powers in some measure akin to himself. If they are not personal, they are at least responsive. Man cannot master the totality of nature, either now or at any future time. Religion suggests to him a vicarious mastery through association with those powers. Religion is man's assertion of hope in the great world. And with this reassurance comes an element of obligation. There is a right way of living which it is necessary to find. Religion becomes a passionate concern for right living, conceived as a cosmic demand.

Religion thus takes the human mind at the point of its farthest reach, i.e., the human soul, and keeps it from slipping back into anything less than the full human stature. In this respect it cooperates with fine art as an "inner critic of the quality of happiness." For its view of the right way of living reminds the human being that he cannot be happy on purely animal or economic terms. It is an enlargement of his ambition, for it indicates how his life may be significant, not futile, even in the vast sweep of the cosmos.

17. Religion and Fine Arts

Religion and the fine arts have always worked together. In a sense, religion has mothered the arts, since all of them — poetry and myth, dance and music, architecture and sculpture, paint-

ing, ritual, and drama — have gained their first important
themes and practice in the service of religion. This period of
infancy and apprenticeship was bound to pass, and all the arts
declare independence and set up secular interests of their own.
But the existence of secular music and painting does not bring
religious music and painting to an end. They remain as a part
of the total fact of art and also as a part of the total fact of religion.

For religion requires art. It needs it even as a language to
express what it has to say about the world, since the most important truth about the world cannot be fully put into literal speech.[1]
It is best expressed in figure and analogy, i.e., in "symbol";
and the language of art is the language of symbol.

But religion differs from art in that it cannot be content with
the language of symbols alone. The ultimate questions about
human destiny are too serious and searching to be dealt with
solely in figures of speech or through the imaginative suggestions
of ritual. There are three questions which require a more literal answer, even though the answer cannot be complete:

(a) Considering the whole universe as arising from a single
source, is that source living and conscious or is it nonliving and
unconscious? Is it more like a human self or more like an impersonal energy of nature? Is there a God?

(b) If this source or reality of the world is living and conscious,
is it concerned with the fate of man? Is there any destiny for
the human soul beyond the career of the body?

(c) Is this source concerned with the right-and-wrong aspect
of human conduct?

All these questions are subject to argumentation and, as such,
fall within the domain of philosophy; we shall meet them in our
final section. But religion does not wait for the debate nor for the
evidences of philosophy or science. Religion exists because of
what men, prior to all controversy, *see to be true* through perceptions which are sometimes called intuitive, sometimes spiritual.
These insights have been peculiarly strong in certain outstanding members of the race whose lives have commended them to
mankind, so that they have become independent persuasive
forces in the building of culture. They are called prophets be-

[1] Cf. section 9 c, p. 23.

cause they have seen the truth in advance of its confirmation by reason, not because their truth is opposed to reason or renders confirmation unnecessary.

But religion could not in any case wait for the conclusion of philosophic or scientific inquiry. It has had imperative social functions to perform. Besides nourishing all the arts in their infancy, it has encouraged man to believe in himself and in his dreams for his future will to power during that long period when he was struggling to get out of the cockpit of poverty, lack of reserves, lack of machines, lack of knowledge, lack of power. It has given to human society its earliest codes of morals and law, and has lent its support to primitive authority when all custom and all leadership were weak It has supervised the primitive plans of education, and has protected the early and crude compilations of history and learning. It has maintained a certain sane unity of the human will by offering men a supreme object of devotion and obedience, usually in accord with the will of the state but not infrequently above the will of the state. And when the issue has come whether men shall obey the state or what they conceive to be the will of God, religion has elicited some of the high occasions of moral heroism, whose meaning for mankind is not yet exhausted.

18. The Peril of Religion

In these important functions of religion lie the possible perils, not of religion itself, but of its administration by fallible human agencies.

Because the announcements of religious seers have had to precede scientific controls and checks, there has been room for dogmatism and for a rigidity of doctrine which has at times made free growth difficult. The prophet, usually certain of the right things, may also be certain of too much. The line between symbol and literal truth is never too well drawn: religion has tended to a certain excess of affirmation, which has not infrequently brought the teachings of the prophets into conflict with science and with each other. And when religious teachers denounce one another's teachings, there is always a doubting section of the public ready to conclude that they are both right in what they denounce.

It is the very importance of religion which has led to such conflicts — to persecutions, intolerance, and holy wars which have
blackened many pages of history. The methods of bigotry have
been cruel and irreligious. On the other hand, a flabby indifference which often usurps the cloak of "toleration," holding
that no religious proposition is of any importance, or that a compromise between right and wrong is better than conflict, has
equally little to contribute to the welfare of mankind.

It is also the importance of religion which has led at times to
the neglect of earthly business and to overemphasis on the otherworldly. Where this is true, the disposition to fight out in this
world important issues of justice may be crippled and a false
patience be nursed which justifies the reproach, "The opiate
of the masses." Further, since religion requires an organization
for its continuance, it may suffer in repute and influence from
the defects of its trustees when they have shown themselves more
human than divine.

Modernity is sharply conscious of these historical troubles
which have attended the immense services of religion to society.
Modern states have sometimes tried to wash their hands of the
whole matter. The new Turkey, after defining itself as an Is-
lamic state, is now experimenting in neutrality toward its numerous internal religions. A weekly journal, *Idjtihad*, published
in Istanbul, included among its announced principles the following statement:

"All religions profess to cure strife and to promote good will and
peace among men. If, instead of this, they promote discord by their
own rivalries, the cure may be worse than the disease."

But two things are to be said of any attempt to dismiss religion
as a future factor of human life and culture: (a) That it is not
the nature of the highest truth to leave men in peace; nor can
its problems be disposed of by external and diplomatic consid-
erations. There is a truth and falsity in regard to the great
questions of destiny. It is not less imperative today, but more
imperative, that men find the right answers, if their societies are
to be sound.

(b) That the errors of religious people and religious groups
are not the errors of religion; and that, as for these errors, the

old Roman proverb is still one of the deepest insights into the meaning of human history, *Optima corrupta pessima*, "The best things when corrupted, become the worst." The very extent of the evils wrought by a misguided religious sense is an indirect evidence of the importance of its natural work. Religion continues, not because its human manifestations are free from fault, but because its work is necessary to individuals and to society.

19. Social Institutions and the Course of History

A just judgment of our civilization cannot be had by dwelling either on its glories or on its perils alone. If we have taken care to face the weaknesses of our position, it is because we are emerging from an era in which the history of culture has been written in a vein of self-felicitation, based on the notion of an inevitable "evolution" of mankind.

This idea of a necessary progress is not wholly unfounded. It is based on two substantial facts. The first, that man is a being who continues to learn from experience, so that the discovery of a defect is an incentive to devise a remedy. The very recognition that a pessimistic analysis of civilization is justified might be the means of preventing a pessimistic prophecy from becoming true. The second fact is the nature of social institutions and especially of the institution of the state.

An "institution" is a more or less settled way in which the members of a given society have come to satisfy their main interests, including property and the family, education and religion, science and the arts, the traditional ways of amusement and recreation. When we say "settled ways" we imply rules, written or unwritten, just as the institution of baseball implies carefully considered rules, revised from time to time.

The revisability of the rules is as important as the rules themselves, for the reason that no set of rules is quite perfect. In fact, a set of rules, say for property or the family, may be regarded as a social experiment; and hence they will vary greatly from people to people and from time to time. As an individual learns from his own experience, so a society may learn from the discovered defects of its institutions, if there is a supervising mind to draw the inferences from these defects. The state is such a supervising mind, a sort of frame-institution to stabilize the rules while they are in force and to guarantee the orderly character of change when it is due. The state may be considered man's announcement that he proposes to bring his social order under his self-conscious control and, so far as this can be done by legislation, to keep it from collapse.

It is certain that decline and death take place within the state. Institutions lose their vitality. The family has periods of strength and weakness. Property rules grow rigid and are broken down by revolt or economic decay. Art and the church have their periods of greater and lesser fertility and influence. But it is just for this that the state exists. As the frame-institution, the state does not intend to die. Its business is "to create a calculable future," to supply durability to the work of perishable individuals, and to revive flagging institutions from its own store of the medicine of immortality, so far as its wisdom permits. It is largely because the political order has never completely broken down, in spite of all the ups and downs of institutions, that the total movement of human culture has been forward.

But these facts do not amount to a complete insurance against the decline of culture, for there are sources of trouble which no state action can reach. The things which most surely advance in the course of history are knowledge, technology, power, and freedom. These are all good in the sense that they make good possible; in themselves, however, they are all qualitatively neutral. They may be used alike for good and for ill. They might all be included under the term "freedom" in a wider sense; and it is the nature of freedom not to be compelled to decency or wisdom by anything except the choice of its holder. Civilization, by the very nature of its advance, becomes increasingly dependent on the inner character of its individual members. This is beyond the reach of the laws.

The situation to which we are now brought by our own progress is that we hardly know how to reach the sources of character in ourselves. There is a real self of man which appears to be submerged under the complexities of modern sophistication so that he cannot find it. His science, made to supply him with means but unable to teach him ends, presents him a picture of his own nature as a thing of cause-and-effect for which no ends are possible. His language is infected by a latent materialism which tends to deny the reality of what cannot be defined in terms of sensation. His very skill in language has become a skill in concealing truth, and his psychological subtlety has lent itself to the propaganda of deceit. He has lost the secret of a type of amusement which is recreation because it leaves him remade, and he believes, on hearsay, that he is the more enjoying himself as his relaxation dips deeper into laxity. He accepts on authority that the bottom of his soul is a den of irrational impulses. He understands the love of Freud but not that of Plato nor of Christ.

Nevertheless, these things are not himself. Nor are their opposites — asceticism, rejection of the world, contempt of power and science, distrust of individuality. Such a cleavage would be as much a threat to civilization as the groping confusion in which we are caught. What we require is to reunite with our freedom and power those inner standards which alone can make us fit to be trusted with power and freedom.

C. STANDARDS OF JUDGMENT

(i) THE DISCOVERY AND FORMULATION OF STANDARDS

20. The Origin of Standards in Everyday Experience

Anyone who has watched a horse munching hay has seen him occasionally shake a mouthful to get rid of a bunch of roots or a tuft of weeds or a strand of musty hay. Occasionally the remnants of a forkfull will be nosed aside, with a push of annoyance, as not up to standard. Any animal of the vertebrate group will show by its behavior its knowledge of the difference between first-rate and second-rate provender. It does not formulate standards, but its memory gives it a basis of expectation and so of criticism.

Thus animals move toward goals which they *remember;* man moves toward goals which he remembers but also *invents.* When he finds something good, he imagines something along the same line but still better — he "extrapolates" or projects. Not satisfied with repetition of an experienced good, he keeps inching his hopes ahead and so advancing his standard. Hence the ends toward which his purposes work are not merely "ideas" but "ideals" in the general sense of mentally constructed goals "nearer to the heart's desire."

Animals play, but man alone inserts into his play the notion of "breaking records." Not so long ago, the record for pole vaulting stood at 11 feet, 3 inches. It was a great day when it took a swift advance and went above 13 feet. Now it is above 15 feet. This is a stage in the evolution of jumping contests, which are as old as human boyhood. All play involves a sort of competition, if it is only that B runs and A chases. One day it occurs, probably to an onlooker, to measure the speed of A, not by the speed of B, but by a conventional distance and a time-piece; thereafter, the contestants race not more against each other than against the "record." Standards begin to be defined in exact terms.

A standard is evidently a requirement which the human mind has extracted from past experience, improved upon in imagina-tion, and set up as a measure for its own current achievement. It surrounds human activity with an invisible incentive. It is the most specific way in which man keeps reminding himself of what he is not, but can be, as well as of what he is. It has some-thing to do with the use of the word "ought": my standard is what I think I ought to reach.

In their nature, standards are aids to effective action. They may become torments if they are set beyond what can be achieved with fair exertion or if, being built on the performance of exceptional individuals, they excite in others a persistent feel-ing of inferiority. There are right and wrong uses of standards, but let us first give attention to their discovery and formulation.

All purposive life is a *trying*. One could imagine a purely con-templative consciousness which could be aware of the world without trying for anything — a mental eye, so to speak, devoid of muscles, able to perceive facts and their qualities but not to change them. But the consciousness we know is, at the same time, perception and effort; and when this conscious effort or striving has an aim which is molded, not merely by the fact of choice which governs all aims, but by an idea of what is prefer-able or worth choosing, a standard has emerged. To have an idea of what is worth my trying for is to have a standard of my own.

Some of these standards lie in the nature of the objects one is dealing with. For example, being in a hurry, I cut across a corner, having an intuitive notion that there is a shortest distance from point to point. In my notion of the nature of space lies embedded the idea of a "straight line," which becomes a standard for the economy of motion. To produce an exact straight line is a high feat of engineering; but meantime, to criticize lines that are not straight, to squint along lines of sight in setting out stakes for a digging, to note fine shadows in surfaces supposed flat — all these crude arts are common to mankind and presuppose that men know what they are aiming at, though they cannot perfectly achieve it.

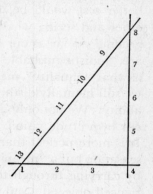

It is sometimes said that standards are a product of social life. But in fact every individual has to work out his own standards. No outsider can instruct any mind what "pleasure" and "pain," "better" and "worse" signify. After we acquire language, we are much influenced by what others enjoy or hate but without always being able to agree. So in our experiences of space, which we share with others, standards would emerge even if

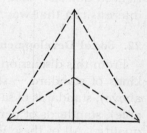

man were a solitary creature. A Robinson Crusoe, if he did any building, would get the standard of a right angle as the precise quarter of the angular space around a point on a flat surface. He might not light on the ingenious trick of the Egyptians for laying out a right angle on the ground by tying in a rope thirteen knots to make twelve equal intervals; then when knots one and thirteen are held together and the rope pulled out into a triangle from knots four and eight, a right angle is formed at four. But he would get a fair approximation to a perpendicular to a moderately straight line by use of the old and familiar principle that the perpendicular to a straight line at a given point means that line which cuts the space on either side of the base line equally.

21. The Standard of Equality

By either method, we use the notion of *equality*, which is itself
a standard of an extremely interesting kind, lying at the basis of
all comparison and measurement. If we are talking about equal
spaces, we can usually tell by the eye when they are nearly equal,
as when a set of glasses are filled to nearly the same level. A
better test would be that of superimposing one stretch on the
other and seeing whether the ends coincide. If they are "con-
gruent," so far as our eyes can see, we may say the two lengths
are "indistinguishable"; and some thinkers would say that this
is what "equality" means. But this cannot be correct, because
we still mentally distinguish between equality and indistinguish-
ability. We not only imagine, but *mean*, a more perfect test than
our own crude vision. In other words, equality is a true ideal.
It is more perfect than anything we can see because it is not a
sensation but a "meaning." It is a standard created by the mind
by carrying through to perfection an interest excited by experienced objects. And this would happen in solitude, if a man's
interests ran that way.

22. Social Developments of Standards

From this discussion we can already see that there are various
kinds of standard — standards of ideal definition (such as the
above), standards of satisfaction (such as agreeable and disagree-
able), standards of performance, standards of personal being or
quality. All of these would arise in solitude, but all are helped
to emerge in social situations and by the use of language. The
last-named kind, standards of personal quality, is especially
dependent on social aid. Let us see how this takes place.

The social situation is inseparable from an atmosphere of
approval or disapproval. Just as the mind introduces into the
factual world the distinction of better and worse, so an environment of minds introduces into one's own behavior the qualities
of better or worse in the eyes of those observers. They cannot
see any action of ours in complete neutrality.

If I set up a target and shoot at it, the target itself comments
silently on my marksmanship; the bull's eye is my own standard.
But a group of onlookers will convey another sort of knowledge,
namely, how my degree of success compares with that of others

who have had the same amount of practice. They applaud or fail to applaud according to a standard which has a social history and to which I have no access except through them. If they tell me I am "doing well for a beginner," I may think better of myself, though the target tells me a depressing story.

The elementary standard-setting situation is that of the parent and child, elder and younger, in which the subconscious trying of the child is directed toward acquiring maturity. Animal imitation (as when the young bird acquires the parental song) involves a dumb standard-taking. In the human context, imitation is eked out by all the resources of language and emotional expression. The child is congenitally sensitive to smiles and frowns, and not so much to the smile of friendliness as to the smile of approval or praise. (Here is baby falling down in her walking because she is looking too intently at the admiring faces to watch her step.)

Perhaps the most important parts of vocal language are not the nouns and verbs — names of things and actions which might be indicated in other ways — but the adjectives, adverbs, and epithets of praise and blame which apply to the invisible standards of performance and character. If we say a man "lies," we judge his speech on the standard of veracity; if we call him a "liar," we go farther and judge his character on the basis of his habitual care for veracity. One is a standard of performance, the other a standard of being.

Now, apart from society, a man has little knowledge of either standard. He knows he can think and that he can run, but he does not know how good a thinker or how good a runner he is. Still less does he know his personal quality — whether he is a good sport or a poor one, a leader or a follower, one who does his share or who drops his end of the log. And yet nothing is more important to him, if he wants to know himself, than to have these judgments, if only to give him a chance to move from one class into the other.

We might say that one of the chief reasons why man is, and remains, a social animal is that he is driven by a necessity of knowing what sort of person he is and can only find out by way of a constant interaction with other men. They are the constant mirrors of his changing self, and their mere glances are forces which help him to maintain his balance of self-judgment. The advance of a people in civilization is accompanied by an increase in the vocabulary of praise and blame; one might measure civilization by the richness of the vocabulary of vituperation. Since there are always more ways of going wrong than of going right, there ought to be more epithets of condemnation than of praise; and it is probably true that, with every new advance in culture, men invent new ways, not only of vice and crime but also of folly, waste, selfishness, self-indulgence, irresponsibility, pride, pretense, hypocrisy, treachery, evasion, fraud, disloyalty, meanness, and all the other exhibitions of defect which afflict mankind. Shakespeare requires several hundred derogatory terms to describe the faults of his characters and their enemies. A contemporary Shakespeare would require several hundred more. A good dictionary of the American language reveals the gift of American social consciousness for a new diagnosis of human error both new and old. Some examples are: fourflusher, goldbrick artist, double-crosser, gangster, socialite, high-brow, stuffed shirt, roughneck.

23. Social Authority Not Final

The use of these epithets cannot be taken as a final and disinterested verdict of character. Children are not in a position to resist the weight of authority with which such comments strike them. If Johnny is called "bad," he is inclined to believe it and may suffer under a sweeping sense of disgrace not understood. But in time one learns that critics have a "point of view," so that if the alleged refined call the alleged unrefined "vulgar," "decadent," the alleged unrefined may call the alleged refined "snobbish," "Puritanical," "snooty," "Victorian." Neither the epithet nor the counterepithet is final.

One learns also that all social epithets are used by way of recommendations to others, and, especially to the young, are not uniformly by way of a claim that they are practiced by the user. It is always easier to recommend than to exemplify.

As a result, the social verdict embodied in an epithet comes to . be received rather as an hypothesis than as a conclusion: each such comment calls for self-examination; the final judge cannot be any external authority, it can only be one's self. And while it requires the sturdiest self-assurance to stand up under a general storm of denunciation; it can be done if one has one's own standards in active working condition. In principle, then, society, though always in the vast majority, can never make a man's self-estimate; it can only suggest it.

24. Free Standards

The important thing for us to observe is that, with whatever caution a set of social standards must be used, their existence is an invaluable asset to every member of the community. They may begin as simple biological reactions, like the snarl of a dog whose possession of a bone is contested, a snarl which says "thief," to which the reply is a countersnarl, like that of Proudhon, "All property is theft." But they loosen themselves from every self-interested and emotion-charged context; they stand as a question put to every man in his solitude: "There is such a thing as a vulgarian or thief; does it describe me?"

They loosen themselves further from every particular personal application and, like the idea of a perfect circle which all men can think and no man can see, *run to their own limit as ideals* which exercise their own command without regard to special social circumstances. Thus, out of the countercharges of thievery and greed, the opposing selfishness of competing groups and classes, there emerges slowly the ideal of the "fairminded" man who, rightly caring for property, cares even more for justice and for an unimpeded fraternity with other men, the man who is truly "liberal" and "magnanimous" without falling either into a mush of concession or a strained contempt of ownership.

The capacity to arrive at such free-riding standards or ideals is certainly an outstanding achievement of the human mind, for which no parallel can be found in subhuman nature. We shall now make a brief excursion into the three main groups of such standards, those relating to thought, to feeling, and to conduct.

(ii) STANDARDS OF THOUGHT

25. Thought as Operating with Ideas Instead of Things

When we use the word thought, or thinking, for a special activity of the mind, we usually mean bringing to mind some-

thing that is not present. "You have lost your dinner pail:
stop and think where you had it last." If you are playing chess,
you think out the possible moves before you make one. In
thinking, you are operating with the ideas of objects, rather
than with the actual objects.

It spares us many a trouble to be able to think out the consequences of various courses of action instead of trying them out:
"If I try to drive across this gully, I shall get bogged in the mud.
If I drive around to the head of the stream, I shall lose three
days' time. If I go down stream, there is a chance I may find a
passable ford but no assurance of it. But yonder are some logs,
enough to rig up a bridge in half a day's time." Thought
searches out the alternative possibilities of action and then
explores the alternatives by way of ideas. The inefficient thinker
might have tried driving across the stream; the one who avoids
that fate may be using common sense, or he may be remembering
an earlier experience of his own which brought grief with it.
Bringing past experience to bear on a present problem is an
important part of what we call "intelligence." It is "learning
from experience" and then using what you have learned.

26. The Two Fundamental Operations of Thought

Here we have two operations of thought. The first, learning
from experience, is an act of what is called "generalization."
Being stuck in the mud for the first time, the observer does not
stop with noting the particular facts but, seeing the relation of
cause and effect, he extracts its general meaning then and there:
"Muddy stream bottoms are treacherous; they are good things
to keep out of." This generality he holds ready for future use.

The second operation of thought is using, or applying, that
generality. One encounters a new case of stream-crossing; one
recognizes the bottom as belonging to the muddy variety; one
attaches to it instantly the quality of "something to be avoided."
Such use of a generality to guide us in a special case is called
"deduction." If we were to analyze in detail this swift procedure, it could be set out as follows:

Muddy stream-bottoms are things to be avoided in driving;
Here we have a case of a muddy stream-bottom;
Here we have something to be avoided in driving.

This formal arrangement of "premises" and "conclusion" (called by logicians a "syllogism") is far more cumbersome than the actual, almost unconscious, passage of thought. Yet, like the slow-motion picture, it shows us the linkages of the process we have instantaneously gone through. By way of our general knowledge, we interpret the facts before us — we see in them qualities which, to our senses, are invisible.

27. Standard of Thought: Truth versus Error

Now thought is incessant. By dint of incredibly rapid and frictionless generalizing and deducing, man lives far more in the world which his ideas show him than in the surface shown by his eyes and ears. What his eyes show as a vague bluish shadow, his thought calls a mountain. What his ears report as a dull rumble, his thought notes as a distant train. Seeing a yellow-red flare among a group of steep chimneys, he thinks "blast-furnace." Feeling a swift tug at his line, the fisherman thinks "a trout." Catching a faint odor on the breeze, the farmer thinks, "Neighbor Jones is burning brush."

The financier is interested in cash balances, but he looks at figures, not at money. In these figures his thought sees the invisible operations of his business. The physician writes a prescription — marks on paper which mean to him a medicine and the way to take it. But these in turn mean disease and its cure, events which no one sees nor feels, but which have to be thought by way of the chemistry of the body. The farmer and laborer are dealing with what they can see and handle; but they too enter into partnership with invisible "laws" — laws of their materials or of soil, fertilization, growth, and slow processes leading to distant results not seen but only anticipated in thought. All such thinking is a risk. If one's conclusion is right, he has "truth"; if wrong, he has "error." The word "truth" is the most general name for the standard of successful thinking.

When man's life is thus immersed in a world of thought, correct thinking is not merely an occasional advantage but of continual and momentary importance. This importance is registered in three ways: in the informal judgments which men pass on the "intelligence" of one another; in the sciences which deal with thinking — logic, which analyzes the methods of right thinking, and psychology, which is interested in our propensities to error, and in the processes of education so far as they are concerned with habits of thinking. Let us look briefly at the first two of these.

28. (a) Measures and Kinds of Intelligence

Language contains a record of informal appraisals of intelligence, not only in degree but in quality. The difference between the sharp and the dull, the clever and the stupid, may be purely one of degree. But the difference between longheadedness and sensitive discernment is a difference between two *kinds* of excellence. The earlier efforts to measure something called "intelligence" proceeded on the assumption that there is a quality which varies from person to person on a linear scale, so that I. Q.'s can be numerically rated. There may be such a factor; but, as more recent studies indicate, it is only one of various factors in what common language terms intelligence. A mind may be very slow and yet uncommonly reliable in its results. Some minds are gifted in seeing likenesses and so in reaching generalization; other minds are gifted in noticing differences and so in avoiding the fallacies of too rapid generalization.

Some minds, again, have an uncommon mechanical intelligence; they quickly get the hang of a new machine; they can detect what is wrong with a motor or a turbine; they have, like Steinmetz, the electrical wizard of Schenectady, an uncanny skill in diagnosing the troubles of complicated instruments. Others are baffled by tools but are at home with animal or vegetable life. George Washington Carver might not have mastered an automobile, but he could make plants grow where other hands would fail and see more possibilities in a peanut than any other man alive.

There is a capacity called "intuition" which is certainly a variety of intelligence and which women are credited with having in greater degree than men. It is a quick perception of the states of mind of other people, of the meaning of an occasion, of the drift of opinion and feeling, of the spirit of groups, of the feelings of animals, in brief of anything that has life and motion. Bergson has well called it "sympathetic intelligence," and has given it a higher importance in truth-getting than the more analytical and mechanical types of thought because it alone puts us in rapport with what is fundamentally real in the world around us. In its highest forms, it is the gift of genius and serves the insights of poets, artists, and prophets. (Some have maintained that intuition is of value on the stock market as well, especially when statistics and charts fail to give reliable predictions; but the likelihood is that there is hardly any side of life in which "mother wit" or a good "hunch" — other names for intuition — is not as important as analytical intelligence.)

29. (b) Logic and the Psychology of Thinking

Since it is the business of thinking to move into the unknown, it is, in its nature, attended with risk, and the varieties of possible error are as numerous as in other forms of action.

Some errors of thought are due to defects of our powers of observation or to the mixtures of thought with imagination and desire. Psychology is particularly helpful to us here in putting us on guard against our own biases. Any strong feeling will tend to warp judgment: love and hatred constitute prejudices for and against their objects; hope and fear incline to wishful or anti-wishful thinking. This is no argument against strong feeling — to take it as such would be a good example of bad reasoning — but it is an admonition to keep a particularly steady head wherever our feelings are strongly involved. To recognize a good trait in someone we regard as a scoundrel may bring into play the standard of justice as well as the standard of truth.

30. Dangers of Generalizing

Generalizing is so much the essence of intelligence that we are likely to forget that we are doing it and become unaware of its peculiar hazards. We catch a couple of fish one day in a particular pool, and we generalize, "This is a good fishing spot." We are disappointed in an item of merchandise, and we avoid that store, generalizing on one experience. We meet in a strange land some one or two persons whom we strongly like or dislike, and these experiences qualify our judgment of an entire nation. There is an intrinsic satisfaction in a generality. It gives a sense of power and control to be able to say, "All Sikhs have black beards" or "All Cretans are liars."

But it is not merely haste or vanity which leads the mind to a premature profession of conquest; it is a *necessity of living* to act on such evidence as we have, even when it is not complete. No one act can prove a person your friend or your enemy; yet you must treat him as one or the other, and the one act may be all the evidence you have. The stray cat is in the same predicament. Give her a saucer of milk, and she will take you on. "Hasty generalization" is a form of fallacy; yet it is, in a sense, our fate. The chief protection is the knowledge that we are doing it, and here the science of logic is of great practical importance.

Care in generalization marks the chief difference between superstition and science. "Boasting brings bad luck; rapping wood will help you avoid it." Here are two generalities, each of which can claim support in experience, for who is there who has not boasted and had bad luck soon after? There have also been people bitten by dogs who, having secured a hair from the dog that bit them, have recovered. There was a time, not so long ago in Europe, when medicine depended on just such thin relationships, supported by occult intuitions of suitable causes for the desired effects. Science gets into the saddle in the seventeenth century chiefly by establishing the methods of responsible generalization.

31. The Inductive Methods of Science

These methods (usually called the inductive methods) consist for the most part of three simple principles:

(a) Physical effects must have physical causes. This rules out the idea that boasting could bring bad luck or that the beauty of an ellipse could be a reason for the orbits of the planets assuming that shape.

(b) If you are generalizing from cases which agree, be sure that the cases are sufficiently different to include all likely varieties. If it occurs to me that heat expands metals, I should try it out, not on iron alone, but on as many different sorts of metal as I can get hold of.

(c) Examine the negative side of your case as well as the positive. If it is heat that causes expansion in a particular case, then no-heat-addition should show no-expansion, and less heat-addition less expansion. And if you could subtract heat and find contraction following, your case would be still stronger.

There are refinements on these principles which we need not here pursue. But two remarks must be made. First, there is no rule which can insure the discovery of the right generalization. The rules given eliminate the major absurdities, but the discovery itself remains a leap of insight. Second, the generalization remains a "hypothesis" until it is verified. Verification consists partly in the repetition of the observations and experiments by others, confirming what the first announcer reported, and partly in drawing further consequences from the hypothesis to see whether these consequences hold good in fact.

It is not quite clear at what point a scientific hypothesis ceases to be a purely probable guess and begins to be an established truth. In some sense, a hypothesis is always on trial. Until quite recently, the theory that light is a form of vibration seemed established, and Newton's theory of corpuscles ruled out. But now the theory of quanta seems to require a modification of the wave picture, and the problem is reopened. From such experiences some have concluded that no generalization is ever quite certain. (We will only note in passing that this statement is itself a generalization, which, if it is true, is not quite certain. And, if it is not quite certain, then some generalization may be quite certain. We shall come back to this.)

Science, then, is a structure of at least probable truth built by observation, generalization, verification. And the rules for selecting hypotheses have so far rid themselves of the weeds of magic that the structure cumulates, gathering strength year by year, its parts supporting one another, and all of them supported by the mastery of nature which they have put into human hands.

32. The Logic of Deduction

Until the seventeenth century, logic consisted chiefly in rules for correct deduction. In contrast to inductive logic, precise rules can be given and successful conclusions insured, provided the premises are valid. The ancient example:

> All men are mortal;
> Socrates is a man; therefore
> Socrates is mortal.

does not pretend to prove that Socrates is mortal, but only that if the two premises are valid, the conclusion follows. If you have no doubt that all men are mortal, this "if" clause will not bother you. But if it occurs to you to inquire whether the generalization is wholly certain, and how we came by it, we should be launched on the inductive logic just now surveyed.

The older logicians, following Aristotle, were interested in the question where the premises came from, but they were inclined to think that not all generalities come from generalization. The proposition, "Every event has a cause," is certainly a generality. But it is doubtful whether it is reached by generalizing from special cases, partly because we use it before there are any special cases. We seek causes instinctively as babies look around for the causes of noises. But to seek causes is to assume that events have them. This idea is therefore not so much a result of experience as it is a frame for experience to grow in. Some thinkers have regarded it as an "innate" or "a priori" idea; others have called it an "axiom."

There were other general truths which the older logicians accepted from revelation or scripture. And possibly the "intuition" we were speaking of could reach general truth without going through the generalizing machinery. If so, deduction can use such premises to reach perfectly reliable consequences and need not wait on induction.

In any event, there is one source of premises for deduction which raises no question of truth, namely, *definition*. This is what gives us mathematics and also the more recent developments of logic. If we say exactly what we mean by a circle and postulate that certain operations familiar in geometry can be carried out, we can derive a group of theorems which are completely certain because they simply elicit what the definitions involve.

And of course these definitions need not be arbitrary — they seldom are. They fix the meaning of numbers or of figures, giving them an ideal perfection. Ideal definition is the chief source of the premises of mathematics, which thus becomes an instrument for the exploration of a world of absolute order and beauty. It is a revelation of the inner richness of these ideas, which are pure creatures of the mind, however suggested by the images of sensation. The certainty of the results of this science and the enormous power which the processes of deduction may gain from the mere form of mathematical statement might be taken as a proud though meager compensation for the difficulty (many believe incurable) of reaching any complete certainty in the concrete sciences.

In this case, mathematics would be the highest form of truth and, so to speak, the standard of standards in the pursuit of truth. This was the ideal followed by Spinoza in his *Ethics*. But we shall leave open the question whether there may not be certainty also of a more concrete sort, something by which men are better able to live than by the abstractions even of that perfect realm of order.

(iii) STANDARDS OF FEELING

33. Evidence That There Are Standards of Feeling

Thought has a definite target to aim at, and there is an obvious importance in hitting it. Thinking which strikes truth may be immensely better than animal instinct. If it misses the target and offers error instead, it may be immensely worse. But how can there be standards for feeling?

Feeling, let us remind ourselves, is that inner stirring which is evoked by the qualities or values of objects — their agreeableness or disagreeableness, their auspiciousness or menace, their beauty or ugliness, their grandeur or dullness, their rightness or wrongness. Feeling has to be free and individual because it is a *direct personal response* to things — it is the chief mark of individuality. Nothing is more descriptive of a person than what he likes or dislikes, what attracts him or repels him. If we expect feelings to vary in this way, are not standards out of place? We are always prepared to believe that what one man enjoys another will be bored by. How a person feels about a given event is his own affair. No outer agency can control it, or set up yardsticks for it — and who wants to?

The answer has to be that, in spite of all this free and almost untamed nature of feeling, there is such a thing as "right feeling" and that everybody concerned with any person is interested in the natural rightness of his deeper feelings — from his family and friends to his nation. For feeling is the mother of action. One might almost define feeling as a perception of quality preparing for doing something about it. A feeling of sympathy, for example, is a sort of inner mobilization for offering help. Just because they cannot do much about it if the normal feelings are not there, parents watch their children with all the more concern to see not only whether they laugh and cry on the right occasions but whether they get properly angry on the right occasions. There is grave anxiety at home if Johnny fails to develop a proper pugnacity when the other fellows put it over on him. Later they will worry whether he has the other feelings which lead him to control his temper, but the first question is whether there is a temper to control.

Trying to regulate a person's feelings from outside is a different and difficult matter. The new boy at school is expected to feel "the right way" toward the success of the school team. His mates watch him to see whether he shows the right degree of "enthusiasm" and "loyalty." This kind of domineering inspection may itself arouse revolt in a strongly individual spirit who refuses to put on any sham emotion. (Cordelia, in *King Lear*, is the classical example of the person who refuses to live up to current expectations in the manifestation of grief and devotion.) No freedom is more important in any free community than the freedom not to pretend any "Heil Hitlers" or any other "Heils" that one does not mean. But the very fact that control may be attempted and that it is so deeply resented is evidence that feelings do have their own standards and that these standards are profoundly important.

34. Feeling as a Kind of Intelligence

Indeed, feeling might be regarded as a deeper kind of intelligence. It is intelligence regarding values as distinct from intelligence regarding facts and truths. As there are morons in the field of intellect, so there are morons in the field of feeling, and the latter are far more socially dangerous, especially if they are, as they may be, intellectually clever. For example, if, as an accident of heredity, we should develop a breed of women capable of marriage but moronic in respect to their desire for children or in their care for bringing them up (and there are such specimens), society would be all but helpless. Would it be too much to say that it is more important to have the right feelings than to have the right ideas? If you try to set up a logical proof that women or men should be concerned with the bringing up of children, it might be hard; and it is not necessary that any parent should be able to give cogent reasons for it. What is necessary is that they should have the impulse which shows itself in responsible care.

After all, a man is only as much alive as the extent of his feelings. If he knew everything and felt nothing, he would, by definition, be indifferent as to his own life or death. Feeling is not identical with "emotionality" or agitation of mind. A man may feel a great deal and show little or nothing outside; the steadier and deeper feelings are in general quiet. The nature of feeling is simply *appreciation;* it is "knowing a good thing when you see it" and also a bad thing, and all the shades of betterness and worseness which the world presents for estimation. To say of any man that he cannot enjoy what is enjoyable is another way of saying that he is only half-alive.

35. How Society Trains Feeling without Rules

This implies that our powers of appreciation are partly in-born and partly acquired. The fundamental "right feelings" are those which attend our major instincts, such as sociability, sex, pugnacity, acquisition. But there are other feelings which belong to the goods which man has developed — the goods of culture — whatever forms of enjoyment or celebration a society has been able to create. These feelings have to be acquired, as the American acquires his enjoyment of baseball, and the assumption is that the normal man inherits from his ancestry the same traits which enabled these ancestors to develop those modes of enjoyment.

It is because of this, no doubt, that simpler societies make so much of unanimous participation in community expressions of feeling. The great occasions of the year — harvest, return of the sun — celebrated with dance, feasting, ceremony, game, pag-eant, assure each member that his neighbor joins him in appre-ciating the meaning of the event. Further, they increase the feeling itself. For when a feeling has an active outlet, especially a more or less formal ceremonial outlet, it develops its full power,

and it is obviously difficult for a single individual to carry out a
ceremony alone. Then, too, any feeling is increased by the sight
of the signs of feeling in others, just as the sight of a panic-stricken
face brings a suggestion of fear, quite apart from any known
cause. If for no other reason, human beings would live in groups
in order *to do justice to the possibilities of feeling*. Even the feeling
of grief at death is incomplete without the social participation
and the dignity of ritual, the aim of ritual being to conserve for
recurrent occasions the most adequate expressions of feeling
which a given community has lighted upon. By such means as
these, early societies maintained a rough agreement of feeling
as well as an agreement of thought.

36. Feeling as Ethical and Aesthetic

This free community discipline of feeling leads to a point
where the stream of feeling divides. One part of the stream,
keeping its connection with action, accepts the budding classification
of types of conduct as good and bad and becomes merged with
the rules of morals. We can understand why the community
begins to emphasize the behavior and tends to forget the feeling.
"Thou shalt not kill" means "No matter how you feel about it,
the destruction of a blood-brother's life will not be tolerated."
Negative standards of conduct are set up, quite independent of
the original feeling. After a few thousand years of this behavior-
measuring, all great civilizations have come back to the insight
that it is the feeling that is most important. "Love your neighbor
as yourself," and then you will do no murder.

The other part of the stream appears to *surrender its connection
with action*. Something happens to the human group which does
not happen to the animals. Man begins to take his expressions
of feeling as spectacles to be enjoyed for themselves quite apart
from their original purpose. The dance had originally something to do: it had to call the gods, invoke the totem, or inspire
the participant with the divine *wakonda*. But in time the dance
makes its own place in enjoyment. The inherent pleasure of its
rhythm, heightened by music, and the perfect mastery of motion,
which brings the unaided human body near to the sense of
flight — these can be taken "for their own sake." There are
few things men do purely as means to an end; they begin to

enjoy the means, and then the means become ends also. This is the meaning of "aesthetic" enjoyment. The word signifies an appeal to feeling detached from ensuing action.

This is one way in which man finds himself an artist and begins to set up standards of feeling in apparent independence of all ritual or ethical responsibility. Art has other sources than the community celebration, and we have already mentioned some of them.[1] What now concerns us is whether art can offer us any standards for feeling.

37. Art as a Source of Standards

That art is expected to do so seems beyond question. Insofar as art is a language, it must be understood in order to be effective. The artist is not intending to vent his personal feelings in a soliloquy; if he puts them into verse, he wants somebody to hear the verse. The medium of art is not only one that seeks permanence; it is one that can be public, enjoyed by many at once. And the artist must somehow get his living from the public which can see something in what he does. If he makes sketches for the fun of sketching and then throws them away, he does not throw them *all* away! The artist may have been a hundred times provoked to write or paint something to the one time that he can get it done — most good artists have experienced this — but unless he gets beyond the dream to the physical deed, he is no artist. And while the vanity of many a modern artist induces him to see how far he can lead a pained and puzzled public by the nose, this is a game which has natural limits. The feeling of the artist is, in its social function, an informal standard for the feeling of his community.

This very fact that the public will trust its artists a certain distance into the obscure and will strain its powers of appreciation toward what it believes it ought to enjoy, but does not — this very fact shows the normal position of art as a standard. The young people who are led in droves through the museums by elders who want them to be "cultured" in their tastes and told what they ought to admire may be permanently alienated from the very word "art" by a stupid and insincere pedagogy; but such educational crimes are a distant homage to a true

[1] Cf. Section 15.

notion of where standards are to be found. Where are they to be found?

There are no rules for art production which can compare with the rules of logic for reaching a better brand of truth. The science of aesthetics can indicate certain sources of natural joy which lie in the harmony of colors, the principles of design, the elements of good composition, the architecture of musical form, and the like. These, like the rules of etiquette, which is itself a form of art, the artist (and the student of art) will need to understand if only that he may safely ignore or subordinate them to the integrity of his work. But the real standards of feeling are not in these rules; they are in the integral works themselves. Men treasure art and put it into public places because, without any announcement of commandments or laws, it does, so far as it is true art, give crude feeling a finer and juster standard.

These works are useless to anybody unless two conditions are complied with. Each must be within his grasp so that something in him responds to it and says, "Yes, that is good." And it must be sufficiently beyond him so that he has to stretch a little to get its full value. The business of art is to haunt a person with the inner tinglings of a nobler selfhood which is not yet in existence but is on the way to be born.

(iv) STANDARDS OF CONDUCT

38. The Limited Range of Legal Morality

Since conduct can be seen, as feeling cannot, it is an inviting field for the application of standards. The profusion of epithets of which we have spoken apply chiefly to types of behavior. The "quitter" is not a man who feels like quitting; he is the man who quits. The Sermon on the Mount defines adultery as "looking on a woman to lust after her"; but law and the general usage of speech reserve that name for a definable act.

On the whole, law deals only with external behavior; and some theories of law hold that it is indifferent to the motives which actuate that behavior. It expects a man to pay his debts; whether he does so because he wants to be honest or whether he thinks it good policy for his business, the law does not inquire. Nor, if he fails to pay, does the law take much interest in whether his failure is due to negligence, bad luck, or an attempt to slip out of an obligation. In other words, whether or not "God looketh at the heart," man does look "on the outward appearance," because that is the only thing for which he finds legal evidence. And, after all, if a man only contemplates a deed and does not do it, whether it be a good deed or bad deed, he should receive no credit for the good thoughts he failed to carry out nor blame for what he actually did not do. It may be to his credit that, having been inclined to murder, theft, adultery, suicide, or what not, he checked his impulse before it got all the way across into action.

It is a fallacy to suppose that either the law or social opinion are indifferent to motives. In the case of homicide, the law inquires carefully whether the act was premeditated; it makes the difference between manslaughter and murder. It would be absurd to say that any state is unconcerned how its citizens feel — whether they obey the laws and pay their taxes solely through fear of punishment or neighbors' opinions or whether they have some attachment to the nation. But because it is so difficult to prove anything about motives, the law restricts its rules to external actions.

The legal order, therefore, in all civilized societies, concerns itself with actions, classified into three groups: the commanded, the prohibited, and the permissible (being neither commanded nor prohibited). And, quite naturally, it is chiefly concerned with what is prohibited.

The legal order is a sort of minimal morality turned into socially enforceable rules. It is supplemented by a moral order which defines the full ideal for the union of feeling and behavior.

These standards for conduct will come in for special discussion in the second and third parts of this text. Here I raise only one general question: — whether there are or can be any stable and universal rules for right action as there are for right thinking; in other words, whether there can be standards of conduct which can compare in certainty with the standards of thought.

39. Generalities about Right Conduct

There is no question that mankind sets up generalities in regard to right conduct just as it does in regard to truth. Man uses these generalities precisely as he does the generalities of science: to deduce from them applications to special cases.

Any rule of law is a generality. A trustee, for instance, must use due diligence in protecting the property of the beneficiary of the trust; if a trustee is accused of negligence, the lawyers will have to apply the generality to the special case. The prosecution will argue, in effect, as follows:

> A right trustee will use due diligence;
> This trustee did not use due diligence (he invested in securities which he could have known to be worthless);
> Ergo, this trustee is not a right trustee.

But the question is, how do we arrive at these generalities? Are they simply formulations of custom, indicating how people in the given community generally act, and therefore having merely a presumable or local rightness? Or are there such things as moral axioms which can be known to be valid without going through the business of generalizing? There are few questions in the range of philosophy more important than this, for on the answer depends the authority of the rules of right conduct which are found everywhere in the tradition of civilized peoples.

There is an intimation that they are something more than prejudices or conventions or changeable social habits in the fact that some moral generalities are found in the traditions of nearly all peoples. The Golden Rule is perhaps the best example.[1] Confucianism, which was brought into coherent form by the Chinese teacher about 500 B.C., takes as its main ethical idea *Jen*, whose character is "man, two alike," meaning equal treatment of yourself and others. Putting this idea into the form of a general maxim, the Chinese sage, with characteristic caution, gave it a negative form: "Do not do to others what you would not want them to do to you." It suggests that the positive form, which taken literally would involve us in endless enterprises in behalf of others, needs some kind of limitation in order to be practicable. Kant tried to put the matter exactly in his famous

---

[1] BR, No. 7, "A Sheaf of Golden Rules from Twelve Religions."

rule, "So act that you could will the maxim of your action to be a universal law"; and he considered this principle equivalent to the very definition of morality and, therefore, valid among all peoples at all times.

On the other hand, nothing is more notorious than the variability of moral judgments among different peoples and even from person to person. The idea that questions of taste are not subject to debate (*de gustibus non disputandum*) many are inclined to carry over into the realm of morals as well. They adopt the view that all general standards of ethics, all moral "principles," are "relative" to time and place and the particular social order.

40. The Meaning of Relativity and Its Cost

The study of anthropology gives us plenty of examples of queer moral ideas which have been held at one time or another. Collections of customs are as interesting as they are weird. There are tribes that make a crime of murder; others that make a virtue of it. There are tribes in which female chastity ends with marriage, others in which it begins with marriage. There have been many experiments in polygamy: Islam, in some quarters, still prefers the Prophet's allowance of four wives to what it sometimes regards as the inferior Western substitute of prostitution. There have been a few experiments in polyandry, though this can have been a general practice only where the scarcity of women was very great. Most peoples care for their aged; some knock them in the head. Most peoples regard it as a duty of parents to take care of all their children; some peoples have regarded it as meritorious to sacrifice some of them; and it has frequently been held allowable to sell extras into servitude or to expose them. Slavery itself has been at times approved and defended on philosophic grounds, as by Aristotle; at other times, it has been condemned as a social abomination.

Today, there are strong moral contrasts between East and West. It is true that the shrinking of the world has finally mixed up East and West, so that all the old twaddle about "never the twain shall meet" has gone by the board as well as the dogma that "there are no morals East of Suez"; what we have East of Suez is a group of well-marked types of morality. But these types are hung on a different balance than our own. The eco-

nomic virtues of thrift, industry, scientific planning, individual
initiative are not the dominant notes of Oriental society; meditation and the search for holiness have a higher authority; the
family as an institution is stronger and subordinates the individualism of its members. The Orient is changing in the direction of the West in all these respects, and in the meantime the
West, it may be hoped, will be learning some of the wisdom of
the East; but each has a long way to go.

Perhaps, after all, social evolution is a perpetual change, and
the only stable truth in respect to all standards is that there is
nothing stable. According to Professor Conklin,

"Such diversity in forms of aesthetic and ethical satisfactions does
not prove that there are no standards of values . . . but it does show
that, in human estimation and practice, values are relative and not
absolute. In this respect, science occupies no position of superiority;
its findings are never to be regarded as absolutely true or, false, but
rather as approximations to truth." [1]

It is an advance in wisdom and toleration when one changes
his mode of expression from "This is true" to "This seems to be
true" or "From my point of view, this is true." The ampler
expression includes the implied acknowledgment that other
seemings may be had from other points of view. And this
advance is characteristic of our modern period.

There is liberation in this insight from brow-beating fixities
like the classic models for art and the Victorian conception of
decorum. Those who do not see things that way are encouraged
to say, "What seems to me beautiful is beautiful for me, and
that is the only beauty I am concerned with." "Every gentleman has a right to his own ideas of spelling." And every
adolescent to his own ideas of right and wrong?

When one reaches this point, he begins to wonder whether
the liberation has not been rather costly. He has rid himself of
inflexible commands; he has shed "principles" as so many superstitions, like the old lists of axioms; but he has also lost contact
with all his fellowmen. For the principle of relativity, taken to
the limit, leaves every man alone with his own standards. It
is not *man* who is the "measure of all things," but each man for
himself is his own set of measures, and there are no common

[1] E. G. Conklin, "Man, Real and Ideal," p. 170.

measures, hence no common judgments, hence no real bonds which hold men together in a truth which commands their united allegiance. Perhaps there is something wrong in the premises of this indulgent and self-indulgent way of reasoning.

41. Limitations of Relativity

Relativity cannot be the whole truth about standards. There is certainly good reason for being suspicious of any formula which pretends to set up an absolute and final truth or law, but to say that a formula needs to be revised is not to say that it is wholly off the mark. It is a fair question whether any one of the formulations of the Golden Rule by Confucius, by Jesus, or by Kant is perfect and unchangeable. But there can be no doubt that some requirement of regard for the interests of others is the essence of all morality, among all nations and races and at all times. If slavery is wrong today, it was also wrong for the Greeks.

In point of fact, the collections of queer customs in which writers on social history have delighted do not prove the relativity they announce. It is true that peoples have had different rules about murder, and some head-hunting tribes have made it a point of honor. But this does not prove that it is purely a matter of social convention whether or not one finds it right or wrong to kill his neighbor. There has never been a tribe which made it a point of honor to kill one's own tribesman! Rome countenanced the exposure of superfluous infants, with remonstrance from some of the Stoic philosophers; but no tribe of men has ever made it a duty to expose all infants, and for the obvious reason that such a tribe would long since have vanished. We shall therefore have to cancel the proud statement of Professor Sumner to the effect that "The *mores* [customs] can make anything right." This is simply untrue. There are moral rules which may be regarded as experimental and variable; others which are necessary and universal because they are the only conditions under which a human society can operate.

42. Relativity Requires an Absolute Rule

The real significance of the valid doubt about standards which are set up as "absolute" is rather the opposite of a general relativity. The whole point of a discovery of relativity is to *get out of relativity*, just as Einstein's principle of physical relativity is a stage in the formulation of an absolute unified law of change. If the alleged natural rights of life or liberty or property are relative to something, then the rule that they are relative to that something is itself an absolute rule.

It is always suspicious that there should be many absolutes, whether in truth or in standards of morals. The correction of these absolutes leads in the direction of finding one absolute instead of many. The Ten Commandments were set up to be ten fixed and eternal rules, but some of them, such as the rule against killing, have exceptions and must be relative. What this limitation points to is that all of them should be merged into one principle which *is* absolute. The search for such a single principle is the origin of the Golden Rule formulations, and if this is not final, the search must be continued. For whatever is relative is relative to some absolute.

This is the reason for the paradox pointed out above — that the person who says that all truth is merely probable intends to make one certain statement, which is not merely probable; he therefore involves himself in a contradiction. So the person who says that all standards are relative means by that statement to offer an absolute standard and involves himself in contradiction. It is impossible for the mind, in however humble a mood, to shut itself out from a point of hold upon the permanent in standards of judgment. The doctrine of relativity is, in fact, a piece of false humility which would rob all men of their prerogative as men — that of a direct hold on something true and final. Whenever the human mind discovers and announces itself as limited and shut in, it is already taking a position outside of the alleged prison. It is the nature of man to know truth as it is and to know the beautiful and the good for what they are, as every mind in the universe, human or divine, must know them.

43. The Union of Feeling and Conduct

One reason for the persistence of the belief that all human standards of judgment are relative is that we think of the mind as a medium through which we look; such a medium, like a pair of colored glasses, will cast its own hue on everything we look at. There are jaundiced minds which, like jaundiced eyes, see yellow where others see white. But every mind, we fancy, has some tint or other, and when one describes another person his very adjectives may betray the color of his own medium. If A describes B as "stingy," this may be because he himself is a "spendthrift." We no longer expect our news sheets, in describing a political event, to tell the same story. Each will represent it from its own partisan position.

In trying, some years ago, to get facts about the French administration in Syria, I was told: "There are no facts here; there are nothing but *versions*." Can there be such a thing as a true history, let us say, of the war between the States; or must there always be a Southern version and a Northern version, or several of each? Keeping our figure of the colored medium, we have come to see that there is no such thing as a colorless view: a man with beliefs must write or talk from those beliefs; one with no beliefs — if such a being could exist — could see nothing truly. Nor do we want any such thing as an unfeeling judgment. If we feel hotly about something, we want to hear or read the words of those who feel equally hot, not of those who feel nothing at all.

For if feeling, as we have said, is a mode of intelligence, the feelingless mind is simply unintelligent. This perhaps gives us the clue to the whole matter. For, while feeling does color our reports of fact, especially of human and social fact, this does not mean that it falsifies these reports, provided there is — as we decided there must be — such a thing as a *true feeling*. We do not want colorlessness nor false coloring; but we do want the true color, and that alone is the full truth!

The mind is not itself a colored medium — for in that case it would stain everything alike, which it certainly does not do. The mind is not a medium at all, it is the thing *which does the looking*. In looking, it applies the standards of quality at the same time as it does the standards of truth. It is these standards of appreciation which lend the color. If they are true standards, they report the true color. If I laugh at something which is essentially tragic, there is something wrong with my standards. Cruelty is the capacity to be unmoved by, or even to take satisfaction in, the suffering of others. It is not "relatively all right"; it is a falsity of feeling, or an even greater falsity of no-feeling. The same may be true of the absence of anger when one ought to be angry; the mind which can see unmoved an event which excites a just indignation is not "seeing things as they are." We are not therefore condemned to relativity by the fact that we are obliged to judge the world by way of our own feelings and beliefs.

44. Self-correction the Way to Final Standards

We human beings are nearer rightness in our standards of scientific truth, I believe, than in most other standards. But even where we are most swayed by our peculiar biases, the power of the mind lies in this fact, that it can recognize the bias and in time correct it. The mind that can say "I am prejudiced" is at that moment seeing beyond the prejudice and is therefore to some extent unprejudiced. This is what is meant by the saying that to recognize a limit is to be beyond it.

If this is true, the fact that our age has become so generally aware of the danger of relativity is the fact which promises to cure the disease. To know the bias of propaganda is to be immune from the bias. To discover that I am wrong is, at that moment, to be right. The man who has lied and who says "I am a liar" is telling the truth. The man who has bad taste, and who comes to see that he has bad taste, must be somewhere on the border of good taste. In sum, the mind, which is full of faults, has the remarkable power of being self-corrective; and this fact makes it a sharer in the quality of final truth. It does not fully possess any perfection; but, on the other hand, there is no perfection which is alien to its nature and of which it does not get a glimpse.

This is what is meant by the saying that man shares in the nature of God; or, as the Buddhist would put it, that each man has his share of the Buddha nature; or, according to the Stoics, that we are sparks of Zeus.

This puts a new item into our definition of man. *Man is the being who is capable of thinking and using a perfect (or absolute) standard.* It is this which makes it possible for him to reach understanding and agreement with other human beings across no matter what gulf of racial or national difference. For as, in the old axiom of mathematics, things which are equal to the same are equal to each other, so, in what we may call the social axiom, men who agree with the same standard agree with each other. So long as we accept relativity as the last word, we may expect Chinese to agree with Chinese more or less, and Americans to agree with Americans, but not Americans with Chinese. But if both can break through *at any point* to an identity of standard, their minds can meet.

Since we have taken parts of our mathematics from India and the Arabs, these groups of minds have already met at this point. And since in art we admire many Oriental works, we have also met in this field. But what may be more important at present is the fact that we are sharing codes of law with China, Thailand, and other Far Eastern lands; and that the School of Comparative Law in Soochow has put out work of value for jurists in all lands. These facts imply that in some points of the principles of law and therefore of the conscience from which law comes, an identity of standard has been caught sight of.

With these beginnings, we can deal hopefully with the remaining relativities. Through his hold on true standards, and only through that hold, man can make a unity of the human species, rather than stand helpless, like an animal, before these varieties of race and culture.

D. MAN AS CREATIVE AND MALLEABLE

(i) HOW FAR CAN MAN GO IN REMAKING NATURE AND HIMSELF?

45. Question concerning Human Possibilities

There was an old wager to the effect that a man could not run a thousand miles in a thousand hours. An average of a mile an hour seems at first sight a safe bet, for it allows much more than half the time to recuperate. But when you consider that it means twenty-four miles a day for over forty days consecutively, one has second thoughts. Not many years ago, it was supposed that the man who undertook it was sure to lose because the bodily processes of repair cannot be hastened beyond a certain point. I am told that this is not the case and that the feat is often done by Japanese runners. But the problem illustrates a common human experience: there is a defined task which seems quite possible, but in our honest efforts to do it we are defeated by something called "human nature," a vague phrase for the sum of the limited powers and hampering conditions under which we conduct our lives.

Hence the fact that man sets standards for himself is not of itself a proof that he can reach them. There is, indeed, a certain presumption — if there is a degree of reasonableness in the make-up of the universe — that a being capable of thinking out standards would not have been produced for nothing. "The target is not set up in order that we may miss it." But the situation is a little different from that. The idea of a perfect circle is not something which we can damage in order to accommodate it to our powers of draughtsmanship: it has to be exactly as it is defined. But no human being has yet drawn free-hand a perfect circle (a proposition which it would be hard to prove unless one were certain of it in advance!).

We are, therefore, proposing to inquire into human possibility: how much can man achieve? What can he make of the world and of himself?

46. Is Man Controlled by Nature?

Nature sets obvious limits to what man can do with his physique: he cannot greatly alter his height; he can extend his life, but not indefinitely. But does nature set similar limits to what he can do with his mind and character? This is an ancient question. Nothing is older than human lament about falling short of good resolves, and nothing more hoary than the explanation that we are held back by some hidden check: the body, a lower nature which wrestles with our higher nature, or the devil himself. But science puts the matter more simply. It points out that, as a product of nature, man and all his doings must be subject to nature's laws. His very trying is a part of the scheme of nature, and it carries on as far as nature bids, no farther.

To put the matter in terms of physiology, man's brain and nervous system govern his behavior; and they in turn are controlled by the whole system of energies which manage the living organism. What we do is thus shaped by nature with the same exactitude with which the motions of stars and atoms are shaped.

We can see this to be true of our *reflex actions:* for the most part they take place in spite of us (try controlling a wink or a patellar reflex). Other types of action seem more our own doing, such as actions prompted by an instinctive drive like fear or anger: they do not "take possession" of us without our consent; but science is not prepared to say that our consent is uncaused, nor even that what we call *"voluntary actions,"* i.e., actions conceived and carried out on plan, are uncaused. For every such act must have its "motive," and motives are not uncaused. Why do we enjoy fishing if not because of our heredity? Granted we always do as we wish and so feel free; but if nature makes our wishes, then nature, with the most perfect absence of intrusion, controls what we do by way of our wishes. And also what we fail to do.

After all, how could there be a science of psychology or of sociology unless there were discoverable laws of human conduct, just as there are laws of the behavior of heat and light? It seems possible to establish a few such laws; there are statistical probabilities in regard to such voluntary acts as marriage, divorce, thrift, and even in regard to the major crimes, including suicide. We cannot predict the behavior of men as confidently as we can predict an eclipse or a chemical reaction, since the conditions are far more complex. But the scientific principle of cause and effect seems to be borne out reasonably well. And many a psychologist feels that he must either assume this strict determination of all human behavior by its causes or else go out of business as a scientist.

Unquestionably this view of things is bound to reduce man's sense of being his own master. His feeling of being free to achieve or not to achieve his ends begins to seem an illusion and, with it, his sense of responsibility for what he does, since nothing that he does could have been otherwise.

The situation is a strange one, for science is the tool by which nature was to have been mastered. Man, the master, is supposed to be free to apply nature's laws so as to achieve his own ends. But now by extending science, he brings himself, the master, within the scope of these laws and finds himself a prisoner at the moment of his triumph. For since the supposed master is himself a part of nature, there is no master except nature.

Man becomes simply a tool through which nature alters some small part of her own pattern. The final achievement of science, the mastery of human nature, would be the abandonment of its original aim, to bring nature under human control. The thought is perplexing and profoundly disturbing.

47. Decision Not a Matter of Cause and Effect

There is no question which runs deeper into our modern world-view than this one: how far is man's life controlled by nature? We shall meet it again (see Part V, "A World-View," sections 334–346). Here we shall simply point out that we cannot reject what we know about our own mental processes merely in order to allow psychology the doubtful privilege of resembling physics. The process of decision is not a cause-and-effect process.

Decision, as we know, is capable of hesitation; to deliberate is to hesitate in the sense of postponing decision. *A causal process cannot hesitate.* A train approaches a half-open switch. Which way will it swing? We are unable to predict, but the train itself does not hesitate. The engine moves steadily onto the switch point and then does without delay what the balance of forces then and there prescribes. A man in a similar situation, not seeing clearly what he wants to do, may refuse to decide until he knows what the alternatives are and what they mean to him. He manipulates the time-factor of his approach to action as a causal process cannot do.

But there is another difference. In the causal process, the possible alternatives are definable in advance: in principle, nothing new can happen. In the activities of the human will, alternatives are invented. Man's delay of decision is not primarily a matter of making up his mind which of the obvious paths open to him he likes best; it is chiefly that of devising something which will suit him better than any of them. In other words, the human mind is *creative.* It puts something into the world which, apart from that process, the world would not have contained.

Wherever minds are, they are the channels through which novelties creep into the course of things, and, so far as we know, they are the only channels. The beauty of inanimate nature is that it can be relied on always to do the same thing in the same way: a "law" of nature is the announcement that a given sequence can be repeated (add water to quicklime and you will invariably have an output of heat). This is why nature can be utilized by the mind. But it is the business of the mind to employ these regularities to produce something different, something of which nature had not dreamed, something which in nature, apart from mind, was not even possible. A good song is nothing but a collection of notes arranged in a certain order. If one had a device for shuffling notes at random, any song you mention might be produced in a million years as one of the "possible" combinations. But nature has no device for producing notes *together*, nor for outlining a particular group of sounds as having a beginning and an end and a single sense; hence, apart from a mind caring for music, a song is strictly impossible. The productions of the mind are, in a literal sense, additions to creation; they may be said to continue the work of creation.

We may, therefore, shake off the bugaboo of determinism and, with it, a certain alibi for our mistakes. There are times when it is convenient to be able to blame our heredity, or nature at large, for our failures. "God made me lazy, and I can do nothing about it."

> O Thou who man of baser clay didst make,
> And with the Garden didst devise the Snake,
> For all the sin wherewith the face of man
> Is blackened, man's forgiveness give — and take!

An immortal alibi and a beautiful fallacy. For have we not already seen that the man who sees himself defective is, at that moment, outside the defect? Whenever he says truly, "I *am* this vile thing," he lies — if he pretends it to be the whole truth. He is that, *plus the man who sees and repudiates it*. The fact of self-awareness and self-judgment is the tool of freedom. Man has the task of shaping his physical world; he has also the task of shaping himself.

We have now to follow some of the methods and accomplishments of twelve thousand years of traceable human self-making in connection with the parallel task of shaping the world around him.

48. Interaction between Man and Environment

The early evolutionists of the school of Darwin thought of the environment of life as a relatively stable set of conditions to which organisms had to be adapted or perish. Almost every kind of animal makes some trifling alteration in its surroundings by way of shelter or retreat; but in general they make the best of the world, the water, or the weather as they find them.

But man has never been content to "accept the universe" to this extent. He carries on a deliberate and increasingly systematic campaign to make his environment over. Instead of adapting himself to the earth, he adapts the earth to himself and then proceeds to adapt himself to the revised environment. Instead of taking creation as a finished event, he considers himself authorized to continue the process. (And since, on the whole, he has improved both the earth and himself in doing so, there is room for speculation that this may have been one reason why Creation was left in such rough shape.)

On the vast scale of nature, what man has done in this way is very small. He has made no striking changes in climate or geography, except in spots where, by burning forests or overplowing prairie land, he has done widespread damage. But the scale of his modifications continues to increase. And it is hazardous to set a limit because it is not on his own physical force that he relies for such change. It is only nature which has power enough to alter nature in a perceptible measure.

But this is precisely the bent of man's genius. Like his capacity to make tools and machines, his capacity to set up an artificial environment for his own life depends on his inventiveness in getting nature to work against itself. Against its winds and storms he sets its trees, made into logs, stockades, boards; against its cold, its reservoirs of heat in wood, coal, oil; against its drought, the flow of distant rainfall; against its heights, the power of mountain streams, as the Swiss trains are driven uphill by the downrush of Swiss waters turned into electric power.

In this process of rearranging the world, man is obliged to alter his own habits. Thus, indirectly, he becomes to some degree his own architect. Those who say, "Man is a thing of nature and not something in contrast with nature," are reporting a large part of the truth but not all of it. To an important degree

— we have now to consider how important — man constructs himself.

49. Self-building, Direct and Indirect

To some extent, and I judge to an increasing extent, man takes himself directly in hand and attempts to change his character.[1] The extraordinary human capacity for self-criticism has its role to play. Whenever any set of circumstances irks a human being, he is likely to confront them with two questions, where the animal would ask only one. He will ask, "What is wrong with this situation?" but he is also likely to ask, "What is wrong with me?" If he reflects, "We have too little food to carry us through the winter," he may also reflect, "I must work harder next season." In the course of centuries, such comments as these, and their consequences, make perceptible differences in human quality.

But for the most part man makes himself in the course of his efforts to deal with things outside himself — his occupation, his hard struggle to conquer the wild or pain-breeding aspects of his environment. He is not "adjusting himself to his environment," but he is adjusting himself *to his work* and to the *conditions which he is trying to create*. He is forever at work on himself as the creature of tomorrow who can live with satisfaction in the world which he is in process of making.

We shall sketch this double process of world-making and self-making in three regions: the struggle with physical nature, with the untamed side of the human world, and with the wider cosmos.

(ii) THE CONQUEST OF NATURE

50. The Motives of Work

It is an ancient question whether, if we were creating a world after our own fancy, we would make one in which there was no necessity to *work*. The traditional idea is that this necessity is a curse, one of the original curses of mankind. Economic science has for the most part accepted the notion that labor is something men do solely because they have to in order to eat. And it adds that there will always be some who have to work because popu-.

[1] Cf. BR, No. 12, William James, "Habit."

lation tends to multiply up to the limit at which the poorest
have only a bare subsistence.

This view of things is hardly in accord with the psychology
of natural labor. It is not in the warmer and easier regions
but in the harder climates and more meager soils that men appear
to be not only most vigorous but most happy. And further, it
is not bread and butter for the poor which keeps men at work
any more than it is the requirements of their creative faculties.
Man's imagination is as likely to make him toil as his stomach;
and his imaginative capacity for using his wealth has always
exceeded his power to produce it. The probabilities are that the
human imagination will develop faster than all possible labor
can provide the materials for putting it into architecture, public
works, devices for the enlargement and adornment of life.

If work were a necessity against which we were in constant
subconscious protest, it is unlikely that it would have played its
immense role in developing human fiber and stamina. A New
England farmer wrestled for two or three hours with a granite
boulder which was doing no harm, but which, in his opinion,
spoiled the looks of his field. By way of apology he said, "They
say it's them rocks thet makes us folks so stubborn." Not the
rocks exactly, but the combination of the rocks with his self-
imposed ideal of a clean field.

There is always a major drive in us which favors the effort
of work, once we are under way. As an evidence of this, there
are few people who do not work harder at their jobs than they
have to, if they are not interfered with and are under normal
conditions. In a complex industrial society conditions are
intricate but not necessarily abnormal. The chief difficulty is
that the man who has the imagination to plan the job seldom
has the fun of working out his idea; whereas the man who does
the work seldom has the fun of having (or sharing) that imagination. When a man works for others on plans devised by others
and with a reward measured in money instead of in personally
witnessed achievement, he is in a different psychological position
from that of the man who works to effect his own plans under
his own direction, as the farmer does.

Yet even here intelligence and a free communication of ideas
can do much, and could do much more, to maintain the natural

incentive. It is still true, even in our artificial economic set-up, that the growing boy hurries to get rid of his toys, find a job, and feel the satisfaction of his first pay envelope. For, however complicated the channel, the underlying drive of the "will to power" is finding an outlet: one is taking his part in a corporate effort to master certain actual resistances of nature. Because of this underlying approval of the campaign for mastery, modern economy, like ancient economy, continues to build men.

51. The Effects of Work upon Character

It is due to Karl Marx and his colleague, Friedrich Engels, that our times have become aware of the profound effect on human character exercised by the economic situation. With the changing instruments of production, the manpower and the wealth-reserve of any society have to be organized anew. If a hunting society cannot behave like a herding society nor a herding society like a settled agricultural society nor any of these like an industrial society, *neither can they think nor feel alike:* they will not have the same heroes, the same prides and prestiges, the same ambitions, the same conceptions of property (and therefore of law), perhaps not even the same forms of the family nor the same ideas of religion.

Anyone can have contemporary evidence of these effects if he can watch over a few years an initiation into any trade. A boy goes to sea; he is not thinking of the effect of his new life on himself — that takes place without his thinking of it; after a voyage or two, he is the same person and *not the same;* he has become "a sailor." Before this time, he could have entered any one of half a dozen other occupations equally well perhaps; after this time it would be harder to change; the ways of the sea have gotten into him.

Facts of this sort have much to do with what we call national differences. The Swiss, the Russians, the Spaniards are different people not more by race, language, customs than by the ingrained influence of climate, soil, and occupation, welded into a mutual harmony so that it would be hard to transplant a man of the soil from one nation to another.

Now we are concerned with this principle, not for the sake of tracing out local differences, but for the sake of finding what

long-time consequences have come into human character everywhere because of the general struggle against nature's resistance.
It is this same hard school of *work* which has been the great
teacher of the race in regard to those qualities which have been
called the "economic virtues" — forethought, industriousness,
respect for fact, ingenuity, honesty, frugality or saving, keeping
of contracts, enterprise, responsibility — an impressive list.

Economic forces do not of themselves produce these virtues. We must
here guard against an easy assertion that it is economic pressure
which produces these qualities in man. There is an "economic
theory" of history (also largely due to Marx and Engels) which
tends to trace most of the characteristics of men and civilizations
to the "economic factor," especially to the necessities of the
current mode of production. A moment's reflection will show
that this theory claims too much.

An economic fact cannot, by its own force alone, produce any
mental change whatever. If privation were able by itself to
produce forethought, the most poverty-ridden peoples would be
the most prudent. If it were true that "necessity is the mother
of invention," the neediest would be the most inventive. Unless
your economic fact strikes on a mind capable of creative ingenuity or disposed to self-improvement, you get no invention and
no moral advance. The hard school of poverty has operated
for hundreds of years in India and China. It has not there produced the energy or initiative of Europe or America. The great
family system in both these countries, with its common family
fund on which all can draw, has stood between the individual
and the direct impact of the argument from personal effort to
personal reward. Poverty in China has led to great industry,
frugality, and care of soil; the same poverty in India has not
led to the use of cow's manure nor the breeding of better stock.
What result will come from economic pressure, or whether there
will be any result, will depend on what is in the mind already,
its whole system of thought, politics, religion, family, community.

52. Work and Cooperation

It is especially mistaken to say, as is often said, that economic
need engenders cooperation. Undoubtedly primitive peoples
do cooperate in fishing, hunting, etc. But equally clearly, the

economic motive taken by itself is competitive. If the product is limited, the more clearly does this competitive relation come out when the hunt is over and the bag has to be divided. It is not the economic self-interest which has brought about the cooperation. It is (a) intelligence, which is able to see that, in hunting, a single individual is unable either to surround or properly track or safely kill his game. And it is (b) a social habit of acting together, already established by the family system, which can here be turned to good economic account. Among strangers, who have no prior grounds for knowing or trusting one another, the advantage of cooperation, even if they are all intelligent enough to see it, does not beget the capacity to cooperate. Hence primitive cooperation arises solely between persons already having some bond of blood.

But what economy cannot create, it can do much to strengthen. No human fraternity is complete until its members have carried through some hard enterprise together. Every personal relationship is deep in proportion to the members' knowledge of one another; and no one knows either what is in himself or his neighbor until each has been up against an obstacle which calls out one's powers of endurance and resource. All the qualities of sportsmanship, fair play, holding up one's own end of the log, accepting one's place and task without complaint, which belong to the teamwork of play, come to full force in the teamplay of work. Hence the economic life, as long as its total temper is good, re-enforces a whole group of social virtues which it has no power to beget.

If the total temper is not good, the economic motive alone will tear the group apart. There will be nothing to ease the contrast between the slacker and the man who does his part nor to settle the uneasy questions of distributing the product. An unequal distribution, which should follow from unequal contribution, will rankle with those who receive less; an equal distribution will rankle with those who have done more. Marx has well said that the industrial society of our time has solved the problem of production but not that of distribution. The problem of distribution is a question of justice and cannot be solved on economic grounds alone. If nothing but economic motives are brought into play, the effort to divide the industrial product may assume the shape of a class struggle in which the fruits of economic progress and the spirit of cooperation are both lost. It is only when man has morality to contribute to economics that economics can contribute to an improved morality.

This is the normal relationship which helps to carry civilization forward:

Every economic evil, such as poverty, at a given stage of sociability and intelligence will instigate an economic advance. This advance, in turn, makes possible an improvement in the moral make-up of society; but it also develops in time a new set of economic problems, which the new moral level should be able to meet. There is thus a hand-over-hand progress: in conquering the problems set by his natural environment, man improves himself. This alternate advance continues as long as human energy and general goodwill and the sense of duty remain high. Drop out these factors, and the advance stops. There is no automatic assurance of human progress on economic grounds alone.

But in any case we can now answer our original question. If we were creating a world and were interested in the improvement of the human stock, we would not leave out of that world the necessity for labor! [1]

(iii) CONQUEST OF THE HUMAN ENVIRONMENT: THE SOCIAL VIRTUES

53. Why Do We Speak of Social Conquest?

For each individual, his human environment is primarily a friendly affair, not something to be conquered. It stands like a protective envelope between him and the rude impact of physical nature. The physical world is unconscious, silent, inexorable, wholly devoid of interest in his welfare. The human group, pooling its powers, puts up a common front against winter, famine, flood; spreads and regularizes the menace of want or danger. At the same time, it has a corporate mind; it can respond to a call for help if nature cannot. So well does modern society play providence to its members that few of them

[1] Cf. BR, No. 9, L. P. Jacks, "Life Functions in a Resisting Medium."

know what it is like to be alone against the big forces of the world.

Hence, instinctively, the human being craves association with his kind. He is drawn to his group without any prudential calculation of the benefits to come to him: he could hardly tell you what they were. He is perhaps not aware that it is chiefly conversation he needs, or that it is only among fellow-men that he can come to his own full stature. He has simply an inarticulate dread of prolonged loneliness and a corresponding reassurance if others of his own kind are around. These impulses, assuming the auspicious character of the human environment, we sometimes refer to as the "social instincts."

But anger also is a social instinct, and fear is partly social. Even when it is an inanimate object that excites wrath, the angry man personifies the obstacle and addresses it as a malicious foe. If one fears in the dark, it is because imagination peoples it with unknown companions. After a few weeks of fairly complete confidence, the human infant begins to notice "strangers" and to adopt the race-old equation of the stranger with the suspect. His world of humanity takes on the fundamental distinction of "friend" and "enemy."

After all, it is only among beings having wills that conflicts of will can occur. Indeed, the old saying that "man is man's worst enemy" says too little; for it is only among men that the relation of enmity can exist. It is only among men that conflicts of will can develop into systematic warfare, with a scientifically implemented purpose of annihilation. And the very advance of human self-consciousness, with its increasing sensitivity and ambition, renders human relations more prolific in rivalries, grievances, envies, recriminations, feuds. Kant put the matter well in his remark that "Men cannot get along without their fellows; and cannot get along with them."

Hence there is much to do to "conquer" the human environment in the sense of creating a "society" — that is to say, a large community in which conflicts are so managed that the dominant fact is not conflict but harmony and understanding. Such a conquest must obviously be at the same time a conquest of one's own reckless self-assertion. But if this self-control goes to the point of suppressing one's self-will entirely or giving up one's individuality to the interest of public order, the problem is not solved but shirked. What we have to achieve, and to some extent have achieved, is a society which keeps its unity while encouraging the growth of that impulse to separateness of mind and interest which we call "individualism."

54. Society as Divided

To see how this has occurred, we must note that what we call society is not one thing but many things. There is the large group or community which serves as a general social medium; and within it are numerous small groups, typified by the family, which serve as an inner and closer environment for the individual person.

Each human being has a general social interest which links him to the larger group with an impersonal tie. A vague loneliness will stir up the latent herd instinct in us, and we make for a crowd, any crowd, no matter what — Broadway will do, or the Quebec Promenade. Robinson Crusoe, excited by a footprint, was not in the least particular whose footprint it was. Social hunger, like hunger for food, may reach a point at which discriminations and choices are out of order.

But the typical form of human social impulse is not the herd instinct, nor is the typical form of human society the herd. There is no human herd. The typical form of human society is the small group. For significant companionship our capacity is limited. Anyone can do with more than one friend, but a thousand begins to be too many. Men find themselves in small companies of intimates, from boys' gangs to political wigwams, religious orders, secret societies, trade unions, amusement clubs, college fraternities, artists' colonies, societies for the promotion of this and that, rotaries, granges. Such groups are selective; and *selection means exclusion*. Intense association takes on an antisocial character. Thus the broad human environment becomes honeycombed by the unsocial sociability of the intimate associations.

Of these, the family is the most important and the most exclusive — the only small group which is represented in animal societies. It puts up such a strong claim for devotion that it often competes with the larger community and weakens it. Plato in his *Republic* thought it necessary to weaken family attachments in order that his ideal state should be strong; [1] and even today, in the great family systems of India and China, the spirit of national unity makes its way with difficulty across the lines of clan loyalty. But every small group, because of its exclusiveness and its disposition to absorb the devotion of its members, tends to detract from the force of large-group unity. Until recent times, European states remained suspicious of private societies, and the "right of association" became accepted, even in England, only in the nineteenth century.

Nevertheless, it is the small group which is indispensable to a truly human social existence, and it is in the small group that the mastery of the human environment begins.

55. The Social Uses of Small Groups

It is chiefly in the small group that human society is *fertile:* this is its great claim to free development. The fertility of the family, in terms of population, is of course indispensable; but beside this there is the *fertility of ideas* and, among them, the ideas of certain elementary social virtues.

In many ways the small group tends to be an ideal society. Was it Thoreau who said that "All the abuses which are the objects of reform are unconsciously amended in the intercourse of friends"? If we talk about "fraternity," here it is; the spirit of "equality" is the very basis of friendly association; and "liberty" is here also, because there is not alone tolerance of one another's peculiarities, but a welcome for them, and openness of expression is the breath of life of the small group. It is the general spirit of "kindness" pervading the small group which disposes of the ever arising conflicts of will. It is not the silly stupidities of mutual retreat from a contested point, it is not "politeness" which governs in the small group — just the contrary; it is the hearty inventiveness which finds ways of satisfying both A and B. We could define the problem of the "conquest of the wider human environment" in simple terms as that of *bringing to it the natural virtues of the small group.*

There are three other social virtues which the small group cultivates: loyalty, reciprocity, generosity. Loyalty is called for

[1] Cf. BR, No. 48, part I, Plato, "The Republic."

when a group member slackens in devotion to the group; reciprocity, when he is inclined to take more than he gives; generosity, when he limits his contribution to the common store.

56. Defects of the Small Group

In these last-named virtues, we have to recognize certain dangers inherent in the small-group pattern. It undertakes to own its members too completely. It wants to absorb their loyalty to the point of preventing their interest from wandering elsewhere. This demand has its justice as against human fickleness, but it may become pestilential when the small group assumes a perfection it does not possess, appeals to "loyalty" to support a crooked deal, to "generosity" to squeeze out support for a foolish project, or to "reciprocity" to carry on a shady log-rolling enterprise. Loyalty to the group then becomes disloyalty to all further social health; as a clan virtue, it is the dangerous virtue.

But, apart from all such abuses, the small group is not sufficient for a complete social life. Even the family in time begins to stifle, and the growing member pushes his way out of it. It is too personal. He requires a severer kind of estimation; he wants to be valued for what he can do, not for what he is. He wants to earn his living and in that process he does not want his family to cut any figure, if his state of mind is healthy. He wants a cold business judgment of his output. He realizes that impersonal competition is what he was born for, and he wants to try his strength in a just but merciless match.

In this wider field, he wants to come into the range of a more abstract set of social virtues, those of justice, fair competition, legality.

57. Emergence of the Individual

This process of getting beyond the intimate and person-regarding atmosphere of the small group, which every man goes through, is one which the race has been working on throughout history. It is the slow process of the emergence of the individual from the group.

The capacity to stand alone, to think alone, to be "independent," to hold to a difference in judgment from one's neighbors, is hardly an original capacity of man in any high degree, though it does belong to the definition of being a self. In fact, though primitive society tends to domineer over all the thoughts of an individual, it finds that it can only continue its own existence by encouraging, and even demanding, a degree of independent personal judgment. The ceremony of initiation in very primitive societies contains, as one of its essential elements, sending the lad off into solitude to get his own hold on himself apart from the tribe, before he is entrusted with the traditional lore. For it is only such an awakened self that can understand what it is he is supposed to carry on. And society thus takes the risk that in stimulating individual thought, it will at the same time arouse a spark of originality which in transmitting the traditions will revise them. From the first, society has taken this risk.

After thousands of years, the small-group atmosphere is fairly cleared away from the larger group. The blood-bond ceased to be necessary as a political tie. The feudal system vanished in its hold on economy with the development of modern industry. When Thomas Carlyle (in *Past and Present*) denounced the heartless "cash nexus" and called for a return to the human and personal ties of the feudal time, it was just the working public that turned a deaf ear.[1] It wanted to go forward into an impersonal type of society in which the bonds were intellectual and legal, a society founded on "rights," not on personal loyalties. As Arnold Toynbee, in his brief history of the industrial revolution, so accurately put it: "Men must separate in order to unite." The graces of personal adherence must be dissolved in order that new ties, based on reason and conscious good faith, may be set up.

The industrial revolution was an economic crisis. But it was none the less a social crisis, turning on a latent moral conviction. It revealed that the whole system of "loyalty" which might, and did, involve all sorts of compromise under fine labels — lying for your fraternity brother, concealing his vices, becoming partner in his crimes, fighting his greedy forays for him — all this had become intolerable at the moment it became unnecessary. Not that the glorious virtue of loyalty could ever become intolerable, but that there must be an independent position for the self-respecting individual conscience from which abuses, masquerading under the name of loyalty, could be corrected. The large

[1] Cf. BR, No. 35, Thomas Carlyle, "A Gospel of Work."

group, in the form of the liberal state as guarantor of human "rights," became the home of the individual spirit of fair play and seemed to promise a satisfactory control of the human environment in the interest of individual growth.

58. Are "Individualism" and the Abstract Social Virtues Enough?

In moving out of the family group, a man does not drop the small group ties. Very likely he founds another family. In any case, he continues to require both the personal and the impersonal types of judgment. For, after all, there is no guarantee that the large society will have an infallible eye for any special talent which John Brown has. He will always have use for the small groups which value him for what he is rather than for what he does. The normal life of man consists in an alternation between the personal and the impersonal, between his home and his occupational group, and so between the regions in which the concrete virtues and that in which the abstract virtues are dominant.

But the chief difficulty with our individualism is that the conquest of the human environment, in the large group, is far from complete. Such legality as reigns there is not adequate to ensure justice nor fairness of competition nor the resolution of those deeper conflicts which lead to war.

Hence many are inclined to judge that it is our individualism which is at fault and the "nineteenth century liberalism" of which it was a part. That liberalism took its problems too easily. It assumed that liberty plus education plus the natural goodness of man were enough to deal with domestic and then with international clashes of interest. Seldom has any important stage of human progress been so short-lived. Its need for correction is everywhere apparent. While John Stuart Mill was penning his noble essay "On Liberty," Karl Marx was already at work on an incisive *Critique of Political Economy*, which foretold the nemesis of a liberty which piled up an uncorrected inequality of status, and saw the end of the era of individualism in a period of class conflict.[1]

These gloomy forebodings are not fullfilled: and individualism has still to show its full social meaning. But neither of these

---

[1] Cf. BR, No. 59, Karl Marx, "The Communist Manifesto."

prophets has the full truth of the social problem. Some union of them would give a rounder version; for humanity can certainly not give up the demand for liberty, nor yet for social justice in the total working of liberty. The present generation has still to write a new chapter, perhaps the most important chapter, in the self-creation of man through the shaping of his social environment by uniting and satisfying these two demands. When this is done, the social virtues developed in the small group and those developed in the large group will find themselves working together for the security of both groups, and of society itself.

(iv) CONQUEST OF WORLD EVIL: THE POSITIVE CONTENT OF RELIGION

59. The Problem of Social Ills

Beyond the fringe of nature which we can conquer and the range of social ills which we can master, there lies the whole wider world which is beyond all foreseeable conquest. These untamed, and perhaps untamable, reaches of nature and society are sources of both good and evil, benefit and calamity, life and death. Scientifically speaking, there may be nothing of chance in nature; but from the standpoint of human ignorance and inability to control, a large element of chance hangs over human fortunes. This means a deficit of justice in the physical side of man's fate. And the same must be said of the social side.

For not only are we imperfect ourselves, but by necessity we are in alliance with imperfect men and imperfect institutions. Power must be given to the state if there is to be any order or liberty but this power must be administered by fallible persons because there are no others. Again, we live subject to the past: we are all inheritors of a world set up by fallible men because there were no others. We enjoy the fruits of their wisdom and hard labor; we suffer the penalties of their follies and crimes. We do not "deserve" either the one or the other. And this infection of the whole meshwork of history by the mixed merits and demerits of mankind is an inescapable part of every human life.

These defects become peculiarly painful at the points where men aspire to be above reproach. It is because society raises the question of justice that it is capable of perpetrating the outrage of a false verdict. Nature does equal damage: nature interrupts the best human plans with illness and death, but it issues no condemnations; it destroys, but it never maligns. Society alone can declare in its judgments, "This is justice; this is the law"; if it is in error, its mistake is doubly evil because it carries the label and repute of rightness. Hence the old saying, *Summa jus, summa injuria* (the utmost reach of legality may be the utmost reach of injury).

These facts do not of themselves destroy the net worth of living. Not many human beings, and no animals, are disposed to give up life solely because of the pervasive element of chance and the deficit of justice. And there is at least one good result which can be ascribed to these facts: men are drawn together because of the constitutional insecurity of the wider world. Not only is there a closer solidarity in the presence of calamity, but men try through charity and insurance to share the uncertainties of fortune. Nevertheless, while human community may be strengthened by the dangers of the common lot, the effect is somewhat like that of alliance against a common enemy — an alienation of mind from the total auspices of life.

60. Various Attitudes toward World Evil

Some are driven to the conclusion we call "pessimism," so far as the course of human history is concerned; however genuine our desires for human good, however substantial our love of justice, the heavy forces of the world, they believe, are against us.

Others, accepting the facts with an honest realism, write off in advance all expectation of a circumstantial justice and school themselves to regard such things with a saddened resignation; their spirit for the further improvement of economic and social life is lamed.

But there are many to whom neither pessimism nor resignation have any appeal. They may reach a very different attitude. Since chance is bound to play a large role in human fortunes, the thing is, they conclude, to play one's chances for all they are worth. If necessary, stack the chances in one's own favor and identify one's happiness with one's good luck. This means that life becomes a game played secretly from a solitary center in which all the shrewd ones understand that they must either do others or be done by them.

This attitude is more often secret than avowed: it amounts to a private individualism as the dominating outlook. If it undertakes to defend itself, it is likely to take on a tinge of "cynicism," the belief that all human nature is essentially selfish, all profession of virtue being a pleasant cloak or rationalization for the bitter fact of strife underlying all human relations.

61. Religion as Adaptation to the World

In a broad sense of the word "religion," all the attitudes outlined above are religious. They are deliberate adaptations of the mind to the world in clear view of the world's evils.

But they are *negative* adaptations; they regard the total frame of life as hostile or indifferent. The word "religion" is commonly reserved for a *positive* adaptation, different in principle from any we have yet mentioned. In this the usual sense, religion is a *resolve to keep faith with the world as if it were just*, whether one sees the course of specific justice there or not. If there is no purpose nor meaning in the world to keep faith with, religion in this sense is simply a cosmic folly. In the eye of the cynic, religion might be exactly defined as "the resolve to keep faith with a faithless world, in order to keep faith with a faithless humanity."

Now it is not our business here to argue out the case of religion. This belongs to later portions of this text (See "The Meaning of Religion for Man," Part IV). But evidently religion plays a critical role in the course of human self-building. For while it is nonsense to talk about "conquest" of the wider environment, it is not nonsense to talk of conquering world evil in the sense of reaching a positive adjustment to the facts of chance and nonjustice which appear there. And to achieve this must make a vast difference in one's will to continue the long human effort we have been tracing. It is this bearing of religion on the enterprise of self-building that we are here concerned with.

62. The Fundamental Dilemma

The great difficulty with being a first-rate cynic is that one cannot put his cards on the table. For he cannot admit to his neighbor that he is going to make a principle of outwitting him if possible, a principle which is implied in consistently looking out for Number One. This is why the acceptance of life as a game of chance is more often secret than professed.

But the cost of maintaining good faith with one's neighbor is high. It is impossible to do this without maintaining that good faith with the universe which, at times, seems so unrealistic. For all human relationships, including the relation between two people, are relationships with third objects. Mind A, being unable to perceive mind B directly, deals with mind B by way of physical objects, space and time, words, ideas, standards — objects which are not identical with either A or B but are common to both. This elementary situation has as a consequence that A cannot serve B directly; he can only help B by way of some third object — it may be food, it may be truth. The development of civilization carries with it the vast development of this indirect service. The scientist may never see those persons whom his discovery helps; he serves an anonymous mankind by serving his own "abstract" third object, truth.

It is this service of third objects, common goals, which draws mankind together; and there is no other way of doing it. Hence the good faith of any man with any other man is, at the same time, his good faith with all other men. It consists in the honesty of that service of third objects which he *has* to profess and especially his respect for truth and fair play and the other virtues, concrete and abstract, which men have come to formulate.

Now what we call a man's "honor," or a woman's, depends on whether the *professed* object of his devotion is the *real* object. This principle acts as a sort of fatality in preventing the direct aim at various social goods we might like when these goods logically come as results of the sincere pursuit of third objects. "Popularity" comes as a logical result of being a good servant of some such object. Hence to go out for being popular, as a direct aim, is a fairly sure way to lose popularity. The candidate for office who *has* to win, and who cannot wait for his competence to put him in office, does not deserve to win. The party which uses every means, fair and foul, to retain power deserves to be out of power. The woman who feels she has to be married and makes a direct drive for it deserves not to be married.

The scholar who needs fame, and who can gain it by a quiet plagiarism, deserves the contempt of all scholars.

On the other hand, he who goes out for the pure service of his third object and thus for the pure service of humanity, and forgets his own interest in doing so, runs a good risk of being overlooked. This is the fundamental dilemma — that the conditions of being worthy of happiness are conditions which forbid the manipulation of fortune in one's favor in order to rectify the nonjustice of a heedless world. Man must forget himself in his object; he must "lose his life in order to save it": but then he does run the risk of losing it! Religion asserts that this ultimate sincerity of service, which looks like folly, is in reality the deepest wisdom.

(v) POSSIBILITIES OF HUMAN CAPACITY: HOW FAR CAN WE GO?

63. General Principles of the Outlook

The two main facts which our study has so far been working out are (a) that human nature is modifiable and has been modified in the course of history, and (b) that man as a species, being self-conscious and self-judging, does take an effective part in remaking himself. He has a malleable material, and he has goal constituted by the standards which he sees. No doubt he knows better, at any time, what he does not like about himself than what he does like; he is better at criticism than he is at directing. But he can always conceive something better than he is and keep working toward it, both in himself and in his young. And if the question is "How far can he go?" the most pertinent answer that can be made is in another question, "Where can he stop?"

The notion of a perfect human being is fairly vague and perhaps fairly distant; it will not be reached by the run of us tomorrow (though many believe that it has been reached once in human history). But as long as the standard is there and is not rejected as a legitimate claim on our efforts, we the human race cannot at any point say, we shall go no farther.

The chief obstacle to the belief that we can keep on with what has been started is the idea of determinism, which we have dealt with. It creates a wholly mythical limit to what can be done; and if we ask the determinist where we must stop improving ourselves, he also has no possible answer.

But it has been our principle not to shirk the difficulties and, having put down the facts which govern the long-time outlook, we have now to come to closer grips with the actual business of improving mankind.

64. Relativities of the Concrete Ideal

There is a definite standard of truth and right, but there is no such thing as an "ideal man" in the concrete any more than there is an ideal picture. One trouble is that not all the excellences of human character can be realized in one person. It might be hard to improve on Shakespeare as a poet, but he is not cited as an outstanding instance of the economic virtues or of political sagacity or of military heroism or of scientific attainment in his time or in social reform leadership. Nor do we expect these things of him. We are sufficiently grateful that he has come far along his own chosen line of excellence. Indeed, if every man could be held to a fairly good job in an all-around identical ideal of humanity, it would be hard to say why God made so many of us. The likelihood is that each one, in accepting the common human standards as a part of his life business, knows that there is another part peculiar to him alone. It is for him to do that task well which no other being in the universe can do. His version of the ideal man will therefore be relative to his own job.

The total effort of mankind at any time is thus broken into a vast number of partial efforts in different lines, which supplement one another. These fall into groups, often into pairs antithetical to each other, which we may regard as specializing in one aspect of a total truth or right. Presumably we shall always have a right wing and a left wing in our parliaments, a conservative and a liberal slant in politics and all other social issues — and this without subscribing to the doctrine of predestination announced in the lines:

> That every little boy or gal
> That's born into this world alive
> Is either a little Liberal
> Or else a little Conservative.

For that matter, the division of mankind into male and female is, at the same time, a biological and a mental division; the man needs the woman partly because their moral specialization is different. Marriage is normally an arrangement in which each admires in the other qualities he does not have and yet needs. And the affection on which marriage is founded is, among other things, a shrewd arrangement of nature whereby each is disposed to take from the other a moral criticism more searching than he is disposed to accept from other sources, a mutual criticism which, in the course of a lifetime, moves each partner perceptibly toward the standpoint of the other.

It is at least conceivable, and I think probable, that the different races of man, while identical in their major standards, have also the destiny to supplement the partialities of one another's moral and aesthetic outlook. The unbalanced helps the unbalanced, and mankind moves forward, as in walking, by the continuous correction of deviations from a central thread.

65. Possibilities of Individual Improvement

Our main concern is with the progress of the race; but the individual is the bearer of the race, and there is no such thing as "the human race" which can act apart from the effects of persons. What the individual can make of himself by trying may or may not modify the germ cells he carries (the question is still open in biology), but it certainly affects the conditions under which his offspring carry on their first steps in living. It becomes a part of "social heredity."

Now the possibilities of each individual are far greater than he can possibly realize — a nice contradiction in terms, which means simply that every decision a man makes between possibilities kills off the alternative possibilities he does not take. If he becomes an engineer, he does not become an artist. Most men have the capacities for half a dozen different careers; and most men have to limit themselves to one or two of the six. Limited by his original endowment, he is limited again by his own deliberate specialization. There are also moral possibilities of a similar sort. A man may become a thief by a simple turn of the pen. Each one has most of the antisocial possibilities in his repertoire as well as their opposites and the nondescript middle region of moral mediocrity. And while the issue of a man's profession is sometime closed, not to be reopened, the moral issue is never closed: a good citizen at seventy may decide to try his hand at crime, and vice versa. Conversion and counter-conversion (from bad to good and from good to bad) are possible at every stage of life; and there is another kind of conversion which may be the most important — from mediocrity of moral level to a significant level.[1]

For most men have unrealized capacities, both for their careers and for their characters. Whatever may be the case regarding those "energies of men" which William James thought were largely unused in most of us, and gave good reasons for thinking so, it is the peculiarity of the individual's moral status that the only limit set to its nobility is set by himself. For moral greatness is something which, by definition, has nothing to do with gifts of nature, and therefore we find it distributed wholly without regard to any other human classification. We rightly make much of the splendor of character among the lowly placed — of Joan of Arc, of Lincoln, of the carpenter of Nazareth, of Socrates, the improvident sculptor — but even a "nobleman" can sometimes be noble, and our own Washington had the disadvantage of coming from one of the F.F.V.'s! The battle is to get men to believe in their possibilities and in the worth of trying. Chiang Kai-shek, in his *Philosophy of Action*, calls on the rank and file of his troops to take on the character of the "Man of the Revolution," whose maxim is "Knowledge is hard, action is easy," meaning thereby that once one has his conviction of the right course, all that remains is to act with simplicity and to disregard the obstacles which deter the timid. That is all! Doing this, says the Generalissimo, places the common soldier at once on the level of the greatest heroes. The history of the world is largely the history of great men who did not know that they were great. They were doing their job with the simple directness of a felt necessity.

> Would we might drink, with knowledge high and kind,
> The hemlock cup of Socrates the king,
> Knowing right well he knew not anything,
> With full life done, bowing before the law,

[1] BR, No. 22, J. H. Denison, "The Transformation of the Self."

Binding young thinkers' hearts with loyal awe,
And fealty fixed as the enduring sun,
God, let us live, seeking the highest light:
God, let us die aright.[1]

66. Possibilities of Improvement in the Human Stock

The processes of natural selection by spontaneous variation and elimination of the unfit had done most of their work on the human frame twenty thousand years ago. The body of Cro-Magnon man was apparently as good as our own, perhaps better. Nature, having turned over to the mind the main task of securing human survival, seems to have regarded the physiological man as a job which each individual could finish for himself, without further alteration in the species. This does not mean that no biological improvements are possible. Almost anyone can imagine a better physical outfit in the direction of some fanciful superman, but few are prepared to indicate how it can be brought about. If nature were to produce a sport in the direction of a higher type, with, for example, a helpful third eye in the back of its head, it would be difficult to secure a mate who would maintain the variation; nor can we conceive that its parents would be happy to see it. The "normal" human type is, to our minds, the ideal animal form, both for general utility and balance and for the artist's conception of beauty.

When the biologist tries to imagine a more responsible sort of improvement, he is likely to suggest a larger head to house a more adequate brain. Ruling out the objections of the artists, who may be prejudiced by classical models, there are at least two disadvantages here. Unless the increase of head size were attended with a corresponding increase in the size of the female pelvic arch, any considerable change would require Caesarean births. And there is no evidence that it is the size of the brain rather than its fineness of texture or its capacity for utilizing electro-magnetic fields which renders it a suitable instrument for the next-needed mental advances.

Instead of improving, there is reason to believe that the human body is deteriorating in some respects with the advance of civilization. It is true that science is giving us a longer span of life, and that improved nutrition and physical habits have increased

[1] Vachel Lindsay in "Litany of the Heroes."

our stature (an average modern man cannot get into an average mediaeval suit of armor). But with our medical arts which keep alive many infants ill-equipped for the physical struggle, and with our institutions for the care of the mentally and physically handicapped, we allow the propagation of congenital physical defects to an extent truly alarming. Nature cares for the stock and lets the individual perish; we care for the individual and let the stock take the consequences.

The progress of science tends to conceal from us the total result, for those whom we encourage to survive we are so far able to maintain. But it has been said that there is no known species of animals whose population contains so large a percentage of defectives as the human species. Science has the direct effect, through its applications, of making our physical existence more comfortable. It enables us to take better care of ourselves if we want to take the trouble. It also enables us to avoid the severer exertions and hardships. It thus conceals from us many a fragility, which in ruder modes of life, might reveal itself before it could be transmitted to descendants.

Not only do we care for our feeblest; we do much to deprive ourselves of our strongest. I need only mention the biological devastations of war, in which the most perfect are selected for possible elimination before their parenthood is fully realized. There is also a disposition for limitation of offspring by parents in heavy social demand because of their abilities. There are others who limit their families for reasons of personal convenience, and the race need not too much lament the loss of their progeny. On the whole, the small-family tendency seems to light on those parts of the population which a superficial eye would select for the more promising offspring.

But we are far from ready to say what part of the stock is "the best." A program of eugenics which considered only the body would be a peril to mankind as long as it is possible for precious minds to be housed in unpromising bodies. A political definition of the type which should be allowed to propagate would be a prospect so terrifying as to justify almost complete haphazard as an alternative — if this were the alternative.

Fortunately it is not. It is far clearer that certain types, such as the feeble-minded, should *not* propagate than that certain others should propagate. Kindness to the defective does not require us to conceal from them the social importance of their remaining childless. A program of *negative eugenics* can be begun. And almost everything is still to be done in the way of rendering more responsible those free choices of mates to which a free society is committed. It is against every scientific presumption that the normally strong selectiveness of the sex impulse should have no biological meaning. Whatever tends to obliterate this selectiveness in the direction of an animal promiscuity throws away, in all probability, the best human method of perfecting its stock.

67. Possibilities of Improvement in Human Society

Those who ask whether and how far the human species can progress are usually thinking, not of the biological improvement of individual or race, but of the social order — the most inescapable, most variable, most beneficent, most faulty and harm-bringing, most malleable creation of man. It is also the most intricate and unanalyzable, so that the direct application of scientific intelligence is almost as likely to mislead as to help. Sociologists ought to be, and as a rule are, the humblest of men, the slowest to propose social panaceas, solely because theirs is the most infinite of undertakings in the field of science. It is not even certain that science, through the method of analysis and law-thinking, can discover the bottom truths of society. For what is living cannot, if Bergson is right, give up its last secrets to analysis; and where the relations between the parts are moral, or in part moral, they are to that extent not based on facts but on what ought to be.

Democracy, for example, so far as it assumes a certain equality among men, is not founded on what men are (for they are unequal in every measurable respect), but on their equal status before the ultimate moral standard, and therefore before any law that might become universal, and on what they may become by the aid of an encouraging and demanding social order.

This ethical element in all social relations is at once the hopeful and the difficult side of their advance. For while science can indicate much of what is desirable and undesirable in institutions, such as property, the family, the state, the best institution will

not work without the injection of goodwill and the sense of duty
into its machinery. And, given these qualities, even a less-than-
ideal organization may devise a satisfactory means to its end.

There is, therefore, in history as a whole no necessary social
progress and no necessary going-under of the Western World.
In some respects there has been a fairly steady advance: man
has increased in knowledge, wealth, technical mastery of nature,
in the art of making records, so that achievements once made
are not lost, in the accuracy of the historical record (which
threatens to become too full for utterance), and finally in a
factor which psychology does not yet know how to measure —
sensitivity.

This sensitivity implies that man's capacity for enjoyment
has increased; he can get more and more varied enjoyment from
the simply physical pleasures (note the elaboration of the arts
of cookery and beverage making), as well as a whole range of
new enjoyments. He is capable of greater suffering from the
same physical injury. He can rise to greater heights and descend
to greater depths. If he gives himself over solely to extracting
the pleasure his organism makes him capable of — a program
of life which no animal could devise — he can make himself
consciously more brutal than the brutes.

For a similar reason, the advance of civilization brings with it
a greater vulnerability of all institutions. It is easier to break
up a concert by a warwhoop than to break up a snake dance.
It is easier to destroy property in a modern city than in a Kaffir
village: the easy targets for vandalism are far more numerous.
And the political institutions are more easily undermined by an
increase of popular lethargy or an unwillingness to give what
they take. It is for this reason that prosperity is a dangerous
condition for a modern state. It invites relaxation of the public;
the caterers whose livelihood is proportionate to the degree to
which they can exploit the heightened sensitivity by enticing
to new enjoyments of luxury, sex, greed, and the love of display
and of power, will not be idle. This is so much the repeated
experience of periods of civilized wealth that some students of
history have made of it a law of *rhythm*, of the periodic rise and
decline of cultures, in which the sensitive and effete are swept
aside or subordinated by sturdier and saner stocks. No one

can say that such rhythm is necessary, for that would be equivalent to saying that degeneracy is necessary. One can only say that the more civilization advances, the easier it is for its beneficiaries to be treasonable to the harder moral conditions necessary to hold that level and take the next step ahead. Incapacity for a disciplined life is not a necessary evil.

But overcoming of the rhythm will require the discovery of an international equivalent of war, at present the chief agent for the mutual destruction of the more advanced sections of mankind. All war has become civil war in the sense that only the highly technical and economically fortified peoples can make effective war: war can break out today only between peoples who already share in the same cultural and technological advance, who have a similar group of needs which brings them into clash over some of the limited goods of the earth, and who are already taking part in the general system of communication which has made us one world.

I say "an international equivalent of war" because modern war is not causeless; it represents a group of unsolved problems. It is not due primarily to bad men nor bad nations nor bad ideologies nor bad parties; these evils take root in the unsolved problems which are partly economic, having to do with standards of living and rivalries among outreaching industrial powers, partly moral, and partly political, having to do with the status of national groups, the rise and decline of national power and territorial control. These are problems for which as yet there is no solution in the scope of international law; they are commonly described as "non-justiciable" issues and are referred to arbitration when both parties are willing to arbitrate. This set of problems will be dealt with in the third part of this text. At present we have only to say this: that the peoples of modern nations do not go to war for issues which are purely economic or purely political; they can be brought to the point of facing the sufferings, the efforts, the destruction of war only when such economic or political issues are represented to them as issues of justice. But an issue of justice is one that justice-loving men can come to accord about. And if an aggressor nation is led into war by leaders who have falsified the issue, the remedy is surely not out of the reach of human invention, for it requires simply the replacement of falsehood by truth, a replacement which can occur in proportion as statecraft in general recovers the honesty which has so largely disappeared from it. In brief, we cannot assume that there are any issues between nations which can only be solved by war.

As in the case of individual improvement, we may say of society that the only limits to social progress are those which are set by man himself. Only in this case it is man as a corporate entity that we mean. The conquest of war and of decadence must be achieved by organized effort, a union of new and more powerful thinking, with cooperation of national powers and an acceptance of a share of world responsibility by each sovereign state. The individual citizen is helpless before efforts of this magnitude.

And yet not wholly helpless.

For it is almost a defining mark of civilization that an idea may be effective at once throughout the entire society. Let a scientific discovery be announced, and it is, in principle, the property of the entire community: the discoverer does not have to carry his idea to the corners of the earth, for society is already organized for its diffusion. What is true of a scientific idea is true to a lesser extent of any significant thought. Let a Tagore write poems in India or a Tolstoi create fiction in Russia or a Sibelius compose music in Finland, and the world knows of these things during the lifetime of their authors. The principle of civilization is that whatever has meaning is, in its nature, the concern of all men. And nothing has so much meaning, through whatever medium it expresses itself, as prophecy — meaning by this word not the foretelling of future events but the rebuke of men for those moral failures which defeat their own happiness and that of their fellows, and an indication of a nobler way of living. There is no argument so convincing to men, and to so many men at once, as the argument of a life which is not adrift but has a direction and an inner stability.

There is this radical difference between the perfection of an individual and the perfection of society. The perfection of society must be gained by slow degrees over a long time: its goal is future and distant. The perfection of the individual life must take place, if at all, in the midst of time and not at the end of it. For moral worth consists in part in dealing with the evils of the environment: when there are no more evils to fight, the occasion for individual courage and stamina is past. Perfection in some respect, at some point, is within the reach of individual action and is, in fact, being achieved every day; and where the best social hope of the next generation is in the demonstration of the possibility of a self-disciplined democracy (one which does not require the hero-leader because its powers of correction are within itself) in which no rights are claimed without an acceptance of the corresponding duties and no privileges for which one is not willing to meet the cost, we may say, quite literally, that the way in which individuals govern their own lives makes or unmakes the possibilities for mankind.

PART II.   PERSONAL ETHICS

Brand Blanshard

Yale University

A. DO WE NEED ETHICS?

68. The Two Basic Questions of Ethics

We are about to make an expedition into *ethics*. The subject is not a new one, for one of the leading questions of ethics has forced itself upon us already. We have seen that man is the sort of creature that, like a sunflower seed or an acorn, must be understood in the light of what it is tending to become; so we have had to ask already, "What is it that man is driving at?" "What are the ends he is really seeking?" We have gained some useful hints of the answer, but if we want those hints filled out, it is to ethics that we must go. For ethics, as someone has said, is the science whose business it is to fix the goal-posts of life.

But ethics has a second task; it attempts to arrive at standards of right and wrong. And we shall have increasing need of such standards as we go on. If the reader's breath lasts through this section, and he arrives at the next one on Social Philosophy, he will find himself in a thicket of problems in which he will need ethics as a leading-string at every step. Is freedom a good thing and, if so, why? Is it ever right to break the law, or to go to war, or to refuse to educate oneself? These are questions of right and wrong. And there is not much point in discussing them unless we agree on what *makes* things right or wrong. We must get clear on that if we can.

Both the great problems of ethics will come in for discussion here, but the second is the more pressing, and hence the better to begin with. What exactly do we mean when we say that conduct is right or wrong?

Some people are impatient with discussions of this sort. All that is needed, they say, is that we should have a clear enough idea of right and wrong to choose the one and avoid the other, and we have that already; why bother about anything more? "The trouble with most of us," they add, "is not that we don't know what we ought to do, but that we don't do it." Nobody has any doubt that to pick a neighbor's pocket is stealing or that stealing is wrong. Nobody has any doubt that, in general, he ought to keep his promises and obey the law and pay his bills; if he admits an occasional exception to these rules, as he does, he seldom has any real trouble in distinguishing the exception that is justifiable from the one that is not. If somebody were to cheat us or spread a ruinous scandal about us and then try to excuse himself by saying that he supposed these things were all right, should we accept his excuse at face value? Not for a moment. We should say that if he is a normal human being he knows that such conduct is wrong and is only deceiving himself or us if he says otherwise. If, then, we know the rules of right conduct already and are seldom much puzzled to see what they require in practice, is it not plain that we have already as much knowledge of ethics as we need?

The true answer to this is No, and in a moment we shall see why. Yet the question points to a fact about our moral knowledge that is curious and important. We know what we ought to do, and yet in a sense we do not know. We do have standards of conduct, and we apply them so unhesitatingly and successfully that it looks as if we must know quite clearly what they are. But try to get from any ordinary man a straightforward account of what they are, and you will wonder how he ever succeeds in making a choice at all.

You hear him objecting, for example, to the Nazis' invasion of Norway. "What was wrong about it?" you ask. "Why, everything," he answers. "They saddled their army on the people, gagged the newspapers, drove great numbers to forced labor, and sent those who had the courage to resist into concentration camps or dragged them before firing squads." "Well," you persist, "what is wrong about that?" He grows suspicious. "Do you really mean to say that might makes right?" "Suppose I did," you go on, "just what is wrong about that?" Such a question may only induce a splutter; but let us assume that he has a cool head. "If you say that might is right," he replies, "you can justify anything. On that theory, a clever person who knew how to avoid the police would be acting perfectly rightly if he amused himself some night by burning down your house or wrecking your car or holding you up and taking your

purse." "Granted; but what's wrong about taking a purse?"
"It's stealing." "Yes, yes, but what's *wrong* about stealing?"
"Well, it means taking what doesn't belong to you." "But why
shouldn't you take what doesn't belong to you?" "Because
you have no right to it." "But suppose I insist that I do have
a right to it, that I have a right, for example, to what is in your
purse if I want it. How are you going to show that *your* claim
amounts to a right and *mine* not?" Here confusion is likely to
set in. "I earned the money and you didn't." "Then if you
hadn't earned it, you would have had no right to it?" "No, I
wouldn't say that. I'd still have a right to it, and you wouldn't,
even if someone had given it to me." "And you also have the
right, I suppose, to bray like a donkey if you want to, and to go
on wearing that fantastic necktie in my presence?" "I certainly
do." "Very well, I repeat my question: *What* gives you those
rights? They must rest on something. How would you defend
them?" "Heavens! I don't know. But let anyone try to take
them away, and I'll show him one way of defending them."

69. We Need to Know What We Are About

Such a dialogue brings out two things. In the first place, it
suggests that, whether we have ever studied ethics or not, we
have standards and strong convictions about right and wrong.
It suggests, in the second place, that we are commonly in a fog
as to the bases on which those convictions rest. We know what
we ought to do in the sense that we have standards in the back
of our minds which we take for granted and use continually
without thinking about them. Yet it is also true that we do
not know them, if knowing means knowing explicitly. If called
on to give a reasoned defense of them or even to state them in
so many words, we should not cut an impressive figure. We
combine unquestioning confidence that truthfulness, generosity,
and promise-keeping are right with an embarrassing inability
to say why they are right.

Now to gain this sort of insight requires hard work. To dig
down to the bases of our beliefs about right and wrong and
expose them to the light of day is something that calls for strenu-
ous thinking; and thinking, Emerson said, is the hardest work
we can do. Is the task in this case worth doing? We return

here to the question we left unanswered a few moments ago. If our standards, in their unexamined state, meet all our practical needs, why not let them rest there, without stirring up knotty problems about their ultimate justification?

One may take a higher or lower line in answering this question. It is on record that when the question was put to the great thinker who founded moral philosophy, he took the high line without qualification. Socrates was accused of producing skepticism and unrest by his continual probing of these matters. He replied: Virtue without knowledge is not really virtue at all; only that conduct is truly good which is chosen because we see it to be good; our minds are given us in order that we may know what we are about; the man who acts from habit or mere conformity does *not* know what he is about; he is acting blindly, and therefore failing to play a man's part. "The unexamined life is not worth living." [1]

To anyone who is interested only in action, such an answer may seem meaningless. To anyone, on the other hand, who has acquired in his own field a delight in knowing for its own sake —to the engineer, for example, who is dissatisfied until he sees just how an engine runs, or to the doctor who feels it a blow to his pride to find a disease that he cannot identify, or indeed to any ordinary boy or girl in whom the healthy desire to know *why* has not been educated out — the answer of Socrates will suffice. Understanding, here as elsewhere, is its own justification. It is obviously a better thing to see and understand than not to do so, even if it never increases one's income by a penny or makes the slightest difference to one's efficiency in office or factory. It is worth while for its own sake.

70. Will Common Sense Carry Us Through?

But to say this is of course not to deny that it has practical value too. Here we have the second line of reply to the question about ethical knowledge. That question was, Do we not know enough ethics already to serve our needs? The answer is clearly No, for there is such a thing as the need to understand, and we do not understand fully enough now. We have next to see that our present ethical knowledge is not even enough for our

[1] Cf. BR, No. 5, Plato, "Socrates' Defense of Himself."

practical needs. There are two chief reasons for saying this: first, our common-sense knowledge often breaks down and leaves us with no guidance at all. Secondly, it sometimes does worse. It lays down rules which prove on reflection to conflict with each other. In these cases all we can do is to carry our thought beyond what common sense can tell us.

Consider the first type of case, in which common sense fails through silence. We must admit, to begin with, that such failure is the exception and not the rule, and that our ordinary, uncriticized standards do serve us surprisingly well. If we had to stop and puzzle out what to do whenever the chance arose to short-change another person or take something from a department store counter, we should be like the well-known centipede which, suddenly coming to realize what a complicated business walking was, ended in a ditch and a nervous breakdown. On these points and a thousand others, our policy is settled; we do not need to give a thought to it; we are saved the trouble by a set of rules that have so ingrained themselves into our habits that we follow them automatically.

Where did these rules come from? Not, certainly, from ourselves; we do not believe that theft and arson are wrong because we have experimented with their many varieties and come gradually to a general conclusion about them. The rules came partly from parents and teachers who, in turn, got them from their own parents and teachers; partly from friends and associates who got them from further friends and associates. This does not mean that all our convictions are borrowed; for then how explain the innovators and pioneers who stand out against general custom? Nor does it mean that what at first are copybook headings need remain so throughout our lives, for we may come to see their validity for ourselves. It does mean, however, that we are all echoes to begin with. Our rules and standards are accepted unthinkingly from the society around us in much the same way as our accent and the cut of our clothes.

If it is asked, "How did society itself come by its rules?" the answer is that it molded and remolded them in the course of a long, slow evolution in which one generation profited by the errors of its predecessors. It took mankind centuries to learn that duelling was absurd and millenniums to reach any clear conviction about slavery. Thus the standards we accept so passively as individuals were certainly not so adopted by the race; they are the accumulated deposit of innumerable experiments, adventures, expensive failures, and flashes of unremembered moral genius. They now constitute a huge storehouse of helpful suggestion, covering the larger part of the decisions we are called upon to make.

71. Sometimes Common Sense Is Dumb

The larger part, but not all. Before some cases common sense stands dumb; and these cases include many of the most important decisions of our lives. Where the issue is one of black and white, as in a temptation to thievery or thuggery, common sense is clear and firm. But suppose the problem is complicated, confused, and far-reaching.. Suppose, for example, that the question is whom to vote for at the next presidential election. This is a problem that involves much human good and ill; it is therefore as truly a moral problem as whether one should make off with someone's purse. But obviously common sense is not a good enough judge here. The parties differ in their views on tariffs, on the conflicting claims of labor and management, on foreign policy, on taxation, on the civil service, on dozens of other questions, and all of these are in the end questions of right and wrong; on none of them does common sense have any clear view, to say nothing of the larger issue which must be approached through these minor issues. Faced by a problem as complicated as this, mere common sense stands silent. Of course many an educated man stands silent too; but at any rate the only mind that can hope to deal with it competently is the mind that has had some training in distinguishing means and ends and in looking to remoter consequences.

72. Sometimes Common Sense Is Inconsistent

Sometimes when we try to get help from the body of accepted rules, the failure is more striking still. The oracle is not now silent; it speaks out emphatically enough but only to contradict itself. The secular rule, for example, conflicts with the religious. Anyone who sees much of moving pictures knows that when the hero catches the villain maltreating the heroine, he does not, as a rule, content himself with saying, "Go and sin no more." The average audience would not have it; they want the malefactor dealt with as they feel he deserves; they must be allowed a little delicious revenge. Now these same people go to church on Sundays and listen in all acquiescence to sermons on such texts as that we should turn the other cheek and forgive seventy times seven. The rule they have accepted from the practice of their society is that men should get their deserts. The rule they have accepted from their religion is that good should be done to everyone, regardless of deserts. Both are supported by powerful traditions which all of us inherit; yet both cannot be true. Where one is confronted by such a conflict of rules, there is only one recourse. One must fall back on moral philosophy and ask what is the ultimate justification of *any* moral rule.

"Thou shalt not lie." "Thou shalt not kill." But suppose a gangster, gun in pocket, is looking for his victim; you know this and know, further, that the victim has just passed this way. The pursuer asks you where he has gone; what should you say? If you tell the unvarnished truth, you have been an accessory to the taking of life. If you put first the saving of life, you must buy it at the expense of truth. One rule or the other must go. Or consider the well-worn case of the switchman. A man's first duty, we hear it said, is to those of his own blood. A man's duty, it is also said, is in every case to prefer the larger good to the lesser. Very well; the switchman looks up one day to see his child playing on the tracks with the express approaching. He can drag the child from the tracks, or he can throw the switch, but he cannot do both. If he obeys the first rule, he will save the child, but wreck the train with its load of passengers. If he obeys the second, he will save the passengers but serve as the instrument by which his own child is destroyed. Now one may be sure that whatever course the switchman adopts at this unhappy juncture, it will not be a course of moral philos-ophizing. But it is also clear that moral philosophy is the one thing that in the end could give any clear answer to his problem.

73. Ethics Then Is Necessary

Common sense, then, is not enough; it is both confused and contradictory. If we are to know what we are about, we must go beyond it into ethics. Hence ethics is in a different position from many other studies. Archaeology, astronomy, Greek, and calculus are all important and interesting subjects; but no one could say that they are indispensable or inescapable, for there are persons who have lived long and happy lives without the slightest knowledge of any of them. But no one can avoid ethics. We have to make decisions daily that involve ethical issues, and we always have some standard, implicit or explicit, reflective or unreflective, that we use in meeting these. We really have no choice, then, whether we shall engage in ethics or not, as we do whether we shall engage in archaeology or not. We are moralists willy-nilly. The only question is whether, since we are committed to ethics anyhow, the views we have shall be reflective and clear or uncriticized and muddled.

Nothing is easier than to fall into such uncritical and muddled views; a little philosophy is a dangerous thing. When we begin to feel doubt about the accepted standards and to hunt for firm ground of our own, we are sure to find pressed upon us certain theories that are attractively simple and sweeping, have attained a wide popularity, and are offered us as the solution of all our major problems. They are very tempting, and some of them contain much truth. Still, most philosophers would agree that in their main contentions they are unsound; and since for some readers they may block the way to other and better views, it may be well to look at them at once. Two of them are of prime importance.

B. ARE MEN THE SLAVES OF THEIR IMPULSES?

74. The Case for Impulse

First there is the view that human beings are the tools of impulse and instinct. We are told that, once we see this, and what it implies, we shall have a wholly different idea of what right and wrong mean.

Ethics, in the past, has been based upon the idea that men were rational. Not that everything they did was reasonable — far from it — but it was believed that they could act reasonably if they tried. Indeed, what doing right meant was subjecting their feelings and impulses to the control of reason. Everyone, when insulted, tends to feel angry and lash out at the one who has affronted him. But the good man is the person who, before he lets himself go, looks at the affair in perspective; if he sees that to let fly at the other man would do more harm than good, he checks his impulse and takes a more rational course. Life is full of temptations to fly off the handle in one direction or another, and we all occasionally let go. Animals cannot help letting go, for instinct controls them completely; and though on the higher levels this may be modified by experience, no animal can peer into the future, foresee results, weigh them against each other, and choose the best among them. Man can do that. That is what makes him man.

To most moralists all this has seemed obvious enough. Yet this the new irrationalism denies; and it does so by carrying the analysis of choice one step farther. Consider the angry man. We have supposed him to control his anger by taking thought and seeing that what would be gained by holding himself in is more worth while than what would be gained by letting himself go. But then, is not the act of taking thought itself a step that calls for explanation? Why did he do that rather than not? In answer, we are told that this too is a matter of impulse. If some people, before they act, let their fancy play upon the outcome, while others act at once, that is a matter of their original make-up; introverts are not less creatures of impulse and feeling than extroverts; it is only that their impulses take a different direction.

But further, suppose a man does stop and reflect; suppose he presents to himself clearly the differing consequences of acting first in one way and then in another; just why, in the end, does he choose one course rather than the other? Is it really reason that makes the choice? Surely not. It is true the angry man's impulse to strike is checked by the awareness of probable consequences; he is dealing with a big, irascible fellow and may get much worse than he gives; or it may flash into his mind how much explaining he would have to do if his friends heard that he had been mixed up in a brawl; or he may be inhibited by an ideal of himself as not the sort of person who resorts to his

fists to clear up a difference of opinion. Granted, say the irrationalists, that the presence of these things in his mind overrides
the impulse to strike; *why* do they override it?

The answer is that they arouse impulses stronger still. The
thought of the possible drubbing arouses fear; the thought of
the painful impression on others stirs into life the man's interest
in having others think well of him; the awareness that the act
is out of line with what he wants to make of himself calls into
action his feelings of self-regard. Thus the "rational" choice
itself turns out to be controlled by non-rational impulses whose
existence at first were veiled. So of other "rational" choices.
We are creatures of impulse through and through. And once
we clear our minds of prejudice and frankly admit this, we shall
see that ethics is beside the point. For it is built on the assumption that we can override impulse with what we see to be right,
and it is now clear that that assumption is false. Impulse is in
the saddle. The attempt to control it only betrays the firmness
with which it holds the reins. Reason is itself nothing but
impulse at one remove.

75. The Argument from Evolution

Distasteful as this view may be, it has gained many adherents,
and this largely through the aid of three powerful supporting
influences. The first is that of the theory of evolution. Before
this theory was accepted, it was commonly believed that men
and animals were quite different types of being, who had been
created separately a few thousand years ago and had remained
sharply distinct ever since. The theory of evolution made it
too clear for doubt that this was not true, that the ancestry of
man went back not only into the darkness of primitive savagery
but much farther still into the very depths of the animal mind.
At the date of the supposed creation, man, or creatures very
like him, had already been on the earth for some five hundred
thousand years. And before this stretched out an almost inter-
minable period of probably millions of years during which life
was slowly climbing up the biological ladder.

What that implies, if you look at it in the large, is that the
overwhelmingly greater number of man's ancestors belong
among the animals. If this is true, we should expect to find

that man's body is full of traces of this animal heritage; and that is just what we do find. The little hard point near the top of our ear is an original pointed tip, now slowly disappearing; at one stage in the life of the embryo the vertebrae at the base of the spinal column are free and make a tiny tail; our appendix, whose only present use is to help surgeons make a living, was a useful magazine for food in the days when forgotten ancestors went on all fours; a biologist has recently distinguished in the body 176 such organs, all relics of our animal past. And it is not only in these useless organs, but in the way the bones are arranged, in the way the muscles are attached, in the architecture of the body as a whole, that the witness of our animal heritage is recorded.

Now if this witness is recorded all over our bodies, must it not be recorded also in our minds? Body and mind have the same genealogy. These undistinguished ancestors are the ancestors of our minds as well as our bodies. For most of them thought was unknown, and impulse and instinct were the guides of life. The power to reflect, like the sense of sin and the sense of humor, is a relatively late acquisition, whereas our non-rational nature, with its stewing passions and instincts, is not merely a legacy from the caveman, but an heirloom that was already ancient when he himself inherited it. If what is oldest in our nature is most firmly implanted there, then our animal impulses are central and our rationality a veneer.[1]

76. The Argument from Cave-Man Outbreaks

What the theory of evolution thus suggested received a depressing confirmation from two world wars. If man really was, like the beasts, a creature of impulse, then he would begin to behave like a beast when the brakes of civilization slackened; and that, it is said, is exactly what he did. Men who came from centers of European culture were to be found in every corner of the continent, killing, raping, looting, and torturing. These things did not occur in some remote cannibal island whose inhabitants were imperfectly emerged from their animal past. They occurred in the most highly civilized countries of the world, as if to drive home by an immense historical irony that the restraints of culture

[1] Cf. BR, No. 31, Friedrich Nietzsche, "The Origin of Morals."

and justice and reason were no deeper than the paint daubed on a savage face. Fathers of families, university students, men supposedly given over to gentle thoughts and ways, found, to their own astonishment as well as the world's, that they could become cavemen almost overnight.

77. The Argument of the New Irrationalism

Between the two wars there developed another and third influence, which supplemented the evidence of the second. The great wars revealed how easy it was, in abnormal times, for the caveman to leap out; the founder of psychoanalysis, Sigmund Freud, showed that even in normal times the caveman is not sleeping. He is still there, said Freud, and still in effective control, but he wears a mask. As we look at our conscious choices and beliefs, we see nothing suspicious about them; they seem to be governed objectively by the facts of the case, and we should resent the suggestion that we were puppets pulled about by impulse and feeling.

It was Freud's chief contention, however, that impulse and feeling may act unconsciously, indeed that in everyone there is a vast subterranean cistern of irrational bias, that our surface life of belief and purpose is for the most part a puppet show controlled by wires none the less powerful because they are invisible.[1] A man habitually avoids dogs and explains his habit to himself and others by evidence designed to show that all dogs are dangerous. But when he is examined by special methods, it turns out that his habit is really due to the repressed memory of some frightening childhood experience with a dog which is still lurking in his "unconscious" and making all dogs fearful to him. A man arrives at a belief in God and supposes that he has arrived at it through evidence. Freud explains that what has pushed him toward it is his childhood need, persisting all unrealized, for the protecting care of a father.[2]

In both these examples we see traces of a process which the Freudians have proved to be disquietingly common. It is disquieting because it carries the irrationalist explanation into the processes of reason itself. It has been assumed in the past, as we saw, that we can be reasonable if we try; it has also been

---

[1] Cf. BR, No. 17, Paul Grabbe, "Psychoanalysis."   [2] *Ibid.*

assumed that if our conduct needs justification, that is to be found in giving reasons for it. If we can offer good reasons, the conduct is justified, otherwise not. Now the contention of the new irrationalists — not of all, to be sure, but of many — is that this process of finding "good reasons" is not really reasoning at all; it is a process of "rationalizing"; and by rationalizing they mean patching together an argument that will satisfy not reason but endangered pride. "Our 'good' reasons," it is said, "ordinarily have no value in promoting honest enlightenment, because, no matter how solemnly they may be marshaled, they are at bottom the result of personal preference or prejudice and not of an honest desire to seek or accept new knowledge." "To the modern student of mind, pure reason seems as mythical as the pure gold, transparent as glass, with which the celestial city is paved." [1] When some crackpot inventor urges his product as the most important discovery of the century, we are apt to smile because it is clear to us that his judgment about it is the reflection of his own special interest in it. We are now told that when the successful man justifies the capitalist system or when the less successful man denounces it, when a preacher pleads for religious belief or a military man for a strong army, his reasons are really devices for the defense of beliefs or vested interests that have been adopted on wholly different grounds.

Now, if all this is true, we shall save ourselves much trouble by admitting it. For ethics is the attempt to find out what justifies conduct or makes it unjustified, and if such attempts are bound to be distorted by our impulses, there is not much sense in making them. We must therefore ask whether it is true that we are dominated in this way by impulse.

Certainly there is a great deal of truth in the view, and we owe a large debt to those who have shown how imperfectly emerged we are from the animal mind. We knew this in general before, but they have thrown a flood of light on the devious ways by which this lower mind reasserts itself. And they have done more than that. They have shown that many mental ills can be cured, and have developed a technique for curing them. It is extremely significant that their chief reliance here has been on the method of self-understanding. They have proved

[1] J. H. Robinson, "The Mind in the Making," pp. 33, 44.

in thousands of cases that when the distorting forces are seen
as they are, they tend to wither and disappear.

78. Surmounting Bias by Understanding It

But consider what this means. It means that on their own
showing we are *not* wholly at the mercy of irrational pushes and
pulls. So long as the man with the irrational fear of dogs
remained ignorant of the source, he continued to be its victim;
but when the source was brought to light as the trivial thing it
was, the fear melted away; he was restored to normal perspective
by understanding his own unreason. If this can be done here,
it can surely be done elsewhere. It is quite possible for an honest
man to recognize, with or without the help of others, that his
vehement defense of the Republicans or the Democrats, of his
own children or his own profession, is charged with bias, and
to discount that bias deliberately. So far as he succeeds in doing
so, he is no longer the slave of bias. To see one's partialities
and prejudices as what they are is at least to go a long way
toward delivering one's self from them; for a conviction that
is seen to be baseless has already begun to lose its hold on us.
Indeed the distinction is a pretty fine one between the man who,
though biased, takes full account of his bias, and the man who is
not biased at all.

79. Irrationalism as Logical Suicide

Any spiritual doctor, then, who gives us at the same time a
diagnosis of hopeless infection by prejudice and a prescription
guaranteed to cure, is acting incoherently. But the incoherence
of the present theory goes far deeper. We are told that whenever we choose one thing rather than another it is instinct or
impulse that moves us; that whenever we adopt one conclusion
rather than another it is not reason that has carried us to the
conclusion but a set of influences from below which have nothing
to do with reason.

But if so, what was it that moved the holders of the theory
to adopt this theory itself? If their own report is to be believed,
what really moved them was not the requirements of the evidence
but a set of impulses that worked in disregard of the evidence.
But in that case, why should we believe their theory? The mere
fact that they have an impulse to accept it is no ground for

supposing it true. Indeed, in other cases where we know that a belief rests on nothing but impulse, we take that as evidence that it is probably untrue. Thus the theory that we are at the mercy of irrational impulse destroys itself. If the theory is true, then it is itself the product of non-rational impulse and has no more claim to truth than any other product of unreason. On the other hand, if in this particular instance its authors have escaped the control of impulse and succeeded in following the lead of the evidence, they can surely do it in other instances. Thus in neither case does the theory have any claim on our belief.

Some people find points of this kind unconvincing; they are suspicious of criticism that turns so largely on logic and so little on fact. This suspicion is really not justified. No more decisive criticism can be made of any theory than that it is inconsistent with itself, since, if it is thus inconsistent, it cannot possibly be true. But there is no need to confine ourselves to this sort of criticism. For the present theory, besides being inconsistent with itself, is also inconsistent with fact.

80. Thought May Remold Impulse

For example, it is just as good a fact that thought molds impulse as that impulse molds thought. Indeed, impulse under the guidance of thought may be all but completely transformed. Consider the instinct of pugnacity. As this appears in the lion or tiger it is an automatic affair; if, under certain conditions, a rival appears, the animal will react with a roar and an attack as inevitably as a slot-machine will react when a coin is inserted. The animal cannot restrain his reaction; he cannot trim and shape it to suit remoter ends because he is unable to think of ends. In a young child the impulse works similarly; if he is displeased, he is likely to pick up his toy, throw it on the ground, and smash it. But he pays the price for this, for a little later he wants his toy and finds there is none to be had. When the impulse arises the next time to smash a toy, he has begun to realize what indulging his temper leads to, and the long process of the remolding of impulse by thought is under way. But it has only barely begun, and the process may go on through level after level of transformation.

When Winston Churchill was a fiery-tempered schoolboy at Harrow, he was asked what profession he thought of going into. He replied, "The Army, of course, so long as there's any fighting to be had. When that's over, I shall have a shot at politics." He was a pugnacious, adventurous youngster who, if report is to be believed, was a handful. A student of his character, writing some years later when he was still a young man, said of him: "He is still the Harrow boy, 'having his shot at politics' — not so much concerned about who the enemy may be or about the merits of the quarrel as about being in the thick of the fight and having a good time. . . . But the sense of high purpose is not yet apparent through the fierce joy of battle that possesses him. The passion for humanity . . . the surrender of himself to the cause — these things have yet to come." No "high purpose," no "surrender of himself to the cause!" Such comments would seem very odd if made about the Churchill of thirty years later, who had charge of his country in its blackest days, and who issued the call to "blood, toil, tears, and sweat." The spirit of the man was built on that youthful pugnacity and adventurousness and would no doubt have been impossible without it.

But was the early impulse unmodified as it appeared in the statesman of sixty-five? Fortunately for the world, it was not. Even his severest critics would not deny to the older Churchill the "high purpose" and "surrender to a cause" which they formerly found absent; and, when checked and guided and molded by these, the manifestations of the impulse were transformed at times into their opposites. The man who loves a fray and who is without responsibility can often let himself go without notably ill effects. But when the threat that stirs him to action is no longer offered to himself alone but to the nation and the form of life to which he is committed, when he knows that a little rashness or brashness, an untimely fit of spleen or one ill-judged experiment in "the gentle art of making enemies" may touch the fate of his people at a thousand points, then his combative impulse, though the same, is also profoundly different. For now it is under the discipline of an end that is visible only to thought, which controls it as the far-off pole controls the movements of a compass needle. Granting that it is still impulse that provides the drive, it is thought that now gives the direction.[1]

We have perhaps said enough about the first of those popular theories that stand in the way of straight thinking in ethics. That theory was that such thinking is of no importance, that what really controls our action is not thought but always, if we look deep enough, non-rational impulse. We have admitted that the theory goes a long way toward explaining the more irrational kinds of conduct. But its main contention is untrue. We have seen that irrationality can sometimes be cured; that the theory of total enslavement to impulse is self-refuting; and that even if impulse does often mold thought, so thought may deeply mold impulse.

C. RELATIVISM IN ETHICS

31. Statement of the Theory of Relativism

We come now to the second popular theory that stands in the way of straight thinking about conduct. Such thinking tries to find what is the right thing to do. But the holder of this second theory would say something like this: "You talk about *the* right thing to do. What reason have you to suppose that there is any such thing? May there not be dozens of possible practices, all of them right? What is right to you may not be right to me. What is right to me may not have been right to the people of ancient Greece; it may not be right to modern Tokio or to the South Sea Islanders. And to insist that among all these conflicting practices only one can be right is absurd. Try to keep your charity alive, and your sense of humor. Remember Chesterton's lines:

> The wildest dreams of Kew are the facts of Khatmandu,
> And the crimes of Clapham chaste in Martaban.

And Kipling's:

> There are nine and sixty ways of constructing tribal lays
> And every single one of them is right.

[1] Cf. BR, No. 64, William James, "The Moral Equivalent of War."

Moral rules are not absolute, but relative: relative to the time and place, perhaps even to the individual person. "Leading a pure and noble life is precisely the same kind of thing as dressing properly and taking off one's hat to a lady. Righteousness, good manners, fashion — they are all one."[1] Now if we found anyone maintaining that his own particular style in hats was the only right one, and therefore that the benighted people who wore fezzes and turbans, derbies and sombreros were all wrong, we should only be amused and should probably set him down as the last word in provincialism. Is not a man in the same boat who holds that, with regard to the treatment of parents or wives or strangers, there is just one right way, presumably his own? Why should dogmatism about fashions in conduct be more respectable than dogmatism about fashions in dress?

82. The Argument from Diversity of Custom

There is a large and easy tolerance in this attitude that makes it very persuasive. And the persuasiveness is increased when we find offered in support of the doctrine a vast mass of knowledge drawn from the writings of such anthropologists as Westermarck, Frazer, Sumner, Howitt, Spencer and Gillen. They have shown that, far from all men's approving the same practices, there is perhaps no single practice that can be mentioned which would meet with universal approval. You can take any major department of human life and show that the practices within that field which are approved by the people of one time and place may be paralleled by opposite practices among the people of another time and place.

For example, how should we treat our parents? In China reverence for parents stands at the top of moral requirements; the son must love, serve, and obey his father during his life and burn incense to him after his death. On the other hand, among the Fijians it was formerly a custom, when one's parents had reached a certain age, to kill them, perhaps by making them climb high trees and shaking them down.

Again, how should husbands and wives treat each other?

[1] C. E. Ayres, *Holier than Thou*, p. 1. Indianapolis: Bobbs-Merrill Company, 1929.

Take the matter of divorce alone. Hobhouse summarizes the practices of about two hundred seventy uncivilized tribes. Divorce was wholly prohibited in about one case in twenty-five; it could be had by consent or at the will of either party in about half the cases; it was permitted at the will of the husband alone in about a quarter of the cases and at the will of the wife alone in about one case in one hundred thirty-five. (It was permitted also under certain other special conditions.) Thus every obvious possibility was somewhere or other realized.

Again, how should we treat the stranger? Among the Arabs of the desert it was the practice to give the stranger the best seat by the fire, the best food, and the most solicitous attention. On the other hand, an authority on the native tribes of Australia writes that "whenever they can, the Blacks in their wild state never neglect to massacre all male strangers who fall into their power." [1] It would be easy to continue this catalogue of conflicting practices; but it is hardly necessary. For if the reader agrees, says the relativist, that a competent anthropologist could make such a list at all, he is agreeing that morality is not one thing the world over but a set of countless conflicting moralities. Indeed, there are *more* fashions in right and wrong than there are fashions in hats.

83. The Argument That Rightness Is a Matter of Feeling

Now such diversity does not prove that all these customs are equally right, nor does it show that there is not some single set of customs that is the only really right one; that remains a possibility. What it does show, however, is that if any man rises to remark that his particular customs are right and all the rest wrong, the chances (and the laugh) are against him. For some relativists, nothing more need be said. But in late years there have been many who have pressed the matter farther. They want to know *why* men should differ so wildly about moral matters, while in many other fields, such as mathematics and physics and chemistry, they differ so very little.

The answer arrived at is this: Statements about right and wrong, good and bad, are questions about values, and whenever we say anything about values we are not making statements

[1] E. M. Curr, *The Australian Race*, I, 85. J. Ferres, Melbourne, 1886–87.

of fact at all; we are only expressing our feelings. And everybody knows that our feelings, our likes and dislikes, for example, vary enormously. No one is surprised when two persons look at a picture, and one of them says, "I like it" and the other says, "I don't." What would surprise us is for one of them to say, "That picture is square" and the other to say "Oh no, it isn't; it is a perfect circle." In that case, one or the other of them would be making a grotesque mistake, for it is obvious that the picture cannot be square and circular at once.

Now the reason why we expect people to agree about moral matters, says the relativist, and are somewhat shocked when they do not, is that we suppose them to be making statements of fact. The truth is that they are only expressing their feelings, and these may be as various as the persons who feel them. When a man says that cruelty is wrong, he is not saying anything that is meant to be true about the act but expressing his own dislike of it. Once we see this, we see how absurd it is for anyone to say that his own practice, or anyone else's, is the only right one, for when he does say it he literally does not know what he is talking about. He thinks that he is talking about a fact and that he is making a true or false statement about this fact, whereas, though he does not know it, he is only putting into words how he feels. That is all that statements of right and wrong ever express. Conduct is not right or wrong in itself, for these depend upon people's feelings. If the Chinese have a favorable feeling toward obeying parents, that makes it right in the only tenable sense of right. If the Fijians have a favorable feeling toward killing their parents, then, since rightness depends on such feeling, that too is right. Thus they are both right. Indeed, everyone is right, provided he seriously approves of what he does. We must be infinitely tolerant of each other.

84. Is Nothing Really Better than Anything Else?

What are we to say of this teaching? If all that is needed to make men's practice right is that it should be "right to them," we must admit that to call any custom really superior to any other is dogmatism. But if we embrace such a doctrine, we should do so in full view of what it carries with it. We have been in the habit of thinking democracy superior to Nazism. On the present theory, there is not a whit more ground for this statement than for the Nazi's statement that Nazism is superior to democracy. We dislike Nazism, to be sure, but if the Nazis like it, that is enough; neither system has the slightest claim to real superiority over the other. That leaves us, perhaps, uneasy. But let us go on. The Nazis invade Poland, close the universities, loot and burn towns, put the people at forced labor, and do what they can to exterminate the Jews. The Poles disapproved of all this; it was "wrong to them." But the Nazis approved of it; it was "right to them"; and since, according to the theory, this is all that being right means, they were as truly justified in their view as the unhappy Poles in theirs. If marauders are ever troubled by the thought of people who feel differently, there is one way in which the rightness of their cause can be placed beyond all doubt. Let them exterminate their enemies utterly, so that nobody is left who fails to approve, and, then, since the favorable feeling is unanimous, they will be right beyond any question.

All this seems clearly to follow from the theory that is before us. The view is tolerant, yes; but unfortunately it is so very tolerant as to leave us no ground for saying that there is anything objectively wrong in treachery, cruelty, or murder. Can we accept this? For the sake of the theory, we may do so in words; but if we are normal human beings, it is a safe enough guess that we neither act on it nor really believe it; indeed most of us would say that the conclusion was monstrous, and that any reasoning which led to it must somewhere have gone off the track. Very well, *where* has the argument just offered gone off the track?

85. "Right to Me" versus "*Really* Right"

It went off at the very beginning with an unnoticed confusion about words. The arguer looked at the savages of Fiji, saw that the custom of parent-killing was "right to them," and proceeded to offer this as an argument for believing that there were many different "rights" in this matter. The fact that it was "right to them" was supposed to be evidence that it was really right. But what is meant by "right to them"? Surely nothing but this — that they *thought* or *felt* it right. And the instant we recognize this, we see that the argument so far is without any force at all.

It proceeds on the principle that if somebody thinks or feels something to be right, it really is right.

Now we should see through that in a moment if anyone applied it in other fields. If we were asked to believe that thirteen was really unlucky because many people thought or felt so, or that slavery was really right because large African tribes accepted it, we should regard the argument as silly. We should say that nothing was easier or commoner than for people to have such convictions and be mistaken in them. Between our thinking that something is right and its really being right there is not only a difference; there is not even any fixed connection.

86. Diversity Does Not Prove Relativism

With this distinction in mind, let us look at the rest of the argument. It points out that with regard to every practice one could name there are diverse and contradictory opinions, and concludes that any claim to exclusive rightness is dogmatic. The practice of inflicting pain on others simply for our own amusement may be self-evidently wrong to us, but there have been many people in many ages to whom it has not seemed so, and if it is not self-evidently wrong to them, there is no self-evidence about it. Now it is clear that where there is difference of this kind, it *is* arbitrary to assume that ours is the only true view simply because it is ours; it is evident that someone has blundered, and it may be we; we must look carefully to the ground of our belief. But granting this obvious demand, does mere diversity of view show, or tend to show, that there is no objective right to be found? The principle of the argument is that where there is contradiction or wide diversity, it must be arbitrary to lay down any one view as true. And here again we have a principle that no one really accepts.

If we were asked whether we were clear that 6 and 5 make 11, we should say, Yes. Someone then points out to us that there are tribes in the South Seas to whom this is by no means clear; they rely on their fingers to count to ten, and when their fingers give out, counting breaks down. If one suggested to them that 6 and 5 make 11, they would doubt it or deny it. Does the fact that on this point there are contradictory opinions make us really doubtful whether our insight is to be trusted, or whether there is any one truth to be found? Not at all. Even here we should of course be ready to re-examine our statement, but if, when we do this, it presents itself again as clearly and distinctly true, there is no need for the violent conclusion that our insight at its very best may still be mere delusion. Such a theory would make a wreck of all our insights, including this insight itself. The sensible conclusion is the moderate one — that something may be self-evidently true without being self-evident to everyone. There is no need to distrust Einstein because there are bushmen, or super-bushmen, who fail to follow him.

87. The Deeper Identities

We have been assuming, so far, that deep diversity of moral opinion is the fact. We have now to ask whether it really is the fact. Consider the often-cited case of the Fijians who killed their fathers and mothers. Here if anywhere, it would seem, we have an attitude and a practice differing hopelessly from our own. But as anthropologists have studied the facts, the case has come to wear a new complexion. It appears that the Fijians who engaged in this practice had a firm and peculiar view about the after-life. They believed that a person continued in the after-life with the same set of habits and faculties that he carried with him at death. It followed that to allow an old person to go on living until his faculties were in decay was to condemn him to dragging out indefinitely a feeble and wretched existence. Was that a desirable future for a person one loved? Would it not perhaps be the kindest thing to inflict on him a brief suffering now and secure his permanent happiness later? The Fijians thought it was. Because they thought so, they adopted a practice that makes us shudder. But does this show that their underlying scale of values, the good they sought by these means to attain, was radically different from our own? On the contrary, given their creed, it tends to show that theirs was the same as our own. We think that we should cherish our parents and concern ourselves about their interests. So did they. We think such concern should display itself in securing those parents' happiness. So did they. It was the very fact that their values and filial attitudes were so similar to ours that made them adopt an outward custom so very different. What the diversity turns out to reveal is not a differing scale of values but a different belief about what happens to us after death. And in ethics it is precisely this scale of values that is fundamental — whether one believes that happiness is better than unhappiness, that others' happiness should count as well as one's own.

It would be interesting to look into other clashes of morals and see whether we should not find in every case an ultimate identity of values lying beneath the surface difference. Socrates thought we should. He would have said that just as it is absurd to suppose that arithmetic is really different for a black man and for a white, an American and a German, so it is absurd to suppose that in the end the standards of right and justice are different in various minds. They may be overlaid to various depths by customs that are due to ignorance, by distorting emotions, and by powerful animal impulses that still are often plainly in the ascendant. Some of us fail to prize the things that others love, such as the vision of truth or beauty, not because we have seen what they see and rejected it as worthless, but because we have never seen what they see at all. Socrates thought if our vision were the same, the things we prized would be the same. And the greatest of his successors have agreed with him.

88. Right and Wrong Not Dependent on Our Feelings

But here we stumble upon the last part of the theory. When we suggest that all normal men would agree on the importance of certain values, that they all would say happiness is good, for example, and intense physical pain is bad, the relativist may reply that this is of less significance than we think. For it does not show that these things are good in themselves; it only shows we all have a certain feeling about them. If that feeling were to change in certain ways, things that were bad would be good, and things that were good would be bad, in the only sense in which they can be either. We do not feel approval toward anything because we see it to be good; we call it good because we feel approval. Is this view sound? Hardly.

First, does it catch our meaning when we state our beliefs about what is good and bad? Take the statement about pain. Suppose that when we are away from home a pet dog gets caught in a trap, struggles long and vainly to get free, and is found dead on our return. We look back on what he must have gone through and put it down as a very bad thing that he should have suffered so. But according to the theory, the suffering was not bad at all, and all we are doing when we say it was bad is expressing our present feelings about it. Nothing in fact was bad until we came home and said our say; and if the dog had remained undiscovered, nothing bad would have happened at all; for it is only as people take up attitudes that good or bad comes into being. And if people could manage to delight in the suffering, once they discovered it, then it would be good, in the only sense in which anything is good. This conclusion has actually been held by able men; but it does small credit either to their heads or to their hearts.

Secondly, if the theory is true, we can never argue about moral matters nor even disagree about them. If Jones says bull-fighting is right and Smith says it is wrong, they are not differing in opinion at all; what is happening is merely that Jones is expressing a favorable attitude toward bull-fighting and Smith an unfavorable one; neither has said that anything is true; neither has denied what was said by the other; neither can do it if he tries. Now is this expression of varying feeling all that goes on when we argue about moral matters? Surely there is more to it than that. When you say, "Bull-fighting is all right," and I say, "No, it is wrong," it is plain that part of my meaning is to *deny* what you have said. According to the theory before us, that is impossible, for such statements never assert anything to be true or false; they merely give utterance to feeling. In view of the fact that moral issues are among our most constant subjects of debate, this denial that there can ever be any difference of opinion about them is most implausible.

89. Retrospect

Now let us pause and take our bearings. We have been trying to dispose of two large lions in the path which threatened to make any advance into ethics impossible. First there was the difficulty about reasonableness; since in all we do we are creatures of impulse, we were told, clear-cut ideas on conduct would be of small use to us if we had them. But we have seen that we are not *merely* creatures of impulse, and that we often do in fact escape from it so far as to do what thought reveals to us as the better thing.

Then came the other great doubt. Is there anything objectively right or good for thought to reveal? Perhaps these things are matters of fashion, of changing whim and taste about which it is proverbially idle to dispute. But this theory, for all its seeming sophistication, turns out to be a confusion, the more tiresome because, after all, it is playing with fire. There is every reason to believe that when we dispute about what we should do, there is a truth waiting there to be found as truly as when we dispute about the right sum for a column of figures. In saying that something is right, we are not merely exclaiming in delight or disgust; we mean to point out a truth which is what it is regardless of how we think or feel.

D. TYPES OF ETHICAL THEORY

90. What Is Right Conduct? An Example for Analysis

We have made some progress. When we are in doubt what to do, we can at least say this: there is *some* act that in the circumstances would be the right one for me to do. I may never find out what it is; I may make grotesque mistakes about it; but at any rate the matter is not to be settled by the taste or whim of the moment. The fact that I want to do something, even that I want to do it overpoweringly, is not enough to make it right.

Well, what does make it right? If we are to learn how to tell right from wrong, we must get the answer to that question. What are the earmarks of right conduct by which we can recognize it when we see it? That is the most important question of our whole inquiry, and we must now deal with it as best we can.

Let us look at the problem in an example, taking a bit of conduct that all of us would approve unhesitatingly and asking just what it is that we find deserving of approval.

In the Spanish-American war, yellow fever killed thousands more American soldiers than the bullets of the enemy. Its slaughter was so intolerable that the government appointed a commission, headed by Major Walter Reed, to look into the causes of the disease. After testing many hypotheses, the commission concluded that what probably caused it was a microbe carried from one person to another by the bite of a certain kind of mosquito. Clearly, if this could be established, the discovery would be of incalculable importance; it would save countless human lives.

But how was Major Reed to prove it? He could note that people who were careful about screens in their windows came down with yellow fever less commonly than those who were not; but of course there was no proof in that. He might experiment with animals by having the mosquitoes bite them and see what followed; but that line too was cut off for, as it happens, animals are immune from the disease. The only decisive course was to have the suspected kind of mosquitoes, which were known to have bitten persons suffering from the disease, bite other human beings, and note the results. But who would want to take that sort of chance? The disease had carried off more than a third of the officers in the commanding general's staff; in some of the epidemics the death rate had been 60, 70, even 90 per cent. Nevertheless Major Reed advertised for volunteers. Instantly he got more than he needed.

He wanted to make sure that the disease was not carried, as commonly believed, by the clothes of infected persons; so he asked his volunteers whether they would be willing to spend some weeks in isolated huts, in a temperature of 90 or more, sleeping in the bedclothes and pajamas of those who had died of the disease, which were still filthy and foul with excreta. The men deliberately elected to do it. When they had come through this ordeal safely, he then asked some of them if they would let themselves be bitten by mosquitoes bloated with the blood of yellow fever patients. Again they consented. This time they promptly came down with the disease and went to the verge of death with it, though fortunately, through good care, they did survive. Their service put the cause of yellow fever permanently beyond doubt. From that time forward it was clear that if you could destroy the mosquito, you would destroy the disease. Within a few years there was not a single case left in Cuba of a malady that had carried off appalling numbers annually.

It is hard to imagine a voice of criticism being raised against what these volunteers did. They did what all would agree to have been right; indeed, many would say that they had gone far beyond the call of duty. Whether one can really do *more* than one's duty is a nice question which we cannot at the moment pursue. But we may safely assume an agreement that these men, at the very least, did right. The question now before us is, What made their action right?

If this question looks easy, the appearance is certainly delusive, for the greatest of moralists have had trouble with it. They would probably all agree that *what* the men did was right. But they would offer strangely different reasons *why* they thought it right. And since the views of distinguished moralists on so fundamental a point are sure to contain a good deal of truth, even where they are not wholly acceptable, we shall do well to look into the principal answers that have been given. There are two main schools of thought on the matter, the intuitionists on the one hand and the teleologists or utilitarians on the other. We shall save time and space by calling their theories the act theory and the end theory.

91. The Two Chief Types of Theory

According to the act theory, what made the men's conduct right was something in the act itself, as opposed to its consequences. But what precisely *is* it in the act that rouses our approval? The answers here are various. Sometimes the answer is simply "the act as a whole." One looks at it as one looks at a fine picture and gains an immediate, unanalyzable impression of rightness and nobility. More commonly it is held that we can find, by analysis, precisely what it is that makes the act right or wrong, and then we can bring all acts of that kind under a rule which will guide us safely in the future. But there is a very wide difference of view as to what makes such rules binding. Some people say they are laid down for us by the authority of the church or the Bible. Some say they do not need such support because they are self-evident as they stand. Some have said that the test is whether it would make sense to ask all men to live up to them. Others, again, have insisted that what makes an act right is not conforming to any kind of rule at all; it is rather the spirit in which the act is done: the source in feeling from which it springs, the splendid courage and generosity, for example, displayed by Reed's volunteers. Among these theories there is, of course, wide disagreement. But they all agree that what makes an act right is something in the act itself.

Over against all theories of this kind stands the end theory. It says that what makes an act right is not what it is like in itself, but what it issues or terminates in; what counts is consequences. If the normal result of sacrificing one's self in searching for the cause of disease were an increase of human misery rather than a decrease, would people go on praising it? Not at all; they would regard it as silly and wrong. If so, says the end theory, if, by reversing the kind of consequences, you can reverse the character of the act, then rightness and wrongness plainly depend on consequences.

But what kind of consequences? Here again we find differing views. Some say that the only results that count are results in the way of happiness or unhappiness; if the net result of the men's sacrifices was to increase the sum of human happiness, their act was right; if not, it was wrong. Others insist that this is too narrow a view, that there are other things in the world besides happiness which must be admitted to be good in themselves; for example, the added scientific insight that the sacrifice made possible.

Here are theories in plenty. All of them cannot be right, yet all of them are more or less plausible, and all have in fact been held by large numbers of persons. Indeed, these and certain combinations of them are the main theories about rightness that ethics has to offer. Of course as they appear in the pages of the great writers they are developed with much subtlety and many qualifications and are combined in varying patterns; but still, these simple and natural theories form the essential components in the ethical thought of Kant and Aristotle, of the founder of Christianity and the founder of Stoicism, of Locke and Price, of Hume, Mill, Sidgwick, Martineau, and Green. Each of them contains so much truth that we cannot afford to neglect it; yet we shall find that none of them covers the field alone. And they hold very different amounts of truth. It will be convenient to have them before us in a table:

Act Theories	*End Theories*
1. Impressionism	1. Happiness as the end
2. The rule theory:	2. The end as a harmony of different goods
a. Rules resting on authority	
b. Rules resting on self-evidence	
c. The categorical imperative	
3. The attitude theory	

E. IMPRESSIONISM

92. Judging Right Action by Immediate Impression

The first of the act theories seems to correspond very well to what goes on in our minds when we call something right or wrong. It points out that when, in our example, we view what the volunteers did, we do not withhold our approval until the thought occurs to us, "That act was of enormous benefit to humanity," or until we have analyzed the act and classified it. Our approval is instantaneous. Even before the description is over, our minds are made up that that was a fine thing to do, and seemingly with the help of no reasoning, dissection, or classification whatever. Indeed, to stop and think in such a case often muddies the waters; first impressions, we are told, are safer; it is best to trust one's intuition. The inarticulate person who relies on "instinct" is often a better judge than the "intellectual" who is running over with reasons and arguments.[1] In the end, we must judge of actions, it is said, as we judge of men — by immediate, unreflective total impression.

We have had the experience, perhaps, of advertising for someone to fill a job and have received many letters of application that made the writers look, from the descriptions they gave, as if they were cut out, to the last detail, for that particular work. Then we begin to see them, and we find that we can tell in an instant that Smith would be impossible, and, also within an instant, that Jones is just the man. If we tried to explain to Smith *why* he was not accepted, we probably made a mess of it; yet we were perfectly confident we were right.

[1] Cf. BR, No. 3, Lin Yutang, "Be Reasonable."

So of our judgments of conduct. It is told of the great jurist, Lord Mansfield, that he was once approached for advice by a young friend who was going out to the West Indies to act as a magistrate, and who doubted whether he was equal to the task. Mansfield's advice, in effect, was this: Give your decisions with confidence, for the chances are ten to one you will be right; but don't try to give your reasons, for the chances are ten to one they will be wrong. Nor was Mansfield the first who would have offered this advice.

To Quakers of the days of Fox and Penn, insight into right and wrong was a kind of mystic intuition; they were so distrustful of the results of analysis that when they had hard decisions before them, they tried to render their minds passive and quietly waited for an inner prompting which, when it came, often proved to be singularly just.

Again, there has been an important school of moralists who were convinced that rules and reason had so little to do with our judgments that they spoke about conscience as a moral *sense*, suggesting that one perceived the rightness of an act as immediately as the blueness of the sky or the taste of a coconut. The view that conscience concerns itself, not with rules and abstractions, but with concrete, individual cases, just as perception does, has been given the suggestive name of "perceptional intuitionism."

93. Intuition No Simple Affair

What are we to say of it? When it points out that our judgments of right and wrong are often passed without conscious analysis or calculation, it is certainly correct. But it makes one great error. It supposes that because we are not *aware* of complexities, the complexities are not there. And it is easy to show that they *are* there, both in the act we pass judgment on and in our manner of judging it.

Look first at the act; is this the simple, unanalyzed thing that it seems to be? Consider the case just used to illustrate this point. You meet a certain person and are at once convinced that for a post you have in mind he would never do. This sort of insight, sometimes called "woman's intuition," has been thought a very mysterious affair because the one who has it may be unable to give any account of it and yet often proves so right. But there is no great mystery about it. You have been meeting persons all your life and forming impressions of them; little by little one particular kind of voice, a special kind of look in the eye, a sly or furtive manner have come to signify, by repeated association, an unlikable and untrustworthy person. You have not explicitly noted the connection, but it has impressed itself nevertheless. When someone with these traits now presents himself, he calls to mind what they have signified in the past; that is, they drag the conclusion along with them. You are not really dealing with the man as an unanalyzed lump or whole; you have analyzed him without knowing it; you have fixed on certain traits which, in your past experience, have come to mean for you certain things.

Now something like this happens when we pass judgments of right or wrong. When we disapprove of someone's failing to keep an engagement, our judgment is not an ungrounded mystic intuition, for we can always, by taking further thought, bring to light something that the judgment rests on — an attitude of indifference toward others, a resulting inconvenience, or what not. In short, ethical analysis has begun. We are already beyond the first type of theory and have entered the precincts of the second, where acts are right or wrong because they fall under certain headings or rules, and where we say not merely, "*This* act is wrong," but "This *kind* of act is wrong."

94. What Is Conscience?

The act, then, on which we pass judgment is not the simple, unanalyzed thing this theory supposes. Neither is the judgment itself. An immense lot of superstitious and uncritical talk has been indulged in about "the voice of conscience." It is a "still small voice" which speaks with infallible accents; it is "a little spark of divine fire"; it is a pure, white beam falling across the darkness in which all our other faculties presumably leave us.

Now the trouble with taking conscience in this way as absolute and infallible is that, sooner or later, we find a case in which two men with equally clear consciences find themselves on opposite sides; then, realizing that our idol is toppling, we are likely to fly to the other extreme and deny that conscience has any authority at all. That conscience does give these conflicting verdicts is plain; let one example suffice. John Woolman and John Newton were contemporaries, and both were prominent religious leaders of their day. Woolman was the saintly Quaker whose "inner light" led him to protest so effectively against the slave trade as to awaken public opinion against it. Newton was the author of some of the finest hymns in the language. But he was also, for a time, the captain of a slaveship; and he has left it on record that some of his sweetest hours of divine communion were passed on this ship when he was separated by a few feet from a weltering cargo of kidnapped human beings whom he was transporting for sale like so many head of cattle. Newton's conscience could apparently take that in its stride; Woolman's protested loudly. To represent both these consciences as divine and infallible is not exactly convincing.

The fact is that conscience, far from being a channel of pure light from on high or a separate faculty of our nature, is simply our mind as a whole making its response to an act that comes before it. And just because all our faculties are at work in it, its verdicts are not independent of the sort of persons we are; every bit of education or cultivation we gain will make itself felt in these verdicts. A man may be obtuse in all sorts of ways and yet have a remarkable gift for calculating in numbers because this gift is so highly specialized that it can work almost unaided by the rest of the mind. But every atom of imagination and feeling and intelligence that one has will enter into one's judgments of persons and their conduct. Other things equal, the richer the mind, the better the conscience.

95. Conscience Not a Single Voice but a Chorus

Conscience, then, is not a voice, but a chorus of voices; and if one attends carefully, one can distinguish the various strains in it. In part it is the voice of habit, protesting against being violated; and that helps to explain why, when snubbed, it so quickly falls silent. A habit continually violated is a habit no longer; the thief, after a few acts of theft, can pilfer whenever he pleases without a murmur from conscience.

In part, conscience is the voice of intelligence. We know very well by experience that breaking promises leads to distrust and disappointment, and when our conscience protests, this means in part that our intelligence has done some swift anticipating and is holding up its red light as a warning of what is ahead.

Again, conscience is partly the voice of feeling and desire — the desire, for example, to be liked and approved. That is something we all want desperately, whether we know it or not. Even a thug needs his gang to assure him that, at least in some eyes, he is not an outcast, for universal detestation is more than any of us can bear. On the other hand, there is an amazing tonic in knowing that others approve and admire us; it is far easier to be a hero if others are looking on than if we know our heroism will never be heard of. In conscience there is something of the tuning-fork, vibrating in unison with communal feeling. "The conscience," says Leslie Stephen, "is the utterance of the public spirit of the race"; we hear in it the voice of society warning us what to do and what to avoid if we are to have its favor, and, blending with this almost indistinguishably, the voice of our own longing to be liked and approved.

These and many other voices may be discerned in the choral symphony of conscience. Put them all together, and what do they signify? They are the voice of our ideal of life, our general design for living, speaking through our various faculties and offering comments on the details of our practice.

96. Some Warnings about Conscience

If we are to catch the true meaning of this voice, there are two mistakes we must particularly try to avoid. Sometimes conscience is conceived as confining itself to protests. Now if it really is the voice of an ideal, it is natural that its tone should be sharper when it speaks to warn or condemn than when we are walking securely in the way it approves. Still, it is unjust to conscience to say that its only word is No. The implicit intelligence that forecasts and threatens ill can also promise good and propose a path to it. With its vetoes and its shaming, conscience can make life miserable for us, and it often does; but it has large powers of benediction too; it knows how to cast a glow over work well done; and by common consent of the great teachers, a conscience at peace with itself is one of the solidest piers on which human happiness can rest.

The second mistake is to suppose that the vote of conscience is always for safety and the status quo, though, from what we have so far said, this might easily be inferred. If conscience is the spokesman of the established practices of one's self and one's group, it would seem bound to veto the novel, however reasonable that may be, and give its blessing to timid conformity. Nathaniel Mather, the young brother of the Puritan preacher, Cotton Mather, leaves it on record in his pathetic journal that he once whittled a stick on Sunday and suffered lasting tortures of conscience as a result. Is not such a conscience a brake on all freedom and joy in life? We must admit that it is. Conscience speaks, as we have seen, with many voices, and sometimes what is heard most loudly is the voice of an irrational tradition, seconded by fear but using all the accents of moral authority.

And there are other inward impostors equally skilled in this sort of impersonation. Sometimes "conscientiousness" is a mask for moral conceit and a way of announcing to the world, "I am holier than thou," as it was for the ancient Pharisees. Sometimes conscientiousness in one direction is a compensation for guilty laxity in another, as when a man who is mean and hard throughout the week is scrupulous in the extreme about his Sunday churchgoing. Indeed, the grossest cruelty has been carried out in the name of conscience, as when good men were burned alive for the sin of intellectual honesty.

97. The Voice of the Ideal

All this, and more, must be granted. But what is the conclusion from it? That conscience is to be thrown overboard? There would be small sense in that. The true conclusion is that we need more and better conscientiousness. It is part of the business of conscience to be critical of itself, to single out the false voices and silence them, to be on the alert to distinguish within itself what is genuine moral insight and what is the dictate of custom or toadyism or fear or conceit or hypocrisy. This has been, and can be, done; and the conscience that achieves it, far from being timid and conformist, is, perhaps, the most revolutionary force on earth. It supplies the very yeast of change and reform because it is never satisfied with the existing state of things, either inside or outside the self. It is the criticism of the actual by the unattained ideal, the growing-point of the moral life, the principle of "divine discontent" in human nature.

To be disloyal to conscience in that sense is to turn one's back on the very polestar of advance. John Newton supported the slave-trade "conscientiously"; but it should be added that loyalty to that same conscience carried him out beyond his old allegiance to an altitude from which he saw his mistake. Conscience is an imperfect light; granted. But that only proves that we should make it clearer, not that we should put it out. The surest way to put it out is to let it die by disregard. The surest way to make it clearer is to take it seriously, which does not mean blindly and uncritically, but with a desire to find and follow the best light it can give.

Let us retrace our steps a little. The long-range question before us is how we should go about it to distinguish right acts from wrong. The first advice offered us was: Look at the act as a whole, and you will see whether it is right or wrong by intuition. We have concluded that this will not do. When we judge that an act is right, it is not in virtue of *everything* about it, but in virtue of some special features which may or may not be expressly noted. These features we have not yet put our finger on. And the judgment itself is no simple thing. We have illustrated this from conscience, which, far from being one "still small voice," is nothing short of a chorus of voices.

F. THE RULE THEORY

98. Judging Acts by Classifying Them under Rules

We said that those features in an act which made us approve it had not yet come to light, and we must now try to bring them to light. Here the second theory comes to our aid. It says that the way we recognize an act as right is to see that it falls under a general rule; if it fits the rule, it is right; if it violates this, it is wrong. A child goes next door to see a playmate and comes back with his friend's toy engine. "Did Jimmy give it to you?" his mother asks. "No, I took it." "Well, you take it back this instant." "Why?" "Because you had no right to take it." "Why?" "Because it's stealing." "Why shouldn't I steal?" "Because stealing is wrong." "Why is it wrong?" "Johnny, what a question! Of course it's wrong. Now you run along and take that engine back."

This, it would be said, is a fair picture of the actual working of our minds. We justify an act by a rule which we assume needs no justification; and once we have classified the act, our minds are clear. The watchman at a railroad crossing reported, after a collision between a train and a motorcar, that he had gone out and swung his lantern in the car's path; he did not state that the lantern was not lighted; was he justified or not in making such a report? As soon as we decide that such suppression of fact is lying, our minds are made up. We know a particularly juicy bit of scandal about X, which would tickle the ears and the malicious fancy of everyone present. But X is a good friend of ours. Should we tell the story or not? If we see this as falling under the heading of disloyalty to a friend, the moral issue is probably settled; we may tell the story all the same, but then we do it against inner protest. We see that it is wrong in virtue of the *sort* of act it is; in principle it is disloyalty.

99. Do Moral Rules Rest on Authority?

Why should one take these rules as decisive? To this the general-rule intuitionist replies that they wear their authority on their face; they are self-evident. We must look into this in a moment. But before doing so, we must glance at another way of defending these rules, which, since it goes beyond the rules themselves, is not strictly a form of intuitionism but is both common and important. Some persons, if asked why they believe they should not steal and lie, point to the Eighth and Ninth Commandments, where it is plainly written, "Thou shalt not steal" and "Thou shalt not bear false witness"; and for them, that settles the matter. If asked why they believe that we should never seek revenge, they point to the New Testament requirements that we should forgive "seventy times seven," which means indefinitely. There are many pacifists who believe that the use of force on other persons is, under all circumstances, wrong, even in self-defense, and who, if called on to support their position, would go straight to the Sermon on the Mount with its injunction, "Resist not evil; but whosoever shall smite thee on thy right cheek, turn to him the other also." There are many persons who, if problems arise regarding marriage or divorce, will turn for guidance to the rules of their church, with no question that these rules are absolute. In all these cases, the rule is regarded as coming eventually from God himself, through the Bible or the church as the authoritative interpreter. They are examples of the ethical position known as authoritarianism.

Now whatever we may say about authority as a means of *determining* right and wrong, it is worth pointing out that, in one form or another, all of us rely upon it in practice. In childhood we rely on the authority of our parents. They tell us that it is unsafe to lean out of windows, to go to sleep in wet clothes, and to sample the interesting bottles marked "Poison" on the shelves of the medicine closet. Here and there are hardy young souls who feel the indignity of such dependence and insist on testing these things for themselves, with the all too frequent result that they are the last of their hardy line.

As we grow up and escape from one set of leading strings, we find ourselves attached to others; for all sorts of problems confront us on which we are called to make up our minds, but of which we have far too little knowledge to solve by ourselves. How can I best invest my savings? What is the meaning of this ache in my chest — has something gone wrong with my heart? How useful are vitamins, and which ones are useful for which purposes? What does the evidence really amount to that I am going to survive death? On such questions as these we appeal to authority unhesitatingly; indeed, there are persons who hold that we never make a really independent judgment about anything, that all the beliefs we have about politics, education, religion, and everything else are impressed upon us by the irresistible authority of our community. A great writer on ethics, Henry Sidgwick, records in his journal that he had a dream one night and found it running in his head on waking. It was this:

We think so because other people think so,
Or because we are told so and think we must think so,
Or because we once thought so and think we still think so,
Or because, having thought so, we think we must still think so.

This is somewhat wild, as a good dream ought to be, but it contains an amount of truth not inappropriate to the dream of a moral philosopher. Our beliefs are, far less generally than we suppose, the achievements of authentic insight, and on the larger issues we appeal to authority constantly because we have no alternative. Is there any reason why we should not do the same in morals?

No reason in the world, we reply. The appeal may be perfectly legitimate. But whether it is or not depends on what we expect authority to do for us. If we expect to gain from it counsel from heads wiser than our own which may supplement our own knowledge and awaken our own insight, the appeal to authority shows modesty and good sense. But if we make the appeal with the assumption that what authority prescribes will be right *because* authority prescribes it, we are suffering from a confusion that may as well be cleared up at once.

100. The Wrong and Right Use of Authority

Why do we appeal to an economist when we want to know about investments or to a physician when we want to know about vitamins? Clearly, because he is in a better position to see the facts than we are; he is a specialist with an eye trained to this sort of thing; and because he has this insight we call him an authority. Now suppose someone suggested that the facts were facts because he said they were, rather than that he said they were because they were facts. Should we not set that down as a desperate muddle? Truth, we should surely say, is found, not made; facts are the facts they are, independently of anyone's say-so. Of course some of us have better eyes and brains to see those facts than others, but if the duller among us ask help from the clear-eyed and look up to them as authorities, it is not because these clearer-eyed people *make* the facts what they are, any more than we do; it is because they are better equipped to *see* them. Does the truth of the relativity theory depend on Einstein's saying it is true, or does he say it is true because, with his better brain, he can see it to be true independently? Obviously the latter.

Now the case is the same with morals. We read the New Testament and find that the greatest of moral teachers has laid down a rule of forgiveness; is this rule right because he laid it down, or did he lay it down because it is right? The latter, once again. Just think for a moment what would be involved in accepting the other alternative; and, for fairness' sake, make the authority the greatest conceivable. If anything is right or wrong simply because a divine being says so, then all that appears to us good and right would be evil and wrong if a divine edict so decreed. But does that really have any meaning?

Let us illustrate from a parallel case regarding truth and falsity. A small boy asked his Sunday-school teacher whether God could do anything. "Yes, certainly," she replied. "Absolutely anything?" "Why yes, of course; what makes you ask?" "Well, if he can do anything, can he make a stone so big that he can't lift it?" The teacher's reply is not recorded, but it ought to have been an unconditional surrender; for there are things that even omnipotence cannot do. It cannot make both sides of a contradiction true, for that is simply meaningless; nothing would be true any more, for true *means* true as opposed to false.

The same holds of good and bad. If we say that the agony of intense pain is bad, it is because we see that it is bad in its very nature; to call it good is to call it what it could not be without contradicting that nature itself. Indeed, if what we see so clearly to be bad is really good, then none of our judgments of good or bad is any longer trustworthy; even the judgment that God is good is rendered meaningless. (Of course intense pain may have good *results*, but that is not the point in question.) Thus in ethics, as elsewhere, truth does not rest on authority; authority rests on the grasp of truth.

If authority cannot provide the ground of our moral rules, what ethical purpose does it serve? It serves a very important purpose. It is our indispensable guide on the treacherous road from apprenticeship to maturity.[1] Its business is not to dictate and legislate and make up our minds for us; that is the kind of authoritarianism which, in the political sphere, has destroyed freedom and growth of mind, and there is reason to think that its working would be the same in morals. The true service of authority is the opposite — to give men so clear and firm an example of the right use of reason in conduct that their own

[1] Cf. BR, No. 4, Walter Lippmann, "The Passage to Maturity."

reason will be awakened and stimulated, and they will achieve responsibility themselves. That is the office of authority in science; the great scientists do not dictate to their fellows; they are rather senior co-workers who say, "Here is my evidence, and here is what I draw from it; look at it for yourselves and see whether you can resist my conclusion." In trying with our feebler faculties to follow these minds, we at once verify their right to authority and educate ourselves; our provisional acceptance of their authority is the means of our emancipation.

That is the proper service of authority in morals also. The teachings of the great moralists are not a code to bind us forever but a set of lights and half-lights seen by able pioneers, who ask us to repeat their insight and see for ourselves if they are not right. They would add that we are really doing them honor if, using the light they offer, we manage to see beyond them; the triumph of authority is to achieve its own supersession. But we shall certainly not go beyond them unless we first understand them.

Originality in morals, as elsewhere, lies more in the capacity to learn than in eccentricity or self-will; "genius," says Professor A. E. Taylor, "is rare and unique receptiveness." Walter Pater has an essay on Raphael in which he shows that the path to the great painter's supremacy lay through an openness of mind and absorptiveness that prompted him to sit at the feet of all the best artists of the day and, in the end, to excel by his very teachableness. "The greatest," says Ruskin, "is he who has been oftenest aided; and if the attainments of all human minds could be traced to their real sources, it would be found that the world had been laid most under contribution by the men of most original powers, and that every day of their existence deepened their debt to their race, while it enlarged their gifts to it." [1]

101. Moral Rules as Self-evident

Let us return to the rule theory. We have seen that there are many persons who support their rules of conduct by falling back on authority; and this was too important a view to pass

---

[1] Cf. BR, No. 46, "Such Is Your Heritage." Also cf. BR, No. 44, A. Einstein, "Our Debt to Other Men."

over. But the true supporter of the rule theory takes a different line. He says that rules are in no need of support, because they are self-evident. This means that everyone who understands them will see at once that they are true, without any kind of proof or argument.

Outside the sphere of morals we are familiar enough with such truths. If we were asked to offer a proof that $2 + 2 = 4$, or that two straight lines cannot enclose a space, or that any figure having a shape must also have some size, we probably could not do it; and even if we could, we should say it was pointless, since nothing offered in evidence would be more convincing than the statement itself. Here, then, we seem to have truths that wear their truth on their faces; they are self-luminous and self-proving.

The theory before us holds that we have the same sort of truths in morals. Some examples have already been given. If more are wanted, we may offer some rules laid down as self-evident axioms by William Whewell: the axiom of justice — each man is to have his own; the axiom of purity — the lower parts of our nature are to be governed by the higher; the axiom of order — we must accept positive laws (i.e., the laws of the land) as the necessary conditions of morality.

Now there are none of us who will not profit by having such rules in mind; life would be intolerably complicated if we had to decide every case without reference to others. If it is clear in one case that stealing is wrong, then our judgment is ready on a thousand other cases that differ from it in no essential respect; and the resemblance is usually easy to see.

102. Criticisms of the Self-evidence View

But sometimes the resemblance is hard to see, and then the difficulties for the theory begin. These rules are supposed to be self-evident; if they are self-evident, they should be perfectly clear; and if they are to be perfectly clear, the terms must be so too. But *are* the terms of these rules clear? Take the first of those just mentioned, Whewell's rule of justice. It says, "Each man is to have his own." But what is meant by "his own"? In general, there will be no doubt; a man's hat and coat and watch would be conceded to be "his own," and therefore if we are tempted to take them, the rule restrains us with a firm hand. But he finds a ten-dollar bill; is that his own? He borrows a book and forgets the lender; is that his own? Is the sidewalk in front of his house his own, or the money he saves by misfiguring his income tax?

As soon as we raise questions like these, we realize that the rule has no answer to them because its terms are so vague. It gives guidance where we do not need it, and breaks down utterly where we need it most. And it is absurd to say that a rule is self-evident when one does not know what it means. In such a case, *what* precisely is evident?

But worse is in store for the theory. Even if its rules were defined precisely, we still could not call them self-evident because they always seem to have exceptions. "Thou shalt not lie." A lie may be fairly defined as the deliberate misrepresentation of facts to another. Do we have here a self-evident rule? If so, it should be universal; that is, it should admit of no exceptions any more than $2 + 2 = 4$ admits of exceptions. Is this the case? If you say Yes, you would prohibit a detective, who is in disguise and on the trail of a criminal, from carrying through his part.

Or, to take a stock sort of case: a man is critically ill and inquires about his sailor son who, you happen to know, has just gone down with his ship. You cannot evade the point-blank question, and yet to blurt out the truth might be fatal. What should you do? Probably most people would soften the rigor of the rule in such a case; and if not, there are even worse cases before which the most die-hard devotee of rules would probably quail.

Exactly the same kind of criticism could be made of the other rules offered us by the theory. "Thou shalt not steal." True in *nearly* every case. But if a ship's crew run out of food and they are carrying a cargo of foodstuffs, are they to starve before they take what is not their own? Rules are good enough things, but so are humanity and common sense. "Pile on the agony" sufficiently and you will find that all these rules have exceptions. The point at which the holder of the rule begins to break is very significant, for this is the point where it becomes obvious that adherence to the rule would be more disastrous to mankind than a breach of it.

Here for the first time the voice of the "end theories" is clearly heard: you are beginning to appeal to consequences. If you justify exceptions to the rule by appealing to consequences, then consequences are clearly relevant, and perhaps if you look closely enough you will see that not only the exceptions but also the rules themselves must be justified by their consequences. But at the moment this must be left as only a significant hint.

103. Kant to the Rescue: the Categorical Imperative

A notable attempt to save the rule theory was made by the great philosopher Kant.[1] He did not believe that moral rules could be made out by either authority or self-evidence, but he was convinced that such rules were necessary if right and wrong were to be freed from caprice. For suppose that we had no rules; what should we then have to rely on? Evidently consequences. The only guidance we should have would take the form: *if* you want to make friends, then act with courtesy; *if* you want to be healthy or happy, don't in the present case overeat. But then suppose someone appeared who said he felt no desire to make friends, and as for being healthy and happy, he had not the slightest interest in them. It may be very unlikely that such a person will turn up, but after all, said Kant, it is possible; and are we to say that for such a man what is plain duty for all the rest of us would have no force at all? That seemed to him absurd. For on this point he felt clear: that duty did not depend upon personal tastes and constitution; whether a man wanted to repay a debt or was interested in the happiness of his creditor made absolutely no difference to his duty of repaying it. Now, if the queerest eccentrics in the world still have duties, and substantially the same duties as the rest of us, there must be rules of duty that apply to all of us alike. How are we to discover them?

It is useless to rely on common sense and proverbs and tradition. "Whatever is worth doing at all is worth doing well"; "haste makes waste"; that is the sort of wisdom one gets from such sources, and one can see, with a moment's reflection, that such rules are not in the proper sense rules at all, for they can be riddled with exceptions. What we want, then, so to speak,

---

[1] Cf. BR, No. 27, I. Kant, "Duty and Ethics."

is a rule to end all rules, a great presiding rule that will serve as a test whether any special rule proposed to us will really hold or not. Now there is one test, said Kant, the failure to pass which will throw any rule out of court without further ado and in advance of any knowledge of cases or consequences. This is the test of self-consistency. If we can see on inspection that a rule is not consistent with itself, that will instantly destroy its claim to give the sort of guidance we want.

How are we to apply this? Let us suppose that we are facing some difficult problem and see how Kant would handle it. We are very far down in our luck and are tempted to do a bit of expert work with a safe or a cash register, confident that we can do it without leaving a trace. What would Kant say? He would say: Look at the act you propose to do and get clear what *sort* of act it is; that will give you the rule on which you are proceeding. That is simple enough in this case; the act is one of stealing, and thus the rule on which it proceeds is that stealing is right. And the problem is whether that rule is reliable or not. Now if it is a valid rule at all, it must not only be valid for me here and now; it must be valid for everyone else; and if there is anything about it which would make its adoption by everyone impossible, then it is no safe rule for anyone. Very well, what about stealing? Could I consistently will that everyone, when tempted, should steal? What would be involved in that is that everyone would be justified in taking anything he wanted. What that means, in turn, is that I have as much right to your property, if I want it, as you have yourself. But if that is true, then nothing *belongs* to anyone rather than to anyone else; there is no such thing as property left; and since stealing means taking another's property, there can be no such thing as stealing. Make the rule of stealing general, and you make it self-contradictory.

This was Kant's famous principle of the categorical imperative: so act that the rule of your action could consistently be made universal. What are we to say of it? We must certainly admit that it is ingenious; and, what is more important, it gives us at the very least a valuable suggestion toward seeing where duty lies. It suggests that when we are tempted we look at our action impersonally and claim no exception or favor; that in imagination we view someone else doing precisely what we propose to do, and that we then ask ourselves whether we should approve *that* person's acting thus.

David, King of Israel, having become enamored of Bathsheba and wishing to possess her himself, although she was the wife of another man, ordered her husband to be placed in a post of danger in an approaching battle, and then when the enemy had done their work, added the widow to his already large collection of wives. This he did without the faintest beginnings of a qualm of conscience. Then the prophet Nathan came to him and told him the parable of the rich man who seized a poor man's one ewe lamb. This tale roused the indignation of the king to the highest pitch, whereupon the prophet turned upon him with the words: "Thou art the man." Instantly the scales fell from his eyes, and in contrition of spirit he confessed that he had sinned.[1]

It would save us much if we could see ourselves as others see us.

104. Flaws in the Imperative

Suggestive as it is, however, Kant's famous principle is of little use in marking out a course for us. His process of thought seems to have been that since any rule is wrong which, when generalized, is inconsistent with itself, it follows that any rule which, when so generalized, is consistent with itself is right. Now this is a muddle. Neither assertion is true, nor does the second follow from the first.

Take the first assertion. Suppose the question is whether I shall try to reconcile two friends of mine who are violently at outs with each other. What is the principle of my action? Presumably that peacemaking is a duty. Could I consistently will that everyone should do likewise? No, for if everyone did likewise, there would be no quarrels to make up, and the peacemaker would be out of work. The principle could not be universalized, and therefore on Kant's theory should be wrong; but it is obviously not. Or take vaccination, or philanthropy, or celibacy. Many critics have pointed out, not without glee, that Kant was a bachelor, and that if everyone were to live as he did the race would forthwith become extinct, and with it the principle of bachelorhood. Was Kant therefore living in sin? Now look at the other side of the imperative: the suggestion that every rule that can consistently be made universal is right.

[1] F. C. Sharp, *Ethics*, pp. 119–120, Century, 1928.

I am tempted to be lazy, and I ask myself whether I could will consistently that everyone should be lazy. No doubt I should be very silly if I did, but it would not be because there was anything *inconsistent* in everyone's being lazy; that is a perfectly possible state of things. Again, I might be the sort of pushing and selfish person who neither wants to help anyone else nor cares whether others help him. He adopts the principle that every adult person should take care of himself alone. If that principle were everywhere followed, society would be a very bleak and dreary affair. But there would be no self-contradiction in it.

Indeed, since Kant made so much of being consistent, it is curious that his own theory should fail rather conspicuously when that test is applied, and that it sometimes tells us to do *both* of two contradictory things. "Thou shalt not kill." He would have to take that as a safe rule. "Thou shalt not steal." That too, as we have seen, will pass. But then what about those sailors who are threatened with starvation on a boat carrying foodstuffs? Shall they obey the rule that forbids them to take life? Then they will have to take property not their own, and that is stealing. Shall they obey the rule that forbids them to steal? Then they will be responsible for taking lives that could have been saved. "Don't steal" means violating "Don't kill"; "Don't kill" means violating "Don't steal." They have to do one or the other, and, according to the view before us, whichever they do is both right and wrong at once.

But enough of these dialectics. The surprising thing about Kant's test is that, in spite of its being so abstract and academic, and in spite of its easy use to approve strange courses, it is so often in harmony with our soberer judgments. If this is true, it is because Kant was feeling the pull of another and sounder theory toward which we too are gradually moving. He set out to judge conduct apart from its consequences, and he found himself dragging in consequences at every turn. What moved him to call stealing wrong in general was not really its inconsistency but the dismal state of society it would involve. Indeed, you cannot even state the principle of most actions without reference to their consequences, for an action *is*, as a rule, an attempt to achieve some consequence; a lie is not a movement of the lips but an attempt to deceive; charity is not mere giving but an attempt to better someone's lot. It begins to look as if rules themselves depend for their validity on results.

Clearly the rule theory will not do. It is better than the impressionist theory because its rules do help us in many cases; but it fails us in time of need. In the attempt to catch what it is that makes an action right, it fails to take due account of consequences. But there is another side of conduct which it also neglects and which, in the view of one important school, is the most essential thing of all.

G. THE ATTITUDE THEORY

105. The Teaching of Jesus on Moral Rules

The theory offered by this school is very impressive. Its leading advocate, James Martineau, was convinced that he had the vast weight of Christianity on his side, that this philosophy of conduct was implicit in the teachings of the New Testament. To be sure, Christianity does not contain an ethical *system* at all in the sense in which the moral philosophers have laid down ethical systems; it teaches by precept, by parable, above all by the transcendent example of the founder himself. This is a far more effective method than that of abstract exposition since, for every man who is open to persuasion by formal argument, there are ten or a hundred who are open to this other kind of appeal. Still, the very things that make this method so effective — its reliance on parable and personal example — make it hard to be sure of one's self when one tries to put the meaning precisely. One can only say that if the attempt is to be made at all to crystallize the Christian ethical theory, few can claim the qualifications of Martineau. He was a deeply sensitive and imaginative mind, a scholar of some distinction, and one of the great preachers and theologians of the last century.[1]

The scene upon which Christianity first arrived would almost seem to have been arranged expressly for a test of the rule theory.

---

[1] Cf. BR, No. 29, James Martineau, "Motives, the Basis of Ethics."

The "scribes and Pharisees," the religious leaders of the time and place, had inherited a great framework of rules which, headed by the Ten Commandments, ran down into a set of minute regulations governing eating and drinking, weekdays and Sabbath, the language one should use, the clothes one should wear, the amount to be given to charity, the details of one's fasting and prayer. These rules were taken with the utmost seriousness. The religious leaders taught that in conformity to them lay the good life and obedience to the will of God; and they vied with each other in the rigor with which they could compress their lives into this iron framework.

To these leaders the teaching of Jesus was a bewilderment and indeed a bombshell, for it blew their framework into a thousand pieces. There was no practice in their entire code that they could count on his keeping inviolate. It was against immemorial rule to work on the Sabbath; but Jesus insisted that, if a farmer found one of his farm animals in a hole on the Sabbath day and declined the labor of pulling him out, he was rather to be condemned for his inhumanity than praised for his strictness about the Sabbath. The rules of the Pharisees required that they should be careful in the company they kept; publicans and sinners were not fit associates for them. Jesus found some of his warmest friends and followers among the outlawed classes. It was an ancient rule of the Hebrews that if a man knocked out another's tooth or eye, he should, in punishment, have his own tooth or eye knocked out. Jesus said that the proper requital for a blow was not another blow but forgiveness. You have heard it said, he went on, still more surprisingly, "Thou shalt love thy neighbor and hate thine enemy. But I say unto you, Love your enemies, bless them that curse you, do good to them that hate you."

And just as he held that one could sometimes break laws with impunity, he taught that one might obey laws to the letter and still be a bad man. Among his people, the Pharisees were at the top of the ladder; the nation was a theocracy, and these were its priests. At the bottom of the ladder, in point of social respect and liking, were the publicans, the persons who undertook to collect taxes from their own people for the hated Roman overlords. Jesus deliberately drew a picture of a Pharisee and a publican, side by side, the Pharisee saying "I fast twice in the week, I give tithes of all that I possess," "I thank God that I am not as other men are"; and the despised publican saying only, "God be merciful to me a sinner"; and he ended, "I tell you, this man went down to his house justified rather than the other." Indeed it was precisely the people who were loudest about keeping all the rules with whom he was most impatient and severe.

106. The Moral Emphasis of Jesus

Now if it was not conformity to rule that made conduct right for him, what was it? He answered: the *spirit or attitude with which the act was done*. If the wrong spirit was there, a scrupulous keeping of rules could not save you; you were really only a "whited sepulchre"; if the right spirit was there, you had something which made the rules unnecessary. "The letter killeth, but the spirit giveth life." The publican's prayer alone counted, because it alone sprang from a humble heart. The widow's mite counted, and the lavish gifts of the rich men did not, because she gave from love and they from pride. It is the same story everywhere. What makes it wrong to strike another man is not so much the physical hurt he receives; this may amount to little or nothing; it is rather the evil passion from which the blow leaps out; and if you feel that, said Jesus, you should rid your system of the poisonous stuff before you lay your head on a pillow.

Similarly, when he gave a condensed description of the good life in the Beatitudes, he did so by listing the needful qualities of heart: blessed are the meek and merciful, the humble and penitent, the pure of heart and those who are hungry for righteousness. In one famous passage he put the matter more simply still. A lawyer had come to him and asked him which was the greatest of the Commandments. He declined to name any of them. Instead, he named a substitute for all of them, something without which, in his view, they were worthless and with which they were no longer needed: *love* for God and man.

107. What the Attitude Theory Means

The ethics of the New Testament, then, is the ethics of a universal love. But does this not make duty impossibly difficult?

Suppose we do not feel this love from which the best action proceeds? Can we get it merely by seeing what a good thing it would be to have it, or even by resolutely willing to have it? Can a man say to himself: "I don't feel in the least loving toward others, but, seeing how essential it is to the highest sort of conduct, I am going to start feeling so tomorrow morning at eight"? Obviously he cannot, and for the reason that he cannot make his feelings to order as he can his acts. Martineau recognized this and attempted, without altering the New Testament teaching, to expand it and show that it was really applicable. We are moved, he pointed out, by an immense variety of impulses, covering the whole gamut of feelings, from black vindictiveness up through the desire for ease and pleasure, the passions for power and gain and freedom, the interest in knowledge, the affection for parents or children, to gratitude for help, compassion for human suffering, and reverence for goodness, human or divine. It is possible, he thought, to rank these "springs of action" in order of moral worth; and then we can say that one action is better than another if it springs from a higher place on the scale.

We say, for example, that Florence Nightingale did right in devoting herself to nursing. Why? Because we see that, in any such action, "the compassion which inspires it is nobler than any love of ease or of self-culture which would resist it." We say that Peter acted wrongly when he denied the friendship of his Master. Why? Because "the fear to which he yielded was lower than the personal affection and reverence for truth which he disobeyed." Thus it is not always our duty to act from love or reverence because we cannot command these high feelings at will; duty rather lies in following the highest impulse that does happen to be present.

Suppose, for example, someone has done a great deal for us. It is an unhappy fact of human nature that the result of such service is often to arouse in the person who receives it a sense of inferiority and a consequent resentment against the very one who helped him. Suppose we find ourselves torn between such resentment and gratitude; what should we do? We cannot act from love, for love cannot be summoned on call. But seeing, as all men must if they look at the matter fairly, that gratitude is better than resentment, we can choose the higher spring of action; we can elect to give our gratitude the right of way. That, says Martineau, is the sort of choice that the doing of duty always means. "Every action is right which, in the presence of a lower principle, follows a higher: every action is wrong which, in the presence of a higher principle, follows a lower."

108. The Truth of the Attitude Theory

Now this theory has caught and reported faithfully something missed by the previous views and yet clearly of the first importance for our estimates of right and wrong. Whatever may be our attitude toward the Christian theology or religion or church, we must concede that, in the insistence of Christian ethics that right conduct does not mean going through a set of motions, that it involves the heart as well as outward behavior, there is central and permanent truth. " 'Thou blind Pharisee, cleanse first the *inside* of the cup, that the outside may be clean also!' — this was the very ground-principle in Jesus Christ's teaching. Instead of attending so much to your outward acts, attend, he said, first of all to your inward thoughts, to the state of your heart and feelings."[1] "Be this" was his command, rather than "Do this." And the inwardness of goodness, the fact that man's outward life is rooted in his spirit and takes its quality from this, the fact that motives count and count so heavily that any judgment of the outward man is impossible unless one sees its inner source — this, which was the great emphasis of Jesus, seems true beyond denial.

How indispensable it is to know the inner source, if we are to pass any confident judgment, may be made clear in an example. A man is walking along a river bank when he sees another struggling in the water. He leaps in and swims out to him, but, in maneuvering awkwardly into position, he succeeds only in giving the struggler a blow with his elbow which sends him under and to his death. What sort of moral judgment do we pass upon the rescuer's action? Does it not clearly turn upon his motive? If he acted out of pure concern for the drowning man, we should surely have nothing but praise for him, however awkward and disastrous his actual procedure was. On

[1] Matthew Arnold.

the other hand, if we learned that this behavior, precisely the same in all outward respects as that which we just approved, sprang from a murderous inward intent, our judgment would turn on the instant to horrified condemnation. Moral action is, in every case, the outgrowth of a state of mind, and we cannot judge the fruit without knowing something of the root.

We must concede much more to this view. Moral education and social reform, to be secure, must proceed from inside out, not from outside in. A boy may be forced to give his seat to a lady and spend some hours a day over his books, but he will never, by such means alone, become a gentleman and a scholar; to do that he must achieve the sort of feeling toward others and the kind of interest in knowledge that would issue in such acts spontaneously. "To learn to like and dislike rightly is the essence of education"; [1] "the whole process of moral and aesthetic education may be said to exist just in learning to like most what is really best." [2]

And it is clearly the teaching of the New Testament that, in social as well as personal life, the key to advance is to "cleanse first the inside of the cup, that the outside may be clean also." The attempts, so often repeated, to prove that Jesus was a politician or economist of some particular stripe are all fundamentally mistaken because they turn his relative emphasis upside down; all external arrangements for him were secondary; he taught that if once men felt toward each other as brothers rather than as strangers or enemies, all these things would be added unto them. Let the individual man have a change of heart, and he will become a new man outwardly; let all individual men be imbued with the love of others, and the inward "kingdom of God" will translate itself into an outward political order of peace and justice; that was his message. And the student of history must agree that so far as the genuine Christian spirit has prevailed, war, slavery, sex and race discrimination, the exploitation of labor, and indifference to human suffering of every kind have tended to melt away. Many today are convinced that if this sort of yeast could be made to leaven the sordid lump of human society, this by itself would be enough to bring our social and political problems to an end.

[1] Bernard Bosanquet. [2] A. E. Taylor.

109. Good Attitudes Not Enough

But would it? Here our doubts begin. Is this not asking more of Christianity than we have any right to expect of it? We have granted that high motives are essential, but are they enough? Take an extreme but perfectly fair supposition. Suppose that all of us were moved by the purest and most generous feelings toward each other, but that unhappily we were all morons; would our purity of motive work out into an ideal society? Must it not be sorrowfully admitted that, with the best intentions in the world, we might live in disease and squalor, spreading our maladies through ignorance to others, stunting our children through miseducation and malnourishment, distributing the goods of the world unjustly, because stupidly, to persons all of whom we loved? Surely acting rightly toward others means not merely having the right motive but also doing the right thing; and nothing is more obvious than that we may do the wrong thing with the best and purest of motives. History is full of such cases.

"When we contemplate Torquemada torturing a heretic for the eternal good of souls, Ravaillac assassinating a monarch for the cause of God and his Church, a Nihilist murdering a number of innocent persons in order to benefit his country by the destruction of an emperor, a pastor poisoning his congregation in the sacramental wine in the hope of securing their eternal happiness, we recognize that such acts are . . . done from the very highest motives; still common sense does not therefore hesitate to pronounce them profoundly bad." [1]

Mere sweetness of motive will not by itself tell you how to vote or how to make your will with fairness or whether to go to college; in hundreds of important decisions it leaves you with no sort of direction. To make these rightly you must have intelligence and technical knowledge. Someone who greatly admired Whistler's paintings once asked him what he mixed his paints with. "With brains, sir," was Whistler's reply. Is it not obvious that if we are to act rightly in our complex world, affection must be mixed with brains?

Of course Martineau saw this clearly and gave, as one would expect, an acute reply. We value brains, he said; we appreciate,

[1] H. Sidgwick, *Ethics of Green, Spencer and Martineau*, p. 335, The Macmillan Company, 1902.

envy, and admire them; but it is mere confusion to say that we give them moral approval, or disapprove of anyone for lacking them. We do not *condemn* the would-be rescuer who only succeeded in drowning his man; we may say he is stupid or clumsy, but these are totally different things. And granting that, in order to vote rightly in an election, one must have some knowledge, we never say that a man who has this is better morally, but only that he is more intelligent or better instructed. To treat competence as if it were goodness and incompetence as if it were badness would lead to the most hopeless muddle; we should then find ourselves praising clever swindlers to the skies and pouring our condemnation on acts of simple-minded good will.

110. Inward and Outward Rightness

There is clearly much truth in this argument. We must admit that we often approve men as acting rightly even when they have acted stupidly and harmfully. Are we therefore to take back what we just said about intelligence being necessary if we are to do the right thing, and about the ease with which good motives may lead us wrong? No, this too is true. Have we, then, contradicted ourselves? Not really; it is merely that we have used the word "right" in two senses; we must now get these senses clear, for the distinction is one of the most important in ethics. This is the distinction between what is objectively and what is subjectively right. When we ask what is the right way to vote, we are not asking what motive we should take to the polls with us; we are asking what to do when we get there; we want to know what we should do that is best for the public good, taking into account the interests of all who will be affected. This is the act that would be *objectively* right, and it is clear that to discover it we need all the intelligence we can command. On the other hand, when we say that the man who leaped into the water with such disastrous results did right, we plainly do not mean that what he did was objectively right; that would be nonsense; we mean that it sprang from the best motive; it was *subjectively* right. We use the term "right" in both senses.

We can now see more clearly the strength and weakness of the sort of ethics before us. It concerns itself altogether with

what is subjectively right or wrong. If two men both act from
the same feelings of compassion, it says their acts are equally
right, even though one of them is Torquemada sending a good
man to the torture, and the other is Florence Nightingale giving
herself to the relief of pain. There is something distorted in
such a picture. The agent's feeling fills too much of the scene.
It is true that subjective rightness is of the greatest importance,
and that we never approve an act unreservedly unless we think
its motive is good.

But our moral concern does not stop there. Why did Martineau suppose that it did? Largely because he failed to see
that even our motives are tied up in the most intimate way
with the consequences in which our acts are expected to issue.
A motive is no mere feeling; it is a desire which moves us to
action, and it takes its moral coloring from the character of
its ends. The motive of the boy who gives his mother a present
is presumably to give her the enjoyment that he thinks will
follow, and this motive is good because its end is good. The
boy who abuses a cat may be moved in part by the desire to
cause the cat pain, and to that extent his motive is bad, for its
end is bad.

Now the mistake of Martineau, and of those who think with
him, is in misconceiving the nature of motives, of conceiving
them as mere attitudes of feeling, of failing to see that the reference to consequences belongs to their very essence, and of
thinking we could judge them without taking this into account.
We could say, for example, that compassion is better than resentment, better as such and always. But surely whether it is better
depends on *what* we compassionate or resent. If one is dealing
with a brutal murderer who would repeat his crime at the first
chance, it is by no means always clear that we should give
compassion the right of way. Love and reverence themselves
will lead us astray if we love and reverence the wrong things,
and the very fact that this is possible shows that these feelings
are not enough. We must look beyond them to the consequences
that their indulgence would produce, and unless that interest
is present in our motive, it is defective, even as a motive. We
cannot be subjectively right unless we want also to be objectively
right.

111. From Act Theories to End Theories

We have now examined some of the leading act theories and found them all wanting. We must look elsewhere for guidance. Fortunately we have not been left without clues as to the direction in which to turn. Over and over again we have found these theories falling short because they neglected consequences. The impressionist thinks that because judgment is passed immediately without analysis or calculation, results do not enter into it, but we saw that conscience may bring to bear an extensive experience of the good or ill fruits of prior choices. We saw, again, that those who cling to rules will nearly always abandon them if the result in prospect is bad enough, and that even Kant, who tried to defend them by appealing to consistency alone, had to bring in by the back door the consequences he had ushered out at the front. Similarly with the attitude theory. It judges acts by their motives; but when we examine these motives we find that the reference to consequences belongs to their very essence.

The theory we are next to examine would put these clues together and say that what they point to is obvious. What counts above all in conduct is neither the motive that it springs from nor the pattern of behavior itself, but the results to which the conduct leads. With this we turn from act theories to end theories.

The line between these theories is one of the great watersheds in ethics. In western ethical history there are two main strands or traditions: the tradition of Palestine and the tradition of Greece. The long line of Hebrew prophets that culminated in Christ insisted that the condition and test of right conduct was cleanness of the inward parts; and the cry that was picked up and echoed by generation after generation of them was "Create a clean heart within me." In comparison, the Greek was a man of action and an extrovert. To the Hebrew, morals and religion were practically one; moral laws were divine commands; disobedience to them carried the most dreadful penalties; obedience was not merely a duty but a sacred duty. How deeply we have been affected by this attitude is suggested by the word "sin," which carries for us, besides the idea of wrongdoing, a dim but vast connotation of divine disfavor.

On the other hand, to the Greeks morals were a secular matter. The sense of sin as we know it hardly existed among them, and the agonized cry of repentance and remorse that came from the great prophets, "I have sinned in thy sight, O Lord," would have left them embarrassed and puzzled. There is no word in the Greek language that can be accurately translated by our "ought" or "right" or "duty."

Yet of course the Greek, like the rest of us, had his view as to what made a life good or bad. What was this view? Put generally, it was as follows; everyone had his part to play in the life of the community, a complex part in which he must try, for example, to be an effective provider for his family, an expert carpenter, and a useful citizen at the same time; and the good life for him consisted simply in filling his station and its duties as best he could.

"As best he could"; but how is one to know what is best? The Greek's reply was characteristic. That activity of any kind is best, he said, which achieves most completely and with the greatest economy of means the end it is meant to serve. What do we mean by a good knife? One that is good *for* its special end, which is cutting. What do we mean by a good general? A man who is effective in his responsibilities, such as supplying and ordering troops, which are necessary to victory. What is a good man? That is an immensely harder question. But when Aristotle came to discuss it in the classic work of Greek ethics, he held that it must be answered by the same method. If we are to know what is meant by a good or bad man, by right or wrong conduct, we must know the *end* that man should pursue. Unlike all the moralists we have so far considered, Aristotle held that the primary question of ethics was not "What is right?" but "What is good?" since only when we had answered that question could the problem of right action be raised with any profit. For the right was a means to the good.

On this assumption, our first task is cut out for us; it is to discover what is really good. Aristotle thought that in an important sense we know this already; for on what principle, otherwise, could we chart our course from hour to hour? But then we may know something without knowing it explicitly, and it may take a good deal of analysis to bring the buried knowledge to light. The method that Aristotle practiced on his students twenty-three centuries ago is as valid now as it was then, although we may not reach his results, and the best way to illustrate it is simply to seize a young American and question him. Let us try this. It does not matter greatly whom we take or where we start; what is important is the way the dialogue develops.[1]

112. A Dialogue on the Good

"I see you're on top of the world today; are things going so well as all that?"

"Never better, so far as I am concerned."

"Go on; let's hear about it."

"Well, I have just the sort of job I like; it's steady; promotion is certain, and I've had several raises already."

"What are you going to do with all that money?"

"Get things I want with it, naturally."

"For example?"

"A roadster. In fact, I've just got it. Second-hand, but with a little tinkering, as good as new; color, canary; will do seventy without pushing; eight cyl . . ."

"What do you want it for?"

"Oh, all sorts of things; trips at week-ends, movies, lifts to the family. Then, too, part of my work is in selling; so it will help me make a go of the job."

"Why are you so anxious to make a go of the job?"

"That's not a very bright question. It's because everything depends on it."

"What, for example?"

"Well, without a job — and a good one — how would you ever lay aside any capital?"

"Why should you want capital?"

"Another strange question. For a thousand things, of course."

"Well, what, for instance?"

"College, if you want to know. I'd like to go to college, and it takes capital to go."

"Why should you want to go?"

"With a degree I could get a still better job."

"And what's the point of that?"

"I'd get a still better income."

"And buy more roadsters?"

[1] Cf. BR, No. 24, Aristotle, "The Nicomachean Ethics."

"If I wanted them. But there are lots of other things I want. I'd have my own house, with all the books and pictures I wanted; in the summers I'd travel, and in the winters . . ."

"Yes, but what's the point of books and pictures and travel?"

"They enlarge your mind."

"You're sure it's better, then, to have an enlarged mind than a narrow one? Why?"

"You come to know more interesting people."

"What's the advantage of that?"

"It enlarges your mind."

"You said that before. You don't mean that you enlarge your mind to meet more interesting people to enlarge your mind?"

"Oh, there are plenty of other reasons for educating yourself."

"Very well, let's have some of them."

"An educated man knows his way about in the world; he knows what to think about politics and religion and literature."

"Why should he want to know his way about in these things?"

"Well, because he'll understand himself and other people and society better."

"And just what is that going to do for him?"

"Well, the man who understands is more at home in the world; he gets on better with himself and other people; he feels more secure; he knows he can keep his head above water and doesn't have to be afraid; he doesn't fly off the handle and make a fool of himself so easily. There is a poem, isn't there, about being captain of one's soul? Well, he's that."

"But why be . . ."

"You needn't say it; I see it coming. The reason for wanting to be captain of your soul is that you'll be much happier so. . . . Well, I'm waiting. I suppose your next move is 'Why be happy?' "

"No, so far as I am concerned, you've reached the end of the line."

"But why?"

"Because 'Why be happy?' *would* be a silly question."

"No sillier than 'Why have a larger income?' "

"Oh yes, there's all the difference in the world between them."

"Now it seems to be my business to ask why."

"Because an income is no good to you in itself; a million dol-

lars tied up in a bank vault is worth exactly zero. The only good
of money lies in what you can get with it in the business of getting
rid of it — not that I'd mind a little more of the business myself.
So 'What is money good for?' is a perfectly sane question. But
no sane person asks 'What is happiness good for?' If you have
that, you have what other things are for. But you don't need a
reason for being happy; it's good in itself; it's the end of the road;
and if you ever get there, you won't want to leave. You'll be
like the little girl in Boston who was asked if she'd like to travel.
'No,' she said, 'why should I travel when I'm already there?' "

If the end theories are right, the person questioned here might
be any of us, for, in justifying our choices, we all fall back sooner
or later on things we prize for their own sakes, and we are all
familiar with the distinction between extrinsic and intrinsic
goods. An extrinsic good is something we want as a means or
instrument to something else. Examples would be a motorcar,
a job, money, even a college education. An intrinsic good is
something that is good in itself, something that would still be
worth while even if it led to nothing beyond. In the dialogue,
the example given is happiness. Now happiness, as we shall see,
is only one of many experiences that have been held to be intrinsic goods, but we have taken it as our example partly because
nearly everybody would admit that it is such a good and partly
because the best known of all the end theories — utilitarianism
— insists that it is the only good. It is to this theory that we
now turn.

H. UTILITARIANISM

113. Pleasure and Happiness

Because of the singleness of its end, utilitarianism has an attractively simple view of what makes an act right. It says: that act
is right which, of all the acts open at the moment, would produce the largest amount of happiness. That seems straightforward enough. However, there are certain questions about it
that are bound to arise, and the theory will become clearer as we
deal with them.

For one thing, what is meant by happiness? Is it the same as pleasure? Yes and no. The three leading utilitarians, Bentham, John Stuart Mill,[1] and Sidgwick, used the terms almost interchangeably as both referring to agreeable or delightful feeling, and it is plain enough that both do refer to the same *type* of experience. Still, the meanings are two, and not one. By pleasure we mean the feeling that comes from satisfying our more immediate appetites, desires, and impulses; we speak of the pleasure of a good meal, a good novel, or a good game of tennis. By happiness we mean the feeling, less intense perhaps but less vulnerable and more enduring, that comes with the satisfying of our more central and long-range impulses, such as the desire for friends, for success, for the full and free play of our faculties. One would hardly speak of fulfilling a life's ambition as merely pleasant, or of one's feeling about a cup of tea as happiness. Yet pleasure and happiness shade into each other in such a way that there is little harm in using either term for their common type; and we shall feel free to do this. When one is awarded a hard-earned degree or is told by a physician that a long-feared operation will now be unnecessary, is it pleasure that one feels or happiness? We could fairly say that the emotion is either or both.

Some people have professed to find the notions of pleasure and happiness obscure. It is true that we cannot satisfactorily define either one. We can say that pleasure is agreeable feeling, but then agreeable means pleasant; so we are defining something by itself. Still, there is no real difficulty here. We all know what we mean by pleasure, just as we know what we mean by time and space and existence, though we could not for the life of us give a proper definition of any of them.

Incidentally, we are clear enough about meanings to see that the modern utilitarians do not mean by the good what Aristotle had in mind. For him, happiness was a mere by-product of the end. The end itself consisted in realizing the full and free play of our faculties, and happiness was an offshoot of this self-realization. If we define a hedonist as a person who believes that the sole good of life is pleasure (or happiness) then utilitarians are hedonists, while Aristotle was not.

[1] Cf. BR, No. 28, J. S. Mill, "Hedonism: Pleasure, the Highest Good."

114. How the Utilitarian Deals with Motives

We are ready for the next question: if utilitarians make right and wrong turn wholly on results, it looks as if they could attach no value to motives or attitudes. And does not that lead to topsy-turvy judgments? It happens from time to time that a man who is hunting in the woods hears a rustle, sees what he takes to be a deer, fires — and brings down a fellow hunter. The consequences of his act are deadly; are we therefore to say that in spite of his innocent intention he has done what is morally wrong?

Let us imagine another extreme case. A group of assassins form a plot against the life of the President; when the time comes to carry it out, one of them takes aim and fires, but, missing his intended victim, brings down one of his confederates on the other side. Here the consequences are probably good; there is one less would-be murderer burdening the earth. Are we to say that the act was therefore right, in spite of its diabolic intention?

This looks at first like a formidable difficulty, but the utilitarian takes it in his stride. To meet it he falls back on a distinction we have already made. The hunter's act was *objectively* wrong, even though we may not blame him for it in the slightest, and the assassin's act may well have been objectively right, even though he is promptly executed. It is well to have names, says the utilitarian, which will apply to acts regardless of motives, and which will reflect a judicial appraisal on the ground of results alone. Does this mean the denial of all importance to motives? No; but it does mean that we deny them *intrinsic* value and appraise them solely in the light of their normal results. We do not blame the hunter because we can see that his motive was innocent, that is, the sort of motive which in the vast majority of cases would produce nothing but good. We call the assassin's motive bad because, however happy the outcome was, we can see that, in this case, it was an accident, and that the normal result would be catastrophe. Motives, like acts, are to be tested by consequences.

115. Is Each Man Out for His Own Pleasure Alone?

We turn to another significant question. Granting that the goodness of a motive and the rightness of an act depend wholly on the pleasure they produce, does this mean that pleasure is the only thing we ever want? Here utilitarians are divided. Some, like Sidgwick, admit that we desire other things, such as knowledge or beauty, but say that when we do so we are confused, since these things, strictly speaking, are valueless; the value belongs to the pleasure they bring with them. Some deny this and say, with Bentham, that if we look below the surface, we shall see that pleasure is the only thing that anyone ever desires. Bentham opens a famous book by saying: "Nature has placed mankind under the governance of two sovereign masters, pain and pleasure. . . . They govern us in all we do, in all we say, in all we think," which means that the end of every act is to gain pleasure or to avoid pain.

Now if this is true, the utilitarian view that pleasure is all we need take account of in judging conduct is virtually made out. For even if there are other things that are good, we can take no interest in them; we are so made that we turn toward pleasure as automatically and inevitably as the moth flies toward the candle. Bentham went on to add a second point: the pleasure we seek is always our own, never anyone else's. This is the doctrine of psychological hedonism, the doctrine that every man is out for his own pleasure alone.[1] One can be a utilitarian without accepting either part of it; yet it has so often been used as a bolster for utilitarianism that some comment on it seems called for.

The doctrine has had a large vogue, not so much among careful thinkers as among popular moralists; and it is not difficult to see why. The world is full of hypocrisy, conscious and unconscious, and the best of us at times throw dust in our own eyes about the motives that are really at work in us. The hero who rushes with such disregard of self into a burning building turns out to be keenly aware of his neighbor's admiring eyes. The gratitude of the man who gives generously to campaign funds may turn out to be only "a lively sense of favors still to come." The Freudians have shown how desperately easy it is to mistake one's own motives, to confuse moral indignation with wounded pride, for example, or to be excessively conscientious in one direction only as a cover for laxity in another. No wonder that many people, after reading a certain amount of this literature, acquire a fixed suspicion of everything that presents itself as high-minded and

[1] Cf. BR, No. 30, George Jean Nathan, "Pleasure as the Highest Good."

unselfish and feel that from their new level of sophistication they are able to "see through all that."[1]

They are often easy to analyze in terms of their own theory; they think their cynicism is reasoned out, whereas it is merely their own little recipe for an easy superiority. In saying this we are of course admitting that there is some truth in their doctrine. No one is free from selfishness. Most of us, no doubt, are more selfish than we know or should care to believe. Still, it is pointless to blacken ourselves unless the facts really call for it, and this doctrine of general selfishness is not borne out by the facts.

116. The Failure of Psychological Hedonism

(a) Consider what is implied by the doctrine. It implies that in their motives all men are on a level, that there is not the slightest difference here between William James and Jesse James, between St. Francis and Jack the Ripper. All of them equally were out for their own pleasure and nothing besides, and therefore to talk of any of them as having higher or lower aims than any other is absurd. If the actions of St. Francis benefited mankind, that was either pure accident or else was a scheme on his part to exploit other people in the interest of his own pleasure. Such a view is shocking. But of course that alone does not prove it false. We must be ready to play with the possibility that our praise for the nobility of purpose of the saints and heroes of mankind is all a sentimental mistake. Such a view collides so sharply with our all-but-certain conviction of some persons' nobility of motive that it must accept a heavy burden of proof.

(b) And it generally carries this badly. Indeed, the man who maintains it is not seldom in a muddle as to what he is arguing for. We are all seeking our own pleasure; just what does he mean by that? Does he mean that we always do what we think will give us the greatest pleasure *at the moment?* If so, he refutes himself whenever he goes to a dentist or takes a very cold shower. Does he mean that we always do what we think will give us most pleasure *in the long run* or *on the whole?* Then he refutes himself whenever he eats what he knows will give him a sick headache tomorrow or risks at the gaming table what he knows he cannot

[1] Cf. BR, No. 31, Friedrich Nietzsche, "The Origin of Morals."

afford to lose. Does he mean that we always do what it gives us most pleasure at the moment *to think of?* Then he refutes himself whenever he absents himself from baseball, which he thinks of with longing, to do geometry, which he detests. If he means any one of these things, he can be routed with an almost embarrassing ease, and if his case seems plausible, it is because he shuffles about without knowing it from one meaning to another.

(c) Still, it remains conceivable that we are all seeking our own pleasure solely, though now in one form and now in another. To show the contrary we must produce a clear case of our seeking something else, such as another person's welfare. It certainly looks as if this were a common enough occurrence. Is the man who carefully draws up a will which provides for the education of his son and daughter thinking of nothing but his own pleasure? It certainly seems as if he were thinking of what would be best for others at a time when he himself would be beyond the range of pleasure and pain. Is the mother who gets up in the night and tends the needs of a sick child thinking of nothing but herself? Is the man who makes a point of kindness to animals concerned only with his own sensations?

To most of us, suggestions of this sort will probably seem so far from plausible that we can only wonder how the egoist goes about it to make them plausible to himself. His line appears to be this: that if we fail to do these things we shall get in trouble with ourselves; what we are really doing is avoiding the pains of self-reproach. This is a line that is said to have been taken by the youthful Lincoln. When he was riding in a wagon one day with some companions, he saw a sow on the bank of a stream making a great commotion because some of her little pigs were mired in the mud and unable to get out. Lincoln, who had been arguing that all men were really selfish, stopped the wagon, ran down to the bank of the stream, pulled the little pigs out, restored them to their mother, and climbed into the wagon again. His companions at once took him to task: how did this fit into his theory that he always acted selfishly? He replied that he did it only because if he hadn't he would have been uncomfortable all day.

Now when one reflects on this answer, one sees that he had provided as neat a refutation of his theory as one could ask. If he had no interest in the plight of the pigs, why should the thought of them make him uncomfortable? If their misery had no importance, why should he blame himself for taking no steps about it? The facts he offered in support of his conclusion were facts that wrecked that conclusion.

The view, then, that all men are exclusively selfish is not convincing. Regard for others, generosity, even heroic self-sacrifice are really possible to men; indeed they are facts of daily occurrence; and there is ground for thinking that, as time goes on, they will become far commoner. For much that passes as cruelty and deliberate selfishness is mere dullness and deadness of mind. It takes a living imagination to enter into the manifold ways in which our conduct affects others; it is hard for a white man to feel as a Negro feels when his hopes are cut off because of his color; or for any man to feel what a young girl feels about clothes, or what an enemy feels about his cause, or what a child does about his childish games and toys. Here, as so often, we should be better men if we had richer and more active minds. And there is reason to hope that, as the race advances and education improves, what lies at the root of three-fourths of the world's selfishness, namely, mere reptilian sluggishness of imagination and feeling, will give place to that livelier sympathy from which springs concern for others.

117. Is Pleasure the Only Good?

We have considered psychological hedonism here because it has often been used as a support for utilitarianism. But most utilitarians have not cared to have its support, partly because of its perverse psychology, partly because its stress on selfishness gives a wrong impression of the utilitarian spirit. There is nothing necessarily selfish about that spirit; Mill and Sidgwick were among the noblest of men; indeed, since the utilitarians hold that we should regard the happiness of others as of equal importance with our own, they have set an extremely exacting standard of social responsibility.

Still, though they reject the psychology of psychological hedonism, they do cling to its hedonism. They insist that, though we can work for others' good as well as our own, that good consists in every case in happiness or pleasure; this is the only thing in the world that is good in its own right. If we say it is good to be wise, that only means that wisdom makes people happier. If we say beauty is good, that only means, if we care about exactness, that beautiful things give to discriminating persons more pleasure than less beautiful things. And so of everything else that we call good.

118. Socrates and the Pig

Is this sound? When the view was stated to Thomas Carlyle, he snortingly dismissed it as a "pig philosophy," [1] and we shall better understand why he did so if we put to the utilitarian a test case which, though extreme, is not unfair. Suppose you had to choose between two lives of equal length. The first is the life of some rich and sensitive human mind, say Socrates, who had all the satisfactions that belonged to such a mind but all its disappointments too, its sorrows, frustrations, and failures. The second is the life of a hygienically kept pig, whose appetite is always satisfied with the most luscious of porcine dainties, and whose time is given alternately to the sleep of perfect health and to ecstatic gulping and guzzling. If you compare these two forms of life with respect to the single point of comparative net pleasure, there is at least a very good chance that the palm will go to the pig. On utilitarian principles, the life of the pig must, in such a case, be pronounced the better. Yet there are few who would acquiesce in that. We know what the delights of appetite are like, but even if the life of the trough were stretched out to treble its length, we should probably not be greatly tempted. We would rather be Socrates with all his troubles than the most serene highness that ever lorded it over a sty.

John Stuart Mill was worried by this odd problem because he saw that it was a crucial case. As a good utilitarian it would seem that he should cast his vote for the pig, but in fact he agreed with everyone else in thinking it would be better to be Socrates; and then it became a problem how he was to reconcile this with his theory. He tried to do it by saying that in voting for Socrates he was still voting solely for pleasure, though for a higher *kind* of pleasure; it was the pleasure of intelligence and religion and a rich and varied human life, while that of the pig was purely

[1] Cf. BR, No. 28, J. S. Mill, "Hedonism: Pleasure, the Highest Good."

and grossly sensual. Both were equally pleasure, but the first was higher in quality.[1]

Mill's instinct here was right, but in making this defense he was really abandoning his great principle that only amount of pleasure counts. We can see this as follows: suppose that the two lives contained the same amount of pleasure; would Mill still choose to be Socrates? Yes, he is ready to admit that he would. But this cannot be owing to the greater pleasure in one life than in the other, for it is admitted that there is no more of this in one than in the other. Hence it must be because of something whose addition to an amount of pleasure does not increase that amount at all; and this clearly cannot be pleasure. Therefore there must be something other than pleasure that we prize.

I. IDEAL UTILITARIANISM

119. This Theory Includes What Is Good in Other Theories

It looks as if utilitarianism must join the lengthening list of theories that we have weighed and found wanting. For it insists that pleasure is the only thing in the world that is really good, and this we cannot accept. We cannot believe that the only thing that makes a great picture better than a poor one, a noble life better than a mean one, the life of a Hottentot better than the life of a pig, and the life of Socrates better than that of a Hottentot is the amount of pleasure produced. That does not square with men's actual convictions and insights.

And yet utilitarianism is very near to the truth. Indeed, if it is willing to make one major change in its outlook, it will come as near to the truth as we can hope to arrive in this study. Suppose it were to give up its dogma about all good being merely pleasure [2] and to admit that beauty and knowledge and friendship and perhaps many other things have a value that goes beyond the pleasure involved in them. In such a position we should at last arrive at the goal toward which our thought has so long been moving. The rule of duty laid down by this theory is as

[1] Cf. BR, No. 28, J. S. Mill, "Hedonism: Pleasure, the Highest Good."
[2] Cf. BR, No. 41, B. Russell, "A Free Man's Worship."

simple as it is sweeping; and if there is anything from our discussion that is to stick in the mind of the reader, let it be this:

So act always as to produce the greatest good.

In this position, which has been called Ideal Utilitarianism,
everything that is sound in the theories we have been studying
seems to be included. The theory accepts the voice of conscience;
but it says that conscience at its best is intelligence, passing judgment in the light of results. It believes in rules; but it insists that
these rules are not laws of the Medes and Persians that must be
obeyed regardless of circumstances; they are useful suggestions
for going right which have been arrived at through long experience and which will hold in nine cases out of ten, but are in no
case absolute. It accepts motives as important but sees that they
cannot stand alone; for a motive *is* a desire for consequences.
And finally, while accepting consequences as the really important factor, it insists that among these must be included
everything of intrinsic value that the act involves, not pleasure
only.

If this is to be our final theory, we cannot afford to be misty
about it. Probably the best way to get clear about it is to imagine
a critical reader who is intent at once to find what the theory
means and to poke holes in it if he can. We shall try to raise,
one by one, the questions such a reader would ask and to give
a point-blank answer to each.[1]

120. Goods Are Many [2]

What is to enter into the account when we talk of the "largest
good"?

The answer is: all the intrinsic goods and evils that our action
may produce. What are these? First, human happiness. This
is not the only good, as we have seen, but it is of prime importance
nevertheless. If we knew that the passage of a bill through
Congress would increase the sum of human happiness, we could
pretty safely urge its passage, even if we knew nothing whatever
about it but this one fact.

Still, we have insisted that not all the values of life can be
compressed within the limits of happiness. Are not knowledge,

[1] Cf. BR, No. 76 F, "Criteria of a True Moral Law."
[2] Cf. BR, No. 33, E. S. Brightman, "A Table of Human Values."

for example, and love, and the experience of beauty valuable in themselves? If a young man is facing the problem whether to educate himself or not, and so far as he can see the amount of happiness would be identical on both sides, does it really make no difference whether or not he lives in ignorance? No difference at all, says the utilitarian. A large difference, say we. Of course the probability is that education *will* add to his happiness; but according to our present standard it is better to have a clear mind than a muddy one, better to understand the world one lives in than not to understand it, even if that understanding does not add a single dollar to one's income or a single degree to one's happiness. So also of a number of other great goods. We shall say more about these in a moment.

121. Dramatis Personae

Whose good is to be considered?

First, one's own. This does not call for much emphasis, since most of us are too preoccupied with ourselves already. Still, one's own good is not only part of the total good; it is the part that for each of us is bound to be most important, since it is the part we can most directly and deeply affect. And for all our self-centeredness, it must be admitted that our concern with self is often singularly futile. Bishop Butler once said that the world would be better off if there were more enlightened egoism in it. Regard for oneself is perfectly proper, but it need not be petty, capricious, and short-sighted; if we raise our sights to our higher and long-range interests, we shall do far better for ourselves as well as for others.

This answers the further question whether we owe a duty to ourselves. The answer is, Yes, we do. If we admit that an instructed mind is better than an ignorant one, then with the choice before us which we shall have, our principle says it is a duty to choose the first. This does not mean that we should always choose what under ideal conditions would be best for us. If I could choose which to have, an understanding of some great philosopher or the pleasure of a story by O. Henry, I would unhesitatingly choose the philosopher. But that does not mean that tonight, weary and with a tiresome cold, I should give myself to a struggle with abstruse philosophic reasoning.

For, given the conditions, I should get nothing but blur and exhaustion from philosophy, while I should at least get some lightening of mood from O. Henry. Circumstances alter duties, and life would become a dreary drudgery if we had to drive perpetually after those goods that are accessible to us only in favored moments.

122. Self and Others

But suppose the conflict is not between two goods of one's own, but between one's own good and someone else's. A friend and I, for example, are offered the use of a ticket to a concert; one or the other of us can use it but not both. I have a mildly musical ear, and I know that I should enjoy the concert; he is extremely musical and I know would enjoy it more. What should I do? Our principle says that my duty, so far, is clear; I should turn the ticket over to him. For I should so act as to produce the largest good on the whole, and this clearly lies in his presence at the concert, not mine. If I admit that enjoyment as such is a good thing, I must admit that it is equally good as occurring in another and in myself; and if I refuse to sacrifice a lesser good of my own for a greater good of another, I am plainly acting unreasonably.

We are bound by our principle, then, to consider the good of others as of equal importance with our own. But how many other people are we to consider? Those of our immediate circle, or the whole world, or some group that falls between? Our principle gives the answer: we are to consult the interests of all *affected* by our action, either for good or for ill. Since our action affects those around us far more than those at a distance, it is clear that charity should begin at home, and that our responsibilities are like the rings that a stone makes in a pool: they are highest near the center and die away as they recede.

Hence there are two characteristic dangers. There are people who overstress their duties to the rim of the circle at the expense of their duties to the center — people who, like Dickens' Mrs. Jellyby, worry about the natives of Borrioboola-Gha to the sacrifice of their own households.

But far more common is the counterpart danger of preoccupation with one's own little group at the cost of everyone outside it. There are parents who will make any sacrifice for their own children but will press the claims of those children unscrupulously against what they know to be the stronger claims of other children. There are employers whose very loyalty to their own families leads them to adopt practices that push the families of their employees to the wall; and there are employees who feel no loyalty except to the working class, holding that, if this class wins out, it does not matter what happens to anyone else. The Nazis admitted the deepest obligations to their own nation and race, while to those unfortunate enough to be born outside this charmed circle, particularly if they were Jews, they owned practically no obligations at all. There have been members of our own legislative bodies who were quite willing to pass tariff and immigration laws whose foreign effect was disastrous for the sake of a slight advantage at home, and there are newspapers who make a slogan of "My country, right or wrong," though precisely the same doctrine, as advocated by a German or a Japanese, would no doubt be regarded as offensive and dangerous. Clearly the reasonable policy here is that suggested by our principle: of responsibility to everyone whom our action touches, but of responsibility graduated in degree according to the seriousness of the effect.

While we are discussing whose good is to be considered, there is another point that should be cleared up. Does our obligation extend beyond humanity altogether and down into the animal world? Undoubtedly it does. For let us remember that we are to take into account all the values and disvalues that our actions produce. And if there is one thing clear about the animal mind, it is that, like the human mind, it is capable of intense pain. Now intense pain is an evil, and a horrible evil, no matter where it happens. In human beings it sometimes has moral effects that help to reconcile us to it; but in animals it is always innocence that is suffering, and an innocence cut off from all such profit. Cruelty is usually a matter of sluggish imagination. If the trapper could experience for five minutes what the animal experiences that chews off its leg in a hysteria of pain and terror in order to escape from a trap, there is little doubt that he would be a more humane as well as a wiser and sadder man.

123. Alternative Right Actions?

May there not be *many* actions open to me, all of which are
right? The answer is almost certainly, No. The act that we
must find and do if we can is that which will produce the greatest
good. It is possible, in theory, that this end could be equally
well attained by many means, just as it is possible that, in a
money-raising campaign, the maximum amount may be raised
in many different ways. But it would be a mere chance, and a
somewhat remote one, if this were true in either case. As a rule,
there will be just one act that is the right one; and all the others
we must call wrong, though of course they will not be subjectively
wrong if we have done our best to find the right one. It follows
that it is far easier to do what is objectively wrong than right.
It follows, too, that in this sense most of us do wrong most of the
time. Indeed, when one considers how many ways there are
of going wrong and how few of going right, one wonders whether
anyone ever succeeds in doing right for sixty minutes together.
His chances are none too bright.

124. Means and Ends

Does the end justify the means?

People who say that it does hold that there are ends of such
importance that one is justified in attaining them in any way
one can. It is so important that one land a certain contract or
make a certain sale that, in order to achieve it, one may gouge,
shade the truth, and even beat the law. It is so important that
a certain nation should get its place in the sun that it is justified
in going berserk, if necessary, in order to attain it.

Put nakedly in this way, everyone recognizes that there is
something wrong with the doctrine. But precisely what is wrong?
This: that it would justify our choosing the greater evil, which is
wrong always and in principle. It tries to make this plausible
by fixing attention on one part of the results at the expense of
others, ignoring the fact that the expensiveness of the means
must be counted as well as the goodness of the end. One may
be convinced that it would be a very good thing that one's
nation should have a dominant place, but if the cost of securing
it is ruin to the rest of the world, then to persist in one's plan is
sheer wickedness, since the good of the end is far outweighed
by the evil of the means.

We cannot rightly pick and choose among the consequences of our action, taking account of the ones we like and refusing to look at the others; we must weigh all the results impartially.[1] To refuse to do this is the typical error of the fanatic. "Peace at any price," "Victory at all costs," "Let justice be done though the heavens fall" — these lend themselves too easily to the uses of the bigot. There is only one end that can safely be sought at all costs, namely, the greatest good on the whole, and that is safe only because the cost has been counted already.

125. Differing Duties

May what is right for me be wrong for you?

Yes and no. Let us suppose that you and I both receive letters from the same man, appealing for help. You have never heard of him before. I recognize him as a person who once put himself to great inconvenience to help me out of a difficulty. In such a case, would the act that was right for you also be right for me? Pretty certainly not. It is one thing to ignore an appeal sent at random by a stranger and another thing to ignore an appeal from one to whom any normal man would feel a debt of gratitude; and thus what might well be right for you would be wrong for me. In order to tell what is right, we must have regard to the circumstances, which are different in the two cases. If you ignore the appeal, the situation produced will be one in which no particular injustice will be done. If I ignore it, the situation produced will be one in which a natural expectation will be met by an unnatural slight. Our duties clearly differ.

But then, in another sense, our duties are the same. If you and I confront precisely the same set of circumstances, then what is right for me will also be right for you, and to say anything else would destroy our main principle itself. For if the circumstances are really the same, then we can only believe that what would produce the greatest good in one case would do so in the other, and to justify some other course would be to justify the lesser good. And that can never be sound. Thus the answer to our question is: What is right for me and for you may differ if circumstances differ; if not, they will be the same.

[1] Cf. BR, No. 48 B, R. W. Emerson, "The Law of Compensation."

126. Rules Again

Are there then no moral rules that hold everywhere alike?

Yes and no, again. The great rule which we have laid down for conduct generally does seem to hold without exception. And we have followed Sidgwick in suggesting that there are certain other rules, perhaps mathematical rather than moral, that hold good everywhere — the rules that one should choose one's own greater good, that one should prefer the greater good of another to a smaller good of one's own, that one should count each man's good as of the same importance as the like good of another.[1]

But this is not the sort of rule that most people think of when they mention moral rules. They are thinking of something more specific, like "Always tell the truth," "Always keep your promises." Are there specific rules like this that have absolutely no exceptions? Apparently not. Such rules will lead us right in ninety-nine cases and mislead us in the hundredth. But it would be a major blunder to suppose therefore that we could throw rules to the winds.

Society is based, for example, on the assumption that we can rely on each other's word; and if we had to suspect deception whenever there would be a slight amusement or advantage in deceiving us, the moral atmosphere would be stifling. The doctor who lies to a patient must take into account, not merely the seeming advantage of the moment, but also the deterioration in trust between doctor and patient; for the patient, once finding himself deceived in this way, will never feel complete security in his physician's word again, or perhaps in that of any physician. A famous doctor writes:

"A single lie spreads. It is difficult to draw the line around it. It spreads in the habits of him who tells it, and it spreads in the community as soon as it is openly defended. . . . A polite lie under a set of peculiarly difficult conditions seems easily excusable. But if we ask: 'Will you say, then, that whenever you wish to avoid hurting someone's feelings or whenever you are in a bad fix socially, it is right to lie?' few are content to answer 'Yes.' . . . A popular writer defends lying under certain conditions. His wife of course reads his books and knows this doctrine. On a visit to Boston she happens to consult me as a patient and confesses that though he is the best husband in the world, she never can tell when he is handing her a benevolent and

[1] Cf. BR, No. 42, H. R. Titus, "Some Principles for Living."

conscientious lie and when he is adhering to ordinary honesty. She knows that he intends everything in the kindest possible way, but she cannot reap all the benefits of his devoted kindness because she cannot tell when to believe him." [1]

Dr. Cabot's view was that the physician should allow himself no exceptions at all, and certainly most patients would rather deal with a man who is known to hold this. At the very least, the correct attitude toward the rule of truth is not "May I deceive in this case?" but "Must I deceive?"

127. Rights

What is a right?

A right is a duty looked at from the other end. Suppose I have hired you to do a day's work at a certain wage. At the completion of the work, it is my duty to pay you what I owe you. The other side of that is that you have a *right* to be paid. Your right is my duty; they are two aspects of the same thing.

How is one to tell whether one has a right of a particular kind, for example, to life or liberty or happiness? In exactly the same way as one decides about one's duty. For example, have I a right to freedom of speech and action? If I have, that means that other people have a duty to keep their hands off when I speak and act as I choose. What determines whether they have that duty or not? The greatest good of the whole. Usually that greatest good will require that I be given a large measure of freedom; occasionally, as in time of war, it will require that my freedom be restricted.

If it is true, as we have seen it to be, that there are no specific duties which hold under all conditions, there are no rights of this kind either. There are no "inalienable rights." The rights to life, property, and happiness, sometimes claimed as absolute, rest on the needs and interests of the community and vary with them. A man normally has a right to keep the land he has bought, but if the community needs his land for a railroad, it may force him to sell, on the ground that to recognize his right is not in the community's interest. Even the right to life is not absolute. If the safety of the country requires that one risk

---

[1] R. C. Cabot, *The Meaning of Right and Wrong*, pp. 165–166, The Macmillan Company, 1933.

one's life in its defense, are one's rights being invaded? Most men do not think so.

128. Morality among Nations

Do nations, as well as persons, have rights and duties?

Yes. A nation, through its government, makes war or peace, and such actions affect men's welfare the world over; indeed, because such actions mean so much in the way of good and evil, a special weight of responsibility rests on the shoulders of governments.

It has sometimes been said that morals hold only between individuals and that strictly there are no rights and duties among nations. Of course, nations have often behaved as if this were true. There has been a widespread feeling that if one man killed his neighbor, that was the height of wickedness, but if a million men organized themselves for banditry and proceeded to rob and kill a million of their neighbors, that was rather glorious. It is best to call this by its true name, savagery. The fact that the world has of late been nearly ruined by it and that large numbers of persons apparently still believe in it only shows that our escape from savagery is incomplete.[1]

Little by little, at unspeakable cost in suffering, men are coming to see that a nation has no more right than a person to lie or burn or steal at the expense of neighbors, or even to stand and watch idly while those neighbors are being attacked. If there is a thief or a thug at work in our community, we see to it that the police, who represent us all, are put on his trail; and anyone who refuses to cooperate by obeying the law and helping to apprehend the outlaw is put down as a bad citizen. The day is coming, and coming soon, when a nation that refuses to take its part in the society of nations and to help in the enforcement of law against international thieves and thugs will be quite justly held up to shame by the world community. That nations have such duties is a plain deduction from the main principle of conduct.

129. Proof in Ethics

How can you *prove* that a course of action is right?

You cannot. You can point out the good and bad entailed by it; but if, when these good and bad results are pointed out to

---

[1] Cf. BR, No. 31, Friedrich Nietzsche, "The Origin of Morals."

another, he does not assess them as you do, you cannot prove your assessment to be the true one. One action may bring great happiness and another great misery, but if you were called on to say *why* happiness is better than misery, what could you say? Indeed, could you ever *prove* to a doubter that an ordinary toothache is bad? No; not because there is anything dubious about the assertion, but simply because it is the kind of assertion that does not admit of proof; it is either clear without evidence, or incapable of being made so by any amount of evidence.

The most important truths in ethics — truths about what is ultimately good — are precisely of this kind. Some people have thought that because moralists are unable to prove these propositions, their science must be dogmatic and uncertain. This is a bad mistake. There are many unprovable things of which we are as certain as we are of anything. Can you prove that you are having a sensation of white as you look at this page or that you existed at all five minutes ago? Try it and you will find that you cannot. And yet you have no doubt of either. For that matter, proof itself depends on the laws of logic, and how are *they* to be proved? No, we can only say of the final propositions of ethics that they are quite incapable of proof in any ordinary sense, and that we can know them to be true notwithstanding. We know that intense pain is evil and that knowledge is better than ignorance with the same directness and certainty with which we know that black is different from white, and that what has a shape has also a size.

130. An Ultimate Difficulty

Our theory of what makes conduct right will now be clear. But are there no real difficulties with the theory? We have found difficulties in all the other views; are there none in this? Unfortunately that is too much to say. While there are perhaps no criticisms strong enough to justify rejecting the theory, there is one which is genuinely troublesome. An example will serve to suggest it.

Suppose that in a frontier community there is an epidemic of horse-stealing, that the whole community is convinced that a certain man is the chief offender, and that he is brought before the local judge. The judge is sure that if he is let off there will be an outcry, and that those who are contemplating similar crimes will be encouraged to go on with them. He believes that if, on the other hand, the man is convicted, the fear of the law will be put effectively into the hearts of intending wrongdoers. In the interest of the community, then, it would seem that the best thing that could happen would be a conviction and a stern sentence. But the judge, on studying the evidence, is forced to believe that the man is innocent. What should he do? If he were to obey our principle and act for the good of the community, would he not have to convict an innocent man? And yet is it not perfectly clear that this would be an outrage to our sense of right and justice?

We must agree that it would. We agree, further, that there must be no tampering with what our moral judgment reports; we must not trim and pare its verdicts in order to fit them into a theory. We must admit, finally, that some of the ablest writers on ethics of the present day, including a distinguished trio of teachers at the University of Oxford, W. D. Ross, H. A. Prichard, and E. F. Carritt, are convinced that, in cases like this, our formula breaks down. They would grant that in general the formula would guide us to the right course, but they would insist that occasionally we perceive an act to be our duty even though, for all we can see, it would produce *less* than the largest good. And if one case of this kind can be produced, our principle is not a safe guide.

131. The Answer

This challenge is arresting but not quite convincing. Let us look at the test case again. The judge should not convict the innocent man, even though failure to convict would anger the public and encourage wrongdoers. Agreed. What this implies, according to the critics, is that it is sometimes our duty to produce what, for all we can see, is a *worse* state of things than some other that we could produce instead. But is it clear that this *is* what our judgment implies? Do we ever really see at the same time that an act would probably make the world worse and also that it is our duty? Many moralists would rule out such a suggestion as self-evidently untrue. It is in any case so shocking that we may well decline to believe it unless the facts plainly force it upon us.

Secondly, *do* they force it upon us? Do we not feel, on the contrary, that in refusing to convict the innocent man, the judge may be doing the greatest good after all? The people are clamoring for the man's conviction, to be sure; there will be a storm of protest if he is acquitted, and perhaps an intensification of the epidemic of crime. But there is much also on the other side. Courts of law are specially set up to sift truth from error in such cases; if they are to do their work, it is of the first importance that their integrity should stand unquestioned in the public mind; and if it were learned that a court of law had deliberately convicted an innocent man, that integrity would be badly smirched.

"Yes," say the critics, "but suppose the judge is confident that the secret never will get out, and therefore that he can convict the man without risk to the court's name for integrity; do we not, even so, think that a conviction would be gravely wrong? We should still say that if the man is innocent the judge should acquit him, even though in doing so he is turning his back on the larger and later good."

We answer: the good results to which an act gives rise are not to be looked for only among those that come later in time. Some acts involve a relation of man to man whose existence is itself a great good and whose absence may be a great evil. When a court, designed to find and follow the truth, deliberately brands as guilty an innocent man, it sets up a state of affairs that might better not exist and would therefore be bad in itself, even if it had no effects at all.

And whether acts have traceable results or not, they do have implications. Think out what is implied in the judge's scrupulous adherence to fact and you will see that it belongs to a larger pattern, a pattern of life as a whole in which regard for truth, respect for persons, disinterestedness, loyalty to the code of one's profession, and many another precious thing all have their parts. The maintenance of this pattern of life, with all the good implied in it, is of immense importance; and the final reason why we feel so strongly that the judge should acquit the innocent man lies not so much in the value of this particular act or its consequences as in the value of the larger framework to which it belongs.

Acting as that pattern requires does lead us at times to choose what, if we look at an act apart from its context, seems to be the smaller good, and yet we can see on reflection that it is more important to maintain the pattern than to gain some limited good by departing from it. We often judge conduct in this way. Why is it that we admire a person who, in a tight place which he could get out of by lying, tells the whole and exact truth? Largely because we feel that this act does not stand alone; it reveals much else about a man; he is evidently guided by principle rather than by fear or impulse or selfishness. But do we not also feel that such conduct is of a piece with a way of life as a whole which would be an excellent thing for mankind, and therefore deserves support and encouragement? We can never pass judgment *finally* on any right act or any good thing until we see its place in this larger whole.

Now for our last question: what are the chief intrinsic goods that have their part in this way of life? We have named happiness, and this must rank high. But there are others, and we shall conclude by looking at a few of the most important.

J. SOME GREAT GOODS

132. Health

First, health. In strictness, this is not an intrinsic good at all because health is a state of the body, and such states are of no value except as leading to states of mind. Yet it is well to give it a place here because all other good things depend on it so directly. Unless the appropriate part of the body is doing its work, one can no more solve a problem or write a poem than one can lift a hundred-pound weight.

This has been denied. There have been many people in the past who believed that body and mind were enemies, and that the way to reach the higher spiritual levels was to ignore and repress the body. This is the doctrine of asceticism. Its believers at times have gone to unbelievable lengths in persecuting their bodies, living on bread and water, reducing their hours of sleep, dressing in flimsy rags, living in cells or caves or on the tops of pillars, even flogging themselves and wearing hair shirts so as not to indulge their bodies in the smallest ease or comfort. In India, even today, there are "holy men" who spend their lives on beds consisting of the upturned points of spikes. They think that in doing such things they are delivering themselves from the lower desires of the body and freeing themselves for higher concerns. Such lives, no doubt, have their value. They prove to the rest of mankind what the human will can do in triumphing over physical obstacles. They could be meditated on with profit by those who think they can do nothing unless the conditions are just right.

But what strikes one chiefly about them is their tragic waste of life and happiness, and the tiresome error from which this springs. The error is to believe that mind and body are enemies at war with each other, that bodily health and vigor are hostile to spiritual life rather than the soil in which the spirit must grow. In starving and abusing their bodies, the ascetics without knowing it were cutting the root of their spirit and denying themselves the hope of the very thing they were seeking.

We know more now about the dependence of mind on body. We know that a mere lack of the right kind of vitamins may stunt the growth of mind and character, that pessimism is often due to nothing more profound than a disordered digestion, that a slight change in the working of our thyroid or pituitary glands may alter our whole personality. Indeed, the experts tell us that if our bodies were to secrete about $\frac{1}{100}$ of a grain of thyroxin less per day, we should be reduced to something like idiocy. When the mind depends on the body in so intimate a way as this, to play fast and loose with health is the merest profligacy. "With health," said Schopenhauer, "everything is a source of pleasure; without it, nothing else is enjoyable. It follows that the greatest of follies is to sacrifice health for any other kind of happiness, whatever it may be, for gain, advancement, learning, or fame, let alone for fleeting sensual pleasures."

133. A Footnote on Fatigue

Everyone would admit this, so far as serious disease is concerned. But often we fail to realize how important are mere freshness and vigor for the higher activities of mind. Take one point only, fatigue. Nervous exhaustion is so common among Americans, with their high-pressure ways of living, that it has been called Americanitis. The results of such fatigue are worth noting. Since it affects the highest brain centers first, the cost, when it becomes habitual, may be very high.

The fatigued person cannot concentrate and hence, where clear and exact thought is called for, is of little use. Because he cannot concentrate, his will, which depends on the control of attention, will tend to be feeble and fluctuating. The fatigued person cannot remember; have you not noticed that often the first sign of fatigue is the loss of ready recall for proper names, and how this extends to other things as the fatigue grows deeper? The fatigued person cannot easily control his emotions; and since the emotions that assail him are usually the corrosive ones of anxiety and anger, he forfeits his peace of mind. Even when he does succeed in doing the same things as others, he does them with much more effort. At a university laboratory tests were recently made, with a number of student subjects, of the amount of energy consumed in fifteen minutes of the same kind of mental work, first by men who had had eight hours' sleep, then by those who had had six. It was found that the expenditure of those with less sleep was about 15 per cent greater. When we consider, further, that our temperament — the habitual mood with which we face the world — is largely a matter of physical freshness, the inference is clear that, if we are either to get or to give our best, it is the part of ordinary prudence to keep our balance high in the bank of nervous energy.

134. Knowledge

There is a poem by Charles Kingsley with the line, "Be good, sweet maid, and let who will be clever." The trouble with such advice is that the person who is *merely* good is likely to be good for nothing; life in these days has become so complex that one must have knowledge to make good will count. For example, if a man is to vote intelligently, he must know something about the causes of unemployment, the effects of high and low tariffs, and the importance of foreign policy. If he is to run an ordinary business efficiently, he must know something about accounting, banking, and law. If he enters a profession such as medicine or engineering, he must have a large mass of technical knowledge at his fingertips. And if he is merely to read the newspaper intelligently, he must know a great many things that a century ago were unknown even to experts.

But when philosophers speak of knowledge as one of the great benefits of life, what they have in mind is not the sort of knowledge that increases one's technical proficiency, important as this is. Nor is it the sort of knowledge that consists of a wide range of information, though this is what the term probably first suggests. Some people are gifted with the sort of photographic memory that can retain innumerable odds and ends of detail; Macaulay, for example, could recite whole books from memory, word for word. But Emerson remarked about Macaulay (not quite fairly) that no one ever knew so much that was not worth knowing. It is clear that a mere ragbag of miscellaneous knowledge

> Of shoes and ships and sealing-wax
> Of cabbages and kings

is of no great value to anyone. The knowledge that philosophers praise is marked by two characteristics which are supremely important, though difficult to define: understanding and wisdom.[1]

135. (a) Understanding

To understand a fact means to know not only *that* it is so, but *why* it is so. To understand a theorem in geometry means to see how the earlier propositions lead on to this one. To understand the American Revolution is to grasp, not only the facts about battles and campaigns, but also the earlier conditions that made these battles and campaigns unroll as they did. To understand the flu means to see precisely why it occurs, what causes lead to it in the way of bacteria, exposure, and so on. If science lays so much stress on understanding events through their causes, this is largely because it is through grasping their causes that we come to control the events themselves; if we know

[1] Cf. BR, No. 24, Aristotle, "The Nicomachean Ethics."

the causes of flu, for example, we can remove them and so
prevent the disease. But if understanding is to be complete we
must grasp effects or consequences as well as conditions. Full
understanding in geometry would involve seeing both the
premises on which a proposition rests and the further implications to which it commits us. So of understanding generally.
It means the grasping of something in the light of its conditions
and consequences.[1]

To find such understanding dawning upon us in a field where
everything was mere brute fact is a satisfying and sometimes
thrilling experience. It is said that Newton, when he was
approaching the end of his calculations and it looked as if the
law that held the universe together was about to reveal itself
to him, could no longer trust himself in his excitement and gave
the calculations over into steadier hands. The reason why such
insight gives so deep a satisfaction is that understanding is the
end and aim of the whole process of knowing. To think, to
reflect, *is* to try to understand; to understand is to see things in
connection, to see how they hang together in a system; and
hence, when the facts of economics or political science or biology
are laid hold of in their interconnection, we have the highest
and firmest grasp of them of which our minds are capable.

The science in which this ideal of system has been most perfectly carried out is the science of mathematics, and the clearness
and certainty of this science have put into the heads of philosophers a dream that has come to stay. May it not be that
the world, if only we had eyes to see, is really a single system in
which there are no accidents and no loose ends, in which everything, as in a perfect mathematics, is implied in everything
else, in which all things conspire to frame a whole that is intelligible through and through? This has been the faith of some of
the profoundest minds of the race, such as Plato, Spinoza,[2] and
Hegel. To them the attempt to achieve this clearness and sweep
of vision was the chief delight of life as well as its major business.
And perhaps there is no one of us who is not a kindred spirit of
theirs in the sense that he has felt at times the fascination that
lies in their high pursuit of understanding for its own sake.[3]

[1] Cf. BR, No. 39, E. G. Conklin, "The Ethical Ideals of Science."
[2] Cf. BR, No. 32, B. Spinoza, "What Are the True Ends of Life."
[3] Cf. BR, No. 40, J. H. Newman, "The Delights of Knowledge."

136. (b) Wisdom

But we have said that the aim of the great philosophers was not merely understanding but also wisdom; and what is that? It is the grasp of the relative values of life, supplemented by practical judgment regarding the means of achieving them. The wise man is the opposite of the fanatic and the hothead, the provincial, the bigot, and the crank. For most men there is a tendency to make mountains, for good or ill, out of their own particular molehills; if they are business men, to measure people by their efficiency and power to make money; if they are musicians, to lose themselves in a world of sound; if they are scientists, to overrate exact knowledge and underrate what is done for us by poetry, art, and religion.

The wise man knows the place of these things in the scheme of life as a whole, and this gives him weight in counsel. He knows that money and possessions are means, not ends. He knows the difference between pleasures of the moment and enduring satisfactions, between being great and being famous, between sex attraction and love, between reverence and superstition, between solidity and show in literature, art, and life. He knows that in the human lot some evils are unavoidable, that loss and disease and old age are bound to come; and he has made his peace with their coming.[1] And so when he is overtaken by these things, he is not overcome by them because he has drawn their sting in advance. He has achieved the serenity of the long view.[2]

When moralists speak of knowledge as one of the great values of life, it is this, then, that they mean — not information, technical or general, but wisdom and understanding; in short, the philosophic mind.[3]

137. Work

Most men who have passed the stage of formal education, however, have all too little time for such high pursuits. They have a living to make, and such satisfactions as they can get must be gained very largely through doing their particular job, to which they are probably devoting six to ten of the best hours

---

[1] Cf. BR, No. 1, Epicurus, "Philosophy for Youth and Old Age."
[2] Cf. BR, No. 25, Epictetus, "Stoicism: Virtue, the Highest Good."
[3] Cf. BR, No. 2, W. Durant, "On the Uses of Philosophy."

of each day. To many of them the necessity for such hard and continuous work seems merely a curse. They go to their work reluctantly; they hate it while they are at it; they can hardly wait till it is over. Now anyone who feels this way about the activity in which so much of his life must be spent is facing unhappiness. Perhaps this is inevitable. There are forms of work, such as the handling of garbage and the cleaning out of noisome sewers, which are repellent to everyone, and from which nobody can be blamed for trying to escape with as few hours and as much pay as possible.

But this does not hold true of most work, for in general one man's work is another man's play. Nearly everything that is done by some persons as drudgery is done by others because they like it. Apart from such extreme cases as those we have mentioned, the distinction between work and play is chiefly a matter of attitude. Work is what you do because you must in order to reach some end that lies beyond. Play is what you do for the delight of doing it.[1] Hence work is translated into something very like play as one's attitude toward it changes, and the things that were done from compulsion begin to be done from interest. Ordinarily youngsters like Tom Sawyer would regard the whitewashing of a fence as hard work, but when Tom persuaded his friends that whitewashing was a great privilege they not only did it and liked it; they paid for the chance. Elihu Burritt, beginning language study in hours of leisure as a blacksmith, had acquired at the age of thirty a reading knowledge of nearly fifty languages. What would be intolerable drudgery to most of us was evidently the spice of life to him. Indeed the scholar and the artist afford the finest examples of how work that is laborious and exacting can be transformed by the spirit in which it is done. "I never knew what was play and what was work," writes Havelock Ellis in his autobiography. "Throughout life people have told me how they marvelled at the amount of work I accomplished. I have been tempted to reply: But I never work at all."[2]

Granting, however, that this sort of transfiguring interest may be achieved by artists and scholars, is it really possible in the

[1] Cf. BR, No. 38, R. C. Cabot, "A Philosophy of Play."
[2] Cf. BR, No. 34, R. C. Cabot, "The Points of a Good Job."

workaday world? Under certain conditions it is, and it will repay us to note what they are. The chief conditions are two. If work is to be fully satisfying, (1) it must be self-expressive, and (2) it must be significant.

138. (a) Work Should Be Self-expressive

Few persons, probably, have taken up ditch-digging for its intrinsic satisfactions, while many have sought to write novels for this reason. Ditch-digging calls for little beyond patience and a strong back; the writing of a good novel demands all one's resources and constitutes a challenge that can be met only by a personality that is thoroughly alive. Now the full and free play of our faculties is itself a delightful thing. We like to meet and conquer difficulties, particularly if this calls out our special powers; for then, to the pleasure of varied activity there is added pride in ourselves and our work. There is not much exhilaration in tending a machine or in doing a thousand times a day what a machine would do better, and because so much present-day work is of this kind, it is important that the hours and conditions of such deadening labor be regulated.

But more satisfying than the best regulated job of this kind is the work which, because it calls out our craftsmanship, we enjoy doing for its own sake, and which we can take an expert's pride in doing well. To feel that one is the best dentist, the best farmer,[1] the best carpenter, or the best cook in the community gives a rare lift to morale. Everyone should find his vocation, if he can, in work that he enjoys, if only because as a rule it is the work that he most enjoys that he does best. It is said that "Pop" Anson, the Chicago baseball star of former days, asked to have inscribed on his tombstone: "Here lies a man who batted .300." William Lyon Phelps, often voted the most popular teacher at Yale, tells how he used to wake of a morning and think with delight of meeting his first class. Somewhere in the east there was dug up a mediaeval astronomical instrument called an astrolabe. On examination it was found to have an inscription which ran as follows: "This astrolabe was made by Hussein Ali, mechanic and mathematician and servant of the

---

[1] Cf. BR, No. 37, W. E. Hocking, "The Satisfactions of Farm Life."

most high God." That is all we know of Hussein Ali. And yet
it seems much.[1]

139. (b) Work Must Be Significant

Besides being self-expressive, work must be felt to be significant.
To keep digging a hole and filling it up again or to keep aim-
lessly writing down figures would, in the end, threaten the
worker with madness. One's work must serve some purpose,
must bring something of value into the world. Persons who
must dance attendance on the self-indulgent whims of wealth,
reporters who must color their stories to accord with a newspaper
policy that they deeply disbelieve in, salesmen whose lot it is
to extol the merits of a refrigerator or vacuum cleaner that they
know to be third-rate, had better look for something else to do.

On the other hand, to know that one is doing an indispensable
job makes up for hard conditions. Mothers who have six children
dependent on their hourly care seem to need the help of psy-
chiatrists less often than those with money and leisure. Among
the professions, as work grows more important it also grows more
satisfying, regardless of the incomes attached. The surgeon
whose skill almost daily saves lives is not commonly heard com-
plaining about his job. Most men would rather be colonels than
corporals, even if they did not get a dollar more.

Of course as one goes up the ladder of jobs the responsibilities
grow heavier, but then the greater the responsibility the greater
the power, and the love of power is one of the deep hungers of
human nature. For the outstanding positions in the community,
the headship of a great company or an ancient university, a
seat on the Supreme Court or in the Cabinet, there is never a
shortage of candidates, even though success would bring increased
burdens and decreased salary. The lightest work that is worthless is drudgery. The hardest work that is essential and responsible is widely and eagerly sought for.[2]

140. Friendship and Love

One of the best known passages in the literature of the world
provides a short list of the virtues and concludes with the statement: "The greatest of these is love." Its author was fond of

[1] Cf. BR, No. 35, Thomas Carlyle, "A Gospel of Work."
[2] Cf. BR, No. 36, Kahlil Gibran, "On Work."

insisting that "we are members one of another." William James says that we are so dependent on the notice, and the favorable notice, of each other that no more fiendish punishment could be devised than that a man should be turned loose in society and that no one should ever notice him. "If no one turned round when we entered, answered when we spoke, or minded what we did, but if every person we met 'cut us dead' and acted as if we were non-existing things, a kind of rage and impotent despair would ere long well up in us, from which the cruelest bodily tortures would be a relief."

It is conceivable, as Clarence Day has pointed out in *This Simian World*, that men should have evolved from the cat tribe rather than the ape tribe; if we had, we should be troubled by loneliness less than we are. But the fact is that we are evolved from creatures so gregarious that isolation may mean death. And it is not enough for us that we should be *with* other people. The man who is friendless in a great city may suffer agonies of loneliness. "A crowd is not company," said Francis Bacon, "and faces are but a gallery of pictures, and talk but a tinkling cymbal where there is no love."

141. Romantic Love

No doubt love, as the New Testament says, is the ideal relation between human beings. But love means different things. Probably, in our own country, its commonest meaning is romantic love, the love of youth and maid. Such love is based on physical impulses whose drive is one of the most powerful and whose satisfaction one of the most delightful known to man. Such love, again, sets the mind vibrating in unison with all the chords and discords in another's mind. As children, we are all egoists. The enlargement of self that comes with love, through the inclusion of all another's values among one's own, is perhaps the most precious experience of which human nature is capable. It is so universally celebrated in poetry, art, and song that there is small danger of our forgetting or undervaluing it.

Indeed, the danger is perhaps rather that, through the constant exploitation of it by fiction, stage, and screen, we should overrate it at the expense of other forms of love. "Love at first sight" may be less deeply based than it seems, and to take it as the infallible guarantee of a marriage made in heaven has led to much unhappiness. "Love and nothing else," as Walter Lippmann says, "very soon is nothing else. The emotion of love, in spite of the romantics, is not self-sustaining; it endures only when the lovers love many things together, and not merely each other." Such love, if it is fortunate, culminates in something less ecstatic but more enduring, friendship.

142. The Bases of Friendship

Love and friendship have much in common.[1] If two persons are to be friends, they must find content in each other's company, suffer pain in each other's failure, and take pleasure in each other's success. Each must find in the mood and temperament of the other something attractive and congenial. But any deep and permanent friendship calls for a larger common area than romantic love. Notoriously, the prince may fall in love with the chorus-girl when the two have almost nothing in common. But friendships are based, as a rule, on common interests in a project, an art, or a cause; one thinks of Marx and Engels, Cobden and Bright, Gilbert and Sullivan, the Mayo brothers, Weber and Fields.

Still, common interests by themselves will not guarantee friendship, and many co-workers have been rivals and enemies. Full friendship must see eye to eye about values, about things admired and liked and disliked. It is not furthered if, whenever we grow enthusiastic about dancing or music or flying or science, our companion can only say, "Sorry, but I find all that detestable." One of the blessings of friendship is that it supplies a sounding-board which, in echoing our own delights, makes them greater. And by a happy correlative law, sorrows when shared grow less. Friends fortify each other like the sides of an arch; they gain contentment, security, reassurance in failure, added happiness in success, and a large increment of courage merely from facing things side by side.

Most of us are sharply limited in our capacity for friendly feeling. But in some noble and imaginative minds, the friendly interest in the welfare and distress of others is not confined to a narrow circle. It spreads out, like the ripples in a pool, to

[1] Cf. BR, No. 24, Aristotle, "The Nicomachean Ethics."

persons far removed; it refuses to recognize limits; where human need is concerned, it draws no lines between Jew and gentile, black and white; nothing human is wholly alien to it. This large concern for human good is the highest level to which morality can attain; and many would say that it was never attained except as the love of man was leavened and widened by the love of God.[1] Others, including some of the most influential teachers of our day, would say that religion *is* morality at this highest level, where one's will is surrendered selflessly to the good of mankind. We could not settle this question without discussing at some length what religion means. And that is another story, which we must leave to a later section of this book.

[1] Cf. BR, No. 45, Tagore, "Love as the Fulfillment of Life."

PART III. SOCIAL AND POLITICAL PHILOSOPHY

Charles William Hendel

Yale University

A. THE DECISIONS OF THE CITIZEN

143. The Urgency of Postwar Social Reconstruction

When war befalls a nation, everything men value is at stake. Naturally enough, their differences with each other drop out of sight in the presence of so great a threat. But the hardest times of all lie farther ahead, when these plain, obvious necessities of common action give place again to the divergent interests of men who are enjoying security once more. At a bound, everyone's thought turns away from national defense to self-interest. The war recedes into a past far distant. The habits of civilian life return upon the people. Those who have risked everything see others going about their usual business of getting and spending as before, scrambling for places and jobs, looking out for themselves, and almost exclusively for themselves. The first reactions of relief from the regimentation of a military economy are likely to be thus extreme. All men want the right to go their own free way. For some this means "free enterprise," to seek their own profit or acquire a fortune. For others it means the simple human rights to life and happiness, a home, a family, working at a job of one's own choice, and a good time when one wants it, not at someone's leave. Why *not* liberty for every one, then — as much liberty as possible?

This nation, though one of the most powerful states of the world, has had to be united with others to defeat their common enemy. All the nations have had to work together intimately, with a pooling of their resources as well as their armies. Nor have they been able to sustain their progress toward victory without summoning to their aid other peoples who have to fight from secret underground places, dangerously and under the very eyes of their oppressors. These oppressed men, women, and children have been joined to the cause, though they are not arrayed in battle or reorganized in states. All these peoples are to be liberated, too, and they are desperately in need of rehabilitation and the restoration of an order of life and the formation of their own governments. They have human and moral claims on the resources of those nations that have more than enough for their own existence. But are the people who are well off going to stick by them? The rush for liberty at home tends to make men impatient with such "foreign" claims and unwilling to restrict themselves for their sakes. They are even apt to become angry with a government which tries to carry out its obligations to the larger community which has, as a matter of fact, come into existence. No, they have had quite enough of "the state" and "government." They want everybody to have all "the four freedoms," of course, but why not let each one get them his own way?

In the tense, critical days of war, a statesman, standing with the people bowed in reverence for the men who have died that their nation might live, can invoke a spirit of dedication to some principle, as Lincoln did at Gettysburg. But will this solemn invocation move men who are feverishly busy competing in the market place or in the counting houses or anxiously looking for jobs? Here is a "time for greatness." [1] It must be the greatness of the whole nation. It is nothing a statesman alone can supply, no matter how great his gifts, for it belongs to the spirit of the people.

144. "A Time for Greatness": Our Decision Today

Where do we stand today, and what will be our decision? It has seemed to many Americans that our "new birth of freedom" in the nineteenth century was more like "a sleep and a forgetting." Lulled by the security made possible by others, men went about safely, enjoying life or doing whatever they liked for profit or satisfaction. In such an era of peace and prosperity, the chief decisions of men seem to be only purely individual ones, their own free choice of what is good for themselves. They expect to choose their own work, as well as a wife, if they want one. They hitch their wagons of ambition to whatever star they fancy. The goals they pursue are their own affair. Of course they run into some moral problems, for whatever

---

[1] Herbert Agar, *A Time for Greatness*, 2nd ed., Boston, Little, Brown and Company, 1943.

they do they are involved somehow with other persons. But these questions of personal conduct appear to be the only important problems of their lives. The decision that religion has called upon man to make regarding his "eternal life" is pushed far in the background, as something that can be left until some later time. But another thing is also neglected. It is forgotten that the individual is only part of a larger whole. All the while his free life of indiv dual choice has depended upon *the soundness of the whole order of his life in the state*. His own survival depends on the survival of that state — he may have to give his life for it. The kind of life he enjoys, whether free or regimented, and all the benefits of civilization — all this depends upon the social system and form of government. And whatever the form may be, it is always true that to make *that whole order possible* many things must be considered besides the wishes of the individuals themselves. If people think *only* of themselves and forget these great necessities of organized life, something goes wrong in the whole society and everyone suffers. And it is not a mere profit and loss account. It is lives sacrificed. Heroic but wasteful measures then become necessary to make up for the neglect of the days when men lived on easy street. War has to be waged to set things right again that need never have gone wrong.

145. Examples of Great Decisions and Actions

There is something to be learned about this from the history of our people. The equal right of men to life and liberty was heroically fought for in England three hundred years ago just at the time of the settlement of New England. People of various beliefs and interests had united to oppose the rule of one man, the monarch Charles I, who claimed rule by divine right. Those rebels were fighting for their rights as men and particularly for the right to have a share in the government. And they were discussing, even in the army itself, these questions of right and government. The record is in the minutes of the General Council of Officers. In the debate of October 28, 1647, one of them put his point in this way: "For really I think that the poorest he that is in England hath a life to live, as the greatest he; and therefore, truly, sir, I think it's clear, that every man that is to live under a government ought first by his own consent to put himself under that government." Precisely that was what their monarch had denied, and he did it bravely, too, even as he stood on the scaffold about to be beheaded. He declared, at that last moment, his own obstinate conviction about the issue: the people were only subjects, with no right to government, "for a subject and a sovereign are clean different things." But disregarding "the divinity that doth hedge a king," those subjects put away their monarchy and set up a free commonwealth.

They had, in fact, moved too fast for the common understanding, and they had not reckoned with their own divisions of interest that remained among them after their struggle for liberty. The royal monarchy returned to power and, with it, an extreme philosophy of absolute authority in Thomas Hobbes' *Leviathan* (1651). Nevertheless, in spite of that reaction, history was changed in the direction of liberty. Englishmen had developed the habit of free discussion about the fundamentals of life and politics. They were learning more about the nature of their rights and the difficulties of any government. When John Locke published his *Civil Government* (1690) he made clear and plain the matured convictions of the English people. And at that time the people, through their representatives in Parliament, made another great decision — to put themselves under a new government, that of a monarch, William of Orange, who was appointed by them, and thus they established a constitutional government with their own Parliament supreme.

Meantime, the same sort of people who were doing these great things in England had laid the foundations of the American civilization. They established thirteen commonwealths in the New World. Jealous by tradition of the power of monarchy, and experiencing the rule of government from afar as arbitrary and oppressive, they revolted, declared their independence, and fought for their liberty, as thirteen "sovereign" states. Once victorious, they were in danger of losing all that they had won, through their divisions and weakness as a mere confederation. They could not survive with separate economies, insolvent and incapable of developing into anything strong enough to last.

The founders of the nation themselves understood the need of forming a larger commonwealth or republic. They had discussed, day in, day out, the reasons for this necessity. They published the arguments and the facts they had in mind. Hamilton and Madison, in particular, worked together on the papers of the *Federalist*. And so, by tremendous devotion and labor, the winning of the Revolutionary War was consolidated into "a more perfect union" with the adoption of the Constitution. The new republic was to have a constitutional government, a government of laws and not of men. Those who exercised rule were to be elected to office, so that the citizens really consented to their government. And behind all these measures was the continuing, vigorous spirit of those early Puritans who had declared the equal right of every man to life and liberty.

Four score and seven years after the American Declaration of Independence, Abraham Lincoln stood on the battlefield of Gettysburg, saying that the Civil War was testing whether this "new nation, conceived in liberty and dedicated to the proposition that all men are created equal . . . can long endure." [1] It all depended on the people, on their dedication to the cause. They were summoned by him, in words immortal, to "a new birth of freedom . . . that government of the people, by the people, for the people, shall not perish from the earth." That war did liberate the slaves in the United States. But it could not have decided anything without the long years of debate before the issue was joined, the Lincoln-Douglas debates and many another public discussion, in and out of Congress, on the nature and principles of the American Union and the government of the United States.

146. Freedom Comes from Free Discussion

This is the lesson of that bit of history: free public discussion is what saves the people and all that they cherish in their community. When the men of Cromwell's army took their daring step of overthrowing the monarchy and setting up a commonwealth, they accomplished what they did towards the eventual triumph of the principle of self-government because they discussed seriously the fundamentals of life in society. The founders of the American Republic did so likewise, with their discussions in the assembly of the Congress of the thirteen states and in such

---

[1] Cf. BR, Nos. 57 and 58, A. Lincoln, "Address at Gettysburg" and "Second Inaugural Address."

publications as the *Federalist*. The debates and judicial discussions for decades before the Civil War defined the issues of a Union, "half-slave, half-free," so that the people knew what was at stake, and what was coming. And before the Second World War, the discussions by public-spirited men as well as by men in office, discussions conducted in the press, over the radio, and in many spontaneous assemblies and forums — these made the eventual unity of action possible. But our own new decisions lie ahead — decisions for peace. A greater discussion still must go on to define what is to be done when the attempt at one-man world rule has been completely defeated. Another dedication is needed for this age and for these conditions. And the victory stands or falls by what we will do.

B. THE PROBLEM OF HUMAN LIFE IN SOCIETY

147. Need and Difficulty of a Philosophical Study of Society

When discussion gets down to bedrock, it is philosophy. In order to make right decisions, we must know our true situation, and we must also know *ourselves*. Socrates was always recalling that commandment of the Greek religion: Know thyself. It means knowing what we really think, what counts most, what makes life worth living and having, what we ought to work for — the first things, the basic things, the lasting goods to which everything else is subordinate. Whatever we believe on these questions, together with the things that happen in our lifetime, makes the history of our time. So philosophy is important because it deals with precisely these essentials.

But the way of philosophy is no easy one. The old saying, "Great things are difficult," is very much to the point here. We have to find our way to the truth by applying ourselves to the stubborn realities of our present life. We must begin here and eventually return here, bringing some wisdom we may have learned through that hard, straight course of thinking which is philosophy.

It generally takes so much to live a decent and worthwhile

life that any man does well to be suspicious of easy solutions of something as large as the problem of human civilization, which is what we are dealing with in this study. First thoughts are likely to be only thoughtless opinions or prejudices. We may think that all we need today is to get the government out of our private and individual affairs so that we can be free once again. But that commits us to individualism. Have we thought what individualism really means, following it out into every detail so that we see the whole social order drawn up in such terms? Or suppose we simply condemn the selfishness of individuals as the source of all evil in our present world, as it was in all those times we know about through history. Well, if selfishness is such an absolute fact, how does it happen that we have *any* family life, fellowship with others, clubs, labor unions, societies, states, nations? There is more to it than these single-term solutions indicate.

148. The Spurious Conflict between the Individual and the State

In that easy kind of philosophy, the real problems are left out of sight while we imagine an exaggerated battle between two great opponents, the Individual and the State. They are represented as lasting enemies of each other; the gain of one is inevitably the loss of the other. Those of the party who idealize the social whole, the "socialists" look forward to a perfect regulation of the lives of men by the state for the sake of social justice. But the "individualists" seek to be free from the government of the state altogether.

Now there is, indeed, a genuine problem about the limits of the authority of government, but it is false and misleading to make "man" and "the state" into two great opposing parties. For the men and the women *are* the state; and conversely, the state is *all* the people. The problems that are really worth bothering about are those that fall *inside the whole organization* of men in the state and society. They are the problems of the relation of some parts to other parts, and individual men are standing on both sides of the fence. The whole state, too, is involved in every issue. That old sham battle of Individual versus Society is not worth discussing, and it is an unworthy distraction from the urgent practical issues, where a decision really makes a difference in the lives and happiness of people. What are these issues today? Here is where we must really begin our philosophy.

149. Some Problems of Life in Our Social Order

(a) *Inequality.* The questions that really bother us are those like *inequality*. We are living in a society which professes to assure all men in it of their equal rights; but we see them discriminated against, some having privileges and others suffering under disabilities. Things are not right in our social order, nor are they right in our own personal motives and ideas of the way to act. We are not living up to our principles. The question then is whether we understand these principles. Or it may be more serious still — are they true? And if they are true, what makes people act as if they were not? Do they secretly believe something else? Is it, perhaps, the notion that men are not really equal, that some are bound to be superior, and that those who are *ought* to have the benefits of their superiority of mind, character, and ability to succeed? Here is something one must get to the bottom of, because it has to do with the whole foundation of human life in society. There seems to be a struggle between two principles, one which works toward inequality, the other toward equality, and this struggle is what makes social life the troublesome thing it is.

(b) *Discrimination against Nation and Race.* But the most superficial view of this situation shows that some other problems are involved. We notice at once that it is not the individuals alone who are unequal. It is not the sheer merit of this or that person which entitles him to his wealth, position, or power in the community; nor is it something that the individual himself could do or not do that puts him at the disadvantage with others which we consider unfair or unequal. Men are treated, not as the men they *individually* are, but as members of some social group, for instance a nation or a race. All of one group are lumped together for the benefits or the disabilities of the discrimination. How does that come about? What can possibly justify it? What is going to come of it? This struggle of whole groups for their rights is another one of the present realities of our situation.

(c) *Capital and Labor.* An urgent problem exists within our great and complex economic order. Men are engaged in widespread business dealings with each other, in industry and commerce, and some groups of men are *managing* other men. This gives them a power over the others. The power is not confined, however, to the actual business of the factory or the commercial enterprise. It has ramifications outside. The economic system itself touches almost the whole of life, and it determines the chances a man has, not only for work, but also for most of his opportunities in life, and even for his bare survival. The power of control that resides in this system is vast, and some individuals have to be at the controls, directing and using this power. They naturally have their own interests and look out for them. It has long been said, and accepted as a supposed truth of economics, that men are ruled by such self-interest. At any rate, the facts of the situation are clear enough.

In the face of this economic power, men, determined to be free, have organized themselves in labor or trade unions to protect themselves. As citizens of a free democracy they have demanded their elementary rights. They have presented their grievances and sought to have them rectified. They have used their bargaining power through unions to gain advantages for themselves. They have appealed to the public for social justice. And they have actively fought for all these things, too, by such means as they have had at their disposal, chiefly the power to strike. The story of "capital and labor" is one of continuing conflict and antagonism between powerful groups *within* our society. The question now is what we are to do about this internal warfare.

(d) *Democratic Government.* Naturally we turn to government when we face problems on so vast a scale as the whole economic and social organization of our life. But government itself is a problem no less troublesome. The overwhelming task of having to fight a war against totalitarian domination has momentarily made us forget that something was wrong with government before the war. It was some kind of weakness or failure to meet the needs of people which brought on the Nazi and Fascist dictatorships that have caused the trouble. Similar defects existed in our own practice of government. Now they are being brought home to us again.

How can we conduct the vast business of our United States

through a government by elected representatives in Congress and a President, with a Supreme Court in the background? Can they all pull together as a team? Will they serve the whole people?

How can there be both democratic *and* efficient government? It is possible to get efficiency if a leader is accepted whose decision is always the law, but such leaders have to look first to the satisfaction of their supporters and afterwards to satisfying the people at large. This tends to make justice play second fiddle to party politics. On the other hand, even when representatives, senators, or the president *aim* to carry out the will of the people for the common welfare, they have difficulty hearing the voice of the people. Through the press, through lobbies, through all kinds of representations, the groups and interests within the state that stand to profit by some act of legislation make themselves heard and get their will done. The people then have a sense that their own government is not only unjust but also inefficient because these interested groups are themselves pulling at cross-purposes.

If it is one thing men must have in a government, it is unity of action and plain, honest purpose. So the political struggles of parties for power are not simply like contests of sport. They have a profound importance and are the concern of every citizen. Through them, individuals, corporations, and groups of all sorts are struggling to obtain government that will work for the good of all.

(e) *Free Institutions.* At a time when the powers of government are at their highest because of the necessity of mobilizing all the forces of the nation, the problem is also urgent of preserving free institutions, besides political democracy. This is one of the things in mind when certain people call for "free enterprise." It holds for labor, however, as well as for business: labor unions must be independent of government dictation. But it applies also to very much more than the industrial and commercial order. The press and all organs of communication must be free; and education must be free, together with the institutions, private, municipal, and state, that carry on the work of education; and religious teaching must be free, and the churches and groups that meet for common worship. Besides these universal institutions, there exist a host of small clubs, fraternal organizations, and assemblies of all sorts for good fellowship as well as common work.

There is a live question today about the independence and freedom of all these cherished institutions in our society. One cannot mark out boundaries for each of these bodies and say: Here is your province, just stay within it, and then you can do what you like inside it. All these institutions reach the public and touch the whole of our lives, especially industry and commerce, communications, education, and religion. Somehow they must all be governed in the interest of the whole community and yet not governed by the government. How is this to be done? How are free institutions to be preserved so that they do not have to surrender to a government when they come under regulation, as they must in any social order? The struggle taking place over this question is less evident to the casual observer, but it is no less real than those more obvious struggles for social justice and true equality before the law. These things are all part of one and the same picture.

(f) *The Many Loyalties of Men and Their Sense of Justice.* And finally, the whole situation is complicated by the fact that every citizen has so many loyalties. The people of the nation are not all nicely parcelled out in these different groups so that we can reckon with a lot of them as a group. They may at one and the same time be members of a political party, a lodge, a union, a business or financial corporation, a farm organization, a college, a church. They feel the claims of each one of these bodies or institutions. They are naturally concerned to have the rights of any controversy worked out fairly and harmoniously for all of them. The citizens are thus involved in *all* social disputes and *all* issues of government. All the decisive questions are of public concern. But in such great matters much feeling is naturally aroused. A judicial attitude is needed which will enable all men to see what justice is for the whole nation. For the right decisions of a government all depend ultimately upon the sense of justice and will of the people.

(g) *Nationalism and International Relations.* But we have talked about these urgent questions as if we were the only people on earth. All these questions lead beyond the state and beyond our

own nation. Economic questions have an international character, and organizations of industry and commerce, as well as of
labor, reach across the lines between the states of the world.
Churches do likewise in their spiritual ministry to man. The
protests of minorities against unfair and inhuman treatment are
made in every quarter. And the rights of man are believed to
be universal rights — the same in America, Europe, Asia, and
Africa. Whatever troubles any state has in respect to any of
these matters has reverberations everywhere else: the failure to
deal adequately with these economic, political, and social
problems in any one nation involves the others. So the various
states of the world are inevitably implicated in a whole set of
international problems. But we have been suffering from a
blind or willful nationalism in this regard. What is to be done
about it? How are the nations to deal with the realities of today
which are *international?* What must be the *relations* of states and
nations to each other so that they will form a peaceful community?

150. Life in the Family as an Ideal and a Problem

In the end, all these questions come down to one large one
which can be solved only within ourselves: What are *our ideas*
of the right way for men to live with each other — both individual men and whole nations — in every circumstance of their
existence?

Sometimes we speak of "the family of nations" as if we wanted
to see the idea of the family realized there, in the wide world,
as well as in our homes. It is also common usage to speak of men
at war as being comrades or brothers at arms, and we often say
that they ought to be more like brothers, too, in peacetime.
The image of the family relationship is thus something of an
ideal, contrasting with the defects of the rest of civilization
around us. In the midst of passions of hate, jealousies, ruthless
competition, and the conflicts of people with each other, the
home seems a great, free haven for man. It is the center of some
kindly measure of love in a world where love hardly counts at
all. Here inequality does not matter, though there is no literal
equality between parents and children, nor in the authority of
husband and wife. For affection and care are the important

things in family life, not rank or power. Those who grow up together have close ties founded on the deepest human interests. They appreciate and share in the same values of life. They are also united "for mutual support," as Aristotle put it, which means not only for economic but above all for the psychological and moral support which men and women find in each other, and young and old likewise. In such an order of life, justice is done with a wise discrimination which is more truly just than the decisions handed down in law because the whole heart is in it, and the good of all persons is really in concern. Hence the family has often been taken as an example of the ideal community, with a unity, peace, and common enjoyment of good which we sorely need in all the other social relations.

But this is not to say that family is itself no problem. Our society is full of unhappiness over difficulties with this closest of all human relationships. Some of the trouble does come, of course, from a sort of invasion of the home by that very outside world which is so full of ills. The problems men have concerning property, money, business, and social position in the wider world are what set members of a family against one another. Brothers quarrel over the division of property. They claim and fight for their rights by recourse to law. Sometimes, too, a man brings home discontent with his work, or his wife resents it because he is not "getting on" in the world, and such discontented people make bad companions for each other, which reflects throughout their family and social life. Worse still is the evil of economic unemployment, which keeps people at home with nothing to do *beyond* the home to make its value appreciated after the day's work. People cannot stay home under such conditions; and without any steady responsibility their very lives disintegrate and fall to a dead, spiritless level of uselessness where nobody feels worth while. Things like these in our civilization contribute greatly to spoil or ruin family life.

Yet this does not mean that we need only to get rid of civilization with its wrongs, and then all will be well with the family. After due allowance is made for the evils that come into the home from without, there are still deep-seated causes of trouble within to make life in the family a problem. There are, for one thing, the plain moral failings of men and women to live as they ought.

Besides, if a simple family existence were all men had of social life, it would become a scene of discontent, unrest, and conflict because they would not be satisfied with so incomplete a life. For mankind has, throughout history, formed itself into the larger communities and states.

Aristotle gave the account of the way men and women, beginning with their union in the marital relation and the family, have naturally gone forward to achieve the most truly human and the fullest life, which is only found in a civilized society.[1] Man is *meant* to live in the state: he is "a political animal." To reduce his life to any smaller compass and purpose would be to repress him and to spoil even his family life. The problem of the home is not to be solved, therefore, by isolating man from all his other problems of society. They all form one great *universal* question: how is man to dwell in community with his fellows, and by what ideas can he direct and govern his life so that it will go right and will be good?

151. The Vision of the Good Life in Society

The true community is not something already in existence somewhere but in *the vision* which men have of the existence that is most truly worth having. It is an ideal, that is, some view of what is right or of what ought to be. Whenever we criticize our social order and the various faults of our human relationships, we have some ideal in mind of the true order and the right way of life. Even when we compare the family favorably with the state or the international order, we do not regard the existing family itself as a perfect model which should be copied in every other social form. We are seeing in the family only some approximation to an idea of a human community which is still to be achieved there and everywhere else in our experience. This is the case with people who think and who have some ambition and enterprise. There are many, of course, who find themselves perfectly at ease and well off and consequently are inclined to be complacent with the *status quo* and to talk as if it were the perfect order of things. They oppose change. They deprecate thinking about the foundations of human life in society and about ideals that will stimulate men to work for a better future.

---

[1] Aristotle, "Politics," Book I, chap. 1.

Thus they have no use for philosophy because philosophy means digging at the roots with a view to better growth and a finer flowering of life in mankind. And that view of the good life is not merely a notion of some crank; it is a well-grounded vision, based on the reason and experience of mankind.

Such a vision, for example, is that enshrined in the tradition of our religion. When men are imbued with a faith in God and regard themselves as having a profoundly important relationship to that Divine Being who is conceived as a God of righteousness and love, they see at the same time a profound importance in the way they themselves live with their fellow men. That insight speaks strongly in their hearts as a commandment, as from God himself: they shall love their neighbor as themselves. And to see that steadily and see it whole is to have a vision of a community and fellowship the like of which the world has never known. Yet it is what a Christian's faith tells him must be, even in this present world. Such a vision feeds no one's complacency but lays an injunction upon a man to go and do the things necessary to fulfill it.

But men can find their visions of the true order of society in other ways, too, besides religion. The great statesmen of history who have had a personal responsibility for the welfare and even the desperate saving of their nations, have had insights that became lessons for men ever after. Take the example of Pericles, the leader of Athenian democracy, as described by Thucydides, a general under him in the long Peloponnesian War which lasted twenty-seven years and exhausted the whole Greek world, so that it afterward fell before a conqueror. Pericles gave an address at the civic funeral held for the men who had fallen in the first year of the war in 431 B.C. He recounted to those assembled for the ceremony all that Athens had meant to them so that their pride and love of country would be aroused. But with that exalting of the state went a more moving and elemental appeal: "it was by courage, sense of duty, and a keen feeling of honor in action that men were enabled to win all this," and did not those fine men who had there fallen deserve of them, the living, that they should carry on?

And then nearly twenty-three hundred years later, Lincoln, in this country, expressed the same human wisdom and inspiration: "the brave men, living and dead, who struggled here . . . it is for us the living rather to be dedicated here to the unfinished work that they have thus far so nobly advanced . . ." [1]

Here is the vision of a *fellowship*, patterned on the experience of men who engage in battle or some great struggle together. Cannot something of this be had by those who survive, and who are to carry on the life of the country? Is the obligation of the citizens to the nation not all the greater because their kin, their fellows, their own people have already given so much for it, and more is still to be done? The state is no abstract entity to the men who have made it live, and it should mean vastly more to those who live on in it. The state consists of home, family, friends, associates of all sorts, all the personal relationships and ways of life together. But the relations must be *personal*, if men are ever to feel a personal duty or obligation to act and to sacrifice for the state. Here is the democratic vision of the true kind of community. It has its applications to the home as well as to all the other forms of relationship which create the problems of our present social order.

It is the business of philosophy to discuss the fundamental and universal questions that lie behind the problems of our time. It aims to reduce the great variety of issues to some common problem in order to see their essence. It looks to the realities first and then studies them *in idea*. It forms some conception of the inspiring visions that men have had of their life in the state and society and draws the conclusions from these ideals for the state of affairs as it now is. One of the values of philosophy is that it makes the important ideas precise and accurate — ideas that are otherwise used without clear understanding of their meaning.

Thus men will argue interminably and get nowhere about the rights of capital or labor or the rights of minorities or the rights of the individual, without knowing exactly what a "right" of any kind is. Nor do they have any common understanding of what law or justice is. Even the meaning of "republic," which is the name for our form of state, is not clear and definite. Government itself — *why* it exists, *what* it is, and what it is *intended* to do — this also is vague and uncertain when people are talking

1 Cf. BR, No. 57, Lincoln, "Address at Gettysburg."

about what government today cannot or should not do. And what is meant by personal liberty and freedom? To reach any solution for the problems of the day, we have first to set our ideas in order and examine life in society with a clear understanding of what we mean to have in life. This is the task of philosophy.

C. THE REPUBLIC: THE PATTERN OF CIVILIZED SOCIETY

152. The Greatness of Plato's Republic and of Socrates

Plato was dealing with the demoralization in Greece after the war — that war whose fatal consequences Thucydides had already forecast in his history. He had witnessed a tragic event in his youth which sent him into philosophy. The man of greatest wisdom and personal integrity whom he had known, Socrates, had been put to death by the state, indeed by the Athenian democracy, in the year 399 B.C. The principles of Socrates were absolutely right; but the people were not ready for them, not educated to see them and to honor and follow a man who was their true leader. It was to be Plato's work to vindicate Socrates, and at the same time to educate the world. The *Republic* of Plato remains one of the great arguments of history. It is basic to all subsequent thought about the way men ought to live with each other in society.

The idea is a simple truth: all men, no matter how high their purposes or ambitions, must learn to think of their own personal lives *as forming life in a community*. But it is hard to practice. Plato himself relies on the dramatic story of the life of Socrates, as well as on reasoning, to bring this truth home. The story, especially of the trial and death of Socrates, is an immortal one.[1]

One scene in the *Crito* shows Socrates waiting in prison for the day when the poison would be administered. Crito, a respectable man of means, visits his friend and urges him to accept his aid in breaking jail. It seemed right to do so because Socrates had been wrongfully condemned by his enemies. The

[1] Cf. BR, No. 5, Plato, "Socrates' Defense of Himself."

escape should be made for his own sake and for that of others too — for Crito's sake and for his own wife and children and for all his friends. It was Socrates' obvious duty to all concerned.

Now whenever men were so sure about what was right, the old "gadfly," as he was called, went after them with questions. Even here, where Crito was trying to induce him to save his own life, Socrates inquired into the right of the matter. The only way for him to do his duty by his wife, children, friends, fellow citizens, and even pay his respects to his enemies, was to act with a view to the *good of the whole state* which contained all these relationships. And the rule of right conduct for every man in the state could be only one thing: to honor the fundamental law of the state, even unto death. Socrates felt a religious obligation to do so. He stayed, therefore, to drink the poison and die — the good citizen and good philosopher.[1]

Such a death for principle cannot easily convince other men who have not themselves been eyewitness to it. Plato devoted himself, therefore, to the task of showing what Socrates' idea meant in every aspect of man's existence in society. The *Republic* is, thus, the picture of the whole of life, organized on the principles of Socrates.

153. The Republic Includes a Philosophy of the Best Life

The *Republic* contains, however, vastly more than a political philosophy, for it is a comprehensive philosophy of both man and the whole of "what is." But it is *focussed* on a question of ethics: what is "the whole course of conduct which every one of us must follow to get the best out of life?" Even this is still a very large question: How to live? It is more than the quite specific one we are studying: How is man to live in society? Actually, that is precisely what Plato has to show — that man cannot get the best out of life unless he lives in such a way that *a social community is possible.* Not only will there be no "best," but there will not even be anything really good, perhaps not even a safe existence for man in the world. Everything really has its value for man in and through his life in community; this is the proposition to be demonstrated in the *Republic.*

The ordinary notions of life are very different. Some people

---

[1] Cf. BR, No. 47, Plato, "May a Good Citizen Break the Law?"

think of it as the enjoyment of the good things they desire. Others are ambitious, and life to them is good when they have scope for their powers to do great things, to embark on enterprises, or to fashion a great and powerful state. A few, and a very precious few, see in life the opportunity to *realize* a knowledge of themselves and existence, as Socrates did. What men admire in themselves varies with these notions of the good of life. Some value strength or dynamic power because it "does things." Only the philosophers, perhaps, value a quite different kind of power, the quiet, wise power of reason. So any argument aiming to show that man's life cannot be a good life unless he considers always the *whole* community and takes only what is his due share of "a common wealth" — such a philosophical argument must encounter some incredulity and opposition from the very beginning.

154. What Is the Function of Property in Society?

Before the true argument for the commonwealth comes, there are skirmishes with the opposition which set the stage for it. They show the further need of a deeper analysis into which Socrates goes later. They bring out the different values that men have in mind when they discuss such a matter as the good of life and the right way to conduct oneself through it. And, incidentally, these first discussions enable Plato to drop hints of a truth which is to be brought into full and clear light later.

It seems to people who are well-to-do in the world that to pay their just debts is all they owe to others. They need not concern themselves about them any further. People who have lawful claims on them are rendered what is due them. But it is interesting to observe, nevertheless, that people who have wealth do actually have something more in mind than money payments. It is characteristic of the best of them to look out for some persons who cannot make any claims on them but whose claims they nevertheless recognize. Thus a good man of wealth wants to have his children and his children's children provided for so that they may live well too, and he stints himself, perhaps, in order to leave them something. This intention has been embodied in the laws of the inheritance of property. There is something estimable, too, in the attitude of such a man who regards his possessions as a patrimony, something to be preserved and improved and handed down intact to subsequent generations as a means for them to live. The man there acts as if property were a sacred trust, and he governs his own appetites and ambitions out of regard for this family commonwealth. Here is a significant contrast between the differing policies of life. One man of property goes in for his own enjoyment; another devotes himself to the property for the sake of others — the generations unborn and unseen, whose claim he recognizes though they are not present to press it.

155. Socrates' Arguments against Retribution towards Enemies

That is all very well so long as it is in the family, but it will not do in life beyond the home and relatives. Man will not fare well at all if he concerns himself for the good of others outside the friendly circle. The rule of the world is: do what is good and helpful to your friends, but do all the harm you can to your enemies. This is, of course, the practice of the world — good for good, evil for evil. The argument of Socrates against this rule is briefly as follows: If people adopt this principle, those who begin as friends will probably stay our friends, and so far, so good.

But precisely because we regard such friendship as being so valuable to us, it behooves us to look carefully to the consequences of the other, latter half of the maxim, "do harm to your enemies." This means that those who are now our enemies will never change to become friends, because the bad treatment they receive only makes them more hostile to us, and they will naturally retaliate and provoke in turn more retaliation on our part, plunging us in a bitter and relentless feud.

Meantime, there are many people in society whose attitude toward ourselves we are ignorant of, for all people cannot be readily divided up into two classes, friends and enemies, as if they were two well-defined political parties. Now we may easily in our ignorance treat some of these people as if they were ill-disposed toward ourselves, when they really are not, and may be even friendly. But our ill treatment of them will convert them from possible friends into quite certain enemies who have a genuine grievance against us. Their own friends, seeing them abused by us, will also resent the injury committed and will stick by them and be against us.

What, then, is the outcome of this rule of retribution? It may preserve the original circle of our friends, but it will most certainly increase greatly the circle of those who are at enmity with us. From such mounting hostilities great hatred grows. Eventually we should have the whole community divided into two armed camps.[1] This cannot be called good or just. For justice ought not to lead to war between men but rather to improved social relations.[2]

A suggestion of a totally different policy lurks in that argument against the policy of retribution. It is that "it is never right to harm anyone." This means that the rule of life is always to act for the good of man, for others as well as for oneself, for friends, too, as well as enemies. This is only suggested. But it draws out the ire of a rough, realistic fellow, Thrasymachus,[3] whose name has come down in history because of Plato's picture of him and the point of view he represents.

156. Power Politics Examined

It was in fact the point of view of those very Athenian diplomats who, according to the account of Thucydides, had already ruined Athens in the recent War: "The law of nature is always that the strong shall command and the weak obey." After their civilization had already suffered a grievous blow from which it was not going to recover, the intelligentsia of Athens, ignorant of realities, were still intrigued with the so-called "realistic" policy and with discussing it seriously.

This is the policy of holding power for one's own interest alone. It means that one party secures the power of political government and by means of it keeps all others down so that they are forced to obey commands. The government is not intended to be for the people's benefit at all. It is all for the continued power and

---

[1] The consequences are even more extreme according to Hobbes (*Leviathan*), who, writing in 1651 during the Civil War in England, did not even leave *friends* standing together but drew the conclusion that the outcome of man's natural principle of life is the war of *every man against every other man*. Hobbes did not follow Socrates, however, in his solution. (Cf. BR, No. 51, Hobbes, "The Nature and Origin of the State," section b.)

[2] Cf. BR, No. 48 A, Plato, "On Justice," sections a, b, c.

[3] Pronounced: *Thra-sim'-a-kus*.

enjoyment of the rulers. They rule exclusively for their own good. They are not to be held to account for what happens to the others.

Of course there is a notion of a higher justice by which men criticize government and call it good or bad, according to the way it measures up to the idea. But men who really have power do not pay any regard to such a notion. They consider that it is one of those conventional ideas of the little fellows to keep themselves from being pushed about by the stronger ones. The weak set up these rules to keep people from doing violence to them, and they solemnly call them the laws of justice and expect everybody to abide by them. Now the strong are perfectly willing to have *all the rest* abide by these laws, but they themselves do not intend to be bound by them and they go their own free way, sometimes boldly exerting their power without hearing protests, at other times making an appearance of doing what is just but, behind the scenes, having their own way. "Just or right means nothing but what is to *the interest of the stronger party*, the party established in power." It is all to their interest that the *others* be just. What else is to their interest is for them to decide themselves, for it is nobody else's business. They have the power — the power to rule and decide — and that is the important thing.[1]

But success is the only proof of this kind of policy. It is worth noting, therefore, how men do achieve success anywhere else in the world. After all, government is an art, and not every ambitious fellow can carry it off along these lines of power politics. The other skills of man may throw light, therefore, on what is required of a man who is to govern successfully. Plato used examples from contemporary Greek achievement. The Athenians were seafaring and engaged in commerce. They also had developed the profession of medicine. Here were examples ready at hand. A successful medical man treats his patients and concerns himself about the health and well-being of his patient. A pilot looks to the proper operations of his ship and its crew and wants to bring them all back safely. Men of such responsibilities have their attention on the welfare of what they are

---

[1] Cf. BR, No. 48 A, Plato, "On Justice." Also BR, No. 31, Nietzsche, "The Origin of Morals," sections f–i.

tending, on the patient and the ship and crew. That is the first condition of their effective work and success. Even a shepherd who is only raising sheep to be sold for food and clothing has to care for his flock. There is no profit in it otherwise. The same thing is true of the commercial magnate whom Thrasymachus admired so much: he has to tend to business and maintain a good reputation for honesty. Thus the really successful men give a great deal of thought to the welfare of others and to the firms or establishments with which they are connected. Why not the same in government? Why is not it too conducted with a view to the good of all who are governed, as well as that of the rulers?

There is one bit of truth in that argument of Thrasymachus. In any organized state the things that men may rightly or lawfully do, as well as those that they are punished for doing because they are wrong, are determined by the laws. This is the legal kind of justice. It exists in every society. But this does not go to the heart of the matter. The question is: what are the law and government *for? What* good and *whose* good?

But men like Thrasymachus do not want to inquire any further.[1] They are satisfied with the notion that those who rule are actually stronger at the moment than those who obey their commands. That is a plain fact. But they do not look beyond that fact to see what must happen in consequence of their interpretation of it. They suppose that they can continue to rule by force or power. But they are really sunk in a fanatic admiration of a certain type of man. They admire self-assertive strength above everything. The great thing in man seems to them the dynamic power that can produce magnificent effects in the world. A man with that stuff of greatness should not be hampered by petty rules of justice. The superman makes himself superior to all laws: he *gives* the laws to everybody else. And this is the ideal — the free, strong, lawless man, and what he does is the life worth living!

It is a fantastic world of grandiose imagination. This is betrayed by the need to introduce most fanciful possibilities, like

[1] The case of Thrasymachus is dismissed at this point. Some philosophers have not been satisfied with Plato's treatment of him and have made out a better case. See Hobbes' *Leviathan* and the various works of Nietzsche, such as *Man and Superman* or *The Genealogy of Morals.*

that mysterious ring of Gyges,[1] which makes its wearer invisible so that he can do what he will to other men unseen and thus get away with anything, as he would not be able to do in real life. Such are the extraordinary conditions that have to be imagined.

But what is the free, strong man of Thrasymachus going to *do* with all his dynamic ambition? He will set forth on big business enterprises and gain political domination. This means that the strong man can find scope for himself only by marshalling the power of many others. He uses them to work and fight for him. This presupposes that a state is already there, all in good order. It is assumed that things are being done decently and regularly; people are going about their business as honest citizens and obeying the laws of justice. All this is assumed. No question is asked concerning how this society comes to be there, all ready for such exploitation.

And here is a further question for the master-hand of power politics: since he cannot govern all alone but must have a few about him to carry out his commands, would it not be required of those officers, even if they were all a band of gangsters (this is Socrates' ironical comment on that sort of government), that they shall observe a rule of cooperation among themselves and not follow the principle of their chief who is always doing the other fellow out of something? They must be, one and all, perfectly loyal to him, although he may not be loyal to anyone! What chance is there of lasting success with that kind of government? It is an insane scheme, without any appreciation of realities.

157. The Necessities of a Civilized Life: the Economy

Men exist in society because no man is ever sufficient to himself. They have many different needs which others besides themselves are able to supply by a division of labor and exchanging goods and services. They learn to produce things in quantity and develop the skill to improve the quality. This economy is simple enough as long as the wants remain equally simple. It ministers to a natural, healthy, and regular life. "Alas, too regular," is the comment of civilized man. This monotonous

---

[1] Cf. BR, No. 48 B, Plato, "The Story of Gyges' Ring."

round of existence is like the routine of the animals — one generation after another living the same old way. It seems like a "community of pigs." A civilized order is one where men *aim* to be *better* off. It is natural to crave luxuries and not be content with the simple necessities.

The logic of this restless dynamic of civilization is a whole stock of things that become urgently necessary to make possible the enjoyment of luxury. Such a civilized life costs more than is at first realized.[1]

There is excess and unwholesome living, and so the practice of medicine is immediately necessary. Moreover, some men enjoy more than their share, others become discontented, and the love of gain in all of them involves them in difficulties with each other that call for skillful adjustment; so lawyers and courts of law are necessary. The resulting expansion, too, of industry, commerce, and the population, through the higher standard of living, leads to encroachment upon other peoples and consequently the necessity of a defense against war. Then the art of war must be cultivated and some men specially trained for it. But this has grave dangers. The soldiers ought always to act as the devoted guardians of the community, and their experience must not give them any habits of life which make them a menace to any of their own people. They will have to distinguish between their conduct toward external enemies and that to their fellow citizens. Hence, more important still than their very proficiency at war is their learning the principles of civilized life and loyalty to their community. For this, an education is necessary which is much more than military training. It has to give them an appreciation of the whole state of which they are a part so that they will understand the specific reason for their military function. Only when they truly understand this will they do all things as they ought and keep their own duties in mind, namely, the preservation of *their community*.

158. The Great Importance of Education, and Its Functions

But an inevitable logic leads further. If the soldiers are doing their part, what about the other people? What is their share? They seem to be only enjoying life and luxury, with their desires

[1] Cf. BR, No. 48 C, Plato, "The Origin of the State."

in full rein; and they may be enriching themselves with the various goods of this world. Now the soldiers are not going to do anything for these people unless they see them, too, devoting themselves to some essential service for the community. It follows that all men in the state must have that same education for citizenship. It should be a liberal education, a balanced education of spirit and body which will enable them to have good health and sound judgment for their part in society.

This universal education is the best means, too, of improving the general economy. For it serves two purposes. The first is that of training the men who are naturally fighters but who need to have their minds enlarged so as to grasp the point of their discipline. The second function is to select the men who are best qualified for that or any other service. The community should find out, through the system of education, who are the proper persons for each type of work: some to till the soil, others to work with their hands, others for the military profession, and a few for the most important duties of all, the supreme direction of this whole social order.

Moreover, this education can do something very salutary for each individual. Education is itself nothing less than the whole of a man's own personal development. If it is rightly directed, everyone can attain to higher levels of proficiency and experience. But it is very important that this be not left to mere chance or accident. Everything that touches the mind and character educates man. The acts of parents at home, the acts of the other citizens in their daily life, the imaginative and colorful portrayals of men and gods in mythology, art, drama, the rhythms and temperament of music and dancing — all these expressions of the human spirit call out some analogous disposition and behavior in those who participate in them. All these doings of man must measure up to an ethical standard, since they actually make men in their image, and that should always be an image of the good man and citizen.

Only the very best men are able to direct all these agencies of education in the community, "men full of zeal to do whatever they believe is for the good of the commonwealth and never willing to act against its interest." How these "guardians" of the state are to be found is a great problem not easily solved.

For the purposes of the present argument they are supposed to be there, doing their work properly.

Now we see all the youth of the land going through a common education by which they are to be assigned to their different places and functions in the social system. Here is a point of difficulty — in getting them to accept these respective assignments. Perhaps it can only be done by the poetic invention of a fine allegory and to give them the right idea:

"All of you in this land are brothers; but the god who fashioned you mixed gold in the composition of those among you who are fit to rule . . . , he put silver in the auxiliaries [soldiers], and iron and brass in the farmers and craftsmen." [1] This looks at first like indoctrinating youth with the ideas of a caste system, but the point follows: "Now, *since you are all of one stock*, although your children will generally be like their parents, sometimes a golden parent may have a silver child or a silver parent a golden one, and so on with all the other combinations." Each child is to be placed in the class of work for which he proves himself competent during his education. If children of craftsmen or farmers have the qualification, they are to be entrusted to the highest offices. The scion of golden parents is likewise to be put where he belongs, regardless of the position or achievement of his family. Each man's place in life is thus according to merit, and besides, the good of the community requires that every individual shall measure up to the job. If this were believed, it "might have a good effect in making them care more for the commonwealth and for one another."

159. The Idea of the Commonwealth

On these two loyalties the existence of the state ultimately rests: the loyalty to the whole community and the mutual fellowship of men with each other. Anyone who has charge of the state must guard jealously both these bases of life in community. They will beware of letting the state become so large or great that these personal relations are no longer possible. They will watch carefully over the tendencies in art, music, literature, lest feelings and ideas be injected which make men feel alien to each other and spoil the unison of their way of life together.

[1] Cf. BR, No. 48 D, Plato, "Allegory of the Metals."

What goes on in the world of commerce has to be watched, too, lest it establish unethical ways of life and destroy the morality of the people. The community should stand fast by its own religion, too, and not go chasing after all sorts of strange gods and cults. For change in any one of these particulars affects the unity of the whole and the mutual sentiments of men toward each other and the state.

Here, then, is the central idea of the civilized community. Every man has something of his own to do in the whole economy, and everyone receives some benefit from his part in it. The right men are in their right places. The best talents of each are called into use to create a community wealth in which each has a share. No better system can exist, both for satisfying the desires and ambitions of the individuals and for making their society strong, enduring, and prosperous. It is a true commonwealth. Its most real treasures are, of course, its citizens. They, on their side, care for and cherish their community. They take only what is their due out of the common wealth. Everything they do is in this spirit of consideration for the whole community and for every other part of it. In their work, their pleasures, their personal relations with each other, everything has its value, in their eyes, in *relation to that whole* of which they are all copartners. In this respect, no matter what be their different ages, occupations, interests, ambitions, affections, they are one and all alike. This principle of life, common to every man, woman and child, is the foundation of their community. And this ideal principle, regarding which they are all in accord, is "justice."

It follows that women have their part to play as well as men. It is usually assumed, of course, that their function is childbearing and the care of the home. But women may prove to be qualified for any of the civil functions. They will all be going through the same course of education as the men. Their capacities and achievements will be tested the same way. If they possess the proper qualifications for military service or government, why should they not have the opportunity to do their equal share? Besides, their participation is very important for the moral unity of society.[1]

[1] Cf. BR, No. 48 H, Plato, "The Equality of Women."

160. Just Government and the Renunciation of Private Property and Family

Great responsibility falls upon those who direct the education and the activities of the people of the state. The hardest thing to contend with is family and class feeling. When a child has to be put to physical work because he cannot measure up to the requirements of a job that is more highly esteemed, there is objection or resistance from his family, who want him better placed. But the merit system must be preserved absolutely inviolate. Family or other influence must never count. This, according to Plato, must be guarded against by having those who are invested with the powers of government *divested* of all private property or estates and wives of their own and children. They ought to marry, of course, and have children, for their offspring are likely to be better stuff than others; but no private establishments of their own.

The guardians who govern the state must all live together according to the basic principle that "friends have all things in common." Their greatest common interest is the good of the whole state, and to that everything must be subordinated, even their own affections. They are not to yield to any private feelings or grant favors. They are not to be distracted by any private interest in their own property. They must guarantee themselves against all such temptation by renouncing absolutely private property and family.

In return for this surrender of these usual engrossing life interests, they gain a richer and greater love of their whole community and a most just care for each and every one of their fellow citizens. In a sense, more than justice is exacted of these guardians. And unless they are able to rise to that higher life, beyond even justice, they cannot rule justly, and the state will not be a truly civilized order.[1]

161. The Value of Philosophic Wisdom

The only persons capable of such a life are men like Socrates, philosophers. Plato devoted a large part of his book to showing this. It is a tribute to philosophy as the best way of life and the absolutely necessary way to save the state. The statesmen

[1] Cf. BR, No. 48 E and I, Plato, "The Republic."

must combine philosophy with their rule or they will misgovern through ignorance of the true goal of all human life. For the true philosopher is one who has knowledge of the ultimate Good, the supreme power that moves and organizes all things aright in the universe. Some grasp of that absolute reality is necessary to a mastery of the art of government.

These philosopher-statesmen do not come up through politics as those who rule usually do. They must be sought out among those finer spirits of men and women who go through the common course of education in the state. They have to be taken through a higher education, beyond the general education for citizenship. Here they become transformed by their love of wisdom. They do not have their eyes on the existing order and its places to which they might be trained. They are out of the competition for these things. They see beyond these appearances to the higher world of Ideas which can only be perceived by the intellectual reason.

The philosophers conceive the vision of the pattern of life at its best. But they must bring that insight down to earth among other men and help them in their daily decisions to come as near as possible to realizing the ideal. And note, it is not *one man*, not even so wonderful a man as Socrates, who is to achieve this bringing of spiritual wisdom to practical application, but a whole company of philosophers. They must search and inquire constantly and discuss their thoughts with each other and in their fellowship they must set the example of perfect cooperation for the larger community which they are faithfully leading towards the good life.[1]

162. The Pattern of the Commonwealth in Summary

The *commonwealth* is the pattern of any true civilization. The first fundamental of civilized living is the principle, working in the minds and hearts of all men, that everything of theirs is "their own" and their "good" in relation to the whole community, and that they are all copartners with one another and have similar duties and shares in the commonwealth.

Justice is a poor word inadequately expressing that whole complex of ideas about man and the state. Justice is at once a

---

[1] Cf. BR, No. 48 F, G, and J, Plato, "The Republic."

basic and an all-comprehending principle. It is the universal ground for every other essential of life. With that spirit in men there is a unity of fellowship throughout the land.

The *economic order* is a just one. The men in their various occupations and professions will do their respective jobs honestly and without transgressing upon each other's duties and enjoyments — the doctor, the lawyer, the merchant, and particularly the chiefs of state whose self-interests are subordinated to the greater regard they have for the state because of the greatness of their responsibility.

The *government* by such men in office is not a government by orders but a government of *laws* which only express the amount of justice already embodied in the body politic.

The true way to get this virtue of justice is by *education*, a universal and a liberal education of body, mind, and spirit. This is a more important essential than the law. It is a function to be entrusted only to the guardians who have a living wisdom.

These guardians themselves must necessarily exemplify the spirit of justice to a superlative degree in all their work and life. They must take heroic steps by renouncing private property and family.

They can be equal to such renunciation only if they have grown to the highest stature of man through *philosophy*, which reveals to them a goal of existence far beyond the things of this world. Philosophy trains men to the supreme rule of reason.

The philosophic statesmen form a specially loyal and devoted body of men through their common love and practice of the ultimate *wisdom*.[1]

And unless all these things are so, there is no true justice anywhere in the relations of men with one another in the civilized society. The extent to which this republican pattern of man and the state is even approximated marks the stage of goodness attained in that society.

On Plato's own view, the actual Greek world was farthest away from perfection. The state of affairs was such that anybody could gain rule, and the tyrannical misrule of unreason dominated. The Athenian democracy had put Socrates to death.

[1] See T. S. Eliot, *The Idea of a Christian Society* (New York: Harcourt, Brace and Company, 1940) for a modern expression of this thought.

Their politicians had wrecked the state. The whole of Hellas was at the point of collapse. When Plato's greatest pupil, Aristotle, was going on with philosophy, the Greek cities and states were subject to the foreign rule of the Macedonian conquerors, and Aristotle himself was actually tutor to Alexander the Great. In truth, Socrates had not come soon enough, nor had the people been prepared to understand him — this was Plato's judgment on his age. It explains why he made education the most important thing in the life of the community. His own work, however, enabled the ideas of Socrates to survive, which they have done fundamentally because their meaning is universal.

163. Some Corrections and Additions to the Basic Pattern: (a) The Value of the Family and of Property

The perfect form of community, Socrates said, is "a pattern in the heavens." Statesmen everywhere should come as near to realizing it on earth as they possibly could. But how much *is* practicable? And is it really the right form after all, if it should happen not to fit men as they now are and their ways of life already established? These are questions which Plato's pupil, Aristotle, considered in his masterpiece on *Politics*.

The family and property and all the other things that men have actually been living by must have some good reason for their existence. Each one has a purpose. It exists because it meets some natural need of man. We ought to pay close attention to these elemental human needs and purposes which really organize men in a community life. The philosopher must keep his eye on them as well as on the sublime perfection and unity of the commonwealth.

The family is so necessary and good that the Platonic plan to do without personal family life and private property, even for the governing group of the state, was all wrong. It would never work. It is not possible so to expand the feelings of parental affection that these rulers will feel it for all the children of the state, as if they were "their own." The expression "their own" loses all meaning when there is no one in particular who *is* their own child. The loyalty to country can only rest upon the love of man for his wife and family, and it cannot be reached without them.

Property has its essential value in connection with family life. It is the natural way of providing means of subsistence. To acquire goods, either for immediate use or as a store to live on in the uncertain future, is quite "according to nature." Maybe some men will devote too much care to acquiring money, as Plato feared. Men are not content to amass the real goods that can actually be enjoyed by themselves or their families but pile up mere money as if it were something good in itself. Yet this is only the vice of some men. It is not a fault of property itself. Private property and the family are thoroughly justified by philosophy.

The right sort of state is one which includes property and the family and, indeed, any other forms of fellowship besides, through which men live and enjoy a life of happiness.[1] The political order is intended only to provide for the safety and welfare of men and these various social relations. It is a mistake to aim at so much unity in the commonwealth that some of these must be sacrificed. And it is forgetting how rich a state is, with all the different kinds of people and talents collected into a community. "It takes all sorts to make a city" (meaning the city-state of Greece).[2]

164. (b) The Variety of Good States and Their Governments

Moreover, there are all sorts of states and each has its distinctive value. It is true that there is one absolute standard to which they must all measure up if they are to be considered well-governed states. Their government must always "have the common good in view." But other additional aims are permissible, if that essential one is supreme, and here some variety is perfectly in order.

When the first families of the heroic times at the founding of the state ruled their people, the thing chiefly prized was their character of "nobility," which is the merit aimed at in aristocracy. At another time or place men rise up who make the state prosperous by their genius in commerce, and who come to value wealth; and the whole society is then organized around

---

[1] Aristotle includes slavery, which we reject for other reasons than he contemplated. See *Politics*, Book I, chaps. iii-v.
[2] Cf. BR, No. 49, Aristotle, "Politics," sections a and b.

that as an end. But the commonwealth must never be forgotten in this separate desire for private and individual wealth.

Again, the great body of the common people may aspire to better things for themselves and set their hearts on enjoying equality, which is the end of a democracy. But they too must not forget the good of the whole state and the need of having men of initiative, capacity, and superior excellence for its prosperity and good government. These leaders do not have to be Platonic philosophers. The men of proved competence in those particular things which are of greatest consequence for the state are the ones who rise to the top. In an aristocratic state, the nobles dominate. The management of a private estate is an experience of responsibility that trains men for government. And men who achieve greatly in commerce naturally gain high office and authority in their state. Those, too, who know how to win rights for the mass of the people in a democracy are established in power there.[1]

165. (c) Practical Justice and Politics

As a matter of fact, the chief practical business of any government is to adjust the claims of the various elements of the population with one another. Every developed civilization has had a long history and passed through many different stages of society. It contains the descendants of the patricians or first families, mixed with the middle class engaged in commerce, and with the great mass of the people who are interested in the goods and dignities they see others enjoying. Each element insists on its own claims, according to Aristotle.

The true statesman gives all the claims a wise consideration — the claims of equality, those of wealth, and those of nobility or family — and he works out a *modus vivendi*, which is a way of life that satisfies all the claims so far as they can be satisfied *and still keep the community intact*. This is no remote kind of justice in the heavens; it is what men on earth can have. And this is practical politics.[2]

166. The Pattern in History

The basic pattern of a civilized community, modified by these and many other corrections and additions, has travelled a long

---

[1] Cf. BR, No. 49, Aristotle, "Politics," sections d–f.   [2] *Ibid.*, section c.

way in the history of our civilization. The term "republic" or "commonwealth" has been used often in political crises to mark out some new and fresh effort of men to establish what they take to be the right order of life in their own time.[1] A case which will be particularly valuable for us later is that in the eighteenth century, just before the founding of the American Republic and the French Revolution, which destroyed absolute monarchy and spread the ideal of the republic throughout the western world. Meantime we have to see the background of this modern example.

D. THE BACKGROUND OF MODERN CIVILIZATION: EVENTS, IDEAS, AND INSTITUTIONS

167. The Christian Religion and Its Social Meaning

We cannot escape history. Our lives are organized through institutions, and these have been fashioned by men according to their ideas of the right way to live under the circumstances of their times. These things have left a deep mark on us and on what we value in our own lives. We must understand this heritage. It is necessary, therefore, to acquaint ourselves with some basic facts and ideas which have made our modern civilization what it is.

Christianity came out of the long experience of the Jewish community with a religion of one God. It was centered, however, on both God the Father and on the person of Jesus of Nazareth. Around this Christ, the redeemer of man who died on the cross, a community of faith formed, not by any political art but by the powerful gravitation of spiritual need, fellowship, and common conviction that a Christlike love is supreme in the world. Christian communities came into being in Rome and elsewhere in Europe, Asia Minor, and Africa, and eventually Europe became Christendom.

The man Paul, once the furious persecutor of the Christians, was a great spokesman and missionary for the new church.

[1] See James Madison, *The Federalist*, No. 10, November 23, 1787.

Writing to the Romans who needed his counsel, Paul gave them his idea of the form of the Christian community:

"For just as there are many parts united in our human bodies, and the parts do not all have the same functions, so, many as we are, we form one body through union with Christ, and we are individually parts of one another." (Rom. 12 : 4–5.)

To the Greeks, also, in Corinth:

"For just as the body is one and yet has many parts, and all the parts of the body, many as they are, form one body, so it is with Christ. For we have all — Jews or Greeks, slaves or free men — been baptised in one spirit to form one body. . . . God has so adjusted the body and given such especial distinction to its inferior parts that there is no clash in the body, but its parts all alike care for one another. If one part suffers, all the parts share its sufferings. If a part has honor done it, all the parts enjoy it too. Now you are Christ's body, and individually parts of it." (I Cor. 12 : 12–13; 24–27.)

"All the parts alike care for one another" is reminiscent of Plato's *Republic*, but there is a significant difference, for this fellowship has, besides, a mystical connection with the divine Christ. That relationship makes all the difference. The meaning of Christ to his followers affects their whole order of life with one another. They are bound to love one another. This duty is something more than justice. It is not the outcome of a philosophical argument: it is not reasoned that *if* men are to realize their own good, they *ought* rationally to love their neighbor. It is a direct command in their hearts and spirits. It is so because the love and sacrifice of their Christ is so actual a thing for them: they *must* do likewise.

The Christian religion transforms the conception of man. For when man sees himself in relation to the Divine Being who has infinite and perfect love, he sees himself quite differently in every other relation. The human person, in himself and in all others, is sacred. Indeed, the whole fellowship of Christians is sanctified. Every duty of life is a sacred one. Men everywhere have a spiritual worth.

In Paul's analogy of the community with the body, he had expressly emphasized that the apparently inferior members of the bodily economy have an equal significance, in the eyes of God, with the more obviously honored and useful members. The very least is as worthy as any other, and everyone shares in the sanctity or honor of the whole. So it is not, as it was with the Greeks, that the values of men are to be judged by their places in the social order. This Christian teaching brushes aside the worldly standards of class and rank: the spiritual worth is equal for all. Here is a source of our conviction about the equal freedom and rights of men.

When the ancient city of Rome, long the seat of a great empire, fell before the barbarian tribes in 410 A.D., a North African convert to Christianity, Augustine, wrote a great book, *The City of God*. That catastrophe to a worldly civilization was but God's judgment upon it. The secular state was a tragic failure, insufficient even for elemental security. In what could men put their trust now save the true God and his spiritual order of life? Augustine thus set the spiritual and the worldly in sharp opposition to each other, and "the world," that is, the state and all its works, was condemned. Here is one of the sources of the modern spirit of reformation: we too judge our laws and institutions by reference to the higher law of God, which is the law of ethical right and reverence for human personality.

Two ways of life in society were open. Augustine had repeated an idea of Paul, telling of "the Christians, whose riches are . . . all in common . . . to be distributed to every man according to his need: 'neither any of them said that anything he possessed was his own, but all was in common.'"[1] Some early Christians took this way of life, accounting no property as their own, but God's, and renouncing it gladly. They dedicated themselves to the service of God. They entered holy orders and formed small communities in which they provided frugally for their physical needs. Their worship in common supplied a social need as well. They taught or they ministered to others with services of charity. This was the way of medieval monasticism and of many groups of Christians in the modern world, who made a covenant to live together according to the pure doctrine of their faith. This idea of covenant and its sanctity has meant much to later times.

Another way of life was that exemplified in the Church itself, which could not live apart but had to take part in the civilizing

[1] *The City of God*, Bk. V, Chap. ix; Acts V.

of Europe. When a people have a cherished faith, they must go out boldly to establish its principles in society at large, where the order of life in which they believe will be made safe and sound. Thus the barbarians, whose waves of invasion had engulfed the old empire, had to be Christianized.' So the Church worked with the political system which still survived. But the Empire itself had to be blessed, lest it repeat the corrupt regime which Augustine had exposed in his day, and so it was called the Holy Roman Empire. Thus the business of Christians was to engage in the work of the world but always regard it as a "vocation," something one is called upon to do because of the talents entrusted to him by God and for which he has to give an accounting, like the good steward in the parable. Here is a source of man's sense of personal responsibility, both for his own work and for the actions of the state of which he is a member.

168. The Sovereign State

The states of modern Europe came into existence because princes with military power established them. This is not to say that political society has been founded on power. There is much else that went into the making of the modern state. Fresh enterprise in industry and commerce had been stirring in the fifteenth and sixteenth centuries, and a middle class was developing. Greater freedom of action was required for commerce than the feudal order permitted. The princes of those busy territories of the empire were enterprising, too, and supported the rising class who brought them prosperity with which to maintain their armies. A general quickening of life also took place in these countries, expressing itself in the arts, in literature, and eventually in modern science.

But most important for the social order was the Reformation which broke up the unity of Christendom. For the reformers were backed by the princes, who had armed forces and resources to maintain them, and consequently the religious issue became a political and military one, and Europe had a century of wars, ostensibly about religion. In these wars, the modern sovereign state came to birth.

169. The New Principles of Sovereignty and Monarchy

Europe was becoming anarchical, without law or authority and with nothing but wars between states and wars within states. An individualistic spirit ruled in the people's as well as in the princes' lives. A controlling force was needed somewhere, lodged in somebody. But the authority of the Empire as well as that of the Roman Church was then almost destroyed. So it was necessary to establish a new authority. The function of this authority would be to compel the religious opponents to come to terms and live at peace with each other. A government was needed to lay down the law for all parties, for the sake of order and prosperity. And the ones to do this were precisely those princes who managed to bring about order in the territories that they could control with their own armies. They established such a *sovereignty* over their respective lands. They were sovereign monarchs. And they became glorified figures in the imagination of men, as the source of the unity, order, law, and peace in their domains.

Not only did Machiavelli pay his tribute to the great political art of *The Prince*, but also the great dramatists Shakespeare and Racine. Thus authoritative monarchy became an institution of the European world. But it was not one world, for there were a number of independent sovereigns, each claiming to have supreme power. It boded ill for the peace of the world.[1]

170. The Right of Property and the Limits of Sovereignty

Yet sovereignty was limited. The political philosophers, who worked out the theory which monarchs were supposed to practice, conceived of the sovereign as a grand proprietor, towering above a number of lesser ones. Just as individual subjects had the unquestioned right to manage their own estates, so the monarchs had their title to the Grand State. But they were bound by that idea of property right through which they enjoyed their *own* titles. They had no right to lay hands on the property of their subjects. Any contribution to the expenses of the state had to be with the people's own consent, an English doctrine which met with general favor in the commercial world.

[1] Cf. BR, No. 50, Machiavelli, "The Prince."

Thus it was dangerous for a monarch to abuse property rights. It was essential also for him to keep faith with his subjects, because that was a principle needed for all business and society.

171. The Liberties and Rights of the People

So much emphasis had been placed on the achievements of those magnificent monarchs who forged by their military strength the great states of Europe that the most important source of their very power was for a long time obscured, even from the philosophers. The kings were strong because they had a strong following, and they had such following because as leaders they were the men of their own nation. There were some exceptions, notoriously in the case of James I of Scotland and his ill-fated son, Charles, but the unhappy fate of the Stuart line simply proves that rule. However, the prevalent magnifying of the sovereignty of the monarch, who was simply one man, ignored this dependency of the ruler upon the people whom he ruled. He reckoned chiefly with the class who had the power of wealth. But the spread of learning, the development of the national language, and the writing of important works in that language made another voice possible, the voice of the people, claiming freedom and the rights of man.

A struggle took place, as we have already seen (Part I), in England from the middle to the end of the seventeenth century, coinciding with the beginnings of American society. It went on all through the following century in the continent of Europe, especially in France, where it came to a head in the French Revolution. It was fundamentally a fight against misgovernment. The centralized monarchical system did not work. Besides, it was armed with a pretension that antagonized the people.

When Englishmen challenged their sovereign's "divine right," they were told by one of their own countrymen, Thomas Hobbes, that the sovereign was entitled to *absolute* right, not on the grounds claimed by James I, but on those of reason. The only way men engaged in a civil war can ever escape from their disorder and carnage is for them all to commit themselves, body and soul, to the Leviathan, the state, and to give all power to the sovereign of that state, making him absolute in his rule. Hobbes thus argued that men must renounce forever their liberty and their rights as free men. By so doing they would gain the things they most wanted, security and peace, and with these boons they could go about their business and satisfy their worldly desires for material goods and enjoyment.[1]

The typical philosophers of that century, who spoke for the liberty and rights of man, were Spinoza in Holland, and John Locke. These men risked taking part in the liberal movements in their own lands. They attacked the philosophical argument of Hobbes. They insisted on the fundamental liberty and equality of man; they rejected the view that the whole of man's life is really ruled by self-interest and selfishness, and expressed their belief in his powers of reason, conscience, and self-government. They taught that government is itself only based on the consent of the people who are subject to its law and authority.

To their argument, the French jurist Montesquieu added a body of impressive evidence from the history of various nations to show that the laws and customs of each people are really the supreme law, and that no monarch, however despotic, can ever overrule them and maintain his power. This notion of a law rooted in the traditions of the people became later the idea of a constitution. And this set of doctrines spread through Europe and America in the eighteenth century and came into expression in the declarations of the rights of man and in the constitutions that are landmarks of our civilization.[2]

E. THE VISION OF AN ORDER OF FREEDOM AND EQUALITY

172. Rousseau's Challenging Question about the Value of Civilization

It was a man of the people who gave the new vision of the modern world. Jean Jacques Rousseau knew very well what

---

[1] Cf. BR, No. 51, Hobbes, "Leviathan."

[2] See Spinoza, *Political Treatise* (1677); Locke, *Civil Government* (1688); Cf. BR, Nos. 52, 55, 56; Montesquieu, *Spirit of the Laws* (1748); *Declaration of Independence* (1776); *Declaration of the Rights of Man* (1789); *The Federalist* and *The Constitution of the United States* (1787); Thomas Paine, *The Rights of Man* (1791); Burke, *Reflections on the French Revolution* (1790).

injustice meant to those who were at the mercy of the rich and powerful. He hated slavery and the spirit of domination in others. He regarded liberty as the right of all. He believed in the fundamental equality of men. So he attacked the system of his day at its most vulnerable point: the inequality of men.

The question was actually put by the Academy of Dijon, in 1755, offering a prize for an essay on the subject, "What Is the Origin of Inequality among Men, and Is It Authorized by the Natural Law?" *Why* are there people separated into rich and poor, powerful and weak, sovereign and subjects, masters and slaves? *How* have these things ever come to be? Is such an order *right?* This is what the question meant, in simpler terms.

Rousseau knew his own mind about these questions, for he had long brooded over them. In the "state of nature," which means the state of affairs in human existence before there is a social system, property, and government, men are certainly *not* unfree or unequal, and no one of them ever has any right over the lives of any others. But the learned world was studying history and seemed to see a justification for the actual order there. Was not inequality among men really the law of history? Men have always lived in society with some persons superior and others inferior, and government and law confirmed these distinctions of rank and class. But Rousseau was convinced that this need never have been so in the past and need not be so now. These were the points he intended to prove.

173. The Wrong and Evil of Inequality

The natural inequalities were not objected to. There are genuine differences that exist in men which make some of them better able to do one kind of thing than another. Everyone has something that enables him to get along in the world, though he may be lacking in others. These differences and inequalities of capacity do no harm. Rousseau was far from repressing spontaneity, initiative, and talent.

But here was the point: the existing order does repress ability by giving undeserved advantage to those who are possessed of rank, wealth, social eminence, or political power. These fixed advantages for some and disabilities for others, *regardless of the merits of the men* who have them, these are the inequalities that are wrong. This throttling of the good in people is the evil of the existing social and political institutions.

174. Ideas about the Natural Way of Life for Man without Political Institutions

The argument was worked out partly from facts and partly by imagination. The records of primitive peoples showed men living in very different circumstances in other regions and exhibiting a very different human nature. Much theorizing had been done about the nature of man and society merely from the limited experience of Europe; but look beyond Europe — to America, to Africa, and to all the world — and then consider without prejudice what man is capable of being, and how he ought to live in society.

Consider that picture of man in a primitive state of nature.[1] Rousseau described one of the things man wants most of all to have in life, no matter when or where he lives. He loves independence. He wants room to be himself, to escape from the business of his workaday existence and from the pressure upon him of so many people in the complex, civilized order. He yearns for a vacation from toil and trouble, to roam the countryside, to live primitively in mountains or by the sea, fishing in streams, hunting, or even tilling the soil, simply for the satisfaction of doing something entirely his own and not dependent on other men, measuring himself only with nature and obeying her rhythms and laws. In that way of life there is a kind of essential happiness.

Yet that is not enough for man. If that is *all* one has, it is but an empty independence. Another side of the happy life is seen when man settles into an abode with his wife and children and has constant attachments dear to him. This is the life of settled affection, so much better than casual impulse. Man is here more of a *person*. He has more to defend against any other's interference, and he will fight for his dear ones with a will that ignores his own safety. They are his own, and through having something of his own besides himself, he is richer in his humanity.

[1] Cf. BR, No. 53, Rousseau, "Discourse on the Origin of Inequality among Men."

175. Free Will in Man and the Making of Civilization; the Evil That Develops in Civilized Man

Then there is the fateful will in man that sends him on beyond the family into the world of civilization, society, the state, and all its works. What characterizes man, as distinct from the animals, is his free will. He has it in his power to give or withhold consent to the impulses and desires of his heart. This will to choose his own way is hardly active in a man living independently of others and very little more even in man living idyllically with his family. But this capacity of free will is the only factor that explains some notable achievements: how man constructs weapons, tools, devices, and builds societies and sets up governments; in short, how he makes civilization. Man is thus able to order his own life to suit himself. Like the "civilized man" of Plato, he is bent on "self-improvement," on being better off than he is. Right here is the danger that, in being free to take his own course, he will get off the true course of nature and so bring more evil than good into life and society. And this, according to Rousseau, is precisely what has usually happened.

Man begins, so to speak, with some natural concern for his fellows as well as the interest in his own existence, for compassion is natural to man. It is present as a moderating influence upon anger and thoughtlessness of others. In the family, these feelings for others are focussed on the persons close to man who become objects of lasting affection, and all this stabilizes the life of man. He may develop greater egoism than before because he now has more that he calls his own, and moreover he cannot but esteem himself when others love him; but this egoism is balanced by his stronger sentiments of love for those other persons. Thus the nature of man stays fairly balanced and harmonious in both these earlier levels of experience.

But in civilized life the condition is appalling. Here man is busy with industry, exchange, and commerce, and competing with others for all sorts of exclusive advantages for himself. He develops an undue egotism without any enlargement of his affections; indeed, they are suppressed. He becomes absorbed in his desires for gain, position, power, and exclusiveness. Here, after all the so-called "advances," is a human being who is *willing* to be inhumane. Man is worse in this state than he has ever been. He is almost a damned and lost soul.

176. A Radical View of the System of Property and Government; and Doubt about Progress

In the civilized system, property tends to mean an exclusive claim on the part of some individual to goods, land, or other valuable things, regardless of the needs of anybody else. As an institution, property represents a jealous intention to exclude others from enjoyment. And government follows suit and fixes, for good and all, the previously existing, unjust social inequalities. And then comes the final folly: once the political state with its military power exists *anywhere*, it becomes the universal type of human society because all other peoples must in self-defense organize along the same lines. War is the inevitable consequence of this political and social system.

That radical argument made history. It fell like a bomb upon Paris and the intelligentsia of Europe. Everywhere men who thought about the matter had made the complacent assumption that the civilized institutions and the culture of their social order were good. They believed in progress forever along those lines. Things were admittedly wrong with the monarchy, of course, but men thought simply intellectual enlightenment would surely mend matters. It was not necessary to be so radical.

But a few philosophers recognized in Rousseau's diagnosis of the evils of civilization a turning point in the modern world. It is not merely individual intelligence that is going to make a decent, moral life for man possible, but a great, radical act of moral transformation in the will of all the people inspired by the vision of a free life in a good society.

177. The Responsibility of the People for Their Social Institutions.

It seems at first sight as if Rousseau were blaming the institutions of society for everything. He himself declared that he believed in "the natural goodness of man." In other words, he rejected the hopeless view that man is fated to be inherently evil, which would make people accept their chains and misery as something they could never escape. He appealed to the gumption and self-reliance of the modern man: if we are in trouble, we are going to get out of it by our own powers of mind and will.

But here is the thought: have we not got ourselves into this miserable predicament through our own fault? People have really consented all along to live under such arrangements. They have allowed these institutions to be fastened upon them, piece by piece, simply by not acting as they ought at the proper time when they could have decided the course of history themselves. Now they must radically change the entire system. The whole business is their own responsibility, and they have to begin directly with themselves. Man, the individual, must undergo a moral conversion. The unbalanced, egoistic, selfish individualist must be made into a moral person. This applies to every man. It must happen to everyone without exception. It is something that must take place in the total life of the people. They all have to find the true vision of themselves and their society and believe in it and act on it. Only so can they ever redeem themselves and their evil civilization. Rousseau's radicalism was thus a first step towards a thoroughgoing reconstruction of the good life.

178. The Essence of the New Order

The title of the book presenting this vision of man in a true society did not reveal its meaning satisfactorily. *The Social Contract or the Principles of Right and Law in Politics* [1] suggests another "contract theory" of government. The book discusses the social compact, sovereignty, law, the people, and government much as many another political writing had done. When it declares "the sovereignty of the people," it seems only to be shifting monarchs out of power and installing the people instead. The change of essential ideas in the system is not immediately visible.

Nor was Rousseau himself satisfied with his book, for he sadly avowed later that it should have been written over again. He then put the case in this short, significant statement: "What is it that makes a state one body? It is the union of its members. And whence arises the union of its members? From the obligation that binds them. And what surer foundation can there be

---

[1] Cf. BR, No. 54, J. J. Rousseau, "Social Contract."

for an obligation among men than the free engagement of the one who obliges himself?" [1] This is the essence of the matter: free men, binding themselves to live in unity and held together by their own personal obligations to each other.

179. The Act of the People, the Social Compact

It is by such a free, moral act that the political society or state comes into being, and it is by similar acts thereafter that it survives and prospers. But how is this act possible? We must "take men as they are" — not imaginary men devoid of passions or selfishness. Then we have to see how they might come to take the step which will establish the right order of civilization, where men can at last live in freedom and equality.

Men "as they are" have a powerful self-interest governing their lives. It is necessary, therefore, to reason with them and satisfy them on this score. They must see how their interest is reconciled with justice and freedom. But that very idea of freedom is really the key to the argument. This is something of interest to everyone. For in the struggle and competition for life in the present world, men want to manage their own affairs and get what good they can out of life, but they have to protect themselves all the while against others. They are never free to enjoy life and its goods. It would be for the benefit of all, then, if they could do something about this danger and the restrictions it imposes. If they could somehow associate themselves with each other in the right way for common protection, they would all have the freedom they desire and need. How can they do this?

The answer is by the "social compact," which Rousseau describes as follows: "Each of us puts his person and all his power in common under the supreme direction of the general will, and in our corporate capacity, we receive each member as an individual part of the whole." The community, as one body, receives the loyalty of every member, and in another aspect every member is an inseparable part of the whole body, receiving from every other one the same pledge of loyalty that he himself gives. The relationship of members is one of perfect equality.

[1] See J. J. Rousseau, *Letters Written from the Mountains*, his reply to an anonymous attack by a member of the government of Geneva after his books had been burned in the public square.

No one gives up more than another. No one benefits at the cost of another. No one rules over another. The rule of life for all is "the general will."

It seems, however, as if the community were already there, when everyone personally pledges himself to obey the will of the whole body. That is, in fact, the paradox of human society: "*The social spirit* which should be created by these institutions would have *to preside over* their very foundation." This spirit of community must first come over men or into their minds and hearts. Even while they are living in their ordinary relationships in the present order, they must have this ideal of the right order animating them, much as the Christian who goes through the life of this world must act with the righteous will of God constantly in mind. Something like this has to happen to men if they are ever to form a genuine society with each other.

And another thing must be realized profoundly — the belief about man which Rousseau expressed in his novel *The New Heloise:* "Man is too noble a being to be made to serve simply as an instrument for others. . . ." In the midst of life's severe competitions and conflicts where self-interest is so powerful, men have to honor this nobility and dignity which alone can call a halt to selfish individualism and make them feel a personal obligation towards their fellows.

But when these things have stolen in upon the spirit of people, there is then an act of the greatest importance which they are called upon to take if anything is to come of their vision. They must *will* that this order shall be established. They must take the decisive step to constitute it. They have to declare solemnly to each other their pledges of common allegiance and bind themselves publicly and commit themselves to the rule of the general will. When they do these things, they make *actual* what was merely a vision of community ineffectively stirring in their individual minds. A social compact with one another is necessary to establish the society which embodies their ideal of the right order.

180. The General Will

That sovereign, general will is not literally the will of the people, merely as it might be expressed in an assembly of citizens. They must be continually imbued with that right social spirit.

But their actual decisions in meetings may be motivated by many other ideas than those of the general good of all. The general will is not truly so unless it is both from the whole body and for the good of the whole body. It is thus an ideal, like justice in Plato's *Republic*. In fact, it is the very same principle, described in terms of will.

181. Freedom

But what is the good of it all? What is gained? Is man, for example, as free as before? He seems wholly swallowed up in society and is certainly no longer at perfect liberty to do as he pleases, for he is henceforth obliged by his own deed to act under the direction of the general will.

But in return for that moral obedience he reaps great rewards and precisely in regard to freedom itself. For now every man is secure in his liberty in relation to every other man. No one can possibly be master over others; no one is forced to obey another; no man is a slave. In this order, an equality is really established in human relations. If one man has a right, all men have that same right. If one has a duty, all have the same duty. No one is favored; no one possesses any unfair advantage over any other. Every man enjoys an equal civil and political liberty. And, to cap it all, man gains "moral liberty, which alone makes him truly master of himself; for the mere impulse of appetite is slavery, while obedience to a law which we prescribe to ourselves is liberty."

182. Law and the Democratic Process

A law which we prescribe to ourselves! This is what the people do when their lives are under the direction of the general will. The first act of men toward a true society was the compact by which they all committed themselves to an order of equality. But one meeting does not make an enduring society. There must be a continuous life in which this original democratic process goes on day after day, year after year. Every definite rule of common life which embodies that intention to do things in common and according to the principle of equality is a genuine law. This is a free society only because the men are ultimately governed by their own laws.

But again the puzzling question arises: Are these the enact-

ments passed by some legislative assembly? Not necessarily.
Many motives enter into the acts of governments so that their
acts are not truly the laws of the people. Montesquieu had
demonstrated that the genuine laws are above the orders and
edicts of governments. Even the will of the people only makes
law when it is for the common good and when every citizen is
equal and free under it. What we have here is the *ideal* of law.
But it is not visionary on that account for, unless men did generally observe such true laws, they could not live in society at all.

183. The Function of Government

Nevertheless, this will be only an empty vision unless this
moral order of freedom and equality is protected and maintained. Men are very far from living in a strictly moral relationship with each other. They do not observe the law that is binding on them. They will not always consider their fellows and
the welfare of their society. Some make exceptions of themselves. Others violate the law from shortsightedness and selfishness. To allow these defections to take place is to make the good
citizens suffer from the derelictions of those who fail in their
citizenship.

Consequently, although the general basis of life is the personal
obligation, occasionally this must be further supported by force.
Hence the agreement to live together "tacitly includes the undertaking which alone gives force to all the other things, that whoever refuses to obey the general will shall be compelled to do
so by the whole body. This means nothing less than that he
(the violator) will be forced to be free." [1] It is the precise function of government to see to this vindication of everyman's
freedom.

184. Education in the Spirit of Equality

But government only intervenes on behalf of the community
and its laws. It cannot *make* the community in any sense at all.
That takes place in the spirit of the people, according to their
degree of understanding of the true and ideal order of their own
life of freedom. And this understanding comes not by argument
so much as by experience and education in fellowship. The
youth of the nation ought

---

[1] J. J. Rousseau, *Social Contract*, Bk. I, chap. 7. Cf. BR, No. 54, sections d and e.

"to play all together and in public, in such a way that there is always a common goal to which all aspire, and which excites their competition and rivalry . . . for it is not simply a question of forming in them a healthy body and making them agile and skilful, but also of getting them used in good season to equality, fraternity, rivalries, living under the eyes of their fellow citizens."

And Rousseau added that men so brought up will appreciate "the truly *personal* qualities of their fellows."[1] Everything depends on that appreciation of the personal qualities of men and on being accustomed to equality and fellowship. If these come early in life, the spirit of freedom and equality will long reign among men.

F. THE MORAL AND POLITICAL PRINCIPLES OF A DEMOCRATIC SOCIETY

185. (a) The Community and the Principle of Justice

Thus, modern democracy has been inspired by the common principles of Locke and Rousseau. It was Rousseau's eloquent belief in the common man's powers of moral responsibility that led peoples in Europe and America to dare to make over their political institutions in order to secure freedom and equality. The English tradition contained the principle of the government of law and the practice of representative government which has made possible an extension of the idea of self-government from a small country to large modern nations. If democracy is to succeed now, it is necessary that there be the widest possible understanding of the moral and political ideas which are the ruling principles of this order — the ideas of equal freedom, law, obligation, rights, and the worth of personality. It is also necessary to deal with the problems that arise from all these ideas.

A nation is a community of men, and, in order to endure, it must have a lasting unity throughout its history. The things that are held in common, the ground of unity, may be many or they may be few, but a certain minimum there must be. Men

---

[1] Rousseau wrote these lines when dealing with a constitution for the precarious kingdom of Poland, just before its third partition in the eighteenth century.

must provide for their material needs through an economy in which all participate and benefit and at least obtain their subsistence. It is characteristic of civilized man, moreover, to desire to better himself and enjoy something that he can consider his own personal good. Industry, commerce, and property are the natural consequences, and it is very evident how much men care about property. They also concern themselves about their security against aggression by others. They take measures, too, to settle any difficulties they may get into over matters of property or for any other cause.

For such protection, and for the judicial maintenance of security, order, and peace, the organization called the state is a necessity. The men whom the state is intended to serve must in turn manifest some care for it, as well as for the basic economy of life that keeps them going together. *That unity of loyalty and interest with regard to the whole order of the community is justice.* This virtue of justice is, therefore, the absolutely basic condition of the existence of a state and social community.

186. (b) Personal Loyalties and the State

It will not do to practice justice only occasionally, for man ought always to be acting as a partner with all the others of his community. Now an enduring partnership would be most difficult to maintain simply from pure reason. But when men have been accustomed to enjoying themselves in natural fellowships, they have a fund of social habits which makes them ready for justice. There is the natural habit of family life and that of uniting in common religious worship from a consciousness of great need. In various other associations, the main interests of men may be their mutual pleasure or doing some work together or searching for some common good.

But the essential thing is that there shall be these social relations, spontaneous and natural, freely formed, and independent of the state. These all form a background of experience of life in society and what is required of man to maintain it. They supply some of the most intimate personal concerns which the state is intended to protect. Thus a man, when he is going through the dangers and sufferings of war, will think of home as something for which he is really willing to make sacrifices, "home" meaning all those associations which are dear to him. That supplies a powerful motive for his duty or devotion. So does the elemental comradeship of battle, and any distress shared in common.

The community is not to be thought of, therefore, as merely so many "individuals," collected into a bundle and labelled "the state." A political society is a complex, collective body containing men and women and families, friendships, and associations of all sorts that are personal in character. The very survival and continuance of the state depend on these contacts of one human being and another, generation after generation.

187. (c) The Supreme Value of Law

The common rules of action that are recognized as needful for the community and therefore what justice requires of all men in it, are found in the laws of the state. The laws have always been, more than anything else, the working fundamentals of the social order. This truth was appreciated even by primitive man, who regarded the laws as having some mysterious and sacred power to do something that man alone is unable to do. It was even more appreciated in the early civilization, when the interests of men were expanding and considerably changing their relations with one another and involving them in unforeseen complexities; their first heroes were the fabulous law-givers, like Moses or Lycurgus, who disclosed to them the laws or principles of right living for the time.

188. Divine and Natural Law

The laws were then considered to be divine and not human, of such supreme value and importance were they. They were not made by the law-givers but only found by them or revealed from on high. Even when the older religions had lost their hold, the Greeks, and later the Romans, still exalted the laws above every human institution. Socrates' account of the laws of Athens remonstrating with him, were he to flee from jail with Crito, was the expression of reverence for law.[1]

Still later, philosophers spoke of justice as "the law of Nature," for Nature was to them something eternal and imperishable and

---

[1] Cf. BR, No. 47, Plato, "Crito."

very great, above all human affairs. In the Christian Middle Ages, that lofty appellation, "the law of Nature," was continued, but it had a synonym in "the law of God." For centuries thereafter, even when men were lax in their religious faith, they would still appeal beyond the laws of sovereigns and states to this supreme law of Nature. It was the moral law by which all kings as well as common men were to be judged.

Law was always an authority *above* government and any human sovereignty. At times it may seem as if the laws are nothing but abstract ideas of philosophy and not really effective, but any acquaintance with history shows that men's regard for law in that high moral and religious aspect has, in fact, moved them to do tremendous things in struggling for a better order of society.

189. The Different Kinds of Law in Society

From the start, this moral idea of law has led the way. But the laws we are concerned with are those various laws actually observed to hold in society. The most important of these laws are those dealing with crime, for crime means a deed so destructive of the community, if generally practiced, that the whole weight of the community must be put behind the punishment of such action. There are also civil laws, like the laws of property, the laws of commercial transactions and contract, the laws of inheritance, and so on. There are also constitutional laws which determine the political powers of government and the duties of men as citizens.

The rules of international action that have been common to the nations of history have warranted the idea that there is even a "law of nations." Some people have been doubtful about the existence of such law and have regarded it as merely an application of the moral ideal of Christianity or some abstract philosophy. But international law has been something of a reality, though less valid and certain than the other forms of law. There is nothing, however, to preclude its becoming a more effective law. In proportion as the larger community beyond the separate states and nations can be more definitely organized to secure some greater common good, international law will have the force of an obligation on the nations and thus possess what is called validity.

190. Law and Government

But what makes any law valid? This is not the same as the question, What makes it right? The "right" of it depends on the justice which it expresses. Laws can be recognized as right, that is, they can express what people know ought to be done, before they are made generally effective. Precisely here is where political government comes in. An additional power of human government is necessary if law is to hold throughout the community.

191. The Leadership Principle and How It May Work Contrary to the Supremacy of Law

The supremacy of law over all men is the true aim of politics. But men easily come to disbelieve this truth because they themselves fall in love with power or tamely worship those who wield it. Hobbes' scornful remark joins with the lessons of Machiavelli to teach a view contrary to the principle of law: "Laws cannot govern, only *men* can govern." It takes a person with a will to act, and laws have their effectiveness only through man. So ultimately all government is simply the government by some man or group of men — a monarch, a body of representatives, a clique, or a class. Thus the principle of personal leadership comes to vie with the principle of law for supremacy.

How that can come about is readily discerned. The men who administer the laws of a society are seen by all as they exercise their eminent and great powers of rule. On the other hand, the laws themselves are unseen factors. In fact they are usually invoked only in the forbidding role of restraining men. But a prince can be very princely in his ways, dispensing a nicer equity between men than the law can, granting special privileges and favors to those who will stand with him, and generally seeming to bring prosperity to the country by his administration. He may even acquire a sanctity from being so magnificent an embodiment of their national hopes. Thus impressed, the people have often come to take a worshipful attitude towards their sovereigns or leaders. This hoists the ruler into the supreme eminence that belongs to law. Then it is merely a *man's* government that holds sway, not the government of law.

But this form of government cannot go very far or long endure.

Machiavelli had advised the prince who would truly hold his power to be regulated by prudence, seasoned with kindliness.[1] Montesquieu demonstrated to the France of Louis XVI the limits of even the greatest despotism. But the rulers have almost never believed such political wisdom. The people, too, have to learn their own lesson the hard way, by experience of the arbitrary rule, injustice, and oppression of their rulers. Whatever a man does who possesses full authority will affect the people one way or another. Every decision means someone's advantage and another's disadvantage. It is always somebody's punishment.

Now when the men have to suffer from the impersonal operation of a law, they will stand it if they do not see it constantly hurting them or favoring others. But when they see favorites, a minority or circle close to the ruler, benefiting, they place the fault where it belongs — on the obvious person who decides and dictates action. Their own hurt or disadvantage makes them rebellious. They ask questions about the ultimate value of such an authoritarian regime for them. Must they accept this kind of government? And what after all is a king or leader but a mere man obviously, subject to partialities and prejudices, and why then should he have such power? So revolution threatens whenever there is no supreme law by which the government itself is governed. And when men have won their independence, what they most want to do first is to restore the rule of law.

Any solution of this problem will remain a solution only so long as the people really do value law above all other authority. If they follow leaders and give them unbounded power, they really scrap their laws or constitutions and all the benefits of order and peace. At any time a constitution can become a mere relic and a symbol, and then something like monarchy or a dictatorship takes its place.

192. (d) Equal Rights and Duties under the Law

It is the impersonal theory of law that all acts are equal — it does not matter *who* commits the deed. Personalities go by the board when it is a question of rendering strict justice. But strangely enough, persons who commit themselves to this lawful order of life come out of it invested with new personal values.

[1] Cf. BR, No. 50, Machiavelli, "The Prince."

For, thanks to law, they possess rights. In the older way of speaking, "the law of nature" granted to all men certain "natural rights" belonging to them by Nature or by God's will, rights which are sacred and inalienable and which no one "has a right" to take away from them. Again, this was all in the realm of moral principle, but it was a fighting creed, and the democratic peoples have made themselves great by believing and acting on it.[1]

193. The Different Kinds of Rights

In states formed under the inspiration of this idea of equal rights under the law, the actual rights that men enjoy may not, of course, measure up to that ideal. Nevertheless, the principle remains true: the rights of citizens are what they are entitled to have under the actual laws of their community. Thus, since an individual's life is safeguarded by the law against crime, there is clearly recognized a right to life for every person. This is the most generally recognized human right.

Then there is the right to property, which varies greatly with the particular form of social order, depending on what is regarded as properly subject to an individual's private control. The right of property is different in English-speaking countries from what it is in those that have followed the Roman Law, and different, too, in nationalist Germany or in communist Russia.

Ultimately, the variation in the rights depends upon the different ideas of justice that the nations have, according to their general ways of life. Nevertheless, we can understand each other's differences because we are all thinking according to the same basic pattern about these matters: the justice of the community is expressed in its laws, and the rights are those which men have under the laws.

Besides the property right, there are many kinds of civil rights. Wherever there is a law maintained in the state, there men enjoy certain rights, and they have corresponding duties to respect the same rights in others. Furthermore, whatever the citizens of a state are entitled to do as citizens are called political rights, such as the right of voting or holding office. These are assured to them by the supreme law of the land or the constitution.

[1] Cf. BR, No. 56, Jefferson, "The Declaration of Independence."

To go one step farther, if the nations of the world have any common sense of justice regarding what happens to people outside their own territories, they must recognize, not only an international law, but also certain rights for all men and nations — the *universal* rights of man. Once again, this seems today only a far-off moral aspiration. But it has always been so with all the rights that men have ever fought for and achieved: they existed first as moral aspirations, then became imperative and general demands, and then, by action, accomplished facts.

Moreover, this continual movement to establish universal human rights has been community-building. As men strive to secure common acceptance of the rights which they believe in, they draw more closely together on common ground. Thus rights enjoyed in a community are a powerful cement of fellowship and strength for the state. That is why it is important for the state to do everything possible for the extension of equal rights among men.

194. The False Notion of Absolute Individual Rights

But what stands in the way of this healthy development is the claim of individuals to have an absolute right to something. This actually makes all good government impossible and often leads in the end to the ascendancy of one man or a party who exercise the authority of government and take all rights away, as in dictatorship.

The notion that an individual has absolute rights is a mistaken interpretation of the truth that all law and government exist to serve men and safeguard their personal rights. What happens is that when a man struggles for his rights, he sometimes thinks only of his own rights, forgetting that all others living in the same society have equal rights with himself. His enjoyment of his rights cannot *be* "right" at all if it spoils another's opportunities. This means that he has just as much duty to respect their rights as they have to respect his. All rights sink or swim together. Well, that is precisely what law provides — an equality of right and duty. A right is no good without law.

There is a further error needing correction in that manner of thinking. No one can claim to exercise any *one* right *absolutely without regard to the other human rights*. Precisely what a man may do, in the exercise of any right, has to be considered with reference to all the others, and that is why there must be courts of law to determine exactly what particular right a man has, and what he must refrain from doing in any given situation. A particular right is thus never absolute solely by itself. The law safeguards equally all rights as well as all men.

195. (e) The Political Principle of Constitutional Government

The Constitution of the United States embodies these conceptions of rights and the law. It is the supreme law of the land. It defines the respective powers of the States and of the Federal Government and, within the latter, those of the Congress, the Chief Executive, and the courts. The actual government is all put *under* the supreme law. But, in order that the human purposes of government would be clearly realized by all parties concerned, the first ten Amendments expressing the popular will, gave a "bill of rights," guaranteed to the people. Yet it is to be observed that this set of rights, too, is only valid under the Constitution or the supreme law of the people. Whether any one of these rights is what any citizen claims it to be for himself has to be settled "by due process of law," and that is the responsibility of the Supreme Court of the land. For the different rights must be made consistent with each other *in practice*, and so particular decisions have to be rendered as to which party has right on his side and which one has to yield.

A constitutional government works only as long as it is understood by the people whose rights it is to safeguard. And the people concerned are not the dead but the living. It does not follow at all from the principle of constitutional government that all the rights of man were completely discovered at one time in a certain year in American history. New developments in a progressive society create new needs of the whole people. The ideas of what all really need for a decent, law-abiding life together may develop with the changing circumstances. Whenever the people as a whole become convinced that a certain kind of action is *universally requisite* for their common life and declare it by law, that becomes a new and lawful right. Such is the true way of progress toward a better future.

It is also the way of maintaining internal unity and self-preservation. The government has to keep the community a "going concern," so to speak, and not merely enforce a set of fixed rules regardless of the result for the society as a whole. Otherwise, the relations of men in the state get out of balance. And there is a further case where new conditions require action limiting the exercise of rights, and that is when the safety of the state is at stake in war, which requires a suspension of certain rights. But this is only a suspension for the emergency, and it has to be made by a law that defines when it ends and when the citizens resume their normal rights again. Always under the law!

196. (f) Authority of Government

Justice, laws, rights — all characterize life in a state, but a state has to include something more. It is not simply an empty box in which these elements are collected. It is the *organization* of the community *with power to keep itself intact and defend itself*. The state has authority from the community for these purposes. It supplies, therefore, the force behind the law whenever justice fails to operate readily for the individuals and associations. The law must then be *enforced*.

Thus it is the function of a government to safeguard law, justice, and the whole order of society. The power of the government must be superior to the prestige or power of any element in the society and be able to overrule them all. It must have the right to make military and executive decisions and to declare what particular laws need to be made by legislation and, further, to make the judicial interpretations of these laws, thereby settling individual disputes and providing precedents for the guidance of the people at large. This is the exercise of sovereignty.

197. The Proper Meaning of Sovereignty

The unity of the social order can be destroyed by private interests or classes or groups. Whenever men are eagerly seeking advantage for themselves in any form, especially in a rapid expansion of the economic life, they are brought into strongly competitive and antagonistic relations with each other which threaten the whole society. In the struggle for wealth and power they are apt to ignore the moral values as well as the common good. This calls for a public authority to hold them to the law, or to the spirit of the law, of the community and to regulate the new ways of business. Only a government can act promptly and effectively in that role. Leaving aside all the dross of pomp and pride which has been associated with sovereignty from its past connection with absolute monarchy, the essence of it is this — that it is the supreme power of *decision* for the good of the community. This power is exercised by the government on behalf of the whole state.

198. (g) The Free Development of Man and Education

The true strength of a community is in its men, women, and children. It endures all things through their united will and spirit. What has been called the "general will" really stands for their implicit pledge to each other (called a "compact") that justice shall always hold among them all. It means, also, that when they individually seek anything *for themselves*, they will proceed to it in a spirit of fellowship and good faith with one another. Without that mutual confidence and loyalty, no agreements, laws, rights, arrangements for justice or government, are more than scraps of paper.

It is essential, then, to call into fullest possible operation the inner dispositions of men to live in justice and fellowship with each other. This is the work of education. It has gone on in society for thousands of years. The customs educate every rising generation in the ways of life by which a society has so far been surviving. These habitual ways of thinking, feeling, and acting are formative of the character and mind of each newcomer growing up to a place in the scheme. And particularly in civilization, art, literature, science, business, play, religion — all these together have a role far more vital and decisive for the fate of communities than government.

But precisely for this reason one must have a special care about education and not leave it to be carried on without thought about its results and purposes. It should be an education of man both to live under law and to be truly himself. For the best in a man comes out only when he has scope to develop his own natural perfection as a human being. It will never do to force him into a mold by drilling or to steal his soul away from him by indoctrination, so that he knows no better than to do simply as he is told. The man needed for a free society is a free citizen, and the way to bring him up is by a free education and development according to his own nature.

199. (h) The Value of the Individual

But if the individual man is given the opportunity to realize his own nature, will he really become social, or will he turn out to be a purely selfish individualist? Free education for life in society presupposes a belief that man, when truly himself, will be a good citizen in the community because it is *in him* to be so. Here we come to the deepest of all principles which was, for example, the heart of Plato's argument in the *Republic*. It is stated there in this way: the possibility of having social justice in the state depends on the virtue within every man himself. And because it is in all men, somehow or other it is possible in their society.

We have here reached "the pulse of the machine" of any civilization. But it is not easy to see because such forces are observable only in their outward works. Now the most obvious factor in the nature of man is what Plato and Rousseau both pointed out: man has a dynamic ambition to improve his lot. He wants to live in a civilized manner and not simply go on a daily round like his forbears. He wants to get ahead and make progress. The expression of this ambition has created our whole material civilization. Of course it has sent some people into a life of softening luxury and others into overvaulting ambition, both of which often wreck states. But the drive to have a good life for one's self should not on that account be stamped out — and cannot be done, in any case. It can only be directed, governed, and moderated some way or other. This dynamic principle in man has to be lived with, and human society must be organized with it, and not against it.

200. The Socratic Idea of the Soul of Man

Socrates is immortal, however, for having revealed another and very different power in man. There is the "soul" of man. What that means, in its simplest form, is this: there is something in every man which urges him, in the midst of his many active pursuits and his enjoyment of life, to seek to possess himself, rather than merely some external goods. For man himself is of far more price than anything in the world.[1] To know himself and enjoy being himself throughout the whole of his experience is something every man wants, though he does not know how to get it. He goes hunting outside himself for the satisfaction of this want and naturally fails every time. He can only attain what he is driving at by being loyal to the whole of his being as a person. This it is that gives him control over himself. This enables him to restrain a passion or to plan some future course of constructive action. This is the principle that enables him to find some permanent good in life and to be happy.

And precisely this is the inner "virtue" that makes justice possible externally in the relations of man to man in the community. It is because man has a power of self-government within that he can hope to have a good government in the state as a whole. It all rests upon this power and value of the soul or person.

201. The Christian Idea of the Worth of the Individual

That sense of the significance of every person was immensely enhanced by the Christian religion. The personal aspect of man gained in value because of the belief about man's relation to God. As a result of this, the Christian could be detached from the goods of this world because he lived in the conviction of an eternal life beyond and above. At the same time, he expected infinitely more of himself in his dealings with his fellowmen in this world. The duties of man to his neighbor were far above those the state claimed. The effect of such religious beliefs was to invest with sanctity both the personal fellowship and the persons themselves who shared it. This belief in the absolute worth of every individual has been the driving power behind the strong and obstinate struggle of modern men for equal rights.

202. (i) The Competition of the Spiritual and Material Principles of Life

The life of man is, indeed, a constant struggle, for it is not an easy balance of the two elements in him that have had a part in the making of civilization. There is an unending competition between the two dynamics. It can be seen in the case of our

[1] Cf. BR, No. 43 A, R. W. Emerson, "Self-Reliance."

views on human rights. It is the way of the world that men get their rights by claiming them first, by asserting themselves, by mustering up enough voices or creating pressure or showing power, so that the rights must be granted. Rights have to be won from others. The civil rights we now enjoy are really all souvenirs of great political battles. Men have even had to go to war to get such rights.

But the religious conception of conduct is quite otherwise. First of all, the sanctity of a person is nothing which that person himself can claim, for it comes from God. No man can give it, and no man can take it away. The rights of man are likewise from God and not at the disposal of man. This means, to a genuinely religious man, that the rights of each person are attributed to him regardless of whether he is able to *make* us acknowledge his claim upon us. The poor, the weak, the aged, the children, and whole nations that are inferior in power — all these have their rights, though they have no earthly way of asserting themselves. So we recognize rights that do not have a force behind them.

But the political realist then speaks in us: it would never pay to conduct the world on such principles. The machinery of social life actually runs on the other motive power of self-interest, with some effort, of course, to obtain justice. The plain fact is that force must be used to secure right in this world. But again the religious voice demurs, speaking of peace: the supporting of right by force is really of no avail, for it can never change the spirit of man. And the retort to this which is not easily gainsaid is: *not* to fight for the right but to yield all from the spirit of love is to expose all society to the wolves. Man lives today with such a perpetual argument going on within him. No one can be very complacent about himself or his civilization when he finds this conflict of principles. The deepest moral issues of life are here, and nothing can be worth while if they are neglected. They must be met.

203. (j) Faith in a Design for Living

In the abstract, it may seem a hopeless business to seek a solution of this great problem of man and civilization. Yet men never give up hope, especially those who see the importance of the problem. Though they do not solve the whole big question at one fell swoop (as with a formula), they do manage to solve some of the particular, practical problems of their lives, and thus they advance step by step toward their goal of harmony. It is as if they discerned some ultimate design for living in human society which they are gradually becoming clear about. The task before us, then, is to see clearly into some of the issues of our contemporary life and find the way toward their solution by the help of the principles which we have here learned.

G. CONTEMPORARY PROBLEMS IN THE LIGHT OF THESE PRINCIPLES

(i) NATIONALISM AND ECONOMIC FACTORS AS FORCES IN HISTORY

204. (a) Nationalism

From the beginning of modern society, two large forces have been at work with which we need to reckon, and indeed more seriously today than ever. They are *nationalism* and the *economic* facts and interests. Their influence runs all through our social order. They are involved, sometimes singly, sometimes in combination, in the particular problems we are dealing with. In some cases they are the direct causes of our difficulties. They are, at any rate, the general conditioning factors of our social and political life and consequently have to be understood first, before we proceed to deal with any special problem by itself.

Nationalism emerged with the breakup of the medieval Roman Empire and the religious division of Christendom in the sixteenth century. Sovereign princes established by their military and administrative genius the modern national state. Through the growing conviction in the eighteenth century that the people, not their sovereigns, really constituted the state, men became increasingly aware of the moral and spiritual sources of national unity. Montesquieu taught in the *Spirit of the Laws:* "Many things govern men: climate, religion, laws, maxims of government, the examples of the past, morals, manners — whence there is formed a *general spirit of the nation.*" Rousseau doubtless had this in mind when he spoke of a presiding of "the social spirit," and he adopted the phrase, "will of the nation," rather than "general will" in his practical works treating of the problems of Corsica and Poland. But Rousseau meant more than "will." The unity of a nation was due to the common sentiments and experience which bring people to a *consciousness* of their membership in one nation. All these expressions — "spirit of the laws," "social spirit," and "spirit of the nation" — emphasized, therefore, a spiritual basis for the nation-state.

Yet it was the French Revolution and war that made nationalism a great reality in politics. The French Revolution had been at first an inspiration to all the peoples of Europe, for its gospel of liberty, equality, and fraternity released the pent-up hopes of multitudes. It caught the imagination of poets and those who wrote the songs of freedom. But then the Napoleon of the Revolution became a would-be conqueror instead of liberator. Liberty of the various nations was not coming to them as a gift on the wings of others' revolution; they had to fight to liberate themselves from the domination of a conquering sovereignty. So the Napoleonic wars produced our form of nationalism — a *fighting* faith of nations.

205. The Vision of the Nation and Its Destiny

Whenever people are under some foreign domination, they cherish and sustain their sense of their own worth by a remembrance of things past, when they once had a greatness of their own. Every nation has such an historic past, a past both of legend and of fact. That history supplies the lacks of their present situation. As the men of the nation look into the past, it becomes colored with their own hopes of a brighter future. They find heroes of their own in song and story; they unearth folklore, folk music, art, language, literature, and all the characteristic ways of life that are peculiarly their own. It was this kind of enthusiasm that strengthened the various nations of Europe in the nineteenth century. A fresh appreciation of the Christian religion, which accompanied that historical spirit, aided the development, for, though Christianity is not national but universal in its aim, its teaching of the worth of men nourishes the sense of the individual value of each nation. So history, literature and the various companion arts of self-expression, and religion all contributed to the mounting consciousness of nationality.

With all that came a new vision. For the distinctive feature of men's consciousness of the nation is the great idea of its *oneness and significance throughout historic time*. The map of the world in space may show them only dwelling in a small place under the sun, hemmed in and oppressed by neighbors; but they see themselves *historically* as a community extending far, from a distant past of common experience, and going on to an unbounded great future, a destiny.

206. The Quality of Nationalism and the Values of the Nation

There is every sort of nationalism, because it is a kind of individuality of whole peoples. History has produced German, Russian, and other European nationalisms; nationalism in America; nationalism in Asia. The kind of nationalism depends, in each case, upon the particular history of the nation. But it depends, also, upon the ideal of greatness that a nation has for itself. If power like that of the older sovereign monarchies is sought above all things, then the nationalism has a domineering character and turns to war or conquests.[1] If the wealth of the nation is the chief concern, then the nationalism may compromise in world politics for the sake of material prosperity. Or it may stand staunchly for a liberal system of commerce, with certain common laws of doing business for all the nations. The nationalism may even have as its ideal the principle of freedom as a common hope and aspiration for *all* peoples. Whatever it is that the nation lives and dies for determines the quality of its nationalism. The choice also decides whether and how long the nation may endure.

207. An Example in German Nationalism

The German peoples were still existing in hundreds of small principalities in the shadowy remnant of the old medieval empire when Napoleon overran and subjected them to his new imperial system. Excepting Prussia under Frederick the Great, there was scarcely a state that enjoyed the character of being sovereign and significant as a power in the world. Yet these

[1] Cf. BR, No. 80, "Shinto," especially section B.

peoples had an inexhaustible cultural history, back through the long Middle Ages, during which the Christian religion was becoming European. In them the modern individualistic spirit had first showed its fighting quality, at the Protestant Reformation. When Napoleon bemeaned them, their fighting spirit was again aroused, and with it came the nationalism that was working elsewhere in almost every corner of Europe and the New World, and in both North and South America. The philosopher Fichte gave rousing *Talks to the German People*. The Germans aided in the defeat of Napoleon at Waterloo. Yet they came out of these events still harnessed to a decadent empire. Meanwhile their imagination in music, art, literature, and research into history had created works of universal significance. Beethoven had expressed the liberty and dignity of man in his music. Kant had taught the freedom of man in science and morality. Artists and scholars were rediscovering the spiritual aspects of the Christian Middle Ages embodied in Gothic architecture. All these things made them conscious of their own worth; but still they counted for nothing in politics. German nationalism was frustrated at the start as a *political* ambition.

Philosophy entered the scene to emphasize the absolute importance of the state. Hegel developed Rousseau's conception of the general will. States exist by virtue of a sustaining will of the great social whole, which has a being and life of its own over and above the individuals who dwell within it. The state is not built up of individual decisions, as by contract or law-making, but represents the working of a big creative idea in history. This idea is, according to Hegel, a thing of "spirit" and expresses itself in all the many forms of life, in the various ranks and classes in society, and in the general culture. But it is never truly realized anywhere unless the state exists *with force* to affirm itself in the world. The state is the agent of freedom for men, and at the same time it itself contains whole reality of their freedom. The individuals must find their freedom in that transcendent freedom of the state. They must learn their own worth through their devotion to the state, which is of supreme worth. They must even rejoice in war as the test of their "ethical health." These experiences are part of a grand "dialectic of the Spirit" in history. In fact, the state itself is precisely "the

Spirit of the People." Thus Hegel aimed to lift the German people to a status of political competence with a doctrine which identified man's destiny with the supremacy of the state. The nationalism turned more and more toward a glorification of the state and of force, which the work of Bismarck, in making the German Empire, only confirmed. It is this political nationalism with which the contemporary world has been reckoning.[1]

208. (b) Economic Factors in Modern History

The modern state had come with a new enterprise, industry, and commerce that revolutionized the existing social system. Sovereigns rose to power in the new system, but they were also limited by the very conditions under which their wealth and power were gained. There was thus an economic order which they had to heed and even respect. It was, in fact, a basis of an international law. For the laws relating to property, contract, and commerce were general in Europe, and, thanks to their observance, the people engaged in these affairs were prospering materially, and especially the monarchs.

After the first sovereigns had thus risen to power through their protection of the class who were thus enriching the state, they adopted a mercantile policy according to their own grand design for the state. This political control over the economy failed to work in the eighteenth century — it was more political than economic.

When the peoples threw over the monarchical controls, they adopted a "liberal" policy to enable individuals to enjoy the rewards of their own enterprise and achievements. The theory of the liberal system of economics was set forth by Adam Smith in his *Wealth of Nations*. This ruled out any subjection of commerce to the state. A general doctrine was later developed that government exists only to safeguard the rights of property and maintain the existing laws. There was little suspicion of the controlling power of property itself in the state — the old lingering fear of arbitrary and meddling government was uppermost. Individualism was the order of the day. It promised peace and plenty for all through self-interest. More people than ever would have a stake in the freedom of commerce and thus in per-

[1] Cf. BR, No. 60, A. Rocco, "The Political Doctrine of Fascism."

mitting "the laws of economics" to work without political interference. This was the laissez faire political economy.

209. The Industrial Revolution and Its Consequences

So much for theory and what men believed. The practical
aspect of the matter was the Industrial Revolution, which
changed fundamentally the whole life of nations. It created a
new political and social situation within every industrial nation,
as well as internationally.

In the beginning, those who possessed capital launched an
enterprise and managed it according to their own self-interest
and for their own profit. This was accepted as right; it was
simply the use of their own property. They employed men in
factories that were "owned" by them and they had some personal
connection with the men and the industry. But the development of power, the use of machinery, and a great expansion of
production brought changes in this respect. The size of industry
made wider investment an advantage, and devices were adopted
for that purpose. The setting up of corporations, with limited
liability but greater speculative possibilities, the trading of
shares in a market, the forming of companies which had no
direct connection with the production of goods and trade, but
which "made money" for the organizers — these and many
other developments produced an economic organization where
there were vastly fewer personal relationships between those
having property interest and those who did the work with machines. Any organization of the activities of men is in itself a
kind of social power; but this sort of organization was growing
to be a power without any responsibility to the public and
having no higher end than private interest.

In a world where individualism was general, the rights of
those people who were in inferior positions were bound to be
asserted. There was an upward movement of labor. A century
or so before, the middle classes of Europe had united against
their absolute rulers and gained their individual rights. Now
the pattern repeated itself, though in less revolutionary form, in
the relations of labor and capital. Individuals organized in
craft and trade unions. They could not be compelled to work,
and they could lawfully quit work when their claims were not

heard or honored as they believed proper. Labor unions have become well-established institutions in our industrial society. The conflict between "capital and labor" is thus a major concern of our times.

210. The Failure of Peace

The working of the liberal system internationally had not been so happy as its proponents first dreamed. It was not realized that, in the severe competitive struggle for national position and power, some nations had an interest in breaking the rules of free economic life. States like Germany which had attained full national statehood only recently had to make up for lost time, so to speak. They were afflicted with all the ambitions that older nationalities, like the English, had fought out at home. They organized a *national* economy for the sake of political power in Europe. The aggressive policies of Germany threatened the peace and were partly responsible for the World War of 1914–18. Since then we have a large legacy of problems regarding the international order as a *political and economic* order which will truly serve mankind.[1]

(ii) PROBLEMS OF LIFE IN THE DEMOCRATIC STATE

211. What Philosophy May Contribute to Contemporary Problems

It is not the business of philosophy to propose any specific measures for the solution of contemporary problems. The actual solutions will require the cooperation of a good many minds with particular experience in the matters to be decided. Some questions are so complex that it would take the evidence and argument of a case decided in the Supreme Court really to do justice to them. There is needed on such questions wise counsel coming from men of responsibility in all walks of life — in the trades, in labor unions, in the offices of management, in the professions, in courts of law and government, in education and religion. It is needed even from the poets, who have a disinterested and sensitive wisdom. What philosophy can contribute is to cast light on these practical matters by presenting the *principles* involved, so that the issues are clearly understood.

[1] Cf. BR, No. 59, Karl Marx, "The Communist Manifesto."

This may help to make men aware of what they are deciding. But it leaves the choice of what is good and right to the citizen, who as a free man must judge from his own understanding and experience of life.

212. (a) The Problem of Freedom of Speech

This is an old question which crops out anew in the tensions of contemporary life. The Bill of Rights in our Constitution guarantees to the people "freedom of speech" and also "freedom of the press." The government is forbidden, by the supreme law of the land, to abridge this freedom. No one can prescribe, then, what shall be taught, spoken, or published, and if any citizen does utter words or express questionable beliefs, he has to be judged by the courts of the land according to the law. If his action proves to infringe upon some other rights of the citizens or endangers the state, then only can he be punished. Otherwise he is at liberty to say what he thinks. The guarantee of such liberty is the law, and it is only by the law that the judgment as to the right of the matter can be pronounced. This affirms the sanctity both of the laws and of the courts that interpret them.[1]

213. The Liberty of the People, the Important Thing

The freedom of the press is a civil liberty, however, of *all* the citizens. The important reason for singling out the press for special attention besides is that the people may thereby obtain true information about what goes on in their own neighborhood, their country at large and, as far as it is of interest, the world beyond. It is not required, therefore, of those who supply the information that they must first submit their messages to an official bureau of censorship before they can issue them; they have the right to issue news undeterred by threats or pressures from a government, or indeed from any concealed power in the society. If their statements are inaccurate or false, others who are free to compete can expose the falsity; if libelous, those who are injured can sue in the courts. In any case, the matter is one of law and trial before a responsible body. So much for those who publish newspapers and journals.

[1] Cf. BR, No. 63, W. A. White, "The Importance of Free Speech."

But the rights belong to all the citizens in order that they may have access to the truth. The freedom of the press is *not* a freedom attached to any commercial enterprise as such. This means that the press, *as a business*, enjoys no immunity, for example, from the general law against economic monopoly or any other regulation that may have to do with labor or trade.

There is sound reason for this in the interest of civil liberty. If newspapers were to be largely controlled by any private interest, the people would have no means of protecting themselves against misinformation and a secret irresponsible control of public opinion. It might even keep opinion from being expressed and generally discussed. The business of a newspaper is one thing; the real freedom of the people quite another. And the law is always for the good of the people. The government has the right, therefore, to act on behalf of their democratic freedom. It has authority, on occasions when it is necessary, to regulate or restrain any commercial enterprise that may deprive the people of their rights and liberties.

214. (b) The Right of Education

Although it is not a written article of the Constitution, another right has come to be universally recognized — the right of all men to an education for freedom. This is a necessity for democracy on a large scale in great nations. A general education is necessary to enable the common man to play his part with understanding. Then a wise leadership will be accepted by the people and not that of demagogues, adventurers, or others who might destroy the nation or menace the peace of the world.

The same principles apply to the conduct of education as to the issuing of news and opinion in the press. Education must never be "tongue-tied by authority," any more than art, science, literature, and religious teaching. The main channels through which the education of the mind takes place must not be controlled by the government for political purposes, nor by any other group in the state or out of it. Education is a right belonging to the people and the whole community. It has its own proper agencies in the state, the schools, colleges, universities. These are fully responsible bodies charged with the duty of performing their fundamental work in the making of man and society.

The essence of genuine education is illustrated in the free inquiry conducted by Socrates. The practice of such inquiry is attended by the same risk as that which cost Socrates his life, for it almost always causes some disturbance among those who will not learn but stand rooted in their prejudices and their privileges as if they were eternal rights. They may oppose, therefore, and put unlawful pressure on free instruction.

On the other hand, with that liberty to teach what is true goes a solemn responsibility on the part of the institutions of learning not to *force* private opinions or supposed truths upon others, either by propaganda or by so arranging matters that no other views can be seen by pupils. Every person in the state, in whatever capacity, is living in society with others, and when he is undertaking to think freely for himself he has to *think of the others* as well, and what the meaning of the lessons he expounds will be to them. Men must go forward in knowledge and equal liberty together — education is a social affair. The claims of society have to be considered, then, no less than the individual's right to speak and teach the truth in which he believes.

215. (c) Problems regarding the Rights of Labor

The rights of labor are still in process of debate. During the early struggles, workers had to fight for their right to assemble with each other and petition when they had grievances. They were entitled to this right by the first amendment of the Constitution. Although that constitutional provision was originally conceived as applicable when the citizens of a republic assembled and, without prejudice to their liberty, addressed themselves to their government to ask for remedy of wrongs, it applies just as well to the relations of employed to employer. On such a right is founded the very existence of a trade union, as a lawful organization of workers.

216. The Right to Work and Its Moral Value

But a new moral right has been developing in the minds of the peoples of democratic states which is part of the unwritten law of society. It is the right of man to work, to have work, and to be able to live a decent life by means of his labor. This is not merely a matter of economics. It is essential to responsible citizenship and to the freedom of the individual.

"As a man does, so is he." This truth about conduct and character applies more generally to the particular vocations of every man. A man's work makes him what he is. In its extreme forms, as in slavery, this was recognized by the Greeks, who regarded physical labor as degrading to man, especially when he could not share in the purposes served or express his own nature in doing so. In modern civilization, whenever labor clearly tends to that same result, there has been legislation to prohibit it. Even so safeguarded, men find very mechanizing occupations too narrowing and restrictive.[1] What distinguishes the so-called liberal professions from these occupations is not simply the finer skills of mind and hand involved but the fact that those who practice them have to do with the welfare of the body or spirit of mankind.

Consequently, when men who labor hard in such jobs seek to rise above the illiberal character of their daily toil by meeting in associations with each other for some larger purposes than wage-earning or gain, it is an expression of their need for higher aims and fellowship. A labor union can offer such social experience and satisfaction. Unions develop into much more than organizations of power for negotiating with the management or the government: they actually become social institutions with liberal interests, and they can well become a school for statesmen.

In like manner, farmers too can develop their free interests and social life through their granges and farm organizations, as well as in their local village societies. Across all these economic lines are the churches that lift up men's eyes to something more than the winning of their daily bread, and thus impart significance to their vocation as playing a part in a Divine Order. These are the ways men can realize their own dignity, even in work which often seems to be bemeaning. Such experiences redeem even the hardest work from seeming slavery.

217. The Idea of Economic Democracy

All this has a bearing, too, on a free and responsible citizenship. There was once a requirement, in the early days of repre-

[1] Cf. BR, No. 18, J. Ruskin, "Tools or Men?"

sentative government, which today seems most unjust but which in its time had some point. It was that a man had to own property in order to participate in the rights of citizenship, to vote, and to serve in the government. The notion was that a man who has known the responsibility for property knows how to assume the responsibilities of office in the state. Now in the present industrial world where so many have nothing but a fluid currency that comes in and goes out week by week, there is needed a *moral equivalent of property*. Learning how to conduct their own affairs in unions or other organizations is something of an equivalent. It has been suggested that this experience can never be equivalent until the full duties of responsibility are shared with management, in an economic democracy.

218. The Dignity of Man and the Evil of Unemployment

But to have no work at all to do is to be deprived of almost all possibility of being a good citizen. Unemployment is a social evil with profound moral consequences. The palliative of relief or a dole is obviously only for a temporary emergency. To keep starvation from the door and to clothe and shelter people are not sufficient. Man must have an open door to opportunity, so that he can gain the knowledge of a trade or skill which will have a more constant value, and in the pursuit of which he can realize the sense of his own worth.

Man is entitled to have work to do which has a value in the whole scheme of things. This is what the right to work ultimately means. The conviction that provision for this is an obligation of the whole community today means that a new right of man has really been born of the economic distress between two wars. Social security, as it is called, is only part of it. The greater purpose is to provide for man the chance to be free and to know his own dignity as a person.

219. The Rights and the Law of Labor Relations

These moral values underlie the struggle of labor for rights in our society. But the struggle itself is a most serious, open contest between parts of the community organized under the banners of "capital" and "labor." The public mind is divided, too, hearing the different claims of both parties and often feeling the cost of the long-continued controversy. An argument about rights has been conducted which has not yet reached its proper conclusion.

As the argument began, the rights of ownership had the advantage, for the old rights of property "were there first," so to speak, while the things workers were asking for appeared to be new and upstart claims. For, at the outset, the rights of capital seemed absolute and utterly incontestible. Men who "owned" something — materials, factory, machinery — surely had the liberty of using these things as they saw fit, and of deciding whom they would employ. Working men might bargain as individuals for better wages or other terms with the owners. But for workers to unite and form a regular union and actually strike against their employers seemed taking an unfair advantage.

Furthermore, the labor movement appeared to employers or property owners as a negative thing economically which simply aimed at distributing the rewards of enterprise and good management without adding anything new to wealth. Moreover, it seemed to level men without regard to those superior qualities of initiative, greater capacity, and character itself which, all together, have made for economic progress.

In such an argument, the workers were at the same disadvantage as those men who first struggled for democracy because the rights they were claiming were not vested ones or already recognized by law. Yet labor had a case along the lines suggested by Locke, Rousseau, and later Marx: that a man only gains true title to property by expending labor upon it. On this view of the matter labor was only claiming what belonged to the workingmen as their own deserts, that is, their rights.

But their moral argument, as we have seen above, did not stop there, for labor was struggling for much more than an increase of wages or greater share of profits. It was striving for social justice, for opportunities, for decent conditions of work and life befitting citizens of a modern commonwealth. And first of all, labor had to win some recognized, lawful status for its own group organizations, through which alone these higher ends would be achieved.

Labor has already gained the right to have organized unions and the right to many practices which will maintain unions as institutions of our society. Unions are now organizations which actually wield great social and political power. Accordingly they have, like all other institutions, their responsibilities to the people. They are accountable to the public just as are the agencies of capital — industry and finance. And the state has authority from the whole community to require all bodies within it to conform to the existing laws and to use only lawful processes of settlement. It has had to intervene on many occasions. The government, acting for the state, has taken steps to restrain economic monopoly, which is itself an unlawful restraint upon trade and a violation of the accepted principle of a free market. The government has also had to step in to stop strikes which endangered the existence of the community. It has had to protect those who are not organized to protect themselves.

The public always feels most the cost of this continual conflict and often indicates a limit beyond which it shall not go, and this public opinion authorizes the government to hold the contesting parties within bounds for the good of all. The situation is rendered very difficult by a certain lack of organization in labor. Differences of policy in regard to the form of labor organization have led to two great groups of unions that dispute with each other. It is hard for the public at times to see the responsible authority and to know what to insist upon. But in any case such occasional intervention is insufficient and unsatisfactory to all parties concerned when the matter is a continuing problem, the problem of the relations of men in nation-wide industry and commerce.

The general principle is clear: that organizations of every sort must come under the law. But this does not mean law only in the sense of some specific act of legislation against monopoly or against strikes. It means law as the general rule of cooperation between members of the same community to whom the life of the community means something, so that they will give as well as take, and deal justly with each other. All we are sure of today is that lawless individualism or lawless organized power, in any quarter, is nothing short of internal war, which is ruinous to society. This is plainly wrong, but the rights of the matter have still to be worked out patiently throughout the length and breadth of the land in every scene of labor relations.[1]

[1] Cf. BR, No. 67, F. D. Roosevelt, "The Four Freedoms."

220. (d) **Religious Freedom and the Problem of Church and State**

One of the most critical issues for centuries has been that of church and state, because the profoundest allegiances, feelings, and convictions are involved. The authority of the state over man for the sake of an orderly social existence is firmly grounded in the experience and reason of mankind, and the state is thus a universal phenomenon of life. But others besides those having civil authority likewise speak with a proper authority because their function is also deeply founded. Religion has been the constant guardian of man's spirit through the long trek from the beginnings of history to civilization, and this guardianship continues through life and in the most intimate recesses of it.

It has been said that the state guards the outer relations, and the religious organization or church the inner ones of life. But inner and outer are not separate parts of man's being. The acts of a religious group will have outer consequences that bring them under the jurisdiction of the state and its laws. Acts of the government in the pursuance of its normal business will also, at some time or other, touch the inward life by determining the conditions under which it may express itself. So the problem of church and state is difficult and unavoidable. It is a special problem for every period of civilization because the changing circumstances upset the *modus vivendi* previously achieved.

221. Religion and the State

In some periods of history, religion has been national and the priesthood actually officials of the state, as in Greece and Rome. On the other hand, the Jewish people were often governed by their religious leaders who interpreted the law of God. The Middle Ages presented the signal instance of a competition for authority extending over centuries. The Christian Church of the West, with its seat in Rome, had done much for the organization of a European order out of the confusion, and even anarchy, in the old Roman Empire. The Roman peace (*pax Romana*) was gone, but the church established "the peace of God" with its ideal of a unity of Christendom. Serving in that political capacity, the church exercised a role really very similar to that of the state. When a great ruler arose, like Charlemagne, whose military and political leadership saved the new-forming Europe from external invasion by the Turks, he reclaimed authority as political head of the new Holy Roman Empire. He recognized, nevertheless, the spiritual authority of the head of the Church Universal or Catholic, and on some occasions the emperors received their crowns at the hands of the pope.

There were two authorities then, both with *universal* control over the same peoples and territories. The emperor had as his symbol the sword, the pope the keys. They were needed together for the secular and spiritual life of all the nations. But the problem of keeping them united and acting in perfect understanding of their distinct, divinely appointed tasks was tremendous. The very importance of each office exaggerated the difficulties of their partnership. Much depended on having an equal quality of statesmanship at all times. Now one party was superior, now another, and controversy followed. Nevertheless, this struggle was only taking place within the one whole Christian commonwealth, the preservation of which was a law for both parties. The bitterest wars of religion only came when *both* of these ultimate, universal courts of appeal had lost their authority, and the national princes of the modern state claimed independent sovereignty for themselves.

222. Personal Liberty

But what was the position of the new churches of the Reformation that came along with the modern sovereign state? The church of Luther was separate and equal with the state, but it had to leave to the state whatever the sovereign chose to treat as his secular business, for the sovereign could decide things by the sword, whereas the church provided only for inner confession and conscience. In Geneva, the church of Calvin was the state: every citizen was a member of the church, and the laws of the state were not merely the common laws of justice but the more exacting, puritanic laws of righteousness. The Church of England was established by act of Henry VIII, asserting his independence of all continental authorities, but the Protestant spirit was free also to form other communions there, such as the Presbyterian, the Puritan, and those of many different sects who argued for liberty and rights. The Roman Catholic Church itself was threatened in the territories of the Protestant princes, so that thinkers of that communion argued, too, for the freedom of religion and the rights of the church.

The ultimate beneficiary of all these events was the individual man, who gained the right of personal liberty. The religious issue was settled by depriving both the church and the state of absolute, unlimited authority. Moreover, in our country, the church and state were separated deliberately, in the Constitution, for the sake of religious freedom.

223. The Resistance of Religion to Nationalism and Defense of the Rights of Man

The problem of church and state has recently been reopened. The religion of nationalism, especially in Germany, has violently attacked Christianity and the whole religious tradition of Western civilization. The dictatorships have tried either to suppress the practice of religion in the accustomed institutions or to force it to take the nationalistic form under state-appointed officials. Jews, Catholics, Protestants alike have been persecuted. But the various religious groups resisted. True to their faith, they would not compromise with any power that destroyed its truth. They have only been made the more solid, therefore, by these ruthless attempts to destroy them. They have made common cause against their common enemy. They have been brought together in suffering and conviction. They have taught others to believe that there must be some way of life and attitude of man toward his fellowmen which must be authoritative for all — some common law of fellowship which is the very least that must be insisted upon if all the nations are to survive. This common conviction is of course very far removed from being a common religion, and farther still from a definite creed. But it is a direction of belief that insists upon certain universal values of human life. Some call this belief democracy, and some call it Christianity. In any case religion is most strongly identified with the rights of man, the rights to life and to a decent life, to education, opportunity, and freedom for all men, regardless of birth, race, or nationality.

224. Church and State Today

This stand on the rights of humanity makes the traditional institutions through which the religion of man is expressed more important than before. Yet this increase in spiritual authority happens at the very time when the political power of the state is at the utmost peak of its control over the lives of men, due to the exigencies of a period of economic distress and two tremendous wars. The clash of these two powers, spiritual and secular, has come already in Europe. But it is now one world, and the struggles in one part of it draw in the peoples of distant parts, so that this social issue in Europe becomes an issue in America and elsewhere. Consequently, the problem of church and state must be thought out afresh, if there is to be peace among men in all the nations.

The argument will have to be conducted in terms of the present situation and its values and, above all, with due appreciation of the living hopes of mankind today. In theory, the old doctrine of the separation of church and state keeps the government from laying violent hands on religious faith; and, on the other side, it keeps any church from laying down the law for the whole community beyond its own communicants. But this law of relationship appears now to have too negative a character. It makes for a purely secular culture and it does not seem to recognize how much the spiritual and the secular institutions can do together for the advancement of humanity. The nations today need a more positive cooperation of both these powers.

The search for the right relationship cannot be avoided. Religion has ministered to the spirit of man oppressed by tyranny and suffering, and it has gained a new lease on life in the contemporary experience of man. But religion is a body of conviction about the whole of man's life, and consequently it tends to reach into every human activity. On the other hand, the continuing stern controls needed by the governments of the various states in order to bring about orderly rehabilitation and an economic development that will sustain their populations, tend likewise to touch everything in human life. We must find *the law of this new order* in some new understanding of the relative authority of the religious and the political powers and with complete respect for the freedom of those persons who subscribe to no creed or established institution. No problem today is more urgent nor more difficult.

225. (e) The Rights of Nationalities and Minorities in the State

Nationalism has taken an extreme form in the exaltation of nation and race, as found in fascism and national socialism or Nazism. Lesser breeds of it are to be found in other nations where it is unavowed or else held in check by other influences of civilization.[1] But in its unlimited form it rears a totalitarian state on the wreckage of all human rights and whatever institutions of society do not lend themselves to the masterful will of those who have seized the power of the state to carry out a fanatic policy. A ruthless nationalism, destructive of civilization itself, is not to be argued about but only stopped in its tracks by decisive defeat.[2]

Nevertheless, nationalism remains a problem even for the well-organized states of the world. Most nations consist of an intermingling of peoples of different countries brought together by wars, persecution, or other factors over a period of time in history. There are smoldering relics of ancient injustices carried on in the national tradition. As long as things go well, these old grounds of discontent are submerged in the national life. But let defeat come in war or suffering under economic distress, and the grievances get a new lease on life. Distant kindred outside the nation make common cause with them and encourage them to claim their rights. These claims may be played upon politically. Thus remnants of some other group or so-called race develop a separate national self-consciousness and ambition of their own *within* the nation-state. This creates the problem of minorities.

Wherever such nationalistic feelings mount, powerful antagonisms develop. The very presence of a minority that seems alien may offend the dominant group and increase their will to dominate. Even passivity on the part of the lesser nationality emboldens the stronger to show its power. And the minority in turn, feeling its inferiority, gathers together all its resources in an obstinate, religious will to survive as a group. So matters drive on toward unreconciled conflict. Disunity is the inevitable outcome.

The state itself cannot compose the dispute unless there arises,

[1] Cf. BR, No. 61, A. Hitler, "Nation and Race."
[2] Cf. BR, No. 60, A. Rocco, "The Political Doctrine of Fascism."

in the public generally, a strong new will, in the face of the danger, to have the state whole and sound, and nationality be damned. In the absence of such an internal recovery of the basic principle of social unity, the solution will have to come from without. It may take the form of an arbitration by other states or acceptance of some international law which may be generally adopted in order to regulate what majorities in *any* state may do to minorities, or, to put it otherwise, to define the *rights* of minorities. But this last solution carries us beyond the state to the international order, as do in fact all the other major problems we have been considering.

(iii) PROBLEMS OF THE WORLD ORDER

226. (a) The Inadequacy of International Law

When the Powers of the world actually plunge mankind into a turmoil of destruction of human life and the finest treasures of civilization, it is apparent that states and nations are not being restrained by any superior law. International law seems to have been swept utterly into the discard. But nearly everything else, too, is annihilated — commerce, the exchange of ideas in science and culture, and all rights and freedom. *Everything* goes when law goes.

Many great nations that have been long jealous of each other and antagonized by differences of "ideology" and race, and engaged in not very noble rivalries, have nevertheless been able to unite in order to prosecute a war against aggressors who destroyed world peace and freedom. This alliance of the peoples who have risen to defend themselves can have no other ultimate purpose than to establish an order where this kind of thing will not be attempted soon again. The war has been fought, therefore, to put a stop to such aggressive lawlessness, and the victory ought to mean an advance towards lawfulness and some greater measure of community.[1]

227. Economics and International Law

This means *re-establishing* international law. For it has existed in the past. Although it was never strong enough to

[1] Cf. BR, No. 65, I. Kant, "Perpetual Peace."

prevent all outbreaks of war, it was sufficiently so to allow civilization to advance. Even when monarchs ruled Europe with sovereign authority in the seventeenth century, they were governed by an international law which they had to respect.

Thanks to certain general laws at that time relating to property and commerce throughout Europe, the nations were prospering. The benefits of that international economy made it the common interest of the various sovereigns to observe these laws. They were all interested, too, in upholding their newly established principle of sovereignty. This meant for each monarch his own unquestioned authority over his territory as well as his independence of any superior authority in the Holy Roman Empire or Papacy. In this connection, it was important that the laws of succession to the throne in each kingdom should be universally honored, just as any other inheritance. Furthermore, the sovereigns were greatly concerned that no established state should be wiped off the map, thus disturbing the balance of power and opening the way to a general conquest. Hence there were a number of common interests which supported the economic and political order of Europe. And there were laws and principles upheld which somewhat reduced the chances of war and made economic progress possible.[1]

An international law, founded on such limited human interests and benefitting chiefly so small a portion of all the people of Europe, would fail of course to do justice to the rights of humanity. It failed even to preserve peace. But the inadequacy of that law was no argument against the possibility of its more successful operation in the future and on a broader basis of interest. This was the hope of nineteenth century liberalism. When absolute monarchs were once overthrown, the interests of the state would henceforth become identified with the interests of the whole people, and, in proportion as the nations came to benefit more and more by the system of free enterprise and commerce, they would all support the laws of that order. Thus international relations with peace and prosperity would become a reality. But something was still wrong with that economic principle of self-interest on which the hopes of liberalism had

[1] For an adequate treatment of this question, see Gerhard Niemeyer, *Law without Force*. Cf. BR, No. 62, A. N. Whitehead, "From Force to Persuasion."

been built. The World War of 1914–18 revealed a deeper fault in the world order.

228. Nationalism and International Law Since 1919

The League of Nations, set up as part of the peace settlement in 1919, was a political attack on the problem of peace.[1] It was the beginning of an organized, international effort to settle the affairs of states with justice and without recourse to war. It was meant to be a charter for common action by all the nations. To give the actions of this political federation "validity," it was provided that when states entered into the Covenant they were obliged to stand by all the decisions of the League and support them by force, if need be. Any aggression by one state upon another of the associated states would call for instant united action. But before military action would be taken by any party, it was expected that discussion of the case would be held so as to prevent such open conflict.

Moreover, some of the causes of war were to be eliminated at the start by the adoption of a new principle of the political order. One of the recognized sources of trouble, for instance, was the subjection of some nationalities to the sovereignty of others, and it was therefore proposed that all nations should have the right to determine their own destinies and the form of their government. This introduced the principle of the self-determination of nations which had somehow to be combined with the principle of sovereignty belonging to the old order and not to be relinquished. The consequence of this was that nationalism gained tremendously in Europe. Every nation believed that it should be recognized as an independent sovereign state. The spread of this conviction released at once all the suppressed nationalistic ambitions and caused new difficulties in international politics.

229. The Abuse of the Principle of Self-Determination

The principles of state sovereignty and nationality have not been so easily kept together as the theory requires. According to the principle of nationality, every nation that can prove itself

[1] The full and accurate analysis of the situation since the setting up of the League of Nations is matter enough for a separate course of study, and what is here mentioned is only to supply enough material to illustrate the principles under discussion.

to be such is entitled to a self-governing, independent existence. This tends to multiply the number of small states. Such a process of dividing up can go on until it becomes quite uncertain which are the real effective units of political society.

Also another factor comes into the reckoning. Such small states are at the mercy of the large powers who really have and exercise a full-fledged, traditional sovereignty. Security requires, then, that the newly divided units must combine again in some way. It sometimes happens that nations which differ spiritually because of their past histories and cultures are nevertheless so closely linked with each other in the same geographic region that they need a continual economic relationship. But such interdependence can hardly be maintained without some political form of union, even though such merging is incompatible with their nationalistic passion for independence and the dignity of sovereignty. To survive, therefore, the small nations have either to federate and form larger political units or else to affiliate themselves with a more firmly established large state.

Though the general economic development of the world has brought about an actual international interdependence, extreme nationalism has attempted to defy this condition of affairs by making the national state so absolutely self-sufficient that it can be free from any dependence on others. In Germany this autarchy led to government management of all industry, commerce, finance, and whatever else affected the resources and available force the state could employ in time of war. Along with that went a policy of economic intervention, deliberately making a number of other states helplessly dependent. Such a policy naturally affected the whole international system of exchange and commerce. Even those nations that were sworn to a liberal policy were forced to counter the attack by similar controls and measures, contrary to their traditional economy. So in fact the independent economic system which had served for centuries as a basis of common interest for law was shattered into a multitude of opposing national economies, not only in Europe but throughout the world. To find a new basis for the resumption of world commerce is one of the problems of those nations which have united to fight all this destruction of the political and economic order of Western civilization.

230. (b) How It Is Possible to Have an Order of Law Restored

But the whole problem of our time is vastly larger than that of making any particular economic and political arrangements by individual governments. It is nothing less than the task of restoring civilization throughout the world. Are governments, however, competent to lay down an economy and law for the whole civilized order? We are apt to think so in wartime when they are already doing so much. If they make war, why can they not make peace? They must obviously make the settlement at the end of the war and begin rebuilding. But on what foundation? That is the question. For there *is* something which the political power of a government can never do, in spite of monarch's or dictator's dreams to the contrary, and that is to *create* a new order or society. The powers wielded by a government can only come from a *social community that already exists*. In the present instance, this means that there must be some sort of *community of nations* really in existence if law and order are to hold in the world. What are the possible foundations for an international community today?

Any community exists because the members within it stand together as one body on some common ground. They find this basis of community in their common interests, sentiments, obligations, purposes, or loyalties. Which among these may we build on for the reconstruction of law and order?

231. The Consciousness of Common Needs and Interests, and How It Can Become an Effective Force for the Community

All peoples now have an acute consciousness of the same needs of self-preservation and security, for a generation that has suffered two wars is urgently aware of that. They all need economic restoration, employment, food, clothing, medicines, the essentials of a subsistence. They can all benefit by the free production and exchange of goods through commerce — an international commerce. They will all be more secure if the minority and majority groups within them live in harmony with each other. And if these urgent necessities are to be supplied to all the nations, some universal rules of transaction and diplomacy are necessary, some laws that the nations will generally observe. That is what a political scientist or disinterested onlooker can see: *identical* needs and interests everywhere.

But this truth will not make a bit of difference in the actions of nations if the people of these nations do not realize that these are common needs and interests, necessary and good for all alike. For it does not follow in the least that if a lot of different nations everywhere want very badly the same things they will go out to secure them together and abide by the common rules of the right way to get their share. On the contrary, thinking only of their own desperate plight, each may try to get there first — America first, Britain first, Russia first, Poland first — all like Germany first, before the war. The truth that these necessities are common must be in the consciousness of the men and women of every nation. Everyone's thinking about his own good and the good of his nation will have to be guided by the principle that they must all march together towards their goals of peace, as they are willing to do in war.

Even more than that is required, however; for men cannot start on common action without making their intentions to do so clear to each other. They must declare and commit themselves and give pledges that they will make the common good their aim and a steady cooperation their method. This is the only way common interests can be made to serve as an effective basis for community.

232. The Moral Force of Obligation or Justice

But the notion of "interest" is much too small for the meaning that is here being put into it. What has been described is really Plato's "justice" or what Rousseau called "obligation" under the "general will." When men actually recognize that all have the same interests, and that others have the same rights as they themselves, then something bigger than interest is already at work in their hearts. They are acknowledging a moral obligation. It is a large obligation to consider the common good and to obey the common law and to respect the rights of other men. Of course self-interest is present. It is there all life long. It is what moves a man to make something of himself. And it moves nations, too, to achievement. But that is not enough to make a community life possible. Unless there is, besides self-interest, this moral force of justice and obligation, the existence of man in society is never good enough to be called "civilized." It certainly will not be peaceful or orderly.

233. An Examination of the Notion that National Interest Is a Sufficient Basis of Peace and Order

Obligation has to be superior to self-interest. But there are many who share the views of Hobbes and Thrasymachus, that self-interest always rules — first, last, and all the time. This means that in international affairs "national interest" is always to be supreme. Yet they actually believe that an international order is quite possible on the basis of such a policy. This notion calls for examination.

Let us consider what it means at this precise moment of history. Nationalism has been rampant, and we have been fighting it in its vicious, destructive forms of Fascism and Nazism. We also have to control and harness this spirit of nationalism everywhere, in our own nation as well as abroad. After we have put a stop to nationalistic anarchy, we want to advance towards civilization, and we are striving hard nowadays to find some common ground in order to go ahead. Any idea that turns the mind back to the exclusively national will sap this common purpose and defeat unified action for it. Of course, no one should ever neglect the needs and interests of his own nation, but the way to do that today is to keep one's eye on what is common to all the peoples and to find some universal principles on which all the nations can unite.

Now "national interest" cannot be such a principle. Selfishness sticks out all over it. Moreover, it does not have the true character of a principle, because there are just as many opposing interpretations of what national interest is as there are nations. This introduces a factor of uncertainty into world affairs, for one does not know what the policy means from day to day. Governments decide upon their policy by guessing at each other's plans and views. The resultant uncertainty arising in international politics is the mother of fear, and fear and suspicion are the sources of war.

This tendency of a national-interest policy toward war is even likely to be increased by party politics. Candidates who are seeking power are tempted to present the national interest in such a way as to win favor for themselves with the public. Politicians do not take the hard way of the prophets, reproving or correcting the false pride of their people. Instead they play up the rights of their nation, proclaiming it the favorite child of destiny, and thus contributing to a general nationalistic excitement in the world. But this is the very thing we are trying to put away from us, and we do not want to invite the catastrophe again.

234. An Example of the Right Way to Proceed — the Foundation of the American Commonwealth

As the founders of the American Commonwealth set out to launch their new state, they believed themselves called upon to declare precisely what they regarded to be their essential interests which they were willing to have the rest of the world scrutinize and judge. In the Declaration of Independence[1] and the Preamble to the Constitution they committed themselves to something definite and reliable. They set forth the principles of their policy as a nation. These have been good principles of cooperation because other people can follow them for their own good as well as we ourselves. All nations may be able to share "the blessings of tranquillity" whenever they adopt principles that will bear public scrutiny, and when they themselves meet all the obligations to which these principles commit them. This procedure in establishing a good society seems the wisest politics we have yet discovered. It teaches the lesson that the "national interest" ought to be openly declared in terms of some universal principles. If the principles stand the test of public inspection, they may then express the common interests of many other nations as well and thus become an international basis for peace.[2]

235. Summary: The Conditions of Peace and Order

The fundamental condition of peace is the existence of a strong sense of community — community of need, interest, principle, and aspiration. Nations have to turn their attention to the common good and recognize that they cannot possibly secure their own good without subordinating their national claims to the good of the whole system of nations. They have to grant other nations, too, an equal right to the necessities and opportunities which they are disposed to claim for themselves. When nations realize that they are existing in a real community, that their

[1] Cf. BR, No. 56, "The Declaration of Independence."
[2] Cf. BR, No. 66, Frank Kingdon, "Freedom in World Institutions."

national welfare requires a still more general welfare, and that other nations have the same rights and duties in the order as they themselves, then something which is over and above interest can move them, namely, justice or moral obligation. Then international law and a genuine civilization exist.

236. (c) The Reality of the Community of Nations and What Is Required to Maintain It

How much of a community of nations have we today, or how much seems possible in the present conditions? It is a larger world than was known before — it is Europe, America, Asia, Africa, and yet *one world*. The people of all corners of the globe are now in contact with each other at many points, and the least action in any quarter produces a reaction throughout the world. There is a worldwide tissue of relationships. The strands are in part the wires of communication. But there are many invisible strands that enable men everywhere on earth to know what good things civilization has produced in every region, so that the demand for these things becomes worldwide. The search for the means of obtaining the goods and acquiring science, technique, industry, and trade is likewise universal. Even the knowledge of the art of war spreads to every corner. The nationalism born of Europe's empires and history has gone into the empires of the East as well as throughout the West. Thus material needs, national interests, and the ambitions for a good life have all become universal.

But something else must keep pace with this spread of material civilization (see above, Section 202). When the economic system extends throughout the world there must be an equally wide understanding of the world-economy as something with *law* in it and not a mere tool for political manipulation. And vastly more is required. Corresponding to that, a network of political and military power on a world scale must be based on knowledge of the traditions and wisdom of the East and West, and North and South, and of the principles of an international order — and all this from a *universal* point of view and not from that of nationalism. Without such disinterested science, knowledge, and philosophy, which a sage of the East has called a knowledge of "what is common to men's souls," the prospective community of nations will have very little substance.

Above all things that make for community are the spiritual aspirations of men which are at the heart of life. In this larger world of the nations today there are superficially fewer obvious common heritages and convictions. If religion is only identified with creed, cult, or institution, there is now less community in the matter of religion. On the other hand, the experience of this World War has brought all peoples together in a profound consciousness of the misery and suffering of humanity and a need of some great religious hope and faith in things to come. And the actual meeting of men of various faiths in such times can produce great appreciation of the various established religions so that the common lessons of piety and love of one's neighbor can be realized.

But the aspirations and faith of the men of all nations need not be entirely other-worldly. A powerful aspiration may be seen in the hope of all peoples for a freedom which they have never yet known. In seeking such high things in common they may learn to pull together and recognize that greater common law in the life of man through obedience to which alone they will achieve their peace and true good.

H. THE MEANING OF DEMOCRATIC FREEDOM

237. A Description of the Ideal Community

The developing theme of this argument has been the freedom of man, the equal freedom of all persons and nations. The vision of the order in which such freedom might be realized is our contemporary ideal. A community dedicated to freedom and equality is a more perfect form of community than anything that has gone before.[1]

Consider what Aristotle had described as making a complete community: common location, customs, traditions, religion, and form of government. These make possible also the common sentiments of right and justice, the moral bases of the community. There arises, too, a high patriotic regard for the state. But the Greek state denied to many persons any good life at all. It

[1] Cf. BR, No. 57, Lincoln, "Address at Gettysburg."

established inferiorities and inequalities. Patriotism was evoked only among the small group of those who were equals in property, position, and power, and the civic bond was far less strong in practice than it appeared in Greek theory, where it remained an ideal. The family counted for less than the theory pretended as a tie holding men to the state, for the spirit of the Greek family, among those of position, was an exclusive and not a generous one, and Plato's condemnation had been a necessary warning. Greek education needed a more liberal character, too, as Plato had discerned. The conservative *Politics* of Aristotle tended to confirm as "natural" all the established practices in regard to property, slavery, and the family, as well as the various forms of government. The only advance possible was to temper one form with another in order to approximate as nearly as possible to the common good. But what *was* the common good? In the last analysis, for that philosophy, it was the good of the *status quo*.

When modern men shaped their theory of the state, they thought first along the lines of those shining examples of the civilizations of Greece and Rome. It is true that they had acquired a different attitude to "the world" through the Christian religion, but when they were setting up the modern state, they repeated the ancient pattern and its notions of property, and they sometimes even justified the rule of absolute sovereigns by analogy with the powers of masters over slaves. But men were now bent on being free in a free society. They had a self-respect and dignity which they would not surrender to sovereign authority. Those who were strong enough, therefore, struggled for their rights and freedom. These were at first the class whose intelligence and powers of management had made the economic order possible. They fought for the freedom to govern themselves. But the idea of freedom was not to be possessed only by men of property. It was seized on by all the people. It caused revolutions and then sent the Western World into the experiment of large-scale democracy.

A society aspiring to freedom and equality looks not to the past but to the possibilities of the future. The men of a community where all are recognized as free and equal persons can dedicate themselves to great achievements because they are inspired by an ideal that calls forth their highest personal energies and loyalties. Instead of the blind alleys of class system and inequality, they see before them avenues of greater life for each and all, where one man's gain will not be at the cost of another. In the vision of a free society, the goods of life are not already appropriated by a few to the exclusion of all others but are still open to all. Thus men can see the chance for personal achievement and reward. People who travel together on the way of life are firmly united under the banner of freedom. They draw closer together, too, as they realize that, through their union, everyone is liberated to a fuller life. So they are quite prepared for the discipline of law which is so necessary to any orderly existence. They are controlled by an inner moral obligation rather than merely by the external authority of a government. They value the whole community's sense of right and want to uphold it loyally, with a patriotism springing from the whole of their being. They make themselves a responsible and self-governing community. United by such deep inner bonds and loyalties, they are formidable to any external enemy.

When all these things are taken into account, the truly democratic community is at once finer and stronger than other societies the world has known. As Rousseau said, it is "the masterpiece of politics," and masterpieces are rarely achieved, being the fruits of genius; genius is an infinite capacity for taking pains.

238. The Equality of Persons and Rights

That is the ideal; in reality there are things in society today so wrong and so important that they can destroy all faith in the possibility of a democratic freedom. Liberty and equality are inseparable from each other. But there always *is* inequality. Everything depends on the attitude of men to this constant fact. Some people consider it "right." They argue, are there not differences among men, differences of mind, character, capacity, genius, and leadership? [1] And should these not be mirrored in the social order, so that each person takes the place for which he is best fitted?

Now it is true, men will never consider a social system right which prevents them from achieving their own place and its rewards. Some want profit and wealth; some want political

[1] Cf. BR, No. 7, E. G. Conklin, "The Question of Racial Differences."

power; some want the enjoyment of social position; some want to be left alone. Yet no one is ever prevented from attaining his own good because of the principle of democracy. In fact, the criticism today is that the prevailing system prevents great numbers of men from having the opportunities to work, to prove their worth, to have a place of dignity in society, and to share in the things that other men regard most highly, and it is therefore condemned as undemocratic. The ideal of democracy contains within it the principle of the Platonic Republic, that men should have only the positions and rewards which they merit by their performance.

But the ideal contains, besides, the Christian teaching that no matter what place a man has in society or what work he has to do in it, be it to labor with his hands or with his head, that task is a vocation dignified in the eyes of God, and it ought to be so in the eyes of all men too who should see their own mortal life in its proper perspective. The equality that goes with liberty is thus an equality of men as spiritual persons.

But it must also have some real meaning in the actual order, and this is found in the common rights of man. When people, no matter how different in capacity, are living near enough to each other in society to need the same things for a decent life as persons, they must have the same rights to these essentials. Equal rights are necessary, therefore, if freedom is to be freedom for all, and all men are to be truly *men*. And whenever such rights are denied, freedom is impaired and human aspirations stifled. The unity of society then disappears fast. Thus the attitude of men today toward this question of equality is going to decide whether or not contemporary democracy will be a good and lasting society.

PART IV. THE MEANING OF RELIGION FOR MAN

John Herman Randall, Jr.

Columbia University

A. WHAT RELIGION IS AND DOES

239. No Society Is without Some Religion

We have already been led at various points to consider that fundamental human enterprise we know as "religion." We found that, along with language, social organization, art, science, and technology, "religion" is a distinctive activity of human living. No being other than man performs any actions which seem even remotely comparable with the practice of religion. Yet of all the many different human societies that history has recorded and anthropology explored, none has ever been discovered in which men did not engage in some kind of religious practices. Together with characteristic ways of making a living and getting along with each other, every human culture possesses certain other well-recognized ways of acting, feeling, and believing which we call "religious." It is through their religion that societies have given human life some satisfying and meaningful relation to the universe in which man lives; it is in religious terms that they have normally expressed their best wisdom in the conduct of human affairs.

This is an impressive fact. It is one which no thoughtful man, trying to understand the world in which he finds himself and the kind of fellow-beings among whom his lot is cast, can fail to take into account. Whatever his own experience of religion may have been, and whatever attitude he may take toward churches and religious teaching as a result of his training or his encounters with men, he cannot afford to neglect the significant and important part that religion has played, and continues to play, in human living. The presence in every society of religious institutions, attitudes, and beliefs is a very important fact about men and their ways of conducting their lives. It is also an important fact about the world in which men live, which seems so uniformly to have provoked men to practice some form of religion. In seeking to understand and appraise that world, we can hardly afford to neglect the fact that it leads or drives men to religion, any more than we can neglect the facts that it forces moral choice upon men, inspires them to create works of art, and stimulates some at least to scientific inquiry.

240. Different Views of Religion

In our own society, there are many who would maintain that religion — and they mean of course the distinctive religion in which they have been brought up: Methodist, Catholic, Lutheran, or Jewish — is an institution ordained of God and bestowed upon men that they may obey God's will and fulfill his purposes on earth.

Secondly, there are many others who would hold rather that religion is a great achievement of human civilization, painfully worked out by men themselves over the centuries in their long search for a clearer and purer vision of God and for a better and more just way of living. For this group, religion is a cumulative cultural achievement of mankind that has come to embody the successive moral and spiritual insights of an impressive line of prophets and saints and religious geniuses.

Thirdly, there are still others who have little or no interest in any organized form of religion or in any religious practices or ideas. Such things have either never meant anything at all in their lives or else have lost whatever meaning they may once have held. This third group are quite content that those for whom religion — any religion — does possess a real meaning should practice it. But they find they themselves have no time for such concerns, just as some men are insensitive to music or possess no appreciation of painting.

And finally, there are of course those who have a contempt or an open hostility for all religious beliefs and practices. These "anti-clericals" and "atheists" base their attitude on evidence that may range from casual contact with hypocrites or fanatics to a serious analysis of the way in which religious institutions have operated in society, both in their long history and in the present day.

241. The Widespread Ignorance of Religion among Americans

What is most novel in the religious situation in our own country today is the very large number of men, especially young men, who fall into the third group, the mass who are quite indifferent to religion, not as a result of some disillusioning acquaintance with it, but out of sheer ignorance of everything that has to do with religion. Probably never before have so many men failed to have any feeling or judgment at all about religion. They just do not care whether religion does any good in human living and human society, or whether the good it may do is outweighed by the evil, because they simply have little or no idea of what religion actually does and means.

Men in other societies have normally been almost completely ignorant of all forms of religion save their own; the average man has been hardly aware that there are others. Because of the great variety of churches and sects in our country, Americans have been spared this particular ignorance. But in a country with a single religion, like Italy, for example, although there have been plenty of people indifferent or actually hostile to it, such men have at least known what it was they did not take seriously or were opposing. In Italy there have long been anti-clericals and even atheists; but they have certainly known what the Catholic Church and religion had to offer men, and what part it played in the life of their country.

Multitudes of Americans today do not possess such knowledge of any form of religion. And this includes not only those who may have been brought up with no affiliation or without much contact with any church. It includes a very large part of those whose parents have been church members, and who have grown up with at least some nominal connection with a religious body. They may have belonged to the young people's society for the sociability it offered; they may have occasionally attended church services. But as to the real meaning and significance of the religious practices they have taken part in, they have not the faintest idea.

This is particularly true of the various Protestant denomina-tions — and of many Jews as well. It is notorious that these churches have not made a very good job of the religious educa-tion of their children. They have resorted to various devices to attract and "hold" their young people; and where there have not been too many competing distractions, some measure of success has attended their efforts. But among these devices, ar, education in the fundamentals of their religion itself has not been very prominent. The Catholics have been much more successful in teaching their members what it is that their religion is and does, though they too have taught little about other faiths. Nearly all of us would do well to realize that we are really in no position to decide whether there is anything in religion or not, or what there is to it, until we have found out much more about the matter than we now know.

To attempt to understand the nature and function of religion in human life on the basis of a casual and rather external observation of what religion seems to be doing in America today is to limit oneself to the evidence furnished by a very narrow experience under conditions far from typical. It is very much like trying to understand what man's great achievement in artistic creation holds for the human spirit on the basis of an experience confined to attendance at Hollywood movies. It is like deciding what music can mean in human life when the only music we have ever heard has been the average swing band.

We should be honest enough to admit that most of us are very ignorant about religion, and that our experience of it has been very inadequate. To make up our minds about religion and to pass judgment on its real significance for human living, merely on the basis of what has come within our own provincial ken, shuts us off from sources of power and vision that are of first-rate importance. And such a snap judgment will blind us to any real understanding of other peoples and other civilizations. For we can never share what is vitally human in the experience of those other great peoples with whom we must live in an evershrinking world, until we understand and sympathetically appreciate how they have all served God, each in its own distinctive way.

242. The Place of Religion in American Life

Our society has not succeeded very well in providing an education in even the forms of religion it professes. It has afforded even less opportunity to find out about what religion has been and has done in other times and other civilizations. This comparative failure is not wholly the fault of our churches, our teachers, and our educational setup. It is really symptomatic of the greatly altered position of the traditional forms of religion in contemporary America. For most Americans, religion has become, during the course of the last two generations, an incidental concern reserved for their leisure time — perhaps for an hour or two on an occasional Sunday. It remains a controlling and dominating interest, as it has been for most other times and societies, only for special groups and for exceptional individuals. Hence for one whose experience is limited to the present scene, and whose knowledge does not extend to other cultures or even to the past of our own, it is very hard indeed to visualize the central place in personal and social living which religious attitudes and practices have normally occupied, and continue to occupy, in most other societies.

The lives and thought of present-day Americans have indeed been profoundly influenced by the great religious heritage which has entered so deeply into the formation of the typical American character and attitudes. An earnest moral idealism, a humanitarian zeal, and a generous interest in setting the world aright — such practical idealism directed toward human welfare and social good is surely characteristic of the latter-day American temper. This is what "religion" itself has come to mean for multitudes today. It is the legacy left in many an American heart by the fading of concern with any particular creed, dogma, or church. It expresses the vague religious life of the "unchurched," of that great body of Americans who, while continuing to feel Christian sentiments, feel also a deep distrust of all "institutionalized" religion, of all churches. It has penetrated, to a far greater extent than they themselves realize, the congregations of those that remain faithful to our various churches. It colors the activities of great historic communions and has produced in them all what may well be called a distinctively American form of the religious life. It might be said that this is what Christianity has come to mean for multitudes of Americans. But it is really broader than Christianity, for it is shared by many American Jews and by various other religious groups that have consciously broken with the Christian tradition.

243. The Place of Religion in Other Societies

But in other times and other cultures religion has not been merely a vague sentiment and a resolute goodwill and benevolence. Such goodwill and such active, practical moral idealism are indeed precious to Americans and to their neighbors in our cruel world. With all its hatreds and its warring fanaticisms, the world sadly needs more of them today. But the great religions, those whose horizons and sympathies have extended beyond the narrow limits of a single nation or a single culture, have offered to mankind, and still have the power to offer, far more than that.

Set any American down in a strange land — in a Moslem country, in one of the Latin American countries to the south, in one of the great Oriental civilizations, or even in the Catholic cultures of the Mediterranean. What is sure to impress him as most novel and most strikingly unlike anything in his previous experience is not merely the different customs and habits of an alien people. It is rather the way in which those customs and habits are caught up and organized in a whole body of religious practices; it is the central place which religious institutions hold in this people's personal and social living. Religious beliefs dominate their views of the world, religious observances govern their actions, religious precepts regulate their relations with their fellows. Religion is the cement that holds their culture together.

If our American be narrowly provincial, he may well at first be repelled by the strangeness of the ways of the "natives." Their ideas seem a mass of superstition, their observances a picturesque but meaningless mumbo-jumbo. Their behavior is unfamiliar and seems often incomprehensible enough. But if he possess a normal American curiosity and thirst for new experience, he will not stop there. He will want to find out about these people; he will try to understand why they act the way they do, and how they look at the world. And if he persists, he will begin to discover something of what a wholly unfamiliar religion can mean and do in human life. He will be led on to reflect on the function of religion in human experience. If he be thoughtful, he may wonder what American life would be like if Americans practiced and lived their religion as easily and naturally as these other peoples seem to do. He may even wonder what his own life might be like were he to take his own inherited religion seriously.

244. The Strength of Religious Loyalties

Such a vivid personal experience of the power which religion possesses in other societies to organize and express and direct men's living makes the reports of travelers and the records of history come alive. This power raises many serious questions. What has been the source of this strong hold which religion has exerted over men's feelings and actions and thought? What has religion given to men, what has it done for them, to create so deep a loyalty? Why have men been willing to undergo great hardships, to leave home and friends, like the New England pioneers, and migrate to a "howling wilderness," rather than give up or forswear their religion? Why do so many communities, even today, set their religious loyalties above all other interests or claims — the Protestants of Ulster, the Catholics of Poland, the Moslems of India, the Jews of Palestine, and all the long list of others? Why have the churches, Protestant and Catholic alike, been able to put up so strong a resistance against the Nazi forces? The days of the martyrs are not yet past.

Religions can be strong enough, even in our world. And men at their strongest — in resolute opposition to injustice and oppression, in the very face of frustration and failure — do hold a faith which we must call religious, which unites them with the resolute men of faith in ages past.

245. The Darker Side of Religious History

But is this strength of religious loyalties, is this faith enough? It is, in fact, the very power of religious feeling, expressing itself in fanaticism, in intolerance, in exclusive claims and in persecution, that has for centuries provoked the most serious criticism of religious ideas and institutions. That cornerstone of the American tradition, the freedom of every man and every group to worship God as God grants them light, was not won in a struggle against any purely secular authority or against any political state. It was painfully achieved against the exclusive claims of religious authorities, against authoritarian churches. The bitterest struggles of all are religious wars, conflicts between rival faiths. "To how many evil deeds has religion persuaded men!" exclaimed Lucretius, patron saint of all anticlericals.

These facts, to which the critics of all ecclesiastical institutions may point, are true enough. Nor has anti-clericalism been confined to Christendom. The pages of history record plenty of cruelties, plenty of intolerance and persecution, perpetrated in the name of every religion that has acquired the power to insist on its exclusive claims. Men have invoked the name of God to consecrate their highest aspirations; they have also called on him to justify their cruelest passions. Consider the tortures of the Spanish inquisition, intended to lead heretics back to the "one true faith." Americans may well reflect that, although religion does not occupy in their own land the central position it enjoys in many others, this fact carries with it certain compensations. Nor is it at all clear that what America needs most today is a single, unifying religious faith, which might well be just as intolerant as those of other lands.

246. Religion as a Whole Is Neither Good nor Bad

This darker side of the way in which religions have worked among men in the past makes clear one very important point. Religion is widespread; it seems to satisfy deep needs in human nature and in human society; it may well be socially indispensable. But this does not mean that everything a religion does is necessarily good. Religion is a fact of human experience, like political action or personal conduct. It is the name we give to a complex set of ways of acting, feeling, and believing; and these ways perform a great many different functions. But they are by no means all equally good, any more than all conduct or all political action is good.

Religion is no more to be judged good, or bad, as a whole than is any other of the great types of human activity. Some religions are indeed better than others, although it is a very difficult matter to pass such sweeping judgments upon the great universal religions which are so deeply rooted in complex civilizations and express such varying patterns of life. But it is clear that within a single religion some of its ways of acting and believing are far better than others. And there is no religion that has not at times embodied in its practices many elements which any sensitive man today would hold to be evil. We are here using "religion" not as a term of praise for something that is by definition "good"; we are using it descriptively to denote things that men do and feel and believe, things that have far-reaching consequences in their lives. Whether the great religions in general, or whether our own religion in particular — whatever it may be — does not on the whole accomplish more of good in human life than of evil, is a question we must postpone until we have examined more carefully the kinds of thing that religions do accomplish.

Recent experience has made clear one point, at least, about the relation between intense religious feeling and some of the unhappier consequences to which it has often led in the past. Men and societies do not need a supernatural religion to drive them to fanaticism and intolerance and persecution. Mighty nations in our own world have committed all the crimes that have ever been charged against religion, without claiming that they were doing the will of a jealous God. They have in fact broken completely with their own religious past and have included their own traditional religions among their victims. A knowledge of human nature and of man's history would suggest that if men had not in the past committed their crimes against their fellowmen in the name of religion and God and church, they would have committed those same crimes in some other name — of race, perhaps, or nation or economic class.

Religious practices furnish the means of expressing any deeply felt emotion — not only men's aspirations and loyalties but also their baser passions, prejudices, and hatreds. Religions can bring to a focus men's rivalries and ambitions as well as their fellow-feeling and benevolence. In one sense, religions are little better than the turbulent human life they express; they are the most intensely human of all the activities in which men engage. It is hardly intelligent to blame the mirror for what it reflects or to think by breaking it to transform the scene.

247. The Development of Standards of Better and Worse within Religion

In another sense, religious practices are a lens rather than a mirror, bringing men's feelings and desires to a sharper focus. For, in expressing even hatred and intolerance in religious terms, men must employ religious symbols; and those symbols are associated with their highest insights and values. The discrepancy thus revealed proves genuinely shocking. It is one thing to give vent to narrow, nationalistic prejudice and war fever in a political address. It is another to express it in a prayer to God: it is then hard not to feel a sense of revulsion. This focusing of men's most intense desires in a prayer to the Most High does something to those desires: it "clarifies" them, we say; it helps to criticize them. It is small wonder that German Nazis recently wanted a new mythology; the Christian symbols must have made them feel far too uncomfortable. It is in this fashion that the religion of a people can serve as an intellectual and moral challenge to their passions: it can be better than their average feelings and attitudes and summon them to a higher level of living.

What is most significant here is that the history of every major religion has contained a long succession of men who have attempted to eliminate the worst elements and increase the better ones. A religion develops its own standards of what is of greatest value in that religion itself. Prophets, saints, and religious leaders arise who seek to purify their religion and to reform its institutions; they endeavor to remold what they find into more "spiritual" form. Religions are doubtless always in need of further reform and purification, like every other aspect of the life of man. But they are reformed and made to serve their function better, less from without than from within, by men themselves nurtured on the best that these religions have to offer. External pressure, to be sure, often plays a large part in forcing churches to listen to their best leaders; it recalls them to their true inspiration. The Catholic Church was itself driven by the Protestant revolt to accomplish a drastic reformation at the time of the Council of Trent; it was forced to a further self-purification by the anti-clerical policies of the French Revolution. But it is religious leaders who carry through the really fundamental and enduring changes for the better. The severest critics of the crimes committed in the name of religion have been prophets within the church, who have appealed to the best in their religion to cast out the worse.

248. Conflicting Religious Claims

We have raised the question of what are the critical standards by which we can judge the value of different religions and of different practices and beliefs of the same religion. Of course, most men assume without much thought that their religion, and their particular form of that religion, is obviously superior to the curious and superstitious practices of other peoples. How could intelligent men, they ask, possibly take any stock in that kind of nonsense? This has been a standing puzzle for the followers of one faith when confronted by those who practice another. This is the attitude of the average Christian when he encounters the observances of orthodox Jews, for instance. He would do well to realize that it is also the attitude of the average Jew toward most Christian beliefs and ritual. And for all but the most reflective and sympathetic this attitude persists, even when they are prepared to admit that, in conduct and moral standards, the man of differing faith is a thoroughly good fellow. If such an attitude is so deep-seated, even between members of the same culture, how much more difficult is it to overcome between members of two different civilizations! — between an American and a Chinese, for example, or an Englishman and a Hindu. Superficially at least, societies and cultures seem to differ in nothing so much as in their religious observances.

Many would, of course, go further. Not only is their own particular and familiar religion superior. It is the one true religion; all the rest are mere idolatrous superstitions. Until fairly recently, this complacency was commonly shared throughout Christendom; it is still the professed position of many historic churches. It was this conviction that they were in sole possession of a truth the world needed that was the original inspiration of the great enterprise of Christian missions to the Oriental peoples. It happens also to be precisely the attitude of the other major missionary religion, Islam, and of the less expansive Eastern faiths as well — which may account for the comparative lack of success of most Christian missions among those peoples.

The presence of different religions, each making such absolute and exclusive claims, poses one of the most serious of all the practical problems connected with religion. It is a problem to which our world will have to give its most earnest attention in working toward better understanding and cooperation in the future. But these claims raise also a most important theoretical problem for any thoughtful mind. How can we determine the validity, the "truth," of our own particular religion and of other great religions? Debate on this question is unceasing, and, when it is uninformed about the many different religions of man, rather fruitless.

249. The Objective Approach to the Functions of Religion in Human Life

Let us therefore postpone for the present the question of whether our own familiar religion is the one true faith — even if it happen to be that common American religion of practical moral idealism. Let us not ask, at this point, whether ours is not clearly a better religion than those of other peoples and civilizations. Let us instead approach the religious tradition with which we may be presumed to have some familiarity, in much the objective spirit of the American whom we placed in the midst of an alien culture. Being of an inquiring mind, he wanted to know why he found men acting the way they did, how they looked upon the world, and what their religious practices and beliefs really gave to them. Let us ask these same questions of religion in our own culture, of our own various forms of Christianity and Judaism. What have they to give to men today? Is there really anything in them?

There is an old story about two men discussing the practices of the different Protestant denominations. One asked the other, "Do you really believe in total immersion?" "Believe in it?" his friend asked in turn. "Why, I've actually seen it!"

It is in this spirit that we are proposing to examine what religions do for men. What differences that can really be *seen* do they make in men's lives? To find out how religions operate in human living and what they have to offer men, we shall start out from religion as something to be seen by an observer. "By their fruits ye shall know them." This kind of knowledge is indispensable for an understanding of the functions religion performs, both in the lives of individuals and in the total culture of a society. For in inquiring into these functions, we are dealing with facts that can be observed and ascertained; they are perfectly "objective" or public matters. They can be, and for several generations now have been, made the object of serious and careful scientific investigation. Psychologists, anthropologists, sociologists, and historians have managed to amass a huge body of information about religion that can be used to correct the inadequacies of our casual personal experience. They have erected upon it a number of well founded generalizations about which there can be little argument. We cannot hope to give an intelligent answer to the question "Is there anything to religion?" without drawing heavily on the results of these scientific investigations.

Merely examining men's religious life objectively will not, of itself, take us to what men have found most significant in their religion. Although we shall set out from religion as something to be *seen*, we cannot of course hope to end our examination on that level. In the next section we shall try to get closer to the heart of religious faith by looking at it, as it were, from the inside. But our present approach from the outside will reveal something of what men's religion has done to them, what part it has played in the rest of their living and in their culture as a whole.

250. Religion as an Observable Social Institution

However great the value of the vision religion enables men to see, the religion that men practice is, at the same time, something that can itself be observed and seen. Viewed objectively, it comprises certain things that men do — a set of characteristic ways of acting and behaving. This is reflected in our common speech. What do we mean when we say of a man, "He is religious" or "He is a Christian"? The first and simplest meaning is, he is a member of some church or religious body; that is, he attends its services, takes part in its rites, recites its creeds, and follows such observances as his religious community enjoins. Thus, he may go to confession, attend mass, and fast on Fridays; or he may observe the holy days, light Friday candles, and follow the dietary laws. Such men, we say, are "practicing" Catholics or Jews. The Oriental religions enjoin a still more elaborate set of public observances. Protestantism, especially in the Calvinistic form that has so deeply colored its attitudes in America, was born of a revulsion against such merely "external" observances. Protestants, like Reformed Jews, have reduced them to a minimum, so that a Protestant is usually not thinking of such ceremonial acts when he asks, "Is Smith a religious man?" Yet even those sharing this Protestant distrust of ritual observances would hardly call a man a Presbyterian or a Methodist who belonged to no church and never attended services.

For a religion is not only certain things that men do; it is things they do *together* with their fellows. It is a social enterprise, a set of organized and habitual ways of acting, an aspect of a group culture, certain characteristic cultural traits of that group. This is true even of what we call a man's private or personal religious life. When we ask, "Is Smith a religious man? Is he a Christian?" we may well fail to be satisfied when told merely that he is a church member. "I don't mean that," we may say; "I mean, is he really religious?" Or we may say of Jones, "He is a true Christian, even though he never goes near a church." We are here clearly referring to a man's personal religious attitude, to his character and principles. But we should scarcely call that personal attitude "religious" or "Christian" if it made no observable difference in his life and did not lead him to do any of the things we expect "Christians" to do. And such an attitude — even the intense inner personal experience and vision of the mystic — is obviously something that has been formed and molded within a particular religious tradition and builds on the attitudes and practices of some organized socially expressed religion.

Thus the most personal religious feeling is really an individualized expression of something that is basically social in character. Even when a man has formulated a purely private "religion" of his own, involving perhaps a set of wholly novel beliefs, we should not call that a "religion" if it were not directed toward some at least of the same concerns as are familiar religions, and if it did not do for him some of the things they have done for men. When we say that one man makes a "religion" out of science, or that business is the "religion" of another, we mean that such men have the same faith in the values to which they are devoted as others place in the broader values of religion.

In their lives those pursuits play the central and organizing role that a living religion plays in the lives of its adherents. We mean that they have found something that does for them some of the *kinds* of things that socially organized religions do. In certain respects, it has a function *like* that of a religious institution.

251. The Social Materials of Religion

In most societies, religion has not existed apart from the rest of men's living. It has been an organized expression of the feelings, activities, and beliefs that have seemed emotionally significant and valuable. Religious practices and attitudes have expressed and colored the entire round of activities in a culture. They have embraced everything in human life that men have felt deeply and provided appropriate ways of acting in which men could share and celebrate together these common feelings. These religious practices have thus "celebrated" and "consecrated" the normal social activities and the accustomed techniques of living. They have also built up strong feelings against any violation of the ordinary and approved procedure. At the same time, religions have given particular expression to men's emotions of need and uncertainty in the face of whatever seemed extraordinary and mysterious, like personal or group disaster.

In simpler societies, the religious life has consisted primarily in ritual, that is, in doing something together with one's fellows in the presence of deep and shared feeling. It has been something lived out rather than thought about, often something danced, performed. Such ritual is naturally concerned with the most important acts and crises of a people's life. It grows up as the appropriate reaction to such social activities as hunting and war, planting and harvesting. Since most men until very recently have tilled the soil, all religions observe as ancient heritages important agricultural festivals celebrating the turning points of the farmer's calendar. These are clear in Judaism and only slightly less clear under the symbolism with which they have been overlaid in Christianity.

All religions have likewise provided appropriate rites for celebrating the significant stages in the life of man. The individual crises of birth, adolescence, marriage, and death, with all they mean to a man and his fellows, have demanded some religious observance suitable to the solemnity of the occasion. Men feel these matters deeply, and their emotion expresses itself in rite and ceremony. Men also feel awe and dread before the mysterious, the unexpected, the unlooked-for, the unfamiliar. Guilt demands restoration, sacrifice, penance, atonement. Men feel the need to do something, to perform some holy dance, some sacrifice, to appease an angry deity. The group remembers those who in the past have been successful in an uncertain world and, remembering, invokes their aid.

The very doing seems to help. It has a power of its own. Magic rites multiply. Men who intensely desire something find themselves doing what they desire. They make rain-like noises in their hope of rain; they celebrate victory in the hope that victory may come. For an agricultural society, the rebirth of vegetation in the spring is of momentous concern; what is more natural than to practice sympathetic magic and, by frenzied human procreation, seek to invoke the fecundity of nature? Winter kills, and spring revives; let man too, in baptismal rite, die and be born anew.

All these religious ways of acting and feeling themselves had consequences: they performed a very important function in the social life of the group that practiced them. They served to bind together and unify that society emotionally, making a tribe, a city-state, a kingdom, or a people into a living and "spiritual" union. They helped that people to be conscious of themselves as a group, to live and work together. They generated common loyalties and ties, a common and shared experience, a common world of the imagination, a common vision of the values of life. Even in their crudest form, they made it possible for that group to be a group and to survive in a hostile world. This function of intensifying shared feeling and loyalties, shared awareness of and devotion to a common purpose, is one of the basic services that all religious celebration and consecration perform. It persists, as a fundamental function of religious activity, in persecuted and oppressed minorities like the Irish, the Poles, and the Jews — like so many of the peoples of occupied Europe today. It is responsible, also, for much group clannishness, exclusiveness, and hostility to other groups.

252. The Refinement and Criticism of Religious Materials

This social bond of shared feeling is really but the raw material out of which the more distinctive and higher functions of religion can be shaped. As civilizations developed, men became more intellectually curious, more interested in understanding, and in reasonably consistent explanations. They deepened their moral insights and began to extend the narrow boundaries within which they insisted that men should act in ways that seemed right. Their religions began to place more emphasis on these intellectual and moral interests. Myths were turned into explanations of the striking features of life and of the world, its origin, and its development. These myths became the answer to man's curious whys, and merged insensibly into a kind of speculative science. Rites, myths, and magic began to take on a moral significance; they came to be the symbols of moral customs and ideals. Reformers arose, prophets and leaders, who sought to remold the old ideas and ways of acting into a form that would answer better these intellectual and moral demands. They in turn faded into the realm of magic and myth; rites gathered about their memory. Sacred books set down the customs and ritual, the messages of the prophets, the aspirations of the more far-seeing leaders. The great civilizations developed corresponding organizations of the religious life, with complex social institutions, elaborate lore, immemorial ritual.[1] Together with ancient spells and rites, sacrifices, prayers, and other forms of worship, they came to embody the successive insights of spiritual geniuses.

Viewed as an historical phenomenon that can be seen, religion has been primarily an organization of man's emotions and conduct. It has been a way of feeling and acting together in the face of the important concerns of life. In societies that have developed an intellectual interest, it has also been a way of thinking and believing; but, with few exceptions, systematic belief has been a secondary and derived matter. Religion was a social force before the gods were born; it has persisted in civilizations like India and China and Greece where the gods have given way to other less personal interpretations of the world.

[1] For some examples of these processes see BR, No. 80 B, "The Divine Mission of Shinto," also sections A and C under Shinto.

All religious traditions contain a host of rites and forms that are obviously survivals from primitive days; they have been successively reinterpreted and invested with moral and spiritual significance.

Judaism and Christianity were likewise organized about primitive rituals and myths, and many of their traditional forms reveal the presence of such "survivals." Yet in them, as in the other major religions, this core of magic rite and imaginative myth has served to organize the emotional and moral life of highly civilized peoples. It has been enriched by the ethical insight of prophet after prophet until its symbols have come to express the highest human aspiration and the most generous sympathies. It has furnished a poetic interpretation of the heights and the depths of human experience, and imaginative wisdom for the conduct of life, a common realm of ideals in which generations can live and move, a wealth of imagery and symbol to inspire the artist. It has focused men's ambitions and aspirations, clarified them, and led men on to new insights. It has given them courage and power and consolation, in communion with their fellows and with the saints who lived of old. It has provided another world for the mind of man to dwell in, a realm of ideals from whose contemplation men return with renewed vigor. The enriching of this realm of insight and imagination to express more and more of human interest, feeling, passion, action, and thought has been the greatest human achievement of Christendom.

253. The Christian and Protestant Emphasis on Theological Beliefs

In most societies, the successive refinement and criticism of these social materials of religion have been moral and imaginative or artistic, rather than intellectual. The primary function of religion has not been to offer the intellectual explanation of anything, to serve as a rival to philosophy or science. Although all religions are rich in myth and legend, this imaginative lore has normally not been something to be believed intellectually, but rather something to be accepted and used, as the religious teacher uses parables, to point a moral or symbolize an ideal. Religion has been regarded in Judaism and Islam as a "law" to be followed; in Buddhism and Hinduism, as a "way" or "path" of life to be pursued; in Confucianism, as a code or standard of conduct to be observed. The Oriental religions have been very practical, concentrating on conduct and behavior. They all take religion, not as a set of beliefs to be accepted as theoretically true, but as a life to be lived, a path to be followed.

Christianity, together with Brahmanism and certain forms of Buddhism, forms an outstanding exception to this generalization. Ever since the Christian gospel, early in its career, began to appeal to men in the ancient Hellenistic world who had come under Greek influence and developed a strong intellectual interest, Christianity has had a marked concern with explanation, with systematizing and organizing its beliefs into a "theology." This concern with theological beliefs increased with the Schoolmen of the later Middle Ages and reached its height in the great Protestant reformers, who insisted that all Christians must hold correct doctrine. They transmitted it to later generations of Protestants, who, partly because they were minimizing external observances and ritual, and partly because they were giving religious expression to a society in which the intellectual urge to understand was very strong, gave a central place to religious beliefs and adequate intellectual interpretations.

The Greek thinkers of the ancient world endowed Christianity, and to a less extent the Judaism that has flourished within it, with a complex philosophical theology, a set of propositions about God and his relation to man, which expressed their own faith in Reason and Knowing. This theology, though rarely understood and often taken as a "mystery" to be accepted on faith, has enabled the Christian beliefs to serve as symbols for intellectual as well as moral values. In the Christian tradition, scientists and philosophers have again and again been able to express their devotion to intelligibility and truth in Christian forms; and great Christian thinkers like St. Augustine and St. Thomas have interpreted God to mean Truth, that Truth which is the source of all other truths.

It has been natural for the religion of a society which, above all others, sets high store by knowledge, science, and understanding, to give intellectual and scientific values a central place. It is natural for it to regard the explanation of the world and of life as a major function of religion. Even today, the average man would probably say that he means by religion the *belief* in God, though he would be hard put if he had to explain the meaning of God which the great theologians have worked out.

Protestants soon came to interpret their distinctive doctrine, that man is saved by "faith," to mean that he is saved by accepting and holding the correct or "orthodox" beliefs about God and man and human destiny. The consequence was, not that Protestants persisted in a rigid adherence to any of the subtle, elaborate, and profound systems of beliefs in which the Reformers — Luther, Calvin, and the rest — expressed their deepest understanding of the world and of man; it was rather that they successively modified these beliefs in the light of their own changing and growing understanding of life. Since for them correct belief was essential to religion, any new knowledge or new experience had to be incorporated in their religious faith.

254. The Resulting "Conflict" between Religion and Science

On the one hand, this emphasis led many Protestants to identify their faith completely with a set of scientific or philosophic propositions about the world as the scene of the moral life. In the eighteenth century this tendency culminated in the reduction of religion to the three ideas of "rational theology": God, freedom, and immortality. In the nineteenth century, it tended to associate religion with the more elaborate systems of philosophical idealism stemming from Hegel, who held that religion was really the expression in symbolic form of the truths he had succeeded in stating in exact and philosophic fashion. For both, it made religion a set of propositions to be believed, essentially a body of *knowledge*.

On the other hand, this identification of religion with a distinct kind of knowledge made inevitable the long "conflict" between the religious beliefs that made up "faith" and man's growing scientific knowledge. No sooner had men incorporated as central in their religion some parts of scientific or philosophic knowledge than new scientific discoveries or new philosophic theories seemed to challenge those already embodied in their religious beliefs. This incompatibility has usually been called the "conflict between religion and science." It could be so viewed only by men who identified religion with theological beliefs, and who furthermore assumed that the function of theology was to give a theoretical explanation of the world and of human nature. Because Protestants have made these assumptions, they have faced plenty of "conflict" with science and philosophy. But that conflict has clearly not arisen between science and religion, for the function of religion, as we have seen, has not been primarily to provide knowledge or explanation at all. It has not even been a conflict between science and theology, for theology does not offer an explanation of the things that science explains. It has been a conflict between newer and more extensive scientific knowledge and older and inadequate science, enshrined in religious beliefs.[1]

Assuredly, there is a place for intellectual belief, for reason and intelligence, for knowledge and truth, in the religious life. If these things are to have a place in our life at all, they must be consecrated in our religion. But to the objective observer of religions, starting from what he can "see," the significant functions of religion in human life do not seem to be to provide theoretical knowledge. The religion of a complex society, especially the religion of the subtle, the reflective, and the learned, will normally express and consecrate intellectual and scientific values. It will normally draw on and incorporate the best scientific and philosophic knowledge available. But religion itself seems to be primarily a way of feeling and acting, not a way of understanding and explaining. The relations of theology to explanation are much closer — so close that any theological formulation will reflect the knowledge of the society in which it is effected and will be strongly colored by the prevailing intellectual methods. But if we consider how theological beliefs actually function in the religious life, it is difficult to see how they could seriously conflict with scientific explanations. In any event, it seems clear that theology has not played the central role in most religions that it has performed in Christianity, and in Protestantism in particular.

In minimizing theological formulations, in subordinating and forgetting the elaborate doctrinal systems which earlier distinguished the historic Protestant churches, Americans seem

[1] Cf. BR, No. 87, A. H. Silver, "Science and Religion."

in fact to have returned to the more normal religious emphasis. The theological differences which once set off Presbyterians as "Calvinists" sharply from "Arminian" Methodists no longer hold much meaning. The differences that remain are largely matters of historical accident and social prestige, which vary from locality to locality, together with certain more subtle differences of attitude and emphasis. Nothing is more common in American religion today than to disparage all theology, to elevate the "religion of Jesus" above the "religion about Jesus," to insist that what a man believes does not count so long as he lives a Christian life. There is a sound instinct in this distrust of intellectual differences in religion; only the confirmed intellectual antiquarian is likely to object, and of all men he should be the first to accept facts. In ceasing to be true to their historic Protestant past, American Protestants have been truer to the great tradition of religion.

255. The Critical Function of Religion

Far more important for religion than any presumed function of providing understanding or knowledge has been its function of bringing men's true desires to a focus and placing them side by side with the highest ideals men know. A religious tradition embodies the deepest insights of a long line of prophets and sensitive spiritual leaders. When the passing needs of the moment are brought into close contact with this store of ethical wisdom, the result is inevitably a "clarification" of what men really want and a criticism of transitory enthusiasms. This is the most valuable of all the social functions of religion.

That some form of religion is indispensable to any society seems no longer an open question. It has been long debated whether a society could get along without any religious organization of its life. Recent experience has made clear that if a traditional religion disintegrates, men will not calmly proceed to live without any religion at all. A new religion, or, if we prefer, a new substitute for religion, will spring up to fill the vacuum and to perform the historic functions of a religion. And this new "religion" will be much worse than the old one it supplants. For it will inevitably express some need of the moment; it will be onesided and fanatical. It will forget much of what has been

learned through the bitter experience of generations because
it will lack what the great historic religions have received, the
criticism and clarification that have been born of centuries of
human experience. The new social faiths of Europe reveal their
rawness and crudeness at every turn.

256. Summary: the Functions of Religion

We have suggested that the three fundamental functions of
religion, for the objective observer, are first, *celebration*, the social
observance, in appropriate ritual form, of the values to which
a group is devoted; secondly, *consecration*, the cooperative dedication to those values; and thirdly, *clarification*, the reflective criticism and appraisal of their significance and worth.[1]

Of these three functions, that of celebration, of public worship,
seems to have been for some time on the decline in American
religion. It is clear that we must accept the religious emphasis
we have inherited and find about us, as the material upon which
to work, with all its limitations. For it is impossible to create a
wholly new religion; one can hope only to work with, modify,
and reform one already in existence. New religions are either
weak, attracting a merely personal following, or else impatient,
short-sighted, and forgetful and uncriticized fanaticisms. The
emphasis on a moral idealism is steadily growing. American
religion may hope to clarify its moral ideal; it would be Utopian
to expect it to transform itself into the analogue of the religion
of the Breton peasant or of orthodox Judaism, with all their
public observances.

B. WHAT RELIGIONS GIVE TO MEN: SALVATION

257. Religion from the Inside

In approaching religion as something to be seen, as an observable social institution, we have thus far been looking on religious
activities from the outside, in rather conscious imitation of our
American set down in an alien civilization and curious about
the unfamiliar ways of the "natives." Let us now try to get still

[1] Cf. BR, No. 82, H. F. Rall, "The Nature and Fruits of Religion."

closer to what religion holds for men by coming at it, as it were, from the inside. Let us ask what a religion gives and means to those who practice it; let us try to get the "feel" of it from the point of view of its actual adherents. How does it look to them? What good do they find in it? What are the rewards and satisfactions of religious faith? Why do men belong to and support churches? Why do they attend services and engage in religious practices, like prayer? Why do they take religious teachings seriously? Why do they feel they ought to make a real effort to lead a "Christian" life?

In other times, for many men the answer to these questions would have been: because it was expected of them; because it was what people did without question. In large parts of present-day American society, however, certainly in our cities, there is no longer much social compulsion to conform outwardly to conventional religious practices. The craving for social respectability still operates, to be sure. In many localities the church attended by the best set flourishes, and purely professional motives have been known to lead physicians and lawyers to become church members. But there has probably never been a society in which men were more free to decide for themselves whether or not religion means something significant in their lives. Those who do accept the responsibilities of professing a religion, accept them because that religion seems to them worth while. It gives them something that they really want; it satisfies needs that they feel.

What are these satisfactions that the practice of a particular religion can give to men? They are clearly many and varied, and doubtless few men feel them all. And they differ widely in importance and intensity. They range from the sheer sociability that can come from taking part in the activities of any group, to the deepest and most enduring satisfactions that the life of man can know. Perhaps for most men the sum-total of the relatively minor and incidental satisfactions of religion is, in actual practice, more important than the central goods which religions profess to give. But let us start by asking, what are those central satisfactions which deeply religious men have found? What does religion offer that makes it, for such men, the controlling aim of human living?

258. From the Observation of Religions to Religious Vision

In Section A above, we considered religion as something to be *seen*. But what we can thus observe about religious behavior hardly exhausts the satisfactions that religion offers men. For religious men are fundamentally concerned with things that cannot be "seen," at least not with the eye of the body or with the instruments of the scientist. Some of these objects of the religious life cannot be "seen" because they have not yet been incorporated into men's practices. They are, as we say, "ideal," meaning that they are the objects not of observation but of aspiration and faith. That great religious genius, Saint Paul, defined religious faith as "the substance of things hoped for and the evidence of things unseen."

However, in most religions men have been convinced that they were not only concerned with ideals as yet unrealized in men's conduct. Their faith has extended to objects which, in their very nature, can never be so embodied, which must remain forever "ideal." These objects belong to another order of being; they "transcend" or exceed the limitations of human experience. As Saint Paul put it, "We look not at the things which are seen, but at the things which are not seen: for the things which are seen are temporal; but the things which are not seen are eternal."

Most men would agree that Saint Paul's distinction is fundamental. Religion embraces not only a host of practices and consequences in living which can be "seen." At its core lies a kind of "seeing," a kind of intellectual vision, of something that is not of this world, although for those who see it clearly it becomes the most important thing in the world. The traditional religious term for this intellectual vision, or faith, is "the vision of God."

A wise student of human life today, the philosopher Santayana, has well expressed this central factor in religion which leads beyond something that can be *seen* to a kind of *seeing:* "In every age the most comprehensive thinkers have found in the religion of their time and country something they could accept, interpreting and illustrating that religion so as to give it depth and universal application. . . . The vistas it opens and the mysteries it propounds are another world to live in; and another world to live in — whether we expect ever to pass wholly into it or no — is what we mean by having a religion."

This "other world to live in" belongs to the things which are not seen but are eternal. It cannot be observed in the way in which we can see a particular ritual of baptism, like total immersion. We hearken to the reports of those who have beheld it with the eye of faith, realizing the while that now we all see in a glass darkly. If we are wise, we shall listen to as many reports as we can, hoping that thereby we too can be led to a vision of God. And we shall try to enlarge our own vision through the endeavor to enter sympathetically into the visions beheld by other men and other religions, and to look through their eyes beyond the things of this world. That is why the body of readings in connection with Part IV of this book contains so many of the efforts of other men in other ages and climes to express their vision of the things that are not seen but are eternal.

The long history of religion, with all its periods of decay, its reformations and rebirths, has been the history of the search for a clearer vision of the things which are not seen, for a more adequate knowledge of God and of the demands he makes upon man. It has not been the history of the finding of more adequate proofs that God "exists," but rather of men's deepening insight into what God is. Those who have seen God most clearly — the great religious geniuses, the saints and prophets — have felt no need to prove his "existence." They have rather done his bidding and enjoyed his peace or proclaimed his judgments and his will. And men have hearkened to them and lived their lives in the light of that wisdom. In religious vision and the fruits it brings, they have found supreme satisfaction.[1]

259. The Language of Religion: Its Symbolic Function

It is significant that, in passing from the discussion of the observation of religions to the question of religious vision, we have found ourselves employing a rather different kind of language. It is not the appropriate language of the social scientist investigating the functioning of religions. It is rather what we should recognize as "religious language." It is not a language about religion but the language of religion itself. It is what

[1] Cf. BR, No. 82, "The Nature and Fruits of Religion," section a.

Plato called "the language of probability." He employed it in his religious and moral "myths" or illustrative stories. It is the language of the Gospel parables.[1] It is clearly different, both in its forms and in its functions, from the literal language found in the statements of science. It is used to convey a sense of what men *feel* about their experience and to awaken in others the same attitudes and emotions. In expressing and communicating this shared feeling, it employs metaphors and "symbols" and religious ideas which different men would understand differently if they attempted to translate them into the language of exact statement, but which have a common emotional and "religious" meaning.

Religious *language* provides a set of *symbols* in terms of which men can express and share the experiences they feel deeply, and relate them to the "things which are not seen." This same function is performed also by all the other practices of religion. This is especially true of the various techniques of religious worship, of rites, ritual, and observance. They are all definite ways of behaving, particular acts to be performed, which carry with them a *symbolic* meaning. That is, they stimulate and communicate to all who perform them certain common and shared feelings and attitudes toward experiences that affect them profoundly and help to awaken religious vision and strengthen religious faith.

Thus the ritual of a funeral service expresses men's common feeling of bereavement and loss. It then focuses the emotions of sorrow upon the enduring and permanent values of which the earthly life of the spirit inhabiting this particular mortal flesh was a transitory illustration. This power of religious symbols, in language and ritual, to express a deeply felt and shared emotion and redirect it toward a vision of the eternal, is clearest of all when men stand in the presence of the death of one whom they have known and loved.[2] There are few indeed, even in our secular-minded society, who do not feel on such an occasion the need and the appropriateness of some religious observances and some expression of religious vision. You cannot bury a man like a dog.

---

[1] Cf. for example, BR, No. 78 E, "The Parable of the Prodigal Son."
[2] Cf. BR, No. 75 F, "The Parable of the Mustard Seed."

260. The Central Satisfactions of Religion

What, then, is that vision which brings the highest satisfactions of religion? To the old question, "What is the chief end of man?" the Westminster Confession of the Presbyterians answered: "To glorify God and enjoy him forever." The great Jewish philosopher Spinoza asked the same question: "After experience had taught me that all the usual surroundings of social life are vain and futile; seeing that none of the objects of my fears contained in themselves anything either good or bad, except in so far as the mind is affected by them, I finally resolved to inquire whether there might be some real good having power to communicate itself, which would affect the mind singly, to the exclusion of all else: whether, in fact, there might be anything of which the discovery and attainment would enable me to enjoy continuous, supreme, and never-ending happiness." And though Spinoza's intellectual interpretation of God differed greatly from the Presbyterians', he concluded his rigorous inquiry with the same religious answer: "From what has been said we clearly understand wherein our salvation or happiness or freedom consists: namely, in the constant and eternal love towards God. . . . Love towards a thing eternal and infinite feeds the mind wholly with joy, and is itself unmingled with any sadness, wherefore it is greatly to be desired and sought after with all our strength." [1]

Joy, love, enjoyment, never-ending happiness — these are the terms in which deeply religious men speak of that "real good" which religious vision and faith give them.[2] In all probability the average man has not ordered his life so exclusively toward a single end and goal; but he too can taste in his religion something of this abiding joy. It is perhaps most familiar to him as "peace" — that "peace of God that passeth all understanding." The beautiful benediction we have inherited from the ancient Hebrew priests expresses it: "The Lord bless thee and keep thee, the Lord make his face to shine upon thee, and be gracious unto thee, the Lord lift up his countenance upon thee, and give thee peace." [3]

[1] Cf. BR, No. 32, Spinoza, "What Are the True Ends of Life?"
[2] Cf. BR, No. 78 H, "St. Paul in Praise of Love."
[3] Numbers 6 : 24–26.

What is this "peace" that men find in religion? One answer is clearly stated in the contrast with which Spinoza concludes his description of man's true good: "The ignorant man is not only distracted in various ways by external causes without ever gaining the true acquiescence of his spirit, but moreover lives as it were unwitting of himself, and of God, and of things, and as soon as he ceases to suffer, ceases also to be. Whereas the wise man is scarcely at all disturbed in spirit, but being conscious of himself and of God, and of things, by a certain eternal necessity, never ceases to be, but always possesses true acquiescence of his spirit." And a Christian philosopher, Reinhold Niebuhr, puts it in the idiom of our own day: "To understand life and history according to the meaning given it by Christ is to be able to survey the chaos of any present or the peril of any future, without sinking into despair. . . . In that case the alternate moods of despair and false hope are overcome, and the individual is actually freed to live a life of serenity and creativity."

261. "Salvation" as the Function of Religion

The traditional Christian term for this abiding good which all forms of Christianity have professed to give men is "salvation." The great majority of Christians would undoubtedly answer, in reply to the question as to why they were Christians, that they hoped thereby to "save" their souls. But "salvation" is a term in the language of religion; it can stand for a problem and a set of feelings and attitudes that are common to men whose ideas and philosophies are as different as those of Calvin, Spinoza, and Reinhold Niebuhr. "Salvation," that is, is a *function* which religions perform; but just what it consists in, and how it is to be effected, is a question on which the profoundest religious insight has varied, and over which the different Christian churches have come into existence.

262. Salvation from the World: Otherworldliness

There are many who would hold that the Christian gospel, as proclaimed by their particular church, promises men salvation for their immortal souls from the pains of Hell in the world to come. For those whose religious concern is genuinely focused on this problem of their eternal destiny, all the other satisfactions which religion can give, all the other functions it can perform in this mortal life here below, cannot fail to seem quite incidental. For them, salvation is an escape from this world into another; for them, the joys of religion will be the joys of preparation and anticipation. "Now we see in a glass darkly, but then face to face; now I know in part, but then shall I know fully."

Most Christians have always professed such a belief about their ultimate destiny; and many, especially in other ages, have taken it with the seriousness it demands. For them religion has given not merely another world to live in, it has revealed the "real" world, by the side of which our ordinary human life is but a transitory interlude. Such "otherworldly" Christians have gathered together in monasteries or in solitary cells, the better to live constantly in the light of the life to come. And the great religions of India and the Far East, likewise viewing the ordinary conditions of human life as something men seek to be delivered from, have established similar monastic institutions for those in whom this concern with salvation from life is controlling.

In present-day America this otherworldly and monastic ideal is confined to very small groups. It is so alien to the temper of American religion that we find it very hard to understand, and need all the help we can get to approach sympathetically those other peoples for whom it was, and remains, a dominating ideal. We are the heirs of the Protestant Reformers who rejected the monastic ideal and an otherworldly religion; we can even feel some sympathy with Marx, who called all concern with the world to come "the opiate of the people." Still, amid the evils of our present world, it should not be wholly impossible to understand, if we cannot share, something of the revulsion with which men in the past, and in the hopeless squalor of the poverty-stricken Oriental lands, turned aside from the miseries and frustrations of living to find something more worth while and more "real."

Interestingly enough, it is among those whose beliefs are poles removed from those of the otherworldly monks — among our disinterested scientists and scholars in their research institutions — that we find the closest parallel in our society to such a monastic ideal. The increase of sheer knowledge their labors bring we should all hold to be a benefit to mankind. But the monk, too, prayed for the world and strove to increase man's heritage of spiritual insight. And his disinterested service of the God of Love produced incidental human fruits of moral energy and purified vision that can well stand comparison with the benefits we gain from our servants of the God of Truth.

The monk who sought salvation from this world was, in his own eyes, choosing the better part; he has told of the deepest satisfactions that religion can give, the intense joys of what Spinoza called "continuous, supreme and never-ending happiness." For him religion surely brought salvation in this world, even as it gave the hope of salvation in the next.

263. Salvation from the Fear of Hell

Popular Christianity, both Catholic and evangelical, has continued to make concern with the world to come its central drive. The "sanction" for its observances and precepts has remained the hope of Heaven and the fear of Hell. Thus, Catholics and orthodox or "fundamentalist" Protestants alike find it very difficult to conceive how men can lead a moral and religious life without the threat of a Final Judgment lurking in the background. In this distrust of the strength of religious faith and moral vision without the enforcing power of a Divine Judge, Protestants have failed to remain true to the insight and faith of the great leaders and churches of the Reformation.

Luther and Calvin alike insisted that "salvation" comes from faith, not from any good works or merit of man. According to Luther, men are "saved" by God's forgiving love in Christ; salvation comes when men realize that God has already pardoned their sins and reinstated them in his favor or grace. The church exists to preach the Christian gospel that the Divine forgiveness is freely offered to all men. According to Calvin, men are "saved" because God in his mercy and inscrutable wisdom has chosen them for "election" to salvation. The church exists to proclaim the Word of God, to train men in obedience to his law, to help them to live the Christian life of holiness and godliness.

In neither case does salvation depend on anything men themselves do, on any human merit. Salvation is not won by leading a Christian life; it must precede such a life as its necessary condition. Freed from all religious fears, the Christian will be at peace. He will practice his religion and follow God's commands, not for the sake of gaining any future reward, but because he truly knows, trusts, and loves God, and finds in his precepts the highest wisdom. He is free to glorify God and enjoy him forever, to enjoy in gratitude and love all the satisfactions of religion.

Popular Protestantism was unable to remain loyal to this clarifying insight of its prophets, and came, instead, to reflect once more the Catholic position that men are saved because of their own actions, because of their "good works." This prudent and common-sense attitude reached its clearest expression in the religious thought of the eighteenth century. Men then held that religion is nothing but the belief that God will punish drastically any infringement of the moral code he has established for men. These eighteenth-century advocates of "rational religion" thus made it completely otherworldly in its beliefs: they reduced religion to certain propositions about the world to come. At the same time, they made it most this-worldly in the practices and moral ideals it sanctioned: they seriously tried to eliminate from the Christian tradition whatever in it seemed to them of no earthly value. Their test was, "Will it make a man any the better citizen?" Out of all the wealth of aspiration, feeling, emotion, expression, symbolism, and poetry of the great Christian tradition, they looked only for an incentive to good citizenship. Men had forgotten the manifold satisfactions religion has to offer. It is little wonder that, at this time, the church played almost no part in men's lives and came near to perishing.

There are few today who would look on the function of religion in such simple, not to say simple-minded, terms. Religion does, indeed, provide a "sanction" for the best in human living; it powerfully reinforces all the incentives for living up to our highest ideals. But we have found out too much about the complex ways in which it does so to take it as a mere policeman's club. We have carefully examined the various means by which different religions have, each in its own way, strengthened their followers in remaining true to their best light. We have carried out detailed psychological inquiries into the complex manner in which character is formed and personality directed. We have thus arrived at a much more adequate understanding of the relations between the practice of religion and the achievement of that sure good which is salvation.

The attempt to make the moral life depend on religious threats, on the fear of Hell, appears today to have rested on a faulty psychology. We no longer try to educate our children by such crude threats. We realize that to entrust the moral direction of men to the policeman alone, even to a Divine Policeman, means that we have pretty completely failed to build up the much stronger forces of morale and self-discipline. And this detailed psychological knowledge we have acquired as to how men's moral standards actually function reinforces the testimony of the great religious geniuses of the race who have approached God, not in fear and trembling, but with joy and ecstasy, who have loved him rather than feared him.

264. The Role of Eternal Life in Salvation

Christians have indeed always been convinced that the freedom and peace, the blessedness and salvation their faith can bring, are things to which the circumstances of time are wholly irrelevant. Human beings can attain a quality of living in which men reveal their total incommensurability with the physical body that sustains their life. The existence of human personalities for a brief interval in time and space seems like a passing illustration of something which "is" in a wholly different way. The significance of that illustration is to be sought, not in the body on which it depends, but in the vision of timeless and eternal ends it achieves. It is not by having died but by having lived, by having found salvation, that the soul of man puts on immortality.

This is the conviction that the experience of salvation has normally brought to Christians. It is in this confidence in the ultimate irrelevance of death to the things that men hold most dear that they have faced the terminus of human life. "Death is swallowed up in victory. O death, where is thy sting? O grave, where is thy victory?" In explanation of this ringing faith, men have elaborated doctrines not always consistent with each other, like the resurrection of the body and the immortality of the soul. Death and bereavement are too insistent facts in human experience not to demand some religious way of meeting them and rising above them.

Hence, for Christians, salvation has involved what is called in religious terms "eternal life" and has brought with it the conviction that what is best in man is untouched by death.[1] Man's "soul" is immortal. But it is doubtful whether such "immortality," however it be conceived, has ever been the exclusive, or even the central, satisfaction religion has brought. Christians, like the adherents of some other faiths (though by no means all) have agreed with Plato that men should so lead their lives that at the close they could face the scrutiny of a searching Judge. But for them, salvation has been primarily a present reality, not something to be gained only in the future. Whatever further it might involve in the future, salvation has been a religious good they could possess in this life, and the abiding satisfactions of religion they have enjoyed here and now. Even when belief in a literal Hell was widespread, the "Hereafter" was not a flight, an escape from the ills of life; it was the one fact that, struggle as men might, was inescapable. Christians have rarely forsaken action in this world to dream of a good time coming. When they have dreamed of the Future beyond the grave, they have usually dreamed, not of Heaven, but of Hell. It is no wonder they have dreamed as little as possible and have tried to put the Hereafter out of their lives and thought.

For Protestants, religion has been, in the first instance, a salvation in this world, not from it. Those who have taken most seriously the need of God's forgiveness have found its more immediate fruits in the Christian life as lived among men on earth. Traditional theological symbols and imagery, as they appear in the familiar hymns, for example, still picture salvation in the terms worked out in the Christian scheme of redemption — like the "judgment seat" and the "bliss beyond compare." But the place which the Hereafter has actually come to occupy in popular religious feeling, in contrast to the traditional fear of a literal Hell, is well indicated in the common phrase, "the Christian hope of immortality."

Most Christians "hope" for some sort of immortality, especially in the presence of the death of their loved ones. They have come

[1] Cf. BR, No. 78 I, St. Paul, "Concerning Earthly and Spiritual Bodies."

to conceive it in social terms, as so much else today is conceived, and find the essential sting of death in its sundering of all human earthly ties and relationships. But Christian faith was, and is, rooted in something far stronger than a "hope." The very fact that for a century men have found it necessary to engage in so much dubious argument in support of "personal survival" is a clear indication that notions of a "future life" have come to play a minor role in the religious life of multitudes of Christians. One has no need to engage in desperate apologetics to prove the "reality" of the really central satisfactions one's religion affords.

265. Salvation from Sin

Whatever role the fear of a future Judge may have played in the popular Christian imagination, the great Christian geniuses and teachers have conceived "salvation" in far different terms. Nor have they ever thought of it as primarily a deliverance from death. There were, after all, many other religions competing with the early Church in the Roman world, all of them offering men salvation from sheer death. What distinguished the Christian gospel, as it has distinguished all the great religions that have enjoyed a perennial vitality, was the *moral* salvation it secured.[1] It brought men salvation from *sin*. Even in announcing the Christian's triumph over death, St. Paul added, "The sting of death is sin."

What the term "sin" means in the language of religion is clearly stated by St. Augustine: "There are two causes that lead to sin: either we do not yet know our duty, or we do not perform the duty that we know. The former is the sin of ignorance, the latter of weakness. Now against these it is our duty to struggle; but we shall certainly be beaten in the fight unless we are helped by God, not only to see our duty, but also, when we clearly see it, to make the love of righteousness stronger in us than the love of earthly things, the eager longing after which, or the fear of losing which, leads us with our eyes open into known sin." [2]

St. Augustine is here pointing to basic facts of our moral experience, familiar to every thoughtful and sensitive man. Man is a

---

[1] Cf., for example, BR, No. 75 B, "The Foundation of the Kingdom of Righteousness."

[2] St. Augustine, *Encheiridion*, Edinburgh, T. and T. Clark, The Works of Aurelius Augustine, Vol. IX, 1873.

"sinner"; that is, he dimly sees and ineffectually gropes after better things. He needs light, he needs a clearer knowledge of good and evil. But he needs more than light, for he cannot by his own efforts live up to the best that he knows. He needs power to direct his will toward what he knows to be good. Man is both morally ignorant and morally weak. He needs moral teaching, illumination as to what is best to do, what is really good. And he needs moral power and strength of character to do it. He needs the "salvation," the "saving grace," which St. Augustine himself found so abundantly in his own Christian faith. These two elements, moral ideals and precepts, and the strength of will to follow them, are what men have above all sought and found in religion. Without them, they are cut off from God and doomed to fall short of what they know to be best. With them, they can "know God" and enjoy eternal life.

266. Differing Estimates of Human Nature: Confidence and Distrust

Different religions, and different teachers within Christianity itself, have placed a different emphasis on these two needs of human nature. Some have felt that man's greatest need is for more knowledge. They have stressed man's ignorance of what is good and have looked to religion primarily to provide men with moral teaching, with an education in the highest ideals men have been able to discern. They have had confidence in man's natural moral power to follow the highest that he can discern, when it has been made known to him. In recent times, such men have emphasized the teachings of Jesus — his statement of the Golden Rule, his proclamation of "love" as the highest human ideal, love to God and love to man, his insistence on the fatherhood of God and the brotherhood of man as the essence of religion.[1]

The author of the Gospel of St. John set just such a high estimation on knowledge. In defining the salvation brought by Jesus, he said: "This is life eternal, that they should know thee the only true God." Clement of Alexandria, who, like all the Greek Doctors of the Church, thought that knowledge was man's greatest need, understood the Christian life to be the

---

[1] Cf. BR, No. 70, "A Sheaf of Golden Rules from Twelve Religions."

search for knowledge and virtue; he took salvation to be man's progressive education by reason.

Others, claiming a more "realistic" vision of human nature, have impatiently brushed aside man's need for a more adequate moral ideal as of little consequence in view of his obvious failure even to live up to the ideals he does cherish. The classic statement of the central experience of moral struggle and failure in human nature comes from St. Paul, the formulator of traditional Christian theology and the first great exponent of Christian distrust and pessimism as to the powers of human nature. "For we know that the [Jewish] law is spiritual: but I am carnal, sold under sin. For that which I do I know not: for not what I would, that do I practice; but what I hate, that I do. But if what I would not, that I do, I consent unto the law that it is good. So now it is no more I that do it, but sin which dwelleth in me. For I know that in me, that is, in my flesh, dwelleth no good thing: for to will is present with me, but to do that which is good is not. For the good which I would I do not; but the evil which I would not, that I practise. But if what I would not, that I do, it is no more I that do it, but sin which dwelleth in me. I find then the law, that, to me who would do good, evil is present. For I delight in the law of God after the inward man: but I see a different law in my members, warring against the law of my mind, and bringing me into captivity under the law of sin which is in my members. . . . Wretched man that I am! who shall deliver me out of the body of this death?" [1]

On the road to Damascus, Paul beheld the vision of the risen Christ and was delivered. [2] No longer did the "flesh" lust against the "spirit": he was freed from bondage to sin and had found moral salvation. "For the law of the Spirit of life in Christ Jesus made me free from the law of sin and of death." And Paul preached to all nations his gospel of deliverance from temptation and moral struggle.

That other religious genius, St. Augustine, for whom likewise moral struggle and temptation and the discovery of sources of moral power had been an intensely personal experience, set forth the stages of man's life without religion, and of the salvation

---

[1] Romans 7 : 14–24.
[2] Cf. BR, No. 78 F, "The Conversion of St. Paul."

it could bring through the moral strength or "grace" it gave men: "When, sunk in the darkest depths of ignorance, man lives according to the flesh, undisturbed by any struggle of reason or conscience, this is his first state. Afterwards, when through the [Hebrew] law has come the knowledge of sin, and the Spirit of God has not yet interposed His aid, man, striving to live according to the law, is thwarted in his efforts and falls into conscious sin, and so, being overcome of sin, becomes its slave. . . . This is man's second state. But if God has regard to him, and inspires him with faith in God's help, and the Spirit of God begins to work in him, then the mightier power of love strives against the flesh; and although there is still in the man's own nature a power that fights against him (for his disease is not completely cured), yet he lives the life of the just by faith, and lives in righteousness so far as he does not yield to evil lust, but conquers it by the love of holiness. This is the third state of a man of good hope; and he who by steadfast piety advances in this course, shall attain at last to peace, that peace which, after this life is over, shall be perfected in the repose of the spirit, and finally in the resurrection of the body. Of these four different stages the first is before law, the second is under law, the third is under grace, and the fourth is in full and perfect peace." [1]

267. Overcoming Evil through the Vision of Good

These passages from great religious teachers, which we have quoted in their traditional language, around which so much religious feeling has clustered, have been read by generation after generation of men and have given them strength and courage and moral power to meet the decisions which life has forced on them. All the central terms — "flesh," "law," "spirit," "grace," "sin," "eternal life," and the rest — are terms in the language of religion. That is, they are religious *symbols*, which point to profound feelings and experiences in human living, but which can be, and have been, subjected to endless reinterpretation, as man's experience has changed and his knowledge has grown. As traditional terms, they may mean little to many modern Americans, who are not particularly concerned with understanding what their experience has in common with the

[1] St. Augustine, *Encheiridion.*

experience of men who lived long ago. But they certainly meant something of basic importance to the men who first set them down and to the generations who have read them in a variety of tongues. These men have something to say to us, and we would do well to try to understand what it is that they are saying.

In its deepest meaning and in the bitterest needs it exists to satisfy, religion is concerned with the attitude men shall take in the face of the insistent presence of evil in human experience. No thoughtful or sensitive man can ignore this fact of evil or fail, in some fashion, to come to terms with it. There are a host of specific physical evils which our science and skill can hope to remove. There are many of the ills of human society which we are confident a better education and better social arrangements could remedy. Toward abolishing as many of these specific evils as may lie in our power, we should indeed employ all our resources; and in fact religion has served as the strongest drive toward this never-ending task.

But there are other evils which will remain despite our best efforts; we can hardly dispose of them by the easy advice, "Go thou and do away with them." There are the physical evils that seem inevitably bound up with the conditions of human existence, like sickness and death and sorrow. For these evils, man need assume no personal responsibility. But they seem to demand more than the Stoic attitude of sheer endurance; they challenge men to reveal their stature as men, as moral personalities capable of using even inevitable evil as an instrument to further growth of character and insight.

There are the still more oppressive evils which are due to man himself, which he inflicts on his fellow-man, both unwittingly and in ignorance, and, terribly and awfully, with full intent. For these sins of others, conscious and unconscious, we cannot escape a certain common responsibility; we have acquiesced in them, we have profited by them, we have provoked them, and done little or nothing to prevent them. Only the hardened individualist will ask, "Am I my brother's keeper?" Most of us in these socially-minded days are convinced that we *are* responsible for the faults of others and especially for the faults of that social system whose guilty fruits we acquiesce in. It does not matter that you or I cannot, of our own efforts, help it. What we are responsible for and cannot help is nevertheless wrong.[1]

And there are those hardest evils of all to bear, those we find in our own hearts and lives. Even in accomplishing what seems to our best wisdom right, we find ourselves compelled to act in ways which we know in our hearts are wrong. There is not an American who does not yearn to do all in his power to bring to a speedy close this present war. But there are few Americans — especially those involved in deep personal responsibility — who like to dwell on what we are doing to the enemy to accomplish this laudable end. We see no other ways in which to finish the job we are convinced we have to do. But we know just how damnable those ways are. And these crimes we are forced to commit in a just cause are but an accentuated form of the tangled web of all human living. The pains and sins committed inevitably in achieving the better are the worst of all for sensitive men to endure.

How, then, can a man live with the evils nature forces on him? How can he live with the evil he has allowed to grow up in the hearts of his fellow-man? How can a man live with himself? It is to these tragic problems that the most profound religious insight has attempted to discover some answer. And until that answer has been found, men have not attained "salvation," they cannot enjoy "peace" and what Spinoza called "true acquiescence of spirit." That abiding good which is the fruit of religious faith is not the "happiness" of the untroubled child, oblivious of the evils of existence and quite innocent of the more tragic facts of life. It is a "beatitude" or "blessedness" of soul, a serenity of spirit that has faced evil and risen above it. It has found deliverance from evil in the vision of a Good that places evil — even the evil in one's own breast, the evil of "sin" — in a proper perspective.

268. Salvation: a Present-Day Interpretation

Bertrand Russell, who is not usually thought of as a religious philosopher, has made clear this deliverance that religious men have called the vision of God: "The world has need of a phi-

---

[1] Cf. BR, No. 74 D, "The Folly of War."

losophy, or a religion, which will promote life. But in order to promote life it is necessary to value something other than mere life. Life devoted only to life is animal without any real human value, incapable of preserving men permanently from weariness and the feeling that all is vanity. If life is to be fully human, it must serve some end which seems, in some sense, outside human life, some end which is impersonal and above mankind, such as God or truth or beauty. Those who best promote life do not have life for their purpose. They aim rather at what seems like a gradual incarnation, a bringing into our human existence of something eternal, something that appears to imagination to live in a heaven remote from strife and failure and the devouring jaws of Time. Contact with this eternal world — even if it be only a world of our imagining — brings a strength and a fundamental peace which cannot be wholly destroyed by the struggles and apparent failures of our temporal life. It is this happy contemplation of what is eternal that Spinoza calls the intellectual love of God. To those who have once known it, it is the key of wisdom. By contact with what is eternal, by devoting ourselves to bringing something of the Divine into this troubled world, we can make our own lives creative even now, even in the midst of the cruelty and strife and hatred that surround us on every hand." [1]

C. WHAT RELIGIONS GIVE TO MEN: FELLOW-SHIP, GUIDANCE, AND FAITH

269. Religion as One Concern among Others

We have been examining that central satisfaction of religion traditionally called "salvation." We have found that it has varied from the promise of deliverance from the pains and suffering of existence itself, in the otherworldly ideals of the great Eastern religions and of some forms of Christian monasticism, to triumph in this world over the oppressive fact of evil, normally through the vision of some Good that lies beyond this world.

[1] Bertrand Russell, *Why Men Fight*, New York, The Century Co., 1917. Compare BR, No. 41, B. Russell, "A Free Man's Worship."

That it can give men salvation, deliverance, and peace is the supreme claim religion makes. And, for men who deeply crave and need such religious "peace," this claim is valid; such salvation is what they find and prize most highly in religion.

But we also noted that, for most men, there are other satisfactions that religions give, satisfactions not necessarily brought to so sharp a focus in an intense personal experience. Few men have passed through the inner struggles of a Paul, an Augustine, or a Buddha; few have so single-mindedly sought a supreme good as Spinoza. And there is no convincing reason why all, or even many, men should. It is natural for the religious leader, devoted to his profession, to proclaim that faith must permeate and control the whole of life. The minister, especially if he shares the vision of the prophet rather than the wisdom of the priest — and what Protestant preacher does not fancy himself a prophet? — is convinced that religion must come first or not at all. But the vast majority of men are not professionals but laymen; and the layman is, by definition, one for whom religion does not come first — in practice, whatever he may profess. Religion is but one of his many concerns, bringing him certain distinctive satisfactions among a variety of others. The healthy-minded layman likes to hear once a week that religion is the supreme satisfaction, that salvation is the chief end of man. He believes it — when he is not too busy to remember.

270. The Layman and the Professional

It is natural for the professional — the minister or priest — to emphasize the importance and universality of those experiences which drive men to seek salvation. In the measure that he can lead men to feel them deeply, they will come to him for the insight and guidance he has to give. Evangelical preachers of religion have always made central the great pains of living from which their particular gospel offered a deliverance. By the imaginative rendering of the fires of Hell, by the endeavor to produce a "conviction of sin" in the interests of "conversion," or by subtler attempts to make men more sensitive to the evil that is bound up with even their best efforts, preachers have always tried to shake the self-satisfaction and complacency of their congregations and to awaken men's religious needs. And since these needs are genuine enough, though rarely so intense as the prophet desires, the attempt is usually successful. Men take great satisfaction in having their wants stimulated, especially when there is at hand a ready means for satisfying them.

But most men never find in their religion "supreme, continuous, and never-ending blessedness" — nor do they really desire any such thing. The emotional strength to meet life, the sense of meaning and significance, the guidance and direction they need — these things that are involved in the development of character and in a reasonably satisfactory adjustment to the natural and social conditions of living, men can and do find in the practice of religion. But they achieve them through less exalted means than the "ecstatic bliss" or "supreme good" which "salvation" has brought to the great religious geniuses. It is these humbler, but no less important, functions of religion that mean most to the average man. They comprise what he may reasonably count on finding in religion.

For it is with religion as with science or art. The average man does not expect to be an original scientist or a creative artist. But this does not prevent both science and art from having things of inestimable value to give him. The satisfactions which inspire the scientific discoverer or the artistic genius are not those which the average man can hope to find in either science or art. He cannot share the single-minded devotion to the passionate search for passionless truth; nor can he take part in the intense joys of artistic creation. Nevertheless, he can hope to share the knowledge the scientist discovers, something at least of the method by which it has been gained and verified and of the practical fruits in which it results. He can enjoy the beauty the artist creates and the imaginative enhancement of his experience which each new artistic achievement makes possible.

The relation of the average man to the joys and the insight of the religious genius is just the same. He is unlikely to share the supreme peace and delight of the mystic or the saint or to acquire the moral sensitivity of the prophet. The expectation that he will, far from leading him to appreciate what religion actually has to offer him, is likely, when that supreme good eludes his grasp, to produce in him disillusionment and revulsion. But religion does have functions it can fruitfully perform in his life.

And if he limits his hopes realistically to what he can reasonably expect to gain from the practice of religion, he will not be disappointed. He will discover what religion has to offer the average man, for whom it is one important concern among others.

271. The Enjoyment of Religion: Fellowship

We have seen that all religion is rooted in social feeling; it is something *shared* with others, and involves a *community* of ideals and *cooperative* activities. Man is a social being, and his religion is an expression of his social nature. In its great visions of the Brotherhood of Man, it is the highest expression of man's capacity for extending his social ties. But to push these bonds of fellowship until they include all mankind, we must first experience how good they are on a smaller and more manageable scale. Religion flourishes in the soil of some particular religious *fellowship* or *community*. In our country this normally takes the form of membership in some church.

It is not surprising that the widest of all the appeals that religion makes is to men's craving for companionship and sociability. Men want a "church home"; and they find that home satisfying to the extent that it gives them a chance to take part in genuine group activities. Such active cooperation with their fellows is for many what church membership primarily means. This is true not only of smaller communities, in which the church is the chief social center of community life. It is true in our cities, whose many social organizations still leave thousands without any real chance for active and genuine participation in social activities. The church offers more than mere "membership," it offers real "fellowship," a real sharing rather than a mere division of labor. In it a man can feel that he really "belongs" and "counts." And so "church activities" have increased by leaps and bounds, most successfully when they are not undertaken for church members or merely supported by church members for others but carried on cooperatively by the members themselves.

It makes little difference whether such "church activities" have grown up to attract and interest and hold people in support of some particular church. And it is futile to ask whether they are genuinely "religious" or not. For the average man, such sheer sociability has always been one of the major enjoyments of religion. Church suppers, Christian Endeavors, young people's entertainments may be distinctive of American religious customs. But the Mexican Indian, the Breton peasant, the natives of Bali or Burma have all found similar satisfaction in corresponding kinds of shared and cooperative activity, in forms of sociability that appealed to them. Such activities are not only invaluable schools in training people to work together and understand each other, in developing social feeling and character. They are also the soil out of which grows genuine religious fellowship and brotherhood. On them is built that unity of shared experience among fellow-worshippers we call "religious communion," which can be extended even to the vision of "the communion of the saints." In this universal and ideal vision, cooperation and friendly feeling with one's neighbor whom one has learned to know are elevated into the human bond uniting all who have ever aspired and striven toward better things, past, present, and yet to come. "For even as we have many members in one body," said St. Paul, "and all the members have not the same office, so we, who are many, are one body in Christ, and severally members one of another." And the great Stoic, Marcus Aurelius, saw all mankind as citizens of the one inclusive "City of Zeus": "We are made for cooperation like feet and hands, like eyelids, like the rows of the upper and lower teeth."

The sense of fellowship, of shared experience, permeates the religious life. The earliest religions were expressions of the social ties uniting a tribe or a people in a common way of living, a common set of aims, and a common reverence. "Incline thy heart to abhor that which the city holds in settled hate, and to reverence what she loves," says the chorus in *Oedipus*, giving voice to this tribal feeling of the Greek city-state. This emotional sense of solidarity with one's city or people, as the Greeks discovered, could be widened by men of broadening vision to the conviction that the whole world is one city. It could also be concentrated into the group fellowship of those united in following the teachings of a single master. Every religious movement has sprung from a devoted band of men gathered about some prophet or teacher and set apart from the world in the practice of his precepts. The teacher, followed by his band of disciples, is the typical source whence has come all new religious inspiration and reform. Such groups move through all the great Oriental religions, and they have appeared again and again in Christian history since the original Master.[1]

When religious feeling and faith are born anew, it is in a community or fellowship that they are embodied, in India, in the ancient world, in our own American history so full of the record of such religious communities. Men united in a common faith and way of life strengthen and inspire each other and assist each member in living up to the best lights of the group. And of their joint efforts there is born something that no one of them could achieve alone. "Where two or three are gathered together in my name," said Jesus, "there am I in the midst of them." The record of the primitive Christian communities bears testimony to the truth of this power of religious fellowship. The converts they made were uniformly impressed by the strength of the Christian love they embodied in their lives, a love that seemed to manifest the presence in their midst of the Holy Spirit.

Religious organizations offer not only this very real and tangible fellowship with the living; they give men a sense of ideal communion with a great tradition. The Jew, in performing the ancient rites of his ancestors, feels himself in communion, not only with all other Jews throughout the world today, but also with that long line who have lived and aspired and suffered since the Lord was served in his Temple. The Catholic feels himself in communion with the holy martyrs and saints of old who likewise drew strength and inspiration from an unchanging faith. In the Eucharist he is sharing the very sacrifice instituted in that upper chamber by the Lord himself. And truly, whoever sincerely practices his own form of religious worship can feel that by that act he is entering into spiritual fellowship with the countless millions who have through the ages sought to worship and reverence the highest they knew.

272. The Expression of Shared Feeling in Worship

The fellowship of a religious community normally expresses itself in acts of public worship. Men gather together with their fellows to do reverence to God. They seek to turn in common

[1] Cf. BR, No. 81 C, "The Unity and Functions of the High Prophets."

from the things that are seen, which largely fill their lives, to the things that are not seen. They wish to renew their sense of the best Good they know and to celebrate that Good in appropriate manner, that it may enter more deeply into their lives. In the face of that Good which is not seen, they feel their own inadequacy and their essential subordination in the scheme of things. Their needs are intensified, deepened, and elevated. They pray to God for help, and in the praying they gain a perspective on their demands and petitions. They seek for clarification, and if the preacher be filled with grace he brings something of it to them. They praise God and give thanks for the power they draw from him.

Into worship there thus enter the feelings of reverence, adoration, celebration, humility, need and petition, praise and thanksgiving, consecration, strength, and peace — all heightened and intensified because they are felt in common with fellow-worshippers. Where public worship is well conducted, all the religious arts and techniques are drawn upon to awaken these profound feelings and to give them expression in satisfying form; even in the lack of skill and taste, sincere feeling can work miracles. Public worship can sustain and enhance all the various satisfactions of religion because it cultivates them and their expression in a shared experience. Communion with God can well be easier and more profound in communion with one's fellow-man.

273. How Can One Best Worship?

Each one of these complex expressions of religious feeling can, of course, also be cultivated in private.[1] For many, such personal meditation and prayer are richly satisfying; every religion provides ways in which men may gain strength and inspiration from the systematic practice of devotional exercises. The great Oriental faiths, like the western monks, have expended much care in working out elaborate regimens, techniques by which men may be detached from the insistent pressures of the moment and drawn upward to the things that are not seen.[2] Most religions, like Judaism, have provided forms in which religious

---

[1] Cf. BR, No. 85, A. Carrel, "Prayer Is Power."
[2] Cf. BR., No. 75 B, section c, "Explanation of the Eightfold Path."

feeling can be expressed in that most intimate of all fellowships, the family.

At its best, public worship can serve to school religious feeling and emotion. It furnishes a training ground on which feeling, will, and imagination are educated, and it helps to form habits and provide techniques for the private practice and expression of devotion. Without the stimulus of such shared expression, the religious life is apt to remain inarticulate and rudimentary; it can easily dry up entirely, so that men "forget God" completely. Or else, in exceptional cases, men become zealots and fanatics, push their own feelings to excess, and in their aberrations disregard the standards for the expression of religious feeling which the experience of generations has built up.

After all, the reason why men perform public worship and attend religious services is because it gives them deep satisfaction. This satisfaction may vary from the profound experience the Catholic feels at the elevation of the Host, when he becomes aware of the real presence of God, to the exaltation of the Protestant at hearing a moving sermon which clarifies his moral insight and leads him to contemplate the Divine. For some, worship is most satisfying when it embodies the storied arts of music, poetry, liturgy, and rhetoric, and is conducted amidst the best that human imagination can conceive of architecture, painting and stained glass, singing and organ music. For others, the austerity of traditional Protestant worship strikes an answering chord — the preaching of an inspired minister or the bare beauty of a Quaker meeting, with its homely but sincere expression of the Inner Light, of Divine Illumination.

What form is most effective in enhancing religious feeling and in drawing the mind to God depends largely on one's early upbringing. Much of the satisfaction of worship comes from childhood familiarity with that particular form. It is good to recapture the feelings first aroused by crude services in the church on the village green or in the garish surroundings of the Catholic Church of one's youth. Even in the musically sophisticated, the old familiar hymns awaken nostalgic memories of worship far away and long ago, which heighten their religious effectiveness. Others, who have experienced a revulsion against the forms of worship once imposed upon them, find themselves attracted and satisfied by quite different ways of religious expression. They are "converted," we say, to a different church. What is most important is that, in our complex religious life, pretty much every conceivable type of religious worship is represented. Somewhere, in some church, any craving of religious experience can receive satisfaction. Since men can take such deep satisfaction in religious worship, it would seem to be the part of wisdom to find that form which one can genuinely enjoy.

274. Religion as an Immediate Good in Itself

To meet and work together with one's fellows for some good cause, to worship together when deep feeling draws men to seek companionship, to consecrate oneself anew with one's fellows to the highest that one knows — these things men find good in themselves. They enjoy doing them, they find immediate satisfaction in such action and feeling. Men do not need to ask the question, *why* they should act and feel in these ways the practice of religion makes available for them. They want and love to do so. Men enjoy religion just as they enjoy music or painting or learning more about themselves and the world. Such activities belong to the enduring satisfactions of life. They are what we call "immediate goods."

If men did not enjoy religious activities, they would never have turned to religion to celebrate, consecrate, and clarify their other fundamental concerns. They would seek what guidance they could find to direct their conduct quite apart from religious feeling and religious fellowship. They would try to arrive at the meaning and significance of human life without reference to religious experience or to the central focus it supplies. The moral ideals they acknowledge and the faiths by which they live would be, as we say, wholly "secular." Religion would not be the great help it can be in facing the problems encountered in human living, if it were not first itself a way of living with an immediate appeal.

Now of course men vary greatly in the satisfaction they find in religion, just as they do in what they find in the various arts or branches of knowledge. Although it seems very doubtful whether any society can get along without what religion does for it, this or that man clearly can — millions do today. Millions likewise get along with no interest in music or in scientific knowledge.. In one sense, religion is, for the individual, like the various arts and sciences, a luxury that can be added to the routines of his daily vocation, to make his life richer and deeper and more civilized and humane. If he be quite blind to music or poetry or to religion, that is too bad; but there is no convincing way to prove to him that he ought to open his eyes and see. He can do his job and live out his life without ever tasting these enduring satisfactions of a civilized and truly human society. If he be wholly insensitive to the great pains of existence, if he can face suffering, sorrow, and sin with indifference or sheer endurance, he will not miss the religious ways of conquering the evil of the world and rising above it.

275. Democracy and Religion

In another sense, however, it is clear that the man who is simply oblivious to any of these great ranges of human experience is not only missing one of the most profound and unalloyed satisfactions of life. He is an incomplete and truncated man; he is not wholly human; he is failing to live up to all that he might be. His education and experience have been too inadequate for him to make the most out of his life. And a society that has allowed many of its members to grow up with no real opportunity to experience and appreciate any one of the major achievements of the human spirit is clearly a very imperfect society. It has a long way to go before it can claim to be "democratic," that is, before it can claim to give every man the chance to make the most of all his powers, to become a well-rounded, whole man. We Americans boast of our high material standard of living. But we can hardly rest content with our "standard of living" so long as we "educate" millions of Americans to think that they can truly/live well without bringing into their lives some of the best fruits of human experience — the pursuit of truth, the creation of beauty, and the enjoyment of religion.

Moreover, any democratic ideal tries to extend the range of men's sympathies, to enlarge the area within which men can cooperate with their fellows and share their distinctive experiences. The aristocrat holds himself aloof; the true democrat seeks to learn from other and different kinds and conditions of men. Now religious feeling and aspiration is one of the most universal of all human experiences. He whose blindness to religious experience keeps him from entering sympathetically into the deepest feelings and aspirations of other men is cut off from the strongest bond that can unite mankind in a shared experience.

The intolerance that expresses itself in narrow and fanatical religions is, alas, familiar enough. But there is an even more obtuse intolerance of those blind to all religious feeling. For the horizons and sympathies of those who know something of devotion to the highest and of humility before its insistent demands can always be broadened. The great religions have uniformly been extended to such a universal human vision embracing all mankind. Those who have never felt either aspiration or humility find it much harder to look beyond their own provincial concerns to all the nations of men.

276. How Religion Helps Men to Live

But religion is not merely something that is good in itself, a set of immediately satisfying ways of acting and expressing feeling in fellowship with others. It is also something that bears important fruits in the rest of man's living; it helps men to face their problems and to make their most difficult decisions. It tells them, indeed, how they should best live. It furnishes them with a plan for guiding and directing their conduct and proclaims the ideals they should aim at. It organizes men's various activities in the light of a central "meaning" of life and of human destiny; it formulates the "significance" of living for men and gives them a driving "faith." And it grounds these ideals in the nature of things, so that they are seen as the central reality in the world in which man lives.[1]

The traditional and symbolic language of religion has familiar terms to express these ways in which religions help men to live. Religion includes not only worship and devotion; it contains also a set of moral teachings and precepts for men to follow, and examples for them to imitate.[2] And these teachings are

[1] Cf. BR, No. 77 F, "What Is Man?"

[2] Cf. BR, No. 74 C, "The Taoist Ideal of Repose and Humility"; No. 75 D, "The Buddha's Way of Virtue"; No. 78 B, "Jesus' Sermon on the Mount"; No. 78 C, "The Parable of the Good Samaritan"; No. 79 D, "The Chief Duties of Moslems"; No. 80 D, "The Imperial Rescript on Education"; No. 81 D, "Actions of the Righteous."

usually held to be not merely the wisdom of some revered and Divine Master; they are proclaimed as the "will of God," as "God's law" for the regulation of human conduct, "revealed" to man through the prophets he inspires to speak his word. Christianity goes so far as to insist that God himself, in the person of his Divine Son, appeared on earth among men to bring to them the light of his teachings and the power of his example. In following the commandments of Jesus, as reported in the Gospels, and in imitating Christ, men are doing the will of God himself, thus dramatically proclaimed. Religious faith for the Christian means faith in the validity of these commandments and in the perfection of Christ's example.

Just how this familiar religious language is to be understood we shall postpone until we come to consider the fundamental religious beliefs. In all religions it has been employed, in all it has been subjected to a great variety of intellectual interpretations. But its central conviction is clear. The aims and ideals which religions proclaim and teach are not merely human hopes and imaginings. They are discoveries about the nature of the world in which man lives. They are not the inventions of a being alone in an alien and hostile universe. They are rooted in the nature of things and in the conditions which determine human life. Man is not, in the words of Bertrand Russell in his *Free Man's Worship*, "a weary but unyielding Atlas," sustaining alone "the world that his own ideals have fashioned despite the trampling march of unconscious power." [1]

In consecrating the moral life and proclaiming it to be the will of God, religions have given it a very different meaning and significance. Man's long struggle for a deeper moral insight and for the knowledge and the power to live the best life he knows is a genuine cooperation with the universe. As has been said earlier, it is a kind of partnership with the world, in which the world *reveals* to man its possibilities, and man *finds* what is best in living.[2] Man's highest standards are commands which the world issues to those with wit enough to read the message aright.

[1] Cf. BR, No. 41, "A Free Man's Worship."
[2] Cf. BR, No. 74 B, "The Wonder and Omnipresence of Heavenly Reason (Tao)." Read also No. 74 A, "The Meaning of Taoism."

The moral life contains intense struggle and bitter frustration, as religions have been the first to recognize.[1] It involves opposition to the unconscious power of many natural forces and the constant effort to overcome many strong forces in man's own nature. It is not to be achieved by sinking back complacently in the friendly arms of a Power, natural or Divine, that will painlessly and without human effort make everything come out all right. Such blind trust and confidence belong with the illusions of childhood; the highest in human living and character is not so easily won. And, strive as he may, man is doomed to remain a "sinner" to the end: his reach will still exceed his grasp. He can never hope to live up fully to the best he sees. To think that he can, and has, is the most insidious sin of all — the one uniformly condemned by religions as "spiritual pride."

But in this struggle man is not alone. The powers he mobilizes are just as "natural" as those he is forced to oppose. In attacking disease, the physician is cooperating with the universe; he is successful in the measure in which he has *discovered* the possibilities of cure and health. And in leading the moral life, man is likewise cooperating with the grounded possibilities the world reveals to him. He uses the highest in himself, that which has discerned the highest in the world, to combat the lowest. And the highest in the world is a revelation of Good which the world itself forces on men. It is, as Plato put it, "the best in existence" which is most real. In cooperation with that central reality, man finds his life meaningful and significant, and from it he draws inspiration and strength and steadiness of purpose. That the highest discoverable in this cooperation with the world is most real and insistently demands to be made controlling in human life is what religions mean by "faith." That highest they call God.[2]

277. The Guidance and Direction of Action

All religions embrace a code for the guidance of living and a set of ideals toward which human life should be directed. The ancient traditions, deeply rooted in the conditions of primitive

[1] Cf. BR, 75 D, "The Buddha's Way of Virtue," especially sections a and b.
[2] Cf. BR, No. 84, John Dewey, "Humanism: A Modern Religion."

societies with their love of prescribed ceremonial, set forth detailed rules regulating most of the activities of life. Much of the concern of early Hebraism or Hinduism, like all folk religions, was with providing appropriate rites of purification — of sacrifice, penance, and atonement — for infractions of this ceremonial law, which were taken as offenses against God or the gods. It was probably in connection with such offenses, religious history indicates, that men first began to feel a sense of guilt and sin and to develop a "conscience."

But such priestly codes lump together conventional observances, ancient tribal taboos, and moral precepts and attempt to enforce them all indiscriminately. Most of these prescribed forms are concerned with the ritual expression of religious feeling, with techniques of worship rather than with the conduct of life. They consecrate customary conventions, not moral standards. It is characteristic of the priestly emphasis in religion to confuse the two, to remain on the level of customary morality and to celebrate what is respectable, not what is best. That is why those who have achieved a more reflective and critical moral insight are normally impatient of priestly religion and its devotion to the "letter of the law." They severely criticize what we today call the "organized religion" of the churches for its failure to rise above the moral limitations of what the community actually approves and censures.

In this way, a living religion gives birth to its own "prophets" — those who appeal from the letter to the "spirit" of the law, convinced that while "the letter killeth, the spirit makes alive." That is, they brush aside as of subordinate value all that is merely conventional and customary and concentrate on "the one thing needful" — the moral ideals that should direct human life. "I hate, I despise your fast days," proclaimed Amos. "Though ye offer me burnt offerings and meat offerings, I will not accept. But let judgment run down as waters and righteousness as a mighty stream." Hosea spoke in the name of the Lord: "I desire mercy and not sacrifice, and the knowledge of God more than burnt offerings." And Micah completes this moralizing of the law into an ideal standard for human conduct: "He hath showed thee, O man, what is good; and what doth the Lord require of thee, but to do justly, and to love mercy, and to walk humbly with thy God?" Justice, mercy, humility — these are proclaimed the moral ideals by which men should guide their actions.[1]

Prophetic criticism thus works to transform a precise code into a set of flexible standards and guiding principles, which are at once more universal in their scope and more broadly challenging than the needs of the particular situation in which the prophet first proclaims them. This very flexibility and universal relevance makes it more difficult to know just what such moral standards really demand. In any particular case, what is it to do justly or to love mercy? Ideal standards need interpretation and application; and so there normally grows up in a religion a new code, a new body of legalistic interpretations.

The Hebrew law, moralized by the great prophets, built up over many generations a rich and elaborate set of precedents and rules known as the Talmud. The Catholic Church, confronted with the task of guiding men's lives through the priest in the confessional, likewise worked out a detailed system of "casuistry" for the application of the moral law in particular cases. In all these schemes of moral guidance, the universal ideal standards of the prophets are naturally reduced to the compass of the limited and relative moral practices of a particular age and society. Men's imperfect moral insight is consecrated as the will of God or the wisdom of the Divine Teacher. The priest, it seems, has conquered once more.

But not wholly. For those standards and ideals of what is best remain for new prophets to appeal to; they are the "spirit" of the law. Is this really justice? Is this true mercy? Is this the best that Christian love can do? The way is open for fresh insight and for new reflective interpretation of the meaning of these ideals in the light of a changed situation.[2] Slavery or war may always have seemed "just." But is this really true? The flexible and universally relevant ideal standards which a religion proclaims should be controlling in life do not furnish an automatic answer to men's moral problems. Their application demands as much of ethical sensitivity and of intelligence and

[1] Cf. BR, No. 74 C, "The Symbolism of Water: The Taoist Ideal of Repose and Humility."

[2] Cf. BR, No. 79 A, "Introduction to Islam, the Mohammedan Faith"; No. 79 B, "Mohammed and the Koran: the Prophet and the Book"; No. 81 C, "The Unity and Functions of the High Prophets."

knowledge as men can muster. The great ethical religions that have enshrined such visions of ideal good are not substitutes for reflective morality, for man's best thinking on the issues of life. They are rather insistent challenges to man to think.

This is a danger as well as a challenge. Detailed codes of conduct, like those of Confucianism [1] or of orthodox Judaism,[2] can hold men to a fairly high standard of external observance. They are open to the charge of "formalism," of a lack of inner devotion to the good they seek to embody in practice, especially if they contain large elements that are purely conventional, matters of mere manners rather than of genuine morality. This was the reproach Jesus brought against the "scribes and Pharisees." But religions which try to rely much more exclusively on the "spirit," on men's devotion to ideal standards rather than on a rigid code, do so at their own peril. Protestantism has often professed to leave to the individual the interpretation of the moral, as well as the doctrinal, teachings of the Scriptures. In practice, of course, the different churches have usually attempted to prescribe a code of conduct for their members almost as rigid as their creeds. But this more or less official interpretation of the content of the Christian life has been peculiarly responsive to the changing moral demands of the Protestant communities. Protestant churches have employed their flexible ideal standards to assimilate whatever pattern of living might seem good in the light of their shifting social experience. They have always justified it as what the Bible really teaches.

In its complacent acceptance of the world, the flesh, and the devil in the last few generations, Protestantism has tended to become an emotional force supporting the various reigning secular social ideals, from business enterprise to Christian socialism. It has offered no real opposition to any deeply felt ideal, for that too must be the present-day meaning of the justice and mercy of the prophets and of the love of Christ. But it has come to afford little independent guidance and direction for life. On the other hand, this very flexibility makes it possible for prophetic leaders to develop an intelligent faith in the best goods attainable in our complex world and to buttress that faith with all the power and devotion of religious consecration. The standards of

---

[1] Cf. BR, No. 76 A, B, and C.   [2] Cf. BR, No. 77 A, B, and C on Judaism.

what is best, enshrined in the great religions, demand uncompromisingly that those who take them seriously must work out what they mean in the problems of living that confront men.

278. Religious Ideals Are "Transcendent"

Religious precepts, like the message of the Hebrew prophets, the Sermon on the Mount,[1] or the Noble Eightfold Path of Buddha,[2] are not detailed programs for the guidance of human conduct. They are rather challenges to men to search their own hearts and scrutinize their way of living — calls to vigorous thinking and serious effort. "The Lord of hosts instructed me not to call holy what this people call holy, and not to fear what they fear. But the Lord of hosts him shall you call holy; He shall be your fear, and He your dread." Nothing short of the Highest is enough. "Be ye therefore perfect, even as your Father in Heaven is perfect." Thus Jesus summarized the supreme religious demand.

But men are not perfect, and even with the power religious faith gives them, even with the help of the grace of God, they cannot incorporate perfection into their lives. Saint Paul, convinced that Christians who had been "saved in Christ" were truly spiritual beings and had been fully released from the bondage to sin, was sadly puzzled at the goings on in the Christian churches, whose members retained the limitations of human nature. To this day, many are troubled and some are revolted by the obvious fact that the followers of a religion always fall short of the highest ideals that religion teaches. The gulf is all the more striking as the ideals are worthy of devotion. "Christianity has never been practiced," we say in our society; "the churches make little serious effort to live up to what they profess."

Human limitations, acquiescence in current blindnesses and prejudices, which would pass uncensored in another, are hard to pardon in those who profess devotion to a noble ideal. And religious organizations, which claim to be foremost in the cultivation of aspiration, bear a heavy responsibility. They should be able at least, we judge, to refrain from endorsing the worst passions and cruelties of men, not to speak of adding hatreds and intolerances of their own. Alas, the spotted pages of reli-

[1] Cf. BR, No. 78 A and B. [2] Cf. BR, No. 75 B.

gious history make only too clear the very human ambitions and pretensions, the quarrels and rivalries and struggles for domination that have infected those wielding religious power. There is no hatred like the *odium theologicum*. We fall naturally into attributing the bitterness of our present conflict to the fact that it is really a "religious" war. Even the higher types of character that religious devotion produces are subject to their own insidious diseases and "spiritual sins," which have been carefully catalogued on the basis of a wealth of examples.

To all who innocently imagine it an easy thing to "follow the teachings" of Jesus (or of Buddha, or any other inspired religious prophet), these facts and criticisms should be an ever-present warning. And those who, whether confidently and complacently or critically and accusingly, actually expect the church to realize the Christian ideal of perfect justice and love in its own life, to say nothing of transforming "the world" on that pattern, would do well to realize that, in this sense, no man and no group can ever hope to be fully "Christian." No great religious ideal can ever be "realized"; no religion with a genuine vision can ever "practice" what it preaches. If it could, something would be sadly amiss with the preaching, with the ideal. Andrew Carnegie is reported to have once said, "I have never had an ideal that I have not completely realized." No religion has ever pitched its vision of the Highest so low.

This is what we mean by saying that the ideal standards of religion belong to "another realm," that they "transcend" the limits of human experience. Men can behold them in vision, and in the light of that vision they can strive to order their human lives better.[1] But men cannot hope ever to understand completely what such an ideal as "perfect justice" or "perfect love" would even mean in all the reaches of life. It is characteristic of such transcendent ideals to be inexhaustible; men can always discover in them new suggestions for the better ordering of their lives and their relations to their fellows.

279. The Value of Transcendent Ideals

The fact that the visions of perfect Good which religions set forth in precept and ideal example are, and must remain, ob-

[1] Cf. BR, No. 78 J, "All Things New."

jects of aspiration rather than of attainment, standards for criticizing men's imperfect living rather than programs to be put into effect, is no ground for complacency. Men and groups of men, like churches, are human and cannot expect to become absolutely perfect, even with the aid of all the resources of religious strength. But this does not relieve them of the responsibility to become far better than they are. It would ill become churches to challenge the common opinion that their members stand, in fact, on no higher level of moral attainment than those who do not unite to cultivate a better way of living. It is rather the part of humility for them to confess that their distinction is not a closer approximation to what is best but a clearer realization of their failure. That, at least, the prophetic critic, the man of keener moral sensitivity and deeper religious insight, has a right to demand. However inevitable their sins of omission, churches devoted to a cultivation of the vision of the Highest should be the first to acknowledge that "all have sinned and fall short of the glory of God." Those men and those organizations in which religious vision burns clearest are the readiest to acknowledge their own inadequacy, and that very confession spurs them on to new effort. Repentance is the first step on the road to the better life, even if in the end the ultimate achievement is a deeper realization of what would be best.

The surprising thing is not that religion fails to get men to live up to the best it has to show them. It is rather that for so many the challenge is accepted and leads to real moral effort and achievement. And for some few, the genuine saints — the saving remnant to whom every religion can point as the embodiment of wholehearted devotion to its ideal standards — the limits of human nature seem almost reached. It is no wonder that every religion cherishes and celebrates the human incarnation of its transcendent ideals in its heroes and saints, counsels the imitation of their enlightened lives, and places the gospels and legends illustrating these achievements of personal character among its sacred writings, along with its teachings of precept and standard. For most people, there is more concrete inspiration in the example of what men can be than in the stern reminder of what they ought to be, more in the life of a Saint Francis or a Buddha than in the preaching of a Jeremiah or a John Knox. And for

some, the greatest inspiration of all is to be found in the selfless
devotion that love for God and man can produce in more ordinary men, like the Buddhist monks, the Franciscan or Jesuit
missionaries, or the Quaker relief workers. Men need such "me-
diators" for their vision of God.

280. The Meaning and Significance of Life.

We have traced the kind of guidance and direction that religions have given men, from the priestly provision of detailed
codes and regulations, through the more flexible and universally
applicable standards of the great religious teachers, to the prophetic criticism of conduct in the light of transcendent ideals of
perfection. And here we come close to a further function of
religion, one which many would put first and make central as
the source of all the others. "My religion," such a man would
say, "gives me something in which I can believe. It gives me a
faith. It is the answer to the question of the meaning of life.
It explains the significance of this great world in which we find
ourselves, and how we men fit into the picture. It tells me what
it is all for, and what it is that makes it worth while. It shows
me what my place is in the great scheme of things."

So central, indeed, is this faith and "meaning" which religion
gives men, that we often speak of any inclusive faith that makes
life meaningful and significant for a man or a group as their
"religion." A popular present-day "definition" of religion is,
"man's total reaction to the universe" or even "to life." "Total
reaction" is here taken to mean a fundamental commitment
that catches up and harmonizes all lesser loyalties. Another
recent "definition" runs: "Religious faith is the unification of
the self through allegiance to inclusive ideal ends, which imagination presents to us and to which the human will responds as
worthy of controlling our desires and choices."

We have seen enough of the many different things that religion
gives man, to doubt the adequacy of any attempt to "define" it
in terms of a single limited function. But these characterizations
do all emphasize the fact that when men say that religion gives
life "meaning" and "significance," that it furnishes a "faith,"
something in which they can "believe," they are pointing to what
religion *does* to them, to what *happens* to them as a result of their

religious attitude and conviction.[1] What they are indicating, we should not in any strict sense call "knowledge" at all. They are talking rather about "what is worth while," about commitment to certain ends of living, about convictions of what is of real and enduring value. They are insisting on a faith *in* something, not on the faith *that* something is — though faith *in* anything naturally raises its own questions about what such faith implies as to the nature of the world — questions which can receive a variety of answers.

281. The Nature of Religious Faith

It is important to be clear that the question of the "meaning" of life is not primarily a question about *facts*, about what *exists*, but rather about what is *worth while*, about what it is all *for*, about what is *good*. For this question is often put in such a way that it seems to demand an answer that will affirm certain intellectual *beliefs* about the facts of existence, about the structure of the universe. Belief in something is very different from belief that something exists. The first is a commitment to certain goods and ideals; the second is a proposition that must submit itself to our most exacting standards of verification since all questions of existence fall within the scope of rational inquiry and its tests of validity.

Belief *in* something, commitment to certain ends as good, is to be sure normally bound up with a great many beliefs *about* the world and the conditions of human life. Faith can hardly operate in an intellectual vacuum; it is rather the crown and keystone of all that men have found out about themselves and their world. The more knowledge men have, the more significant will be their central allegiance, and the more clearly will they see how their controlling ideals are relevant to their actual living. Indeed, it is precisely the knowledge and understanding of experience to which a central faith can give meaning and significance. Such a religious commitment provides a means of estimating the relative value of different pursuits and different bits of knowledge; it organizes them in terms of their relevance to its central demands.

Men must have considerable acquaintance with, and experi-

[1] Cf. BR, No. 83, William James, "The Will to Believe."

ence of, life before they can in any significant sense find it to have "a meaning" as a whole. To the child, his different pursuits and activities are each "meaningful" enough; but it is only later that he comes, if at all, to harmonize his various scattered ends in the light of a single unifying set of loyalties and convictions. The kind of "faith" that can make clear what it is all for, and make it all worth while, is born only of experience; and to acquire it is a long and painful process. Religious teaching can help in this hard task of learning from experience by setting before the child, preferably in the form of examples and illustrations, the kind of meaningful faith that other men have found. But it is doubtful whether he can grasp what this "really means," as we say, until he has learned it from life for himself. The single "meaning of life," if he really achieves such a unification of his purposes, will then come to him as a fresh discovery of his own. In religious terms, it will be a "revelation," which will transform what were before merely certain beliefs *about* the realities which are not seen, into a faith *in* them and a loyalty to them. Then the various things he knows about himself and his world will fall into place and make sense in the light of what he has discovered to be really worth while.

Such a religious faith is said to "explain" the significance of life, but not in the sense of providing a reasoned theory about it that sets forth the nature of God and his relation to the world, or the nature of man and human destiny. Most religions do include fundamental beliefs about these matters. But such "theological" ideas are the product of men's reflection upon the fact of faith and upon the visions of their great teachers. They are philosophical interpretations of religious commitments and convictions — questions which naturally interest the thoughtful. Religious faith rather "explains" the significance of life by making it "plain" and clear to see, by "revealing" it when experience has generated the need for it. Faith brings the conviction that what men behold in religious vision is the real thing in life and the central reality in the world. In committing ourselves to such a supreme Good and understanding the meaning of life from the perspective it gives, we are, as we have said, cooperating with what is most real in the universe. It is this ideal perspective born of religious vision, and this sense of partnership with the best the world contains, that give to life that central and unifying meaning which men find in their religion.

282. The Situation We Face Today

In a stable society, life normally follows some meaningful pattern. Such a society is a going concern, with a complexly organized scheme of acting, feeling, and thinking. Its social and cultural habits or "institutions" regulate and direct all the basic relations in which its members stand to each other and to their world. The pattern of their daily living is provided by the various activities in which they normally take part without much question — their family obligations, their way of making a living, their intercourse with their neighbors, their recreations and diversions. The vast majority want to do these things and find satisfaction in doing them well and successfully. To hunt, to fight, to be wise in counsel, to have strong sons — these make up the life of a man. To possess skill in the chase, to be brave in battle, to be loyal and just to one's fellows, to be able to make cunning weapons — these things are good. It is all so clear as to require no debate. The things to be done are meaningful and significant, they all fit together into a familiar and well-rounded pattern; they need no reason why, their value needs no questioning. Thus activities and goals or values come as integral parts of a complex habitual way of doing things. Beliefs and ideas interpret an experience that is meaningful in its own terms because it embodies a functioning pattern of living. Men find life significant by taking part in these living institutions of their culture. They are at home in their world, they are adjusted to the conditions of their living, they have a sure sense of direction and purpose.

The religion of such a society normally celebrates and consecrates this meaningful pattern of living, intensifying the emotional satisfactions men find in it and giving it a religious sanction. The powers more mighty than man respect these ways and perhaps even practice them. It seems but natural for any being to act and feel thus. Or such ways are the law of God, and in following them men are doing his will. For the healthy-minded and "well-adjusted" member of such a society, religion is but one among many institutions that mold his character and make him what he is.

But in the complicated culture of a great civilization, offering so many possible patterns of living that individuals are thrown back on their own resources and have to make their own choices, finding "the meaning of life" becomes a conscious problem. This is especially the case when the older patterns and institutions are breaking down and giving way to others, as in the days of ancient Rome. A constant succession of such "ages of transition" has distinguished our own Western society since the outgrowing of its medieval forms. It has been most of all true since the rise of industrial technology and the impressive scientific enterprise plunged the Western nations into a fundamental revolution and even, as many think today, into a desperate crisis in all the old familiar ways of acting and thinking.

What past ideas are still certain? What way of life still offers a sure good? Men have lost their sense of being at home in a familiar world, they no longer have a sense of purpose and direction. They have lost their old faith, and unless they have found another their life seems "meaningless" and hopeless. America, more than most other societies today, is still a "going concern" — though where it is going is not so clear—and for us there is still plenty of hope. But even in our land, there is confusion, uncertainty, cross-purposes, doubt of the future. And multitudes of Americans are living, as we say, on the surface of life, hurrying from one meaningless activity to another, pursuing rather empty pleasures of the moment, and finding very little real satisfaction in any. They have little faith in the immediate job they are doing and still less in anything extending beyond it.

No doubt much of this familiar complaint is exaggerated; those with some gospel to preach tend to insist on the great pain from which they can promise salvation. Probably most Americans do not suffer greatly from their lack of faith, if such be indeed their plight — as yet. But Europeans have certainly suffered, both from the loss of their old faith and from the new ones that have rushed in to fill the void. We know only too clearly the kind of faith at which many have clutched because of their desperate need for something reassuring to cling to, something to sustain them and give their lives a direction in a world where everything dear and familiar seemed to be going by the board.

We Americans have been engaged in a great common enterprise, bending all our energies to a cause in which, as rarely before, the ideals we supposedly cherish most deeply are at stake. A war with such high issues, it might have been expected, would bring to an intense focus our central and consuming loyalties. Here would be the chance to make everything we did significant in the service of a burning faith. There has been plenty of devotion and earnest labor for what we call the "war effort." But of faith in any further ends to which that "effort" might be directed — of anything approaching a religious faith in fundamental commitments and convictions, which might make the war itself significant as one step in a continuing devotion to supreme Good — there has been little evidence. The men in the armed forces have done their job with heroic and dogged determination. But there seems little reason to think that, when that particular job is over, they will see any further service they wish to devote their lives to. Few of them seem to understand what it is they have been fighting for so magnificently.

283. The Power of Faith

In such a situation, which the war merely brings to a sharper focus, the kind of direction that religious faith can give to life stands out more clearly than in those more "normal" times when life gets its meaning and direction from an unchanging pattern. Many have doubtless learned to live from day to day in our shifting society and do not consciously miss a sure purpose which they never enjoyed. Many more — perhaps the great majority — find anchorage still in the simple and enduring human relations — in love, marriage, and parenthood, in friendship, in a job or profession they can genuinely enjoy. Many of the most sensitive and thoughtful have given some measure of organization and meaning to their lives by devoting them to worthwhile social causes — by working, through political or labor channels, to abolish the grinding slavery of poverty, to reconstruct our social arrangements, to prevent the recurrence of war. And a few have found, in the Marxian gospel perhaps, as inclusive a faith as traditional religions have given.

But all too many have found neither a worthy ideal around which to organize their lives nor even a moderately satisfactory adjustment to the conditions of living. With no sure direction, they are at the mercy of every shock to their feelings or even of every passing disappointment. They have not the emotional strength to meet even the normal crises of living; they go to pieces because they have nothing to fall back upon but their own personal desires and cravings. Men need something bigger than themselves, more important than their own fortunes, in comparison with which what happens to them is of minor moment. They need something "real" with which they can associate themselves. In commitment to its demands their private ambitions are merged in a broader purpose; in thus losing themselves they find what they really are and genuinely want to come to pass. Only by being seized, as it were, by something much more real than one's passing desires, can one hope to develop into a real person. For the select few, a purely private commitment may be enough; it matters not that the whole world is against them or does not understand or care. But normally men gain immensely in steadfastness and strength in the company of others who share the same faith. Men hate to be alone, above all in the presence of the Divine.

The psychiatrist, the physician of sick minds, knows only too well what happens to the delicate organization of human personality when it possesses no goal or purpose outside its own chaotic impulses and drives. Such a personality is not "integrated," he says. It rushes off in every direction, lacks strength and stability, vacillates between false exhilaration and fits of misgiving, self-abasement, and despair. Men must harmonize their different impulses and purposes into an organized or integrated self, with a central drive and direction strong enough to persist through the changing situations of life despite the buffets of fortune. Men must adjust this self to the real world by gaining, through attachment to objectives of lasting value, a perspective upon their place in it and their proper relations to its demands. They need to unify the self through a faith in something that lies beyond it.

Whatever introduces this unification and perspective can serve as such a faith. But, the psychiatrist adds, that faith we call religious, in an enduring Good that relates men's scattered interests to a controlling aim, is one of the surest ways of winning integration and strength of character. There are other and humbler objects of attachment, other loyalties, that can produce a healthy and "well-adjusted" personality. But if we are not content, as physicians alone, with mere strength and health of character — if we are concerned with worthy character and real personality — then we shall consider carefully the kind of "real world" we want to be "adjusted" to. The most lasting satisfaction is to be found in a self unified and adjusted through a genuinely religious loyalty to what is best.

284. Substitutes for Faith in the Highest

Men and societies need faith in something. We are only too familiar these days with the pathological symptoms of lack of faith, in individuals and nations. But equally, merely to have "a faith" is far from enough. The quality of that faith, and what it is directed toward, make all the difference. Men cannot live at all without finding "a meaning" in life. But they cannot live well if that meaning is petty and self-centered and ungenerous. They can live best only by faith in the best that men have discerned.

The greatest temptation today is to try to live by faith in less than the highest. We need hardly dwell on those "total" social faiths that have swept so much of our world, those secular substitutes for religion that have arisen in response to the deep need to escape from hopelessness and despair. In being exclusive and divisive, in setting man against man, in consciously appealing to passion and prejudice and hatred, in restricting their fellowship within narrow limits, they are clearly pathological reversions to the worst features of primitive religion. We should scarcely call them "religious" at all, despite their incidental performance of some of the functions of religion, did we not remember that religions also have betrayed these unlovely traits.[1]

The Germans have found "a meaning" in life, which to those who share it seems better than no faith at all — though in the

---

[1] Another important modern substitute for religion is the Japanese national cult of Shinto. See BR, No. 80.

end it will doubtless come to the same thing. But all peoples have for a century seen the "religion of nationalism" grow by leaps and bounds, until devotion to one's country, patriotism, has become the strongest human loyalty in our modern world, the ultimate commitment. The older and more universal Christian loyalties have often been content to narrow themselves to such tribal compass. Men have been able to convince themselves that devotion to the true good of their nation is itself a form of devotion to God. It would be, ideally, if the national purpose never fell short of the stature of God. In this way, Christianity has managed to accommodate itself to national feeling. But when a higher and broader religious vision has come into collision with this new religion of nationalism, the issue has been at best tragic and at worst disastrous. For how can a man serve two masters?

The social and secular faith of the Communists seems to stand on a higher level and to exhibit more of the characteristics of a genuine religion, however dubious we may be about its embodiment in practice. It has had a more universal vision, cutting across national boundaries — though it has hardly included all men in its scope, and from its comradeship of the workers of the world it has not cast out hate for the common enemy.[1] It has a strong sense of human cooperation with the universe, of its own faith as rooted in the nature of things and destined to be realized by the providential "dialectic of history." And Communism has enjoyed, though usually without full awareness of the fact, a genuinely transcendent and unattainable ideal — the vision of a society founded on justice, not organized injustice, and planned and ordered by intelligence, not wrecked by man's stupidity.

But entirely apart from the wisdom of its principles of political and economic organization, which we are not here considering, whether Communism can remain an adequate religious faith is, for Americans at least, open to grave question. Not only has it displayed, like all strong new faiths, a fanaticism, an intolerance, an *odium theologicum*, which older and more experienced religions have managed to overcome and outgrow. Religious history suggests that in the course of time, with the growth of self-criti-

[1] Cf. BR, No. 59, Marx and Engels, "The Communist Manifesto."

cism, this faith, like so many others, may well learn tolerance and wisdom, and come to incorporate many of the other commitments by which men have lived. Not only has the Communist faith been embodied in Russia in a social and political organization and policy, in what we may well call a "church" — the Party — which has, in practice, exhibited all the wisdom of the serpent, all the dubious devices by which men, assured of the rightness of their ultimate aim, have convinced themselves that the shortest and easiest ways to it are justified. Not only is its ideal of a just society alloyed with a subordination of the worth of individual personality and its sensitive insights, which the religious vision of the West has learned to cherish as a supreme good.

Even at its best, the Communist vision is concentrated on worldly success and remains rather narrowly social. It is a response to the most insistent and bitter need of our day — for economic salvation — and for that very reason tends to neglect or minimize other enduring human needs, especially those more personalized. In an intelligently planned society, it is convinced, all things will be possible. And such a society, it holds, if not yet completely achieved, is nevertheless just around the corner. In it there will be no need to rise above evil through a more ultimate vision, for evil will have been overcome on earth. Such a social ideal, when truly generous and humane, can indeed serve most of the functions of a genuinely religious faith, so long as men are devotedly striving to realize it. Whether it can withstand failure or success and the complacency of partial achievement is not so sure.

Especially "success." Under the impact of war, the Communist ideal seems to have narrowed to the familiar pattern of nationalism and to have sacrificed its broader vision to the immediate needs of the Russian peoples. How much of "Communism" or of the Communist faith will be left when the battle is over is an unresolved question. Doubtless that flaming new faith will become an established national church, appropriately celebrating what has been won, and men will piously repeat the once revolutionary slogans. But whether even Russians will find them an adequate answer to the "meaning of life" remains to be seen.

285. Faith in a Spiritual Ideal

Any vital religion in our modern world, so desperately in need of social direction, must consecrate and give full expression to men's social idealism. The Hebrew-Christian tradition, with its insistent demands that men pursue mercy, justice, and active love toward one's fellow-man as the highest good, holds resources to inspire and sustain such social idealism. This central fact has been illustrated again and again in its long history. For millions of Americans religion has today come to mean primarily the service of God through devotion to the ideal of a just society in which brotherly love shall reign among men. Few sensitive religious leaders in our churches have failed to be touched by this vision of a "more Christian" social order, or to recognize the church's "social message" as an essential part of its mission. And many have come to make that "social gospel" central and have tried to mobilize religious feeling in support of working for a society built upon individual worth, human brotherhood, mutual service, and the love of mankind.[1]

Assuredly, laboring to establish God's Kingdom, striving with Christ to bring about the reign of justice and love, are duties for the Christian; other religions have other symbols, drawn from their own prophets, for the same drive to give our society an ethical direction.[2] Religious consecration can bring strength and power to generous and humane, if not always fully enlightened, social programs. In fact, much of the force behind our most promising social causes comes from such religious inspiration, and religious leaders have been prominent in most of them.[3] Religious consecration brings also its own clarification. In the presence of the best insights of prophets and teachers, the narrowness and one-sidedness of purely secular social ideas stands revealed. "Christian" socialism shows a sensitivity to the many needs of human nature lacking in the more narrowly concentrated Marxian gospel.[4]

These forms of faith are surely more genuinely religious than the social faiths so strong in Europe. Men can find in them the

[1] Cf. BR, No. 77 G, "Anticipations of Universal Peace"; No. 78 D, "Jesus' Parables and Sayings about the Kingdom of God."
[2] Cf. BR, No. 76 G, "Motse on Universal Love."
[3] Cf. BR, No. 88, A. H. Silver, "Religion and Social Justice."
[4] Cf. BR, No. 89, Charles O'Donnell, "Moral Principles of a World Society."

meaning of life without abandoning a universal vision. Something of their drive must form a part of any present-day religious commitment. But can social reform or social reconstruction in themselves fully exhaust faith in the Highest? Taken alone, worthy as they are, are they not a kind of second-best? Those for whom the social gospel has come to form the essence of religion have thrown themselves into practical work in secular social movements, like labor organization or the drive for peace, some into great enthusiasm for the achievements and promise of Communist Russia. Indeed, the uncritical ease with which many such religious leaders have identified the winning of such temporal goals with the establishment of the "Kingdom of God" has led to growing doubts of the religious adequacy of any faith that remains on a purely social level. Is religion exhausted in the pursuit of such finite ends?

Social idealism seems an incomplete and truncated religion, even for the social reformer. A commitment that pins its hopes to practical success in controlling and remolding society is apt to lack the deeper faith and the profounder insight that can come from a more "transcendent" ideal. It will have little to sustain it in the face of failure, no stamina with which to confront disillusionment. It will have no weapon against the cynicism bred by the "success" of its social crusades.

The great religions have offered men a transcendent or "spiritual" ideal that goes beyond their finite ends, and raises them above the mere search for material goods, for social goods, even for others. They have given an aim for living that can stand in the face of outward failure, and an incentive for striving on to victory against insuperable odds. They have shown a victory that will not, like merely temporal ends, turn to dust and ashes in the grasp. They have set their goal so high that none may fall into complacency and the pride of attainment; yet they have avoided despair by promising that he who honestly strives will not be lost. They have counseled feeding the hungry and healing the sick; but they have had a vision beyond such easy winning. Men need for their fullest satisfaction such a transcendent ideal — more than abolishing poverty, more than establishing a juster social order, more than bringing peace upon earth. If they have it, they can wrest victory out of the very jaws of defeat.

For in disaster finite ends are revealed as finite, and man sees himself in his true stature as a "spiritual" being, with a vision that can transcend the limits of time and space and the petty conditions of existence. Man can behold what he finds most real in the universe and commit himself to its demands. For religious men, this ultimate to which faith aspires, this ultimate that eludes definition and yet is shadowed forth even now in existence, is conceived as Divine. This object of faith and vision they call God.

D. FUNDAMENTAL RELIGIOUS BELIEFS

286. Faith in the Divine

Starting with religion as something men do, as certain activities they perform, we have been led to consider the vision of what is highest and best that inspires them to do it and makes the entire round of their living meaningful and worth while. Faith in what men see in religious vision, faith in the Divine — what in our tradition is called faith in God — has always seemed the core of the religious life. We normally speak of different religions as differing "faiths"; and when a man has become indifferent to religion, we say "He has lost his faith."

Faith in this sense means loyalty, attachment, commitment to what we "believe in" — remaining steadfast and true to it. To have faith means to be "faithful" to something. We judge that we can tell the most important things about a man from what he is faithful to, from what he genuinely believes in. And experience has taught us that we can tell what a man really "believes in" — perhaps better than he can himself — from a close knowledge of what the course of his life is directed toward. For a man's central allegiance — any faith controlling enough to be called "religious" — must reveal itself in his actions. We are justifiably suspicious of those who proclaim their "faith" but fail to give any concrete evidence of it in their lives. Such men may follow the practices of a religion, they may give intellectual assent to its creed, but they do not really "believe in" it.

Moreover, faith involves more than mere allegiance. When we have faith in another man — in a friend, or in some human leader — we are not only ourselves faithful, loyal, and devoted. We have trust and confidence in him, in his skill perhaps, above all in his character. We entertain certain expectations of how he will act and what he will do. We are convinced he will not fail us or betray our "faith." We can count on him; he will not let us down by falling short of what we expect of him. And when our faith goes beyond these human embodiments of excellence to the things which are not seen, to the Divine, we still have the same trust and confidence. That Highest we have found will not play us false. We can rely upon it, in the expectation that it will never fail to bring inspiration and strength and direction into our lives. This is the conviction that religious faith brings. Men not only discover a supreme Good which demands to be controlling in their lives, but this Good is also revealed as the central reality in the universe. It is not only the chief end of man, it is what the universe is for. It is what makes the world itself significant and worth while.

It is clear from this brief analysis that religious faith is primarily a matter of a man's *attitude* as expressed in his *actions*. It is what a vision of the Divine does to a man, and what he does in consequence — perhaps in the doing gaining a deeper vision. Loyalty, commitment, trust, confidence — these are what we call "practical" attitudes. They are first developed in working together with other men in that intimate devotion to a common enterprise which we call comradeship and even fellowship of spirit. They are appropriate to the give and take of human relationships at their best and finest, when men sink their personal ambitions in the shared desire of each to contribute most effectively to a common task. Few men have missed the taste of this experience of genuine cooperation in some engrossing job, some group cause, some dangerous task — perhaps on the field of battle. Most men experience it first in the ties of the family, which is why those ties have been able to serve in many religions as symbols of the Divine. If only those relations could be made universal and extended to all men! And so men try to think of all mankind as brothers, and the Divine itself seems to them best suggested by the image of a perfect Father.

287. Faith Uses Human Images

It is because these practical attitudes that go to make up religious faith are most clearly realized in the relations between man and man at their best that faith is normally cultivated and deepened in religious fellowship and communion. And it is significant that these attitudes, shadowed forth in human fellowship, are just those which, in clarified form, men take toward the Divine. They feel toward the highest Good they can discern the same kind of devotion and allegiance that the good embodied in another human personality calls forth. In ordering their lives, they place the same kind of hope and confidence in that highest Good which they place in a trusted human comrade. Hence it is natural for their faith to express itself in a conviction of partnership, of fellowship, of cooperation with the Divine. Their deepest feelings are directed toward a Divine Comrade, who seems not less but more human than the best of men — more "human" in realizing in perfected and unalloyed form the qualities which the best men would like to see take hold of their lives — perfect mercy, perfect justice, perfect truth, perfect love.

In our familiar Western religions, this partnership, this cooperation with the Divine, has been felt and expressed as partnership with a Divine Personality, with God. The average man has thought of God in very personal terms, as a loving Father, just and merciful, stern against sin, but patient and full of forgiveness for the repentant sinner.[1] Such a way of conceiving God has made it seem natural that men should feel toward God as they actually do. To such a being men would indeed give their allegiance; in him they would repose their confidence. This is the way they have seen the Divine; this is the way God has revealed himself in their experience. Popular piety, with a touching, if naive, simplicity of feeling, has often pictured God as rather narrowly and crudely human. The wise have understood these childlike ideas as appropriate to the limited experience of the common man, natural expressions of his commitment and trust.

The philosophic theologian has always recognized that here were symbols, concrete imagery, expressions of emotion and

[1] Cf. BR, No. 77 D, "Attributes of God in the Prophets and the Law," and No. 77 E, "The Character of God as Portrayed in the Psalms."

popular imagination. The wisest theologies have insisted that the face of God remains veiled to mortals, and his ways past finding out.[1] But men have thought of the Being to whom they pray as somehow like the best they have learned of human good and human perfection; and so their ideas of God have of necessity varied from age to age with their enlarging experience of the Divine. Eastern religions, like Brahmanism or Buddhism, have held that human personality is much too limited and finite a thing to serve as an adequate symbol for the Divine and have therefore rejected the conception of a personal God. But even here the techniques men have actually employed in their worship have inevitably approached the Divine in personal terms.[2] It is impossible to give voice to penitence and contrition, to thanksgiving and praise, without feeling the presence of One who hears — just as it is impossible to pray without addressing the prayer to Someone who can answer. The very ways in which men have learned they can best express their consecration to the Highest lead them naturally to feel toward that Supreme Good as to a Divine Companion. The resulting conviction of fellowship and "communion" with God strengthens all those "practical" attitudes which we have seen are the essence of religious faith.

288. Religious Beliefs Are Symbols

We have tried to analyze this central aspect of religion, faith in the Divine, because it illustrates clearly the place and function of religious "beliefs" in the religious life. Every religion involves certain ways of believing, as well as ways of feeling and acting. Faith *in* the Divine is associated with particular beliefs *about* the Divine, about God's nature and his relations to men and to the world. Faith in God is primary and central. If such religious vision, commitment to what it discerns, trust and confidence were lacking, men would have no beliefs *about* God. Men must find such faith in their own experience, even when, as normally, it comes to them first as faith in what other men have revealed of God, in what the religious geniuses, the saints and prophets, have discerned of the Divine and exemplified in their lives. This faith is a finding, a discovery, a revelation.

[1] Cf. BR, No. 44, Einstein, "The Lure of the Mysterious"; No. 74 B, "The Wonder and Omnipresence of Heavenly Reason."
[2] Cf. BR, No 73 A to C.

But every vision of God comes to men with a particular and limited experience, living in a particular society with a religious heritage of its own, and with its own way of looking at the universe and man's relation to it. Hence every vision of God is clothed in an imagery, in a set of symbols and beliefs, furnished by the experience of the culture in which men behold it. The Divine reveals itself in the different ways in which different men can best grasp its meaning and import.[1] Some see it as the One of Hindu speculation, others as the loving Father in Heaven of Jesus' revelation. Spinoza beheld it as the rational Order of Nature, Plato as the Idea of the Good.

These different conceptions are all "symbols," we say, meaning that they are ways of suggesting what God has seemed to men to be *like*. They are each bound up with a particular tradition or a particular, or even personal, way of understanding the world. They are the ideas men have found most helpful in feeling and thinking about the Divine. They are the human components in religious vision, the human lens through which the impingement of the Divine on man's life is brought to the focus of a clear image.

These ways of looking at the Divine are symbols men have learned to use in worshiping God together, in consecrating themselves to his service, and in clarifying their ideas about him. They are aids or instruments men employ in carrying on these central activities of religion. Some symbols are material, like the flag, which serves as an instrument for arousing devotion to our country. Others are acts to be performed, like standing at attention when "The Star-Spangled Banner" is played. Still others are intellectual, like the idea that America is "the land of the free" or the embodiment of the "democratic ideal." Religious beliefs are "intellectual symbols" which point to or suggest the supreme realities that men have found in their own experience. When men wish to express and strengthen a common feeling and purpose, they must use such symbolic means, which arouse in each man the deep feelings of devotion and commitment to what they suggest. Without such shared beliefs, men could hardly practice their religion in fellowship and cooperation with others.

[1] Cf. BR, No. 68, Ramakrishna, "The Unity of Religions."

289. The Function of Religious Symbols

Beliefs about the Divine operate in the same way as the other techniques of worship and devotion. These intellectual symbols not only serve to intensify the social bonds between those who share the same vision of the Highest. They also help to strengthen and reinforce the central attitudes of religious faith, which we have found to be allegiance to and trust in God. And they deepen men's insight into the demands of the Divine upon their lives. For example, when we conceive the best standards of Good we can discern to be "the will of God," or when we take love for our neighbor as a Divine "commandment," we are employing the symbols "will" and "command" drawn from our experience of social relations. We are using these human symbols to strengthen our devotion to those ideal standards and to fortify our resolve to make them controlling in our actions. They are like the commands of a perfect Will to which we have given our allegiance. At the same time, these symbols we use intensify our conviction of partnership and cooperation with the central reality of things, of fellowship with the Highest. That Highest seems to us to be like a Will with whose purposes we can merge our own.

This is the religious function of belief in the symbol of "God's will"; this is how that belief actually operates in the practice of the religious life. Reflective men may well be led to ask, in what sense love toward one's fellow-man can be said to be the Divine "will," in what sense God "has" a will, and how far it is to be understood as like a human will. These are all questions of philosophic inquiry, and those who have asked them have come to many different ways of construing the philosophic meaning of the Divine Will. But the religions which have found the symbol of "the will of God" to be effective in their practices have never been in doubt as to the *religious* sense and meaning of that belief — which is, to intensify devotion to and fellowship with God. And had "the will of God" not been discovered to possess this vital religious function, philosophical theologians would never have been led to raise their questions about its theoretical interpretation.

Again, the Christian proclaims, "I know that my Redeemer liveth." This affirmation of faith in the Divine is couched in the symbols of one of the most complex beliefs of Christian theology, its theory of Christ's "redemption" and "atonement." This theory, rooted in man's moral experience of sin and salvation, has been elaborated in different ages in countless subtle ways, each of which has involved many complex beliefs about what is just in the relations between persons. Each "doctrine" of the Atonement has, therefore, reflected the moral sensitivity of some particular society toward its characteristic social arrangements. These varied theories have all played their part in developing the significance of the ideal standard of "justice," and in clarifying men's insight into what is really just.

But they are all irrelevant to the *religious* function and meaning of the conviction which the affirmation expresses, that the revelation of the Divine in Christ can bring "salvation" to those who genuinely have faith *in* that revelation. This belief operates to intensify in particular the attitudes of hope, trust, and confidence. At the same time, it is clear that the "knowledge" the Christian claims is not "knowledge" in the ordinary sense, something that could be refuted by an appeal to observation or argument. It is a conviction of value, an expression of faith *in* Christ and in his revelation of the Divine.

290. Religious Beliefs Express and Strengthen a Practical Commitment

These illustrations from one religious tradition bring out the *religious* functions performed by the beliefs about God with which faith *in* God is clothed. Such beliefs are ways of expressing the "practical" attitudes of commitment and confidence which make up that faith itself. They are symbols which men use to foster, strengthen, and clarify their faith in the Divine. Hence, whatever symbols, whatever beliefs about the objects of the central and primary religious vision can be used effectively to express, enhance, and deepen faith in God, can play a genuine part in the religious life. The beliefs we find most effective in thus serving our faith will be the most adequate symbols for us to employ. The standard for judging such religious beliefs is their adequacy in performing their proper religious function: differing beliefs about God are better or worse helps for expressing, strengthening, and clarifying faith in the Divine.

Such beliefs are not properly said to be "true" or "false," for the function of faith, as we have pointed out, is practical; it is not to give men "truth" or "knowledge." Faith is a *practical* response, in our attitude and in our actions, to what is revealed in religious vision. The beliefs or symbols faith uses can of course be said to be "true to" that vision and experience, in the sense of being an appropriate or adequate expression of it. This is the sense in which we say that the idea of a Divine Shepherd, in a great religious poem like the Twenty-third Psalm, is "true to" the confidence we repose in the Divine.[1] And religious vision may indeed behold a Supreme Truth. But it is a vision of "the Truth that sets men free," not a knowledge of truths that can be demonstrated or verified. The function of such a central liberating "Truth" is so different from the function of the truths that go to make up our ordinary knowledge that it would probably be much less confusing not to speak of "religious Truth" at all. If we do, we must be careful not to lose sight of the specific religious function of such "Truth" and of the beliefs that express it.

One of the most perplexing and disturbing facts about the religions of man, one which has led to most of the evil consequences that can be charged against too narrow a religious faith, is greatly clarified when we realize that religious beliefs are to be judged, not by their literal truth or correctness as a series of propositions about facts, but by their adequacy and effectiveness in performing their *religious* function of strengthening faith. For what beliefs best serve one man's faith in the Divine may be quite incapable of doing so for another. The beliefs employed in one religion are for the most part not those used in another. Even within the same tradition and culture, the beliefs effective for one age prove inadequate for a changed experience or a changed way of understanding the world. Though the familiar symbols may be retained, their meaning must be modified to take account of these changes. Even at the same time, and among men devoted to the same highest Good, different individuals will find different ways of conceiving God effective for them, depending on their experience and on their degree of philosophical reflection. The distinction we have made between

---

[1] Cf. BR, No. 77 E, "The Character of God as Portrayed in the Psalms."

the philosophic theologian and the common man has obtained in all religions, and will no doubt persist until all men are equally wise.

When those who use one set of beliefs take their own symbols as alone "true" and judge all others to be simply false and wrong, then religious faith is apt to develop the poisonous weeds of intolerance, bigotry, and fanaticism. There have even been times when men fought bitterly about which was the "true" form of worship. Most of us have come to realize today that different men can best worship God in different ways; [1] we do not quarrel with those whose devotion is strengthened in a manner other than ours. We are glad that they have found whatever forms will satisfy their various needs. Could we only see that beliefs about the Highest, like other forms of devotion, are to be judged as we have learned to judge varying types of worship, we might likewise rejoice that different men, and different religions, have been able to express their vision in ways that have proved adequate for them. We Westerners, accustomed by long tradition to think of God in personal terms, might even come to feel a fellowship in faith, if not in specific belief, with those great Eastern religions which think of the Divine as an impersonal Principle of Good. [2]

For when we see religious beliefs as essentially symbols for the attitude of faith in the Divine, we can use those symbols to unite ourselves with our fellow men. Religious symbols may bring men together in shared feeling and a fellowship of faith, however they may differ in their intellectual interpretation of what the symbols point to. An enlightened and generous faith would not only enter into the communion of a common worship with all who employ the same symbols to shadow forth that faith. It would be able to respect the differing worship and symbols of others and to see all men's religious symbols, all their varied beliefs, as pointing to a common aspiration after the Highest and a common devotion to the best insight revealed to them. [3]

[1] Cf. BR, No. 68, Ramakrishna, "The Unity of Religions."
[2] Cf. BR, No. 73 C, "The Indwelling Presence of the Supreme Being," and 73 D, "The Parable of the Salt."
[3] Cf. BR, No. 69, "Mental Hospitality."

291. The Intellectual Commitment Involved in Faith

We have been at some pains to point out that religious faith is a practical commitment to the Divine and to its insistent demands upon human life. It is not primarily an intellectual commitment to any particular theoretical interpretation of what the Divine is. It is a way of living, of feeling and acting, not a way of explaining. It involves beliefs about God and his commandments; but these beliefs are symbols faith uses for its own purposes, which are directed toward living rather than toward knowing and understanding. Faith in the Christian revelation of God, in the ideal standards of mercy, justice, and love, involves the religious man in no single and uniform intellectual interpretation of what such standards are or how they function. As we have seen, it does not even commit him to a particular way of applying those standards. That is an insistent task which calls for the best of human intelligence and wisdom.

There is, to be sure, a sense in which any faith in the Divine does involve a certain intellectual commitment. To have faith *in* anything does imply that we are making an affirmation of *value:* this is the best we have found. We are denying all views which would reject the value of what we are committed to. Faith in the Divine does mean the rejection of any position which would maintain that there is no "meaning" to life or that the universe discloses no central reality which can make living meaningful and significant for man. Faith denies that man's vision of what we have been calling the Divine is a mere matter of man's own wishful thinking, with no roots in the nature of things. Religious faith takes for granted the central reality of its object of attachment and the possibility of human partnership and cooperation with that reality. It is these convictions which it uses human symbols to express. These assumptions seem to be minimal conditions of religious faith, the least it can be taken to imply about the nature of the universe. The universe does disclose a compelling Good which makes man's life in it meaningful; man's greatest good lies in cooperating with the Good at the heart of things. Faith in the Divine commits one to such beliefs about what is good; it involves these convictions of value.[1]

[1] Cf. BR, No. 86, Georgia Harkness, "Evidence for Belief in God," especially section f.

292. Beliefs about Human Nature Are Practical

We have so far been speaking of those fundamental religious beliefs about God and his commandments that work to strengthen and clarify faith in the Divine. Religions normally involve and utilize other fundamental beliefs as well, beliefs about the nature and destiny of man, and about the world and its history. What we have been pointing out about the beliefs that enhance the faith in the Divine applies equally to these other fundamental religious beliefs. They are all symbols that play a part in the practice of religion and not intellectual answers to theoretical questions of understanding. They "explain" certain facts about ourselves and our world by making them plain and clear, by focusing our attention upon them and their religious significance. They do not "explain" them in the sense of offering a scientific analysis, or reasoned philosophical theory about them. Like beliefs about God, they express fundamental convictions of value.

Thus religious insight has thrown much light on human nature, its ideal possibilities and its practical limitations. That insight has been expressed in many beliefs that have tried to give an adequate conception of man's high stature, together with a condemnation of his shortcomings in actual achievement. Pascal's vision of man's greatness and his weakness is the classic example of the attempt to do justice both to man's capacities for envisaging ideal possibilities beyond the actual and to his powers of using these capacities in a way to shame the beasts. Man has been seen as a "child of God," "made in God's image"; he has been viewed less favorably as a "son of the old Adam," as condemned by "original sin" to wickedness and extinction without Divine help. In the individualistic West, human personality has been viewed as so supremely valuable that men have found it inconceivable that the hand of death itself could destroy it. In some Eastern faiths, personality has been seen as an ignoble limitation and an evil to be escaped from even in this life by merging oneself in an impersonal Reality. But whatever shade of confidence or distrust men have placed in themselves and their powers, religious vision has never ceased to throw new light on the old question, "What is Man, that Thou art mindful of him?"

Take the belief that man is the child of God, which represents one of the two poles between which religious estimates of human nature have oscillated.[1] This faith in man's powers of growth and development has played a central part in much recent religious feeling; many would hold that it is basic in the teachings of Jesus. What does it mean in religious practice? It means that in every man there lies the possibility of developing higher capacities, the moral and spiritual qualities of character. There is little actual evidence that such energies exist latent in *all* men; this is a faith, not a reasoned conclusion. In the lives of the great majority there is no proof or indication; more often than not our experience with human nature as it is seems to point to the contrary. Those who share this faith shrink from denying potentialities of higher things to even the most degraded brute of a man; they feel that they could not remain true to their own best nature if they did treat him as the beast he seems to be. They may be wrong in this faith; it may turn out that mankind, as a whole, is utterly incapable of learning to control the savage that dwells in human nature. But they still dare to affirm that this surface animality is not all, that latent capacities are present in man's nature; and to that faith they dedicate renewed efforts to call them forth.

Or take that belief about human nature which has been most widely shared in the great religions that have risen to a universal vision, the belief that all men are brothers. Religious insight has differed as to the capacities for growth men possess. But whether men are united in a common power of achievement or in a common weakness and impotence, in a common need for deliverance, that men are united in human brotherhood has been a conviction of all the religions that have outgrown their original tribal limitations.[2] When Paul proclaimed to the men of Athens, "For God made of one blood every nation of men to dwell on all the face of the earth," he was speaking what, to our best anthropological knowledge today, is literal scientific truth. He was speaking, however, not as a scientist concerned with extending knowledge, but as a religious teacher concerned with

---

[1] Cf. BR, No. 76 C, "Human Nature and Human Duties," No. 76 E, "Mencius on Human Nature and Goodness"; No. 77 F, Judaism, "What Is Man?"

[2] Cf. BR, No. 70, "A Sheaf of Golden Rules from Twelve Religions"; No. 76 D, "The Golden Rule in Confucianism"; No. 81 A and B relating to the Baha'i Faith.

men's attitudes and behavior. He wanted men to take human brotherhood seriously. He was expressing a practical commitment.

293. Intellectual Interpretations of Religious Beliefs

We have been trying to point out that religious beliefs have their own *religious* function, which is to express and clarify men's practical religious commitments. They can stand on their own feet and be judged by their adequacy in performing their own function. They are essentially independent of all questions of philosophic or scientific "truth." Religious beliefs offer no explanation of anything in rivalry to science or philosophic inquiry; they furnish data for such inquiry, not competition with its conclusions.

The thoughtful man will naturally reflect upon these beliefs about the Divine object of religious faith and vision which prove so effective in clarifying his vision and enhancing his faith. He will seek to "understand" them; that is, he will try to "interpret" them, to fit them into his general scheme of understanding and into his whole fund of knowledge about the world and human life. Every religion contains, among the ideas it uses, the results of such past attempts to understand and interpret its fundamental religious beliefs. Along with the vision of the Divine, revealed in its saints and prophets and expressed in the most adequate symbols they could devise, its sacred literature comprises bits of the knowledge of their day and scraps of philosophic interpretation which are clearly not on the same level as what their religious genius has beheld.

The Christian tradition, we have seen, since it has expressed the faith of societies in which there has been an unusually strong intellectual interest and desire to understand, has come to embrace a great wealth and variety of such "theological" interpretations of its central beliefs. These interpretations have incorporated successively most of the great philosophies and schemes of understanding the world that were familiar in their day. Thus, the theology of the Church in ancient times was naturally formulated in terms of the Platonic philosophy, which, with its own religious insights, had come to seem the best way of explaining the experience of men for whom religious faith was central. The different Christian churches have all regarded some parts of these philosophic efforts to understand as belonging with their genuinely "fundamental" religious beliefs. They have incorporated them into their "creeds" and "confessions of faith" and expected their members to "believe" them.

As a result, many of these intellectual explanations of religious insight have themselves come to acquire a genuine religious function. Starting as efforts at philosophic interpretation, they have been turned into symbols serving the faith in the Divine, which can then furnish the occasion for a variety of further interpretations in terms of some other philosophical language. Thus, Origen elaborated the Christian doctrine of the Trinity. He used the ideas and the language of the Platonic philosophy, then widely accepted, to give a speculative explanation of the Christian vision of the nature of God and of God's revelation in Christ and in the life of the Christian communities. But in the practice and the controversies of the early church, the Trinity came to express the fundamental Christian convictions of value. From a theory it became a "doctrine" or teaching, and at the Council of Nicaea it was proclaimed a "dogma" or authoritative belief. Its original explanatory value was forgotten, and it began to gather all those accretions of feeling and meaning which have made it a central religious symbol in the Christian tradition. The Trinity thus became a way of conceiving God which itself challenged interpretation in terms of quite different philosophies from the Platonism in which it was originally expressed.

It is clear, therefore, why religious beliefs have been interpreted and reinterpreted in the course of their long career. We have seen how the ideal standards of Good revealed to religious insight are normally applied in detailed priestly codes adapted to the narrow and limited needs of a particular society. When conditions and problems change, prophetic criticism must call men back from this inadequate application to the standards that are basic and challenge men to attempt a fresh application.

What is true of the moral vision of a religious tradition is equally true of its intellectual beliefs. When science grows and philosophies change, and men come to feel the need of fresh interpretations in terms of their new ways of understanding, there is needed a similar return to the religious beliefs that are really "fundamental." We have been suggesting that those religious beliefs are "fundamental" that perform a genuine *religious function*, in contrast to those that merely give an intellectual understanding — those that express and enhance religious insight and faith, not those that construe that insight in terms of some particular philosophy that may now be outmoded. The need for new interpretations of the beliefs actually functioning in practical commitment to the Divine is a problem always confronting a religion with an extensive "theology." Never was the demand more insistent than today.

294. Central Problems of Faith: (a) Is God Transcendent or Immanent?

Faith in the Divine raises, for thoughtful men, many intellectual problems. The most important are those suggested by the enduring aspects of human experience which men face in any society, like the fact of human aspiration after a better way of living or like the insistent fact of evil. Reflecting on these broad features of human experience, men seek to elucidate and make clearer the meaning of their faith and to think of God in ways that will throw the most light on these universal facts of experience. These are really the central intellectual problems involved in religious faith itself, the perennial problems of "theological" thought.

How, for instance, shall men understand the relation between themselves and the object of religious vision and faith? Is the Divine a Good so perfect that it lies impossibly beyond them? Does it beckon — or command — them to strain after it from afar? Does it enter man's life only to condemn every possible human achievement as worthless in comparison with its own infinite Perfection? Or is the Divine rather a Presence that is close at hand, filling the hearts and souls of men, ever ready for men to turn to in their need? Is God to be found in the common relations of life — in the love of a mother for her child, in the devotion of friend to friend, in the sacrifice of the soldier for his comrades? Were the Stoics right in holding that "God is for one mortal to help another"? Is God the central Reality of which we ourselves are but particular finite expressions, so that the Divine is what we really are in our true nature, as the great Eastern religions have maintained? Was St. Paul adequately expressing our relation to the Divine in saying that "in God we live and move and have our being"?

In the technical language of theology, this issue is phrased as the question whether God is "transcendent" or "immanent." Is the Divine "transcendent," that is, does it exceed or lie wholly beyond the limitations of human nature? Or is it "immanent," that is, does it "indwell" human nature at its best and suffuse all life with its presence?

This question of the relation of God to human experience is very intimately bound up with the value we assign to man's capacities for achievement. Those who distrust human nature tend to emphasize the transcendence of God; those who have confidence in man's power to conceive and follow an ideal tend to think in terms of "Divine Immanence." Those most impressed by the moral perfection of the Good they have come to see raise it far above actual human experience and contrast it sharply with man's limited attainment. Thus the moral prophet finds in God primarily the transcendent Good before which all men fall short. Those impressed by the sense of trust, confidence, partnership, that religious faith involves have always emphasized the nearness and "immanence" of the Divine in their lives. The mystic, in whom such a feeling of cooperation and even of union with God is strongest, normally finds the Divine filling the world with its presence and close at hand in the depths of his experience.

It is clear that the way we understand God's relation to man is really an expression of which aspect of our experience of the Divine we find of greatest importance. Aspiration towards a perfect Good, coupled with condemnation by that Good, and trust and fellowship with a Reality we have found close at hand are the two poles between which men's attitude of practical commitment to God moves. Transcendence and immanence are the ways of thinking of God which express these two sides of religious faith. The experience of different religions, different ages, and different men has varied on this basic conviction of value. Consequently, men have at times laid the emphasis on God's transcendence, at other times on the Divine immanence.

The fact that faith in God combines these two practical attitudes seems to point to the wisdom of conceiving God as both transcendent and immanent. The side of faith which emphasizes aspiration and commitment to an ideal standard makes it natural to think of God as a transcendent Good. We have emphasized the role in the religious life of such a transcendent or truly "spiritual" ideal. On the other hand, the side of faith which involves hope and confidence and cooperation makes us think of the Divine as a very intimate and central part of our experience. After all, it is men who achieve even the most transcendent vision and exemplify its power in their lives.

The great religions have tried, in their reflection about the Divine, to give due weight to each of these aspects of its relation to man. To overlook either is, in the light of the experience of the race, to miss an essential element in religious faith. Those who have found in their faith the peace and blessedness of salvation have normally been filled with a sense of the Divine Presence and of oneness with God. What the nearness or immanence of God has meant to men who have felt it profoundly is made clear in passages from several of the great religions included in the *Book of Readings*.[1]

295. Central Problems of Faith: (b) The Problem of Evil

Overcoming evil, especially the evil in man's own nature, and rising above the evil that cannot be overcome have always been the central practical problems of religious faith. Understanding the meaning of the presence of evil in the same universe that contains the revelation of the Divine has always been the most difficult theoretical problem raised by the fact of faith. Indeed, it is evil, and human or moral evil in particular, that has been the greatest obstacle, as well as the greatest incentive, to faith in God. It is the desire to rise above evil and to obtain a proper perspective upon it that has provoked the profoundest religious vision of the Divine. At the same time, many have felt, "How can I believe in God, how can I have trust and confidence in him, when life contains so many terrible things, so much injustice and hatred and cruelty!" Disillusioned about their fellow-men, some have despaired of God; how can mercy and justice and love be the most real things in the world, when they seem to

---

[1] Hinduism: BR, No. 73 B, C, D. Taoism: BR, No. 74 B. Confucianism: BR, No. 76 B. Judaism: BR, No. 77 E. Christianity: BR, No. 78 G. Islam: BR, No. 79 C.

have so small a part in man's actions? How can there be any meaning in life, any central direction? [1]

This problem has been made especially acute in our Western religious traditions by the way in which God has been conceived. For, in order to magnify the central reality of the Divine, these religions have thought of God as "all-powerful," and as "maker" of heaven and earth. To strengthen the power of the Divine in their lives, they have made it the only power in the universe and therefore responsible for all that takes place. These beliefs about God raise the question, why should a God, at once perfectly good and all-powerful, permit, or even have created, evil in his universe? Theologians, starting out from such a conception of God, have been committed to the task of trying somehow to justify the ways of God to man. The Eastern religions have not escaped this problem. But they have made central man's own responsibility for all the evil he encounters and have emphasized the way of deliverance from the pains of life. [2]

Western thinkers have wrestled with the problem in the terms set for them by their belief that God is at once supreme Power and supreme Perfection. Some, especially those in the long Platonic tradition, have, like the Hindus and Buddhists, denied that evil is "real" and considered it rather as an imperfection or lack of complete reality. [3] But this purely negative and relative conception of evil hardly does justice to the facts of experience and has never satisfied those with any moral sensitivity to the very positive side of the worst evils, human guilt and sin.

Most attempts to explain evil have abandoned either the perfect goodness or the perfect power of God, or both. Few have consciously held that God is less than wholly good. Traditional Christian theology, to be sure, has attributed ways of acting and motives to God which hardly measure up to the standards of human goodness. These ideas are intelligible only as symbolic renderings of the way experience does treat men. But in their profoundest grapplings with the problem of evil, men have in the end refused to betray their vision of the Divine perfection. They have rather sacrificed God's absolute power, which is in

[1] Cf. BR, No. 103, H. E. Fosdick, "What about Evil?"
[2] Cf. BR, No. 75 A, "The Greatness of Buddha"; No. 75 C, "The Parable of the Lost Son"; No. 75 D, section a, "The Foundation of Self-Culture."
[3] See Part V of this book, sections 358, 360, 365.

any event impossible to construe save as a symbol for the controlling reality of the Divine in human life. They have held that God finds it best to conform to the conditions human life imposes for realizing the best human goodness. The generally accepted answer to the question, Why does God permit evil? is, in the word of St. Augustine, repeated by subsequent Christian theologians like St. Thomas: "He judged it better to bring good out of evil, than not to permit any evil to exist." Evil is not itself "really" good; it is not "unreal." But evil is all for the best; it is the condition for attaining the highest good.

296. The Meaning of Evil Is Practical

This is hardly a satisfactory explanation of why evil should exist in the universe, or why it is a necessary condition of the highest human good. The ground of God's judgment St. Augustine wisely found "inscrutable." And there is general agreement today that there is no answer to that question of understanding why there is evil, any more than there is an answer to the question why the universe contains good, why it reveals the Divine. The human mind has been able to find no "reason" why the world, or man's experience of it, should possess any of the pervasive traits they do. Religious men must in the end express their natural piety to the source of their being by calling such ultimate facts "the will of God." We cannot understand them in the sense of being able to explain why they are there.

We *can* understand them, however, in the sense of being able to discover what they *mean* in human experience, what they make possible — and impossible — for us, how we can use them in the problems of living. We cannot explain why there should be evil. But we can understand the *meaning* of evil. And, like all the questions raised by religious commitment to the Divine, the "meaning" of evil is in the end a practical rather than a theoretical problem. Rather, the only kind of reason we can discover for the fact of evil, as for the fact of good or for the fact of the existence of the universe itself, is what it makes possible.

While St. Augustine, therefore, scarcely explained the reason why there should be evil in the world, he did state the answer of religious faith to the profounder question of the meaning of the fact of evil in our experience. When we say, speaking in the symbolic language of religion, that God permits evil in order that out of it there may come a greater good than would be possible were there no evil, we are saying that evil is to be understood, not as an isolated fact, but as a means to the best that can be made out of it. The world puts the problem squarely up to us. The *meaning* of evil lies in what we are able to do with it. That meaning depends upon us, on our own attitude and actions, on how we face the particular evils that come to us, and how we use our faith in the Highest to overcome them and rise above them. The significance of evil in our lives is to serve as a challenge to us "to bring good out of it," with the help of God — in cooperation with the Divine to which we are committed.

And, although we can find no "reason" why the conditions of human life are what they are, it is still true that under those conditions men can, by their use of the evils they encounter, achieve a greater good than if they lived out their lives wholly innocent of all knowledge of evil. Every human triumph in invention and knowledge is a practical overcoming of the physical evils of existence, every success in the better ordering of human relations is an overcoming of some of the evils men inflict on each other. The stimulus evil opposes is a necessary condition of the adventure of living; without it, men would have been driven to create none of their magnificent cultural achievements.

In its deepest meaning, life transcends mere adventure and reaches tragic heights.[1] The ultimate overcoming of inescapable evil must take place in a man's own soul and involves what he does with himself in the face of the evils that cannot be eradicated. The supreme use of evil is, in the end, to deepen our vision of the Highest. We should all agree that such achievements of character are the best that man can offer to justify his ways to God. We cannot conceive the highest human living without including in it this element of overcoming and triumphing over evil. Whether the life of a being who could achieve the highest without ever encountering evil might be still better than the best human life is surely an inscrutable question. That being would not be a man, nor would his life conform to the conditions of human existence. The best human life has faced evil

[1] See BR, No. 104, Rabindranath Tagore, "The Problem of Evil."

and risen above it. This is the conviction of value expressed in the religious "solution" to the problem of evil. This is the practical attitude toward evil that follows from commitment to God.

297. The Ground of Fundamental Religious Beliefs

The basic convictions of value which go to make up religious commitment and trust, like the fundamental conviction of the Reality of the Divine itself, rest ultimately on the revelation men have found, or the insight they have achieved in their experience. It is doubtful whether any of the long line of "proofs" or arguments advanced for the "existence" of God [1] or for the basic judgments of value which faith in God involves have ever brought conviction to any who had not already in some sense "found" God and encountered the power of God in their own lives. But equally, for those who have once discovered for themselves the meaning of the Divine, no amount of new knowledge, no new way of understanding the world intellectually, can shake their faith in the Reality of what they have found. Further knowledge and reflection may well lead them to think about God in new terms and may even make some of the symbols of traditional belief seem inadequate. Thus the older image of God as a king seated upon his throne no longer satisfies many, even as an image, in our modern democratic society. But although the growth of men's knowledge may lead them to alter their beliefs about the Divine, it normally serves only to strengthen their faith in the Divine — if they have really "seen" God.

The Divine is something men "find," something they come to "see," something which is "revealed" to them in their experience. It is not something they arrive at through rational argument or demonstration or through an intellectual search for the explanation of the nature of things. When such philosophic inquiry does arrive at a supreme Truth, thinkers like St. Augustine or St. Thomas or Spinoza have normally been convinced that, in terms of their way of understanding, they have found *what* God is. But they could hardly "recognize" that this first principle of knowledge is God, if they had not already found God in the practical commitment of their faith. Men no more find God

[1] See BR, No. 86, Georgia Harkness, "Evidence for Belief in God."

by argument than they find by argument the beauty with which Plato was convinced the Divine is closely allied. Argument can, at most, point to the Divine and tell men where to look. When men have seen, it can clarify their beliefs about what they have beheld.

The functions of religious vision and faith are so different from those of any enterprise, like science or philosophy, that tries to extend our knowledge and our interpretation of experience, that it is difficult to see how such divergent activities could ever come into serious competition. There can be, for example, no conflict in general between "religion" and "science" as explanations of anything. For whenever we are concerned with explanation and understanding, we are engaged in scientific or philosophic inquiry. Religion is no more a way of explaining things than is art or political activity: explanation is not the function of these enterprises. Even when we are explaining something in art or religion, we are engaged in inquiry. Theology, conceived as an explanation of something, is a philosophical, not a religious, enterprise, and is bound by the standards of such inquiry. A religion may embrace and use among its symbols an explanation; the religions of groups interested in explanation normally do. Further reflective inquiry may then find a better explanation. But the ensuing conflict will be, not between "religion" and the new explanation, but between an older and now inadequate explanation and a more adequate one.[1]

Religious beliefs, as we have seen, are symbols which faith employs; and it is as symbols that they perform their religious function, even should they incidentally happen to be scientifically "true." They can perform that religious function just as well if there is no scientific evidence for their "truth"; they will perform it no better if some scheme of science can "demonstrate" their validity. One might well ask, Are not fundamental scientific beliefs — the "theories" of physics or psychology, for instance — likewise symbols employed in the practice of scientific investigation, whose validity depends upon their fruitfulness in guiding inquiry rather than on their literal "truth"? Our most careful analyses of scientific procedure would seem to point this way. Men have a natural desire to bring the beliefs in

[1] See BR, No. 87, A. H. Silver, "Science and Religion."

terms of which they try to interpret their faith into harmony with these scientific symbols of the moment. But the religious beliefs we have distinguished as "fundamental," on the ground that they express and serve men's basic convictions of value, will in all likelihood remain essentially irrelevant to questions of literal truth.

298. Harmonizing Religious Beliefs with Other Beliefs: Rational Theology

Nevertheless, religious faith does not operate in a vacuum. Many of those who share it do have an interest in explanation and truth. In the major cultures, such men have managed to work out imposing schemes of understanding the world and man's place in it. These schemes usually embrace the same basic convictions of value already consecreated in the religion of that society. They normally attempt to interpret and criticize its religious beliefs. They try to introduce some order and harmonious relation among these beliefs, through a rational reinterpretation of what we call "mythology." This intellectual interest began among the priestly class, probably as part of the task of teaching the tradition to new recruits. The wise men of India and the early philosophers of Greece carried it further, to a reflective interpretation of those religious beliefs that seemed to them intellectually and morally fundamental.

When a scientific enterprise emerged in Greece, thinkers like Plato and Aristotle applied its methods and concepts in interpreting the Divine. Both developed a "rational theology," in which they tried to demonstrate the necessity of a first principle in their scheme of science which they could identify with "the deathless and eternal and divine." They held that the fundamental way of understanding anything is to find what it does, what it is directed toward or is good for. Thus the world as a whole is to be understood as directed toward and as making possible the highest Good. The ultimate meaning of the universe consists in the rational vision of the Supreme Good at which all its processes are ultimately aiming — what Plato called the "Idea of the Good," and Aristotle the "Unmoved Mover." In Greek thought the object of religious allegiance was thus seen as the highest principle of explanation and understanding; what men aspire to was at the same time what all the processes of the universe are aiming at. For the Greeks were convinced that what gives most of understanding is most divine.

When Jews became familiar with this Greek philosophy, they tried to combine these intellectual visions of God with what their own insight had revealed of the Divine. It was the Jew, Philo of Alexandria, who worked out the main outlines of subsequent Christian theology. And when the Christians came to give a philosophical interpretation of the religious beliefs involved in their faith, they likewise identified God with the supreme object of the reigning Platonic thought, the notion of the "Logos" or intelligible order of Ideas. When, much later, in the thirteenth century, men, seeking a fuller science of the world, studied Aristotle, they in turn identified the ultimate principle of his scheme of physical science, the "Unmoved Mover," with the God of the Christian tradition. St. Thomas, best known of the medieval formulators of rational theology, concludes each of his demonstrations of the first principle of his science with the words, "and this all men understand to be God."

The religious practice of the Western tradition, strongly influenced by Greek thought, has thus normally expressed and consecrated intellectual and scientific values by viewing God as the supreme Truth. The subtle and learned have identified God with the basic principles of successive schemes of scientific understanding — with the Logos, the Unmoved Mover, the Order of Nature of the seventeenth-century scientists, the First Force of Newtonian thought, the Absolute of idealistic speculation, Creative Evolution, Cosmic Energy, Space-Time. Scientists and philosophers have been able to use the principles which were central in their understanding of the world as religious symbols for the Divine.

To harmonize religious and scientific beliefs by identifying their objects is not the most important intellectual problem of religion. It is doubtful how much the average man has ever cared about this concern of the philosophically-minded to achieve intellectual consistency. But it is a human desire, deeply embedded in our scientific culture. And there is little doubt that what has so often been accomplished in the past can be effected once again, if men have the will. Religious thought can doubtless once more interpret Hebrew myth and Platonic symbol, this time in terms of the myths and symbols of our science, of its ultimate organizing principles. Thus men's intellectual and religious allegiance will be brought together, their philosophic understanding united with their religious vision.

This harmonizing enterprise would be much easier should our science become once more what the science of the Greeks was, a genuinely inclusive science that could explain human life and experience in terms of the same scheme of understanding that made the rest of the world intelligible. The task was especially difficult during the reign of Newtonian mechanics, which was obviously inadequate to explain man's human and social life. It is hard to find anything in mechanics that can serve as the symbol for the Divine. So long as men regarded Newtonian mechanics as the final way of understanding their world, any "rational theology" seemed impossible, and critics like Hume and Kant buried the whole attempt with elaborate funerals. But Kant also showed that mechanics explains only one aspect of experience. His criticism opened the way for men to return again, in the idealistic systems of the nineteenth century, to schemes of understanding which, just because they did seriously try to explain the life of man, were able to arrive at ultimate principles of understanding which could be identified with God.

And now physical science itself has, in our generation, pushed on to much more complex schemes of understanding and to more fundamental principles than those of mechanics. The speculative dogmas of nineteenth-century physics have today either crumbled or been revealed as postulates of inquiry. In our present-day philosophies it seems once more possible to understand man's life and the processes of nature in terms of the same set of concepts. Hence, it is no wonder that these philosophies are beginning to find a place for God in nature, and that reflective physicists are once more undertaking the elaboration of a rational theology. As we achieve again an adequate philosophy of nature, which does not leave human life an unintelligible anomaly, the ancient enterprise of reinterpreting religious beliefs in terms of our latest scheme of understanding seems destined to rebirth. This is of course primarily an enterprise of philosophical understanding. From the standpoint of the religious life, what is important is not the particular way in which it is carried out, but the fact that it can still be done. Our philosophies and our more unified science once again provide a central place for the reality of the Divine.

299. Harmonizing Religious Beliefs with Other Beliefs: Faith and Reason

Even when rational theology has been most successful in discovering some scientific or philosophical first principle which it could use as a symbol for the Divine, men have never found it enough to limit their religious beliefs to what can be thus demonstrated or rationally established. It is very hard to pray to an abstract principle like the Unmoved Mover or the Supreme Being or the Absolute. The concrete ways in which men think of God in practicing their religion do not come from such schemes of scientific or philosophic understanding. Even when, with Greek science, men understood the world in terms of the "Good," the character of that Good — for Christians, its qualities of perfect mercy, justice, and love — they learned, not through scientific demonstration, but through religious insight. St. Thomas was expressing this distinction when he held that, while rational theology can demonstrate the existence of God, certain of God's attributes, like goodness, and certain of God's relations to the world, the essential Christian beliefs about the nature of God come from "Faith," not from "Reason." They were revealed in Christ. Without the aid of this revelation given through the teachings of the Church, Reason cannot alone reach these insights into the character of God, though it can understand their meaning once they have been given.

This is the difference traditionally made between the beliefs of "revealed" theology and those of "rational" or "natural" theology. It is really the basic distinction we have been drawing between the "fundamental" religious beliefs that are involved in the practical commitments of faith and the "subsidiary" beliefs that fit them into our body of knowledge. We have been pointing out that, while any adequate scheme of understanding the world must find a place for the central reality of the Divine, the "Divine" or Godlike character of that central reality must be learned from what St. Thomas calls "Faith" or "revelation." The fundamental convictions of value involved in religious faith in the Divine come from the insight or vision man's experience reveals. They are ultimately independent of any rational theology.

The most influential defense in modern times of this independence of "fundamental" religious beliefs was made by Kant. He showed that the scheme of Newtonian mechanics, which he thought was the scientific truth about the world, contained no adequate intellectual symbol for the Divine. But at the same time, by careful analysis he made it clear that this scientific truth is a human interpretation of but one side of our experience and is not the whole story about the universe in which we find ourselves. The beliefs involved in other aspects of our experience, like art or religion or the moral life, while irrelevant to Newtonian mechanics, are not to be discarded because they cannot be judged as literal truth. Religious beliefs are those which are really essential to religious faith, not merely those which can be rationally demonstrated.

Kant thought his criticism of rational theology had made impossible any further attempts to demonstrate religious beliefs by the methods of natural science. As we have seen, the working out of other schemes of understanding, first in idealistic philosophies, and more recently in our science itself, throws doubt on this supposed negative result of his analysis. But on the positive side, nearly all subsequent intellectual interpretations of religious beliefs have followed Kant in emphasizing their primary function in connection with religious faith. Kant himself founded religious faith on man's moral experience. This has proved too narrow a foundation. While the practical and moral commitment to a Supreme Good is undoubtedly central in religious faith, present religious thought would emphasize, as we have done, the great variety of kinds of experience involved in the religious life out of which faith grows. But if we no longer have to draw the distinction between Faith and Reason quite so sharply as Kant did, we still understand religious beliefs primarily in terms of their service to faith, to the religious side of experience.

300. How Intelligence Best Serves Faith: By Clarifying Religious Values

The function of religious beliefs is primarily religious rather than explanatory; the fundamental convictions of value involved in the commitment of faith are independent of the various ways we try to interpret them rationally. But this does not mean that thinking is unimportant in the religious life. Intelligence enters in fact very intimately into the faith of thoughtful men, and there is all the difference in the world between a faith held unreflectively, and one maintained critically and intelligently.

If we have any intellectual interest, we shall certainly try to use our best knowledge and philosophy to interpret the meaning of the various ideas that play a vital role in the practice of our faith. We shall try to harmonize those beliefs with our other ideas. We may even embrace, or attempt to work out, a new "rational theology," taking some ultimate scientific concept as a symbol for the Divine. These are, after all, ways of expressing the high regard in which we hold truth and knowledge. Now intellectual clarity is hardly the chief value most men seek from their religion. But clear thinking is so fundamental a good that it deserves all the prestige and power men can give it. One of the ways we can lend religious support to critical intelligence is by trying to make our religious beliefs consistent with the rest of our experience and knowledge.

Religion must express and organize and consecrate men's most careful thinking, as well as their deepest feelings and best actions. The great religions have indeed embraced and given direction to all these sides of human experience. This is the chief reason why it is important to think of God in terms of supreme Truth as well as of supreme Goodness. If, in consecrating the highest values men have found, religion fails to include the values of knowledge and intelligence, so that truth must be sought elsewhere and is not caught up in religious devotion, then the life so consecrated will display little intellectual quality, and its ends will not be truly good. If religion has no place for intelligence, then it will remain caught in fanaticism, or bogged down in moral sentimentality and intellectual confusion.

For this is without question the primary function of clear

thinking and intelligence in the practice of religion: to criticize and clarify the values involved in religious commitment. What does "the Divine" really mean? What does God demand of us? What is our best understanding of those transcendent ideals we take as "his will"? What do they compel us to do in ordering our lives and our attitudes toward our fellows? Our insights into the nature of the Divine come to us, to be sure, by a kind of vision or revelation. But to understand their significance for our experience demands the hardest kind of thinking, to say nothing of the utmost of intelligent action.

Intelligence is fundamental in the never-ending task of trying to organize our lives and our society in the light of what we recognize as Best. How can we best work to make the will of God prevail? Intelligence is essential in determining what the Best can mean for our day and generation. What would be a just society under present conditions? What does human brother-hood mean for us concretely? What does God's will command today? But after all, the most important function of intelligence in the religious life is to deepen and extend our understanding of what is really Best — of what God's will really is. It is to help us to know God, not merely to take his name in vain or to use him to some good purpose.

The history of religious thought makes clear that the chief role of intelligence in religion is not the finding of better demon-strations, in terms of the latest science, *that* God is. It is rather the continued criticism and purifying of our ideas of *what* God is, of what are his "attributes," what is his will. What is the "true God"? What are the supreme Goods that are to organize our lives and give them significance? Despite our best insight, our knowledge of what the Divine bids us do is all too limited and inadequate. Our visions of God need all the widening and deepening we can give them by intelligent reflection.

In this process of clarifying through intelligence the Good to which we are committed, we can learn much from the visions other men and other religions have beheld of the Divine. And one of the greatest services intelligence can perform to faith is in teaching us how we can best learn from faiths other than our own.[1]

[1] See BR, No. 72, "Values of an Anthology of Religions."

E. THE COMMUNITY OF RELIGIONS

301. Religions Are Many, but Religion Is One

The religions of men exhibit a bewildering variety. Each of the great traditions is itself split into a number of sub-varieties. The major cultures, like China, or India, or our own Western world, all contain a multitude of groups each practicing its own distinctive faith. And when we consider the past, with its long succession of reformations and reformulations, new visions and new cults, within each separate tradition, it seems that variety and change are as characteristic of men's religions as of their other institutions. Religion is clearly not like science, which at any one time is the same for all men. It seems to be much more like art, which likewise reflects and expresses the many differences between and within cultures.

Yet despite its infinite variety of forms, there is a sense in which all art is one. All these different kinds do the same thing, they perform the same *functions* in human life. The African sculptor, the Greek architect, the Romantic composer, the modern painter have, in the end, all been working at the same enterprise: to create something that would be immediately satisfying and artistically significant. Hence, a sensitive man can sympathize with the human achievement of each of these types of art; an artist can receive fresh inspiration from them all.

Religions differ just as widely as the arts in the means and devices by which they have sought their common end. But like art, religions all do the same things for men; they display a *unity of function* in the services they perform in the lives of individuals and of societies. As we have seen, those functions are complex and can hardly be reduced to a formula. But we can summarize them as the expressing and cultivating of what men together hold sacred — as man's quest for the Divine and his attempt to order life in its light.

Serious acquaintance with the great religions of mankind reveals the close sympathy of aim existing between the higher levels of all faiths, past and present. Such knowledge suggests that, while "religions are many, religion is one." It is one, not

in beliefs, not in experiences embodied, not in forms elaborated
with loving care, not in spiritual insights attained, not in ideals
striven for. It is one in the function it performs. It is one in
feeling deeply and interpreting profoundly the significant
moments of human life and in consecrating them to the Highest.
The various faiths of mankind seem like differing languages
through which man has been seeking to express, however inadequately, his faith in the Divine, his hope, his aspiration and commitment. They are tongues in which man has endeavored, as
best he might with the knowledge at his command, to relate
himself emotionally and practically and intelligently to the universe of which he is a part and to his fellows from whom he is
divided.

302. Do the Major Religions Really Agree?

Each religion expresses, in its own symbolic language and
actions, the common quest of mankind for the Divine. All
religions agree in the function they serve in human life. But
do the great religions display a still further agreement, not only
in the common quest to which they are devoted, but also in the
spiritual insight they have achieved? Do they share certain
universal convictions of value? Do they conceive the Divine
in the same way? Do they express the same transcendent ideal
of what is the highest Good?

From ancient times many have been convinced that they do.
The Platonic philosophy of the Roman world maintained that
all religions, rightly understood, are really devoted to the same
Good. As Plutarch put it, "There are not Greek gods and barbarian, southern or northern; but just as sun, moon, sky, earth,
and sea are common to all men and have many names, so likewise it is one Reason that makes all these things a cosmos; it
is one Providence that cares for them, with helping powers
appointed to all things; while in different peoples, different
honors and names are given to them as customs vary. Some
use hallowed symbols that are faint, others symbols more clear,
as they guide their thoughts to the Divine."

This conviction that all religions at bottom amount to the
same thing was revived at the Renaissance by Platonists like
Pico, anxious to demonstrate the agreement of Christianity,

Judaism, and Islam. It was proclaimed during the last century
by various leaders in the Oriental faiths. The Brahma Samaj
was founded in 1828 in India to teach the harmony and unity
of all religions. The outstanding Hindu religious teacher of
the nineteenth century, Ramakrishna, maintained: "God is
one, but many are his aspects. . . . Divers are the ways and
means to approach God, and every religion in the world shows
one of these ways. Different creeds are but different paths to
reach the Almighty. . . . Every religion is but one of the paths
that lead to God. A truly religious man should think that other
religions are also paths leading to truth."

On its more reflective level, Hindu thought has generally
maintained the unity of religions. But the recent movement
that has made this conviction most central in its religious teaching
came rather out of Islam. About the middle of the last century,
Baha'u'llah proclaimed in Iran the gospel of the unity of mankind
and of the teachings of all religions. The fundamental purpose
of religion is to promote concord and harmony between men
and nations. Devoted to working for a world commonwealth
based on the organic unity of man, which it sees as the consum-
mation of the process of human evolution, the Baha'i faith
upholds the principle of an unfettered search after truth and
teaches that religion must go hand in hand with science. But
the first step is to recognize the unity of God and of the teachings
of his high prophets.[1]

But we hardly need to go to the religious insight of universalizing Oriental prophets to find men holding that there is no real
disagreement between religions. It is common enough to hear
in our own land the view that religions are all really trying to
do the same thing. They are trying to teach men how to live
better. The ways they do it, we are told, and the points on
which they differ are of little moment. Anyhow, they all believe
in the Fatherhood of God and the Brotherhood of Man.

303. Religions Hold Many Fundamental Beliefs and Values in Common.

In understanding the diversity of religions, nothing could be
more important than to realize that they are in truth bound

[1] See BR, No. 81, "The Baha'i Faith," especially parts A, B, D, E.

together by their common functions — that they are all expressions of men's common quest for the Divine. If we really grasped the significance of this fundamental fact, there would be no further place for the animosities, prejudices, and mutual intolerances that have blackened the pages of religious history. Now one way to emphasize the all-important fact that differing religions have a common aim is to insist that, on all the points that really count, the various faiths of men are alike. And for those with a passionate religious interest in maintaining the unity of the religious experience of mankind, this will indeed be true. For such men will naturally select, as the "points that really count," those elements of feeling and belief, those convictions of value, on which there seems to be substantial agreement.

That there are in the developed religions plenty of such shared elements is made clear in the *Book of Readings*. However they have conceived the Divine, all religions have felt toward it in much the same way. Thus, as the readings illustrate, all have given expression to that sense of the indwelling Presence of the Divine which we symbolize as the immanence of God.[1] Again, there are certain universal principles of human living, like the golden rules[2] and the law of compensation,[3] that appear in some form in all the great religions. And no religion has a monopoly on any of those transcendent ideals of the highest Good: justice, mercy, compassion, active good will, self-sacrifice.[4] Religious teachers in all the great traditions have proclaimed them as ideal moral standards.

These fundamental religious feelings and this universal moral wisdom may well be the most important parts of man's various faiths, the highest expressions of his religious insight. It is certainly the distinctive insight of the prophets of the religious unity of mankind that the preceding statement ought to be true, that all religions should make fundamental what they share with others. And in trying to enter sympathetically into the religious

---

[1] For readings on Divine immanence, see footnote at the end of section 294 in this book.

[2] See BR, No. 70, "A Sheaf of Golden Rules from Twelve Religions."

[3] See BR, No. 71, "A Treasury of Sayings concerning Compensation (Karma)." Also No. 73 E, "Compensation and Reincarnation in Hinduism"; No. 75 D, "The Buddha's Way of Virtue," section c on Karma; No. 79 E, "Reward and Future Life" (in Islam).

[4] For examples, see references mentioned above in Sec. 276.

life of other peoples, trying to find some basis for fellowship with them, it is surely wise to begin by building upon likenesses rather than by aggravating differences.

304. Religions Form a Community

But whether it is equally wise, or even in the end possible, to stop with the insights common to all religions is more doubtful. After all, the religious means men employ in celebrating the Divine and consecrating their lives to God are very diverse. Each religion possesses not only characteristic symbols, beliefs, and practices of its own. Each has won its own distinctive religious insights, its own convictions of value. To hold that only those insights and goods which are shared with all other religions are "really important" is to express one's own faith in the importance of sharing. And it not only makes devotion to human brotherhood and to the unity of mankind central in one's own commitment to the Divine; it also bases that brotherhood and unity on what men have in common, on what is alike in their beliefs and their ideals.

In our warring world, to foster brotherhood and cooperation between men of different faiths is a religious aim of the utmost importance. Whatever genuinely and effectively furthers it is surely worth believing in. But to express that all-important commitment through the belief that in everything that really counts men and their faiths are alike, raises many questions both intellectual and practical. Intellectually, it is doubtful whether such a disregard of what is distinctive and unique in another religion can in the end lead to any real understanding of the men who practice it or the insights of their faith.

Practically, it is difficult to conceive any genuine cooperation between faiths on such a basis. For those beliefs which men actually hold to be fundamental, and those values which are controlling in the practice and commitment of any one faith, by no means coincide with those that are shared with others. Those that are distinctive may appear to philosophic interpretation as one set of symbols among many others. But they are really essential to the faith of their adherents. Men find it very difficult to sacrifice, or even to minimize, what is vital to their own commitment, however genuine their interest in cooperating with other men. Practically, it is probably unwise to expect them to cooperate at such a price. For better or worse, the faith in religious unity is not yet the central faith of the great majority in any religion. Those who do make it central, at the cost of subordinating what is unique, are apt to find that, far from having in that way succeeded in uniting religions, they have rather proclaimed a new one.

Finally, and most important of all, to find important in other religions only that which is already embodied in one's own, hardly fosters the highest respect for those other faiths, and may well lead in the end to their disregard and neglect. For why should one pay attention to the insights of other faiths if one is convinced that they really agree completely with one's own? Why should one feel a compelling urge to learn from them?

To see all religious beliefs as the symbolic renderings of deep human experiences and aspirations in the presence of the Divine, frees one from the vain attempt to reduce the wealth of religious life to a core of philosophical truth common to every historic faith. The experiences of men have varied from age to age and from clime to clime, and even in the face of the universal crises of all mankind, birth and love and evil and death, men have felt with subtle but inescapable shades of difference. It is of the very nature of poetry and metaphor, of the symbolic language of religion, to be literally untranslatable into another tongue. The attempt to find a common prose in which to state all this imaginative symbol leads to a blurring of that which clear thinking would keep distinct, to the loss of the rich overtones so fraught with feeling. To reduce religions to their highest common denominator cannot but lead to an impoverishment. It is to forget the many other factors that enter into the practice of a living faith and to misconceive the way in which such faiths must function.

Consequently, in seeking to foster cooperation between religions, in seeking to enter into fellowship with those of another faith, it is not enough to remember that all religions serve the same function, or that they share many important beliefs and values. It is just because every form of religious life enshrines something that is uniquely precious, something that could be expressed in no other way, that it is the part of wisdom, and indeed a religious duty, to strive so far as possible to enter into that insight. A true understanding of how religious faiths are distinguished thus makes sympathy and cooperation possible and imperative, without leading to intellectual flabbiness and spiritual impoverishment.

Religion is indeed one. But all religions are not alike, even "at bottom." Religions do not form a "unity." They form rather a *community*, in which each plays its own unique and indispensable role in the common quest of the Divine. Cooperation between religions does not mean the forgetting of differences. It certainly does not demand the sacrifice of the distinctive insights of any faith. Rather, it points to the possibility of stimulating ever more creative interrelations between different faiths, in which the very fact of those differences will contribute to a deepening and extending of the vision and insights of each.

305. The Claim to Exclusive Validity and Final Revelation

The most difficult obstacle in the way of such fruitful cooperation between religions is the persistence in our world of faiths, each claiming to possess the sole and final revelation of God and his will. It is of course natural for men to consider their own faith "better" and more adequate than others. Presumably, had they discovered one still better, they would have adopted it. A man must remain loyal to the best he has found, if he has really found it in his own living experience; though this does not free him from the religious obligation to criticize and clarify that faith and to seek to enlarge and deepen it. But this natural loyalty to our own vision need not lead us to deny the value of other visions. We can have it and still recognize that men and societies with a different experience may have found a different revelation of the Divine more adequate for their needs. And closer acquaintance with another religion may even suggest that in some respects — in some practice or belief, in some insight of value — that religion has found a better way of serving the Good to which we ourselves are committed than does our own. This is one way in which religious vision is normally extended.

It is quite another thing to maintain that one's own faith is not only better than others but is the only "valid" faith, the only one whose standards of what is Good have been revealed by God, the only one whose beliefs are "true." As the social scientist and the psychologist can explain, such an attitude is also "natural" enough, men and their group loyalties being what they are. But the student of human ways will also add that such confident and intolerant dogmatism is most characteristic of "primitive" societies and of group loyalties that have not yet learned the wisdom to outgrow their narrow ignorance and prejudice. It is "natural" only for men with little experience and less knowledge of other groups with differing faiths.

Such arrogance is also responsible for most of the crimes committed in the name of religion against those with other loyalties. Through bitter experience, men have slowly and painfully come to realize that this claim to possess an exclusive and final revelation of the Divine is the most dangerous pretension any group can make. It has led to heresy-hunts, persecutions, inquisitions, religious wars *ad nauseam*. Against it, our long political experience has compelled us to build up constitutional guarantees of the freedom of religion, which we rightly regard as the most fundamental of all the freedoms of man, because those who attack it will respect no other human right. And against it sensitive religious prophets have had to inveigh, as the highest and worst form of religious pride and the most consuming sin of which a religion can stand convicted at the bar of history.

Whatever earlier theories they may still retain, the traditional religions have begun to learn the wisdom of "toleration" in practice. The lesson has been forced upon them by human experience and has been proclaimed by their own best prophets. Today it is chiefly the new social faiths that are displaying the ignorance and folly of their youth. America in particular has in the past been blessed with the presence of many different faiths making exclusive pretensions to validity, no one of which has proved strong enough to gain a privileged position or to use the state to enforce its claims. In consequence, these conflicting dogmatisms have been compelled to learn to live together in peace and amity. Out of this fortunate experience has developed the American tradition of religious freedom and the strongly rooted principle of the separation of church and state. We have recognized officially a plurality of religious institutions and have insisted that no one of them should have any special privileges before the law.

Religious freedom was first born of expediency and then converted into a cherished principle as men came to realize the fruits of its wisdom. It has gradually developed, in the democratic experience of America, from a mere negative defense against intolerance into a positive ideal of active cooperation. For multitudes of Americans, the traditional diversity and sectarianism of our religious life have come to suggest the possibility of a genuine community of religious faiths. And for some at least this emerging community of American faiths has already begun to point toward a future community of all the faiths of mankind.

Exclusive religious claims are still maintained by various groups — in theory. But for the most part they have become the expression of a smug complacency rather than of a persecuting zeal. This self-satisfaction can be deadening enough. Where such pretensions are still taken seriously, they make cooperation difficult: it is hard for a religion which believes it has the last word to seek light from another vision. In our modern world, however, with our rapidly growing experience and knowledge of the wealth of insight enshrined in other religions, such claims become increasingly difficult to take literally. In breaking them down, it is the beliefs and values that other religions hold in common with our own that form the entering wedge. Men whose aspiration is so much like ours cannot be wholly outside the pale. Then, once we have realized how much of what other faiths have seen resembles, under different symbols, our own vision, we are led on to consider seriously their distinctive insights. How far the barriers of ignorance and prejudice have already been undermined is clear from the dwindling number of those who would today hold all other faiths to be mere superstition and idolatry. It seems incredible that a century ago such men were in the vast majority, certainly in Christian churches.

But where the claim to exclusive validity is really central in religious faith — where it is what we have called a "fundamental" religious belief — mere increase of knowledge is hardly likely to shake it. It is more apt to provoke a new defense. This is particularly true where dogmatic certainty is embodied in an authoritarian church, in which the claim to be the sole path to salvation is a fundamental conviction of value. Men for whose religious commitment that claim is central cannot give it up; to abandon it would lead to the collapse of their entire faith.

Yet even here we have found that cooperation is possible in practice, in terms of the moral ideals which are held in common and the visions of the Divine which are shared. For the belief in an authoritative and final revelation is fundamentally a *religious* belief. The primary function it performs in the faith of its adherents is *religious:* it strengthens their practical commitment to what they see as God's commands. The further implications of that claim with regard to the inferiority of other faiths are really secondary. Dangerous as they have proved in the past when such authoritarian churches have been in a position to enforce them literally, when deprived of that power, as under American political conditions, these same churches have been willing and able to compromise on putting them into practice. To make the claim is essential to their faith; to enforce it on others is not. They can exercise charity; God, too, is patient with evil. These ecclesiastical claims may clearly create grave problems for others, as the long conflict between church and state bears witness. But these are political, not religious, problems. The religious problem they create is primarily one for those who make them. Is the kind of certainty and strength they confer worth the limitations they impose, the being cut off from all other sources of religious insight?

306. Religious Toleration and Cooperation in Religious Freedom

There are two alternatives to the claim to possess the sole and final revelation. The first, fairly well established with regard to religious faith — though hardly equally so with regard to other faiths taken more seriously — is the negative principle of toleration. The second, whose possibilities we are just beginning to explore, is the positive principle of cooperation in religious freedom. Toleration rests, in the last analysis, on a recognition of our ignorance. As Reinhold Niebuhr puts it, "However we twist or turn, whatever instruments or pretensions we use, it is not possible to establish the claim that we have *the* truth." In the emphatic words of Cromwell, "By the bowels of Christ, remember that you may be mistaken." To recognize the limitations of even our best insight and vision is the beginning of wisdom, as it is the part of humility. We too may fall short, even as other men.

The ideal of cooperative religious freedom does not rest on the mere acknowledgement of possible limitations to our own vision. It rests rather on the challenging opportunity a multiplicity of faiths affords to see further and learn more. We should welcome and seek the utmost freedom for other forms of religious life, in all the wealth of their variety, just because in them we can look upon the Highest through eyes that have seen what we have not, and find fresh visions of the Divine. The more such visions we can share, and the more spiritual insights we can make our own, the more we can enrich our own faith, and the more we can learn of what is truly Best. The principle of cooperation in religious freedom does not demand merely that men should be free to practice their religions without interference. It means something much more positive. Men should be freed from ignorance, narrowness, and shortsightednesss to cultivate the fullest possible development of their various visions of God, in the hope that they may thus add to that store of religious insight which is the treasured possession of the race. For revelation has not ceased; it is progressive and cumulative. The active, searching, and free life of the spirit can be confident that it will win new visions of the Divine.

Moreover, religious vision is *shared* vision; it is a fellowship of faith. Religious freedom demands that it be freed from all self-imposed barriers and shared as widely as possible. If it be genuinely free and genuinely religious, how can that fellowship stop short before the fellowship of all men's faiths? In the last analysis, cooperation in religious freedom means the opportunity for the various paths men have followed in their common quest for the Divine to converge towards a genuine community of religions, a world faith in which each religion shall play its own distinctive part. This seems to be the form which in our day expresses the ancient religious ideal of the brotherhood of man.[1]

[1] See BR, No. 81, The Baha'i Faith: "The Principles and Plan of a World Commonwealth."

307. Do We Need a World Faith?

What kind of convergence toward a world faith lies within the realm of possibility? What does the ideal of a community of religions mean concretely? Does it mean we should look forward to, and work towards, the eventual emergence of a single universal religion shared by all mankind? Should such a religion somehow embrace all the insights of present religions, organized around the fundamental ideal of human brotherhood in the pursuit of the Divine? Should it bear to each existing faith something of the relation which Christianity holds to Judaism and to the other religions of the Roman world whose insights it also incorporated?

To ask these questions is to raise doubts as to whether this is even a worthy ideal. It is conceivable that in the dim future, if a common and universal culture should ever spread all over the world and absorb into itself all local and national cultures, something like this universal religion might be the eventual outcome of the development of a world civilization. Such a unification of culture seems at the moment remote enough. Surely few today would even welcome it, unless the only alternative were sheer anarchy and chaos. But granted the possibility, our present experience points rather to the further universalizing of all the great world religions. Such a culture would be extraordinarily complex and would doubtless, like our own, create the need for many different forms of religious expression rather than for a single all-embracing faith.

The ideal of a cooperative community of religions seems to point rather to a closer fellowship between existing faiths, in which each might learn from the visions of the others and thus deepen and enrich its own spiritual insight. In our rapidly narrowing world, in which civilizations once remote and isolated are being thrust into each other's arms, it seems not unlikely that some such cultural cross-fertilization will take place. But in any process of cultural assimilation, distinctive religious ideals, just because they are so basic and so deeply rooted in a particular civilization, are normally the last to be absorbed. Thus it seems improbable that the high value Western religions have come to set on human personality, the outcome of our long pursuit of the ideal of individuality, will ever take a central place in the

Eastern faiths, unless their whole societies should be revolutionized to foster individualism in personal relationships. Conversely, an equal revolution would be needed in our own institution of the family before it could play the major role it does in some of the Oriental faiths.

308. Learning from the Insights of Other Religions

Should the various religions enter into more of a cooperative community, how could we then reasonably expect them to learn from each other's insights? The direct borrowing and incorporation of wholly novel beliefs or ideals from another tradition in which they are deeply and intimately embedded is a long and slow process. Until the values they express have been actually worked into men's lives, it is apt to be both artificial and superficial. The various attempts already made to combine elements from Eastern and Western traditions into new semi-Oriental faiths, like Theosophy or New Thought, have proved neither very popular nor very impressive. They have appealed mainly to those with a craving for the exotic.

It is more likely that when men approach another faith sympathetically, they will be first attracted by its distinctive ways of expressing ideals and beliefs already fundamental in their own. Liberal Christians have found very congenial the Hindu and Buddhist emphasis on the Divine immanence.[1] But they will now encounter these familiar ideals pushed further, perhaps in a new and different direction. They will incorporate this new extension of meaning, not in the alien symbols in which they have found it expressed, but by enlarging the application of their own traditional symbols in the direction indicated. Thus an appreciation of the mystic contemplation so strong in the Hindu faiths would suggest to Westerners, not the adoption of Hindu techniques like Yoga, but rather the more intensive cultivation of the resources of mysticism in their own Western tradition. Again, should the Hindu faiths come to learn from the Western ideal of active benevolence abounding in good works to men, they would doubtless emphasize it in the forms proclaimed by their own teachers.[2]

[1] See BR, No. 73 A to D.
[2] See BR, No. 73 G, "The Leading Ideas of Mahatma Gandhi."

Nor is this mutual learning, made possible through genuine cooperation, merely a matter of coming to share and absorb new insights. Just as a man sees much more clearly what are the distinctive goods in his own national culture after he has become familiar with what is best in others, so fellowship between faiths can lead to the deeper realization of what is uniquely valuable in one's own. Cooperation with men exemplifying the best ideals of the active and energetic West may well lead Hindus to understand and appreciate the values of Christian forms of good-will. But it may also stimulate them to a criticized and clarified but strengthened cultivation of the characteristic values of the "spirituality" of the Hindu tradition. This is what we mean by saying that a genuine community of religions would bear fruit, not merely in the sharing of religious visions, but also in the further creative exploration and development of what is unique in each.

In these ways, cooperation between religions should make it possible to understand, enjoy, and make use of the symbolic and imaginative wealth, not only of our own but of all the great religious traditions, without binding us to the limited experiences they have severally expressed. In the end, our own faith must be attached to a spiritual ideal that meets the needs of our own life. But it has always been the function of religion to enlarge the experience of the moment and lead men into a broader world. Surely no more promising way of extending our own sympathies and enhancing our own insights exists than that offered by the revelations of the Divine that have come to other men with other needs, and by the imaginative and artistic symbols that have embodied their aspiration and devotion. And by thus entering into genuine spiritual fellowship with the community of men's faiths, we can give tangible expression to our own commitment to the great religious ideals of human brotherhood and peaceful cooperation among men.

PART V.   A WORLD-VIEW

William Ernest Hocking

Harvard University

A. PHILOSOPHY AND THE TOTAL WORLD PICTURE

309. The Need of a World-View

We began our study with an account of man, a unique creature in the midst of an infinite universe. We continued by examining several phases of the kind of life man has worked out, ethical, political, religious. We have now to consider the universe itself, the total environment of all this human thought and enterprise, not assuming that we can know all about it, but that we can know something about it, and perhaps the most important things for the guidance of human living.

In our first study of man, we found it to be characteristic of his way of thinking that he has a vague notion of his total world. Given some notion of the total world to start with, however sketchy, everything a man learns fits into it and also helps to give further shape to the notion. Let us illustrate.

Imagine a person trying to get a good idea of some modern city, say Chicago. Let us show him a number of places in the city but blindfold him in going from place to place — the Loop, the North Side, the stockyards, Hull House neighborhood, the Art Institute; he would have a bundle of impressions but no single idea even of the exterior of the city. If he had first seen a rough map or had caught a glimpse of the city from a plane, each of the items would find its place and contribute its share to a growing total-idea.

Similarly, in building a conception of the universe, the adding together of separate details, without some rude notion of the whole to begin with, would never give us a world-view. When a person is lost, it is not because "he does not know where he is" — he always knows that — but because he does not know where the rest of the world is, the points of the compass, the wider landmarks of the region. Every spot, without its "bearings," is a lost spot; every part, without its whole, is a lost part. Like any animal, the human being must begin with particular facts; he must deal with what is before him and around him. But because he is human, he sets these facts from the first in a frame-conception of the world he lives in.

Naturally, his early conceptions of the whole are more imaginative than literal. They express themselves in broad gestures toward the immensities, the stars and the sky, with signs for "the beyond" and the "unknown." And with these purely physical outlines, man develops some suggestion of the quality or character of the whole, as friendly or hostile, as favorably disposed or at least approachable. These early pictures are various and far from consistent with each other; yet they are something better than pure guesswork. They are like scientific hypotheses, more or less plausible guesses held subject to correction. They are still more like the judgments we make on meeting a person: though open to revision, they report a genuine total impression which the person (or the universe) has made upon the mind — in short, an "intuition."

310. Building from the Detail toward the Whole

Once there is such a frame-idea of the total world, every item of experience, however insignificant, adds a stroke to the world-view. Whether it is only such a trifle as stubbing one's toe or getting a whiff of fresh air or seeing a mongoose tackle a cobra, or whether it is an important success or failure, a birth or a death — the full story of the experience in each case must be something like this: "The kind of universe I live in is one which permits toe-stubbing, successes, greatnesses, etc., to happen."

Now these daily experiences sum themselves up into a total of their own: "my experience." Moreover, each person by aid of language annexes to his own experience that of many others: group memory adds itself to individual memory, and we have "the experience of a tribe." When we speak of "human experience" or simply of "Experience" without designating whose experience, we have in mind an ideal aggregate of the experiences of all individuals — a corporate, cumulative, and certainly majestic totality.

Would such a totality be equivalent to "the universe"? Obviously not, so long as there is much of the universe which no human being ever experiences or could experience. Group experience moves toward the whole but makes no claim to arrive there.

However, man is not content with the casual collection of experiences as they come; he explores. He develops techniques for systematic and aggressive expansion of experience, as a part of the work of science. This exploring process is in various stages of advance. The geographical exploration of the earth's surface is well along toward completion in outline. Geological exploration of the crust has made good progress; but aspiring to include the past history of the world as an explanation of the present state of things (thus widening the notion of experience to the cracking-point), it encounters numerous puzzles. Astronomical exploration is well begun, though the "time-shell" of what we can observe is even more appallingly inadequate as compared with the enormous time-intervals we wish to know about. Atomic and infra-atomic exploration is in its infancy.

Allowing all these explorations, and the conjectures based on them, to come under the broadening name of "Experience," this method of moving from part to whole is not, of itself, in a position to construct a world-view. Indeed, its advance uncovers new and more intricate reaches of the unknown. If this, the so-called "empirical" method, were the only one, we could look to the completion of its task only in the most distant future, if ever. Experience can give substance, detail, and color to our world-view; of itself alone it cannot build one.

311. Building from the Whole toward the Detail

It is man's *thought*, aided by his imagination, which lays down the first sketch-outline of totality, outrunning every reach of experience. The eye lights on a horizon, but thought leaps beyond the horizon. And as it reflects on the nature of space, it sees that there is no point at which it can stop. All things within our reach are *related* to us; but these same relations of distance, time, effect, connect these things with further things, without limit.

Since man's adjustment to this totality has appeared to him a matter of great practical importance, he has had something to do about it (which we have come to call his religion); and through these activities, he has independently given some shape and clarity to his notions of the universe, as the preceding part has amply illustrated. As if working from an artist's rough sketch, he has built from the whole toward the detail.

This business could not wait until the sciences had put into the picture their carefully drawn strokes. It had to be there at the start, encouraging man about his future, enabling him to believe that the world was on the side of his dreams. Hence, religion had to be in operation before it could have any advantage of scientific criticism; and since its interest was quite as much in the qualities as in the facts of the world, it could move far without coming into any comparison with the results of developing science.

But if religion moves from the whole toward the part and science from the part toward the whole, the two would be bound to meet somewhere. And since they are two ways of finding the truth about the same object, they are bound in the end to agree. They are naturally supplementary. With the diversity of the two programs and of their guiding interests, it is less to be wondered at that their reports fail to coincide at all points than that they have shown so large an amount of agreement. Let us note some of the facts about past difficulties of adjustment between the two reports.

312. The "Conflict" between Science and Religion

Much of the alleged conflict has been a difference of language. Religion has had to coin its own language and, in order to say anything at all, in its difficult region, it has been driven to the language of analogy, poetry, myth, symbol. The sciences have often fallen afoul of religious statements because they mistook figurative speech (as in the Genesis story of Creation) for literally meant world-history.[1]

However, in the course of time, points of actual discord in matters of principle began to appear. To religion, physical power is not the only, nor the supreme, sort of power: in its view, the deepest powers of the world are purposeful, mysterious, awesome, maintaining in ways not known to us control of everything in physical nature: God would not be God unless the

---

[1] See BR, No. 87, Abba Hillel Silver, "Science and Religion."

physical world obeyed him. Hence, for religion, "miracle" is a responsible and natural feature of the world-view, meaning by miracle a special suspension of the usual physical order or law by a higher and spiritual control for a significant purpose. For example, it would seem to be in order to regard healing the sick as partly a matter of medicine, but partly a matter of magic or prayer; so with raising crops, success in any hazardous enterprise, protection in danger, and so on.

To science, once it became fully conscious of its methods, miracle was felt to be a threat to its existence. Miracle could not be proved impossible; but it became a matter of scientific conscience to try every other explanation first. Thus, when science took its modern stride, from the seventeenth century onward, it set itself resolutely against every plea for the *exceptional* in nature. It undertook to expel from its domain every sign of spiritual activity, every purpose of supernatural agents, every "final" cause.[1] There were to be no more evil spirits to fear, no demons, no witches, no devils — so far, a good relief to mankind. And, on the other hand, there were to be no more good spirits, angelic or divine, no hand of Providence operating in the affairs of men in this world. (And as for any other world, science knew nothing about it.) Miracle, in its entire range, was to be banished; the old supernatural garret was rid of its bats and the old sky of its radiance.

313. What Does the Alleged Conflict Amount To?

The early phases of the encounter between the religious and the scientific view of things could take the simple form of a jurisdictional dispute: which events are to be ascribed to supernatural powers and which to natural causes? Thus, in the cure of disease, in which from time immemorial spiritual causes and spiritual aid have been invoked, Greek scientific medicine came into clash with popular superstition. We find the great Greek physician, Hippocrates (about 400 B.C.), taking exception to the prevalent idea that epilepsy is a special form of divine visitation. He wrote:

"As regards the disease called sacred, to me it appears to be no more divine than any other disease, but to have a *physis* (a natural process)

---

[1] See BR, No. 95, S. B. L. Penrose, "How and Why: The Kinds of Cause." Also see No. 96, Aristotle, "Four Types of Cause."

just like other diseases. Men regard its origin as divine from ignorance and wonder, since it is a peculiar condition and not readily understood. Yet if it be reckoned divine merely because wonderful, then instead of one there would be many sacred diseases. To me it appears that they who refer such conditions to the gods are but as certain charlatans who claim to be excessively religious and to know what is hidden from others." [1]

But when science reached the point of claiming the whole field of nature as its own, it could no longer be thought that there was a region of supernatural control, as on the theory ascribed to Socrates, that "the gods have reserved to themselves the most important events." [2] The sphere of religion would be outside of nature. God, and any other world or realm of spirits that there may be, would constitute "the supernatural," as something additional to the world we can see and measure. The outstanding difference between the two world-pictures would be simply that the religious universe *has more in it*.

Now science has no way of disproving the existence of supernature. The militant science of the seventeenth and eighteenth centuries simply reported that it did not find any such supplement to the existing world; and that, since supernature if it exists does not interfere in the course of events, it, science, has no use for any such supplement in its business. This sounds like a peaceful settlement. But if all miracle, as the impact of the supernatural on the natural, is banished, the question is bound to rankle, whether a realm of supernature, which can be dismissed as superfluous in scientific affairs, can retain its significance for mankind.

Certainly there is no more important issue in the make-up of one's world-view than this one: whether one's universe is to include something more than "nature," and *what can be meant by this something more* — whether the real world is the more complex (and richer?) or the simpler (and poorer?) affair.

It should be pointed out that the great scientific innovators of our modern age — Copernicus, Kepler, Galileo, Newton — did not regard themselves as hostile to religion or as outside the church. None of them felt that he was rejecting the concep-

---

[1] Charles Singer in *Science, Religion and Reality*, edited by Joseph Needham, pp. 95 f.

[2] Xenophon, *Memorabilia*, chap. 2.

tion of God; though some of them believed that they were offering a better idea of God and of His relations to nature.

Instead of thinking of God as one who intrudes piecemeal into the processes of the world around us, it was proposed, especially by Bruno (1548–1600) and Spinoza (1632–1677), that his action might be *total* rather than particular. Special miracle does not occur, they thought, because the whole physical universe in its regular activity is a single deed of God, a single miracle continuously carried out. To use Spinoza's language, God and Nature are two names for the same thing.

To many minds, this identifying of God and Nature seemed like a preservation of religious language while denying the religious fact. God, immortality, and human freedom are, in their view, matters of too great moment to be merged with even the most beneficent aspects of nature and the processes of scientific advance. On the other hand, many a scientist and many an independent observer of human affairs have judged that just insofar as religious interests separate themselves from men's natural and secular concerns they become dangerous: to rely on supernatural aid rather than on human efforts extended by science has had an injurious effect on human enterprise and character. Otherworldliness, they say, accounts for the economic and social backwardness of many highly civilized regions of Asia; whereas, in the West, the great advances in the improvement of the human lot in modern times have been due to the application of science. They therefore call for continued and exclusive trust in the methods which have so signally proved their value to mankind.

This vital question will be involved in the discussions of the study now before us: we shall not here prejudge its outcome. But we may point out two obvious facts:

One, that modern science has operated within a world-view whose larger outlines have been inherited from an era dominated by religion. While science may revise to some extent that world-view, it can hardly shake off the frame-idea into which its items of truth have entered, and there is no assurance that any adequate world-view could be derived from science alone.

The other, that the religious world-view has no stake in setting up a type of hostility between supernatural and natural, such as would wean human interests away from natural secular concerns: it would rather include the natural in a wider whole.

314. The Role of Philosophy

We are taking religion and science as typical sources of material for our world-view. But there are many others. The mind of man has a speculative bent, and all his activities, arts, and politics furnish suggestions about the nature of the whole he lives in. It is this abundance of rumor about the world and the diversity of report which give philosophy its final task, that of *bringing coherence into the total view*.

President Hadley of Yale once waggishly defined philosophy as "the ever-recurrent attempt to reconcile our scientific knowledge with our prejudices." Like most good caricatures, this saying has truth in it. Whatever science has established must be accepted, since science is nothing but organized truth (but science is good at revising its own views and holds little as "established beyond recall"). "Prejudice," if we mean by it strong convictions about the world from intuitive sources, is essential to get the building started, to frame it in and supply its meaning. Philosophy is not alone a reconciler and critic of views taken from elsewhere; it uses their inconsistencies and defects of statement to lead to its own proposals about the nature of the universe.

The especial responsibility of philosophy is to bring *the care for literal truth, sound evidence, and accurate thinking* into the larger aspects of the world, so that science and philosophy together may constitute a single body of reasoned truth.

This does not mean that philosophy has to reject myth and poetry from its report of the world: Plato is sufficient evidence to the contrary, for Plato has given us numerous delightful myths to complete his accounts when reason had begun to falter. It means that philosophy must carry reason as far as reason will go. It must know what can be proved and what cannot; it must know what is myth and what is literal. If there is a sphere of truth which must be left to probability or to faith, it must indicate that sphere. If there are limits to reason, it must furnish a reasoned chart of those limits. It must everywhere keep faith with the scientific spirit and, seeking for certainty, make clear the area in which certitude has to give way to conjecture.

We shall now go about the task, asking first what are the main ingredients which we must include in any valid world-view.

B. WHAT IT TAKES TO MAKE A WORLD

315. The Need of Discovering the Ingredients of the World

The best way to learn how an object is made is to try to make it. It is perhaps true that no one fully understands the structure of a boat who has not built a boat. For this reason, we more fully own the things we have made than the things we have bought; for we have a mental as well as a legal ownership.

We cannot try our hand at building a world; but we can follow an ancient device and attempt to imagine ourselves engaged in the work of world-construction. It seems probable that many of the creation myths are less attempts to say how the gods actually went to work than attempts to bring vividly to mind what the *necessary ingredients of the world are*. Many of these stories are playful, and represent the deity as using materials at hand to give them shape according to his artistic whim, as the god Knum in the clay region of ancient Egypt beside the cataracts was represented as a divine potter, making his molds and then conferring life. The question of the origin of the clay is not raised; and the presence of day and night, space and time, are taken for granted. It was a much deeper thinker who (according to an undated papyrus in Turin) pictured God as creating time: "I make the hours and the hours come into being."

But leaving the ancients aside, we can take at least this from their efforts to state what it takes to make a world, that *things* are not enough. The Chinese designation, "The ten thousand things" as a phrase for the world, is a fair starting point, but it pretended to be no more. Let us begin with this indefinite notion and attempt — not too systematically — to set up a list of some of the necessities.

316. The Sorting of Things into Kinds or Classes

Meaning by a "thing" any identifiable and tangible object, it would indeed require a good number of things to make a world. But their value for that purpose would depend on what *kinds* of thing they were. To be impressed merely by the numerousness of the things around us is to be in a state of stupidity or bewilderment. Even an infant begins to sort the "buzzing, blooming confusion" into the kinds that affect his vital interests: they are foods or not foods, persons or not persons, moving objects and not-moving objects.

These interest-classifications tell little about the outer world itself. Later on, the mind begins to observe things on their own account. It sees:

First, *that things themselves come in kinds*. That means (a) that everything we meet has *qualities* (such as shape, size, position, color, hardness, smell, taste) which separate it clearly from its neighbors; and (b) that (since it has an outline) there may be numerous others like it in the world. One orange is enough to suggest the possibility of a million others of its kind. And to learn about one specimen is to learn something of all of them — an immense economy.

It may be somewhat accidental — but if so it is for us a fortunate accident — that the natural kinds (species, genera) are fairly well separated, not confused by innumerable intermediate gradations. Naturalists can almost always find missing links, as between the apes we know and the men we know: but these rarities do not greatly clutter the present world, so that we can name our kinds with some confidence. There are intermediates between birds and reptiles, trees and shrubs, but for the most part the kinds are clear-cut and well separated.

Second, in this fact of "kind" we have found two features of the world, always present, and hence always together: *quality* and *quantity*. A thing could not exist without some quality (or descriptive character). And there must always be enough of it, in quantity, to occupy a place in the world. Then there is always another quantity, the number of specimens of the kind (though this is usually unknown), as the number of flies, trees, electrons.

Third, objects of a kind not only appear alike but also *behave alike*.

A bullfrog can be described in terms of his shape and color and anatomy: but with these qualities go his leap, swim, croak, etc., equally characteristic. We usually take our *defining qualities* from what we can see or hear, i.e., from distance-perception. It is just as well to be able to recognize a rattler before we are near enough for him to go into action. But always the action of that kind of thing is within our interest. Our classifications are ways of foretelling what the kind can be expected to do, or what we can expect to do with it. Such expectations imply that there are among things regular and dependable types of change; or, as we commonly put it, there are *laws of action*. Water over fire will boil; eggs in boiling water coagulate; iron in fire turns red, then white, then melts — rough law formulae from rough observation. And such laws are as important a feature of any world we could begin to master as are the things themselves.

We have, therefore, five ingredients of our world: things, their qualities and quantities, their behavior, and the *laws* of their behavior or change.

Things and changes are observable, and occupy the primary places in language as nouns and verbs. Laws are invisible; they are objects of thought: they are imputed by the mind to the actions and reactions of things: we expect repetition of the same behavior under the same conditions — rubber balls to bounce and unsupported books to fall — perhaps because a world which most of the time met expectations is the only kind of world we could survive in. Some would say that the laws thus imputed are not really in the objects but in our minds. But I put this question to the reader: could this expectation persist and aid our formation of habits in dealing with things unless the objects carried out, as it were, their side of the bargain? We shall include laws among the ingredients of our world, hard as it is to imagine what a law consists of.

317. Force, Energy

Ought we now to include *forces or energies* among our ingredients to indicate the causes of change? It is not a part of our usual world-view that change follows law of its own accord: it does so because it has to; its behavior is "caused."

Now energy is as difficult to imagine as is law. The tendency in physics is to drop these conceptions except as mathematical expressions. Force is regarded as a quantity measured by the product of mass and acceleration; energy is one half the product of mass and the square of the velocity, a measure of the capacity of doing work. Physics does not deny that these quantities stand for objective facts; there is such a thing as stress, and there is also such a thing as a variable capacity to do work. The attitude of the physicist is not that of ruling these objects out of the world, but rather of washing his hands of the problem of their nature. While he freely uses these factors, he transfers the problem of their inner nature to philosophy, and philosophy will accept it, at least to the extent of including these among the materials for world-building.

318. Space, Time

There are certain other ingredients not mentioned but implied in those we now have: the backgrounds against which things and changes are outlined — space and time.[1] Things are in general located in different places; and the imaginary lines traced by their motions in space are so far distinct that no two are in the same place at the same time. A physical particle may thus be identified by this line of motion, its "world line." An explorer of a cave who unrolls a string as he goes leaves a part of his world-line behind him; so each moving body can be imagined as leaving an invisible line in space as it moves — unbroken and absolutely individual.

Our space is a three-dimensional region, which is usually considered to be changeless, since all change must be measured with reference to assumed changeless reference-positions and directions. Time gives us another dimension of the world in the sense that, in order to specify an event, we have to fix the time as well as the place. It is no use being at the right place a day too late. The operating world is thus often referred to as a four-dimensional manifold.

There is, however, one radical difference (among several) between space and time. A motion can take place in any direction in space, forward or backward, with equal ease, so far as the nature of space is concerned. There is only one direction in which an event can move in time, namely, toward the future. And all events move together in the same direction in time. The

[1] See BR, No. 94, W. M. Dixon, "The Enigmas of Time and Space."

moving picture may show the reversal of any actual operation; but our observation of the reversal still runs to the future, otherwise we might get back to the beginning of the hour and have seen the whole show in no time at all.

In a sense, space and time are in contrast to all things and events. *Space is not a thing, nor does time "march on,"* for it is not itself a process of change. (If time were a process of change it would have a rate, which means that so much of it would occur in a given time; we should therefore have to have another and changeless time to measure the rate of the changing time. Hence time does not "flow" nor "march" nor "fly" — it has no rate; it is that by which all rates are measured.) For a world composed of things and events, space and time would be two kinds of nothing. They are often conceived as a vast world-room, a perfection of emptiness, within which all the world-show plays itself away forever. We can imagine the show to vanish and all its properties; we have difficulty in imagining the world-room to vanish. (It is worth trying.) In spite of its being a vast nothingness, it resists imaginative abolition even more vigorously than its substantial contents. This fact has an important bearing on the nature of space and time, as we shall have occasion later to notice.

319. Intervals, Patterns

Some light on that nature can be had by considering the fact of "intervals," which I think should be listed as a separate ingredient of the world. An interval is, roughly, the gap between things or events. Suppose that the distance between earth and sun were nothing but empty space; still the amount of that interval is a matter of life and death to this planet. And what is thus measurable cannot itself be nothing. In music there are "rests," intervals supposedly without sound. But here again the interval is measured with extreme exactitude, and woe to the horn that blares in on the silence.

The Chinese classic called Tao Teh King, ascribed to the wise man, Lao-tze,[1] contains an exquisite passage on the importance of intervals or emptiness in the world. In Chapter XI, "The Function of the Non-existent," we find the following verses

[1] See BR, No. 74 A, "The Meaning of Taoism."

in the translation of Paul Carus: "Thirty spokes unite in one nave and on that which is non-existent [the hole in the wheel's center] depends the wheel's utility. Clay is molded into a vessel and on that which is non-existent [its hollowness] depends the vessel's utility. By cutting out doors and windows we build a house and on that which is non-existent depends the house's utility."

Space and time intervals are as important in making the world what it is as are the things and events they separate. When all the intervals are considered together, they give us the "pattern" formed by the distribution of things in space and time: pattern is certainly an ingredient of the world. If (as Sir Arthur Eddington has proposed) there are a finite (or limited) number of electrons in the universe, we might describe the entire course of physical process throughout all time as the changing pattern (or "configuration") of these ever-shifting units.

320. Fields as Infinite

Returning now to space and time, we may say that they are the *fields* within which this shifting of patterns takes place. How great are they? We can assign no limits. When we try to do so in imagination, we have to admit that a boundary is a line between the inside and the outside; and that outside the supposed boundary can only be more space and more time.

This was the discovery that Bruno made when as a boy of twelve he made his first visit to Vesuvius, some twenty miles from his home town of Nola. Vesuvius looked gray in the distance; but when he stood on its slopes he found them green, whereas Nola, so far as he could make it out to the northward, had assumed the Vesuvian gray. "What if every horizon," thought Bruno, "were a new center? Then there could be no final horizon, and the universe would be infinite."

So with the attempt to think a beginning or an end of time. There must have been something before the beginning in order that anything should begin; for from nothing, nothing can come (*ex nihilo nihil*). To religious tradition, this meant that before the world began, God is. To the growing insistence of science that we must follow the chain of causes backward as far as it will go, it meant that the physical process had always been going on, that there had been no beginning. But even if there had been a beginning of things and events, would time have begun with them? Or would the beginning have to take place *in* time, and therefore assume a prior infinite and empty duration? To these questions it is almost equally difficult to answer yes or to answer no.

Infinity is something we cannot banish from our world, and something which so baffles our thought that it has been regarded as "inconceivable" (see for example Herbert Spencer's account of "Ultimate Scientific Ideas" in *First Principles*). This may mean that our minds are inadequate to deal with truth. Yet this can hardly be the case, since it is only our thoughts, not our senses, which discover and assert the infinitude of space and time. And we cannot forget that the mathematical methods of dealing with infinite series have made steady progress during modern times, and especially in the nineteenth century. The paradoxes of infinity, which Immanuel Kant so beautifully laid out in his *Critique of Pure Reason*,[1] probably indicate, as he suggested, that we have made some false assumption in the way we have stated our problem. His suggestion was that space and time were not objective facts, which submitted to being measured as so much land; but they were precisely *mental* things, forms by which our minds perceive the patterns of sensation. We shall return to this theme in due course.

321. Consciousness, Mentality, Life

So far, the ingredients we have assembled go to make up the world of *physical* nature. We have omitted everything that has to do with the mind, unless space and time are mental, which we shall regard for the present as an open question. It might be imagined possible to make up a world without any minds in

---

[1] In the third part of the *Critique*, he set out several pairs of contradictory assertions (antinomies), in which each member of each pair could be defended by a process of plausible proof. The antinomies which here concern us were:

The world has a limit in space;
The world has no limit in space.

The world has a beginning in time;
The world has no beginning in time.

The matter of the world is infinitely divisible;
Matter is not infinitely divisible.

it; it is quite easy for the world-builder to forget that his own mind is occupied in making up this list. I suspect there is an illusion in the idea that we can quite well conceive a world without any consciousness in it and then bring consciousness or mentality in as a sort of afterthought. It is hard to see how consciousness could originate in a world which for ages had gone on without it; no successful explanation has ever been given of how mind or consciousness could arrive in a non-mental world. We shall, therefore, include mind as a separate ingredient.

And while it seems easy to think of a world with no mind in it — a purely physical world — this is a successful bit of imagination only as long as we forget *ourselves* who are doing the thinking. And there may be some things we have put down as ingredients of the world which would not be there unless the mind were there to perceive them. Take, for instance, the noisiness of noise or the saltiness of salt. Noise as a vibration of the air might be there whether there were any mind to measure it or not: but the sound we hear seems to imply the ear and the hearer. Salt as a union of sodium and chlorine might exist in a mindless world; but would it *be salty* if there were no tasting tongue? We need not decide these questions at present. I only point out that if we try to omit the mind from our ingredients, several other things are likely to go along with it.

We may now call this somewhat random list of ingredients a job. We may draw up our rough list as follows:

Things
>   Matter (Substance)
>   Quality, Quantity

Behavior
>   Motion (Change)
>   Force ⎫
>   Law   ⎬ (Causality)

Fields
>   Space, Time
>   Interval, Pattern (Relation)

Mind
>   Consciousness

In this table I have put in the first column the crude terms of ordinary speech, and in the second the more carefully defined ingredients, found by simple analysis.

We may now ask how these ingredients belong together.[1]

C. HOW THE WORLD IS ORGANIZED

322. The Ingredients Not Separate

However separate may be the names of the ingredients of the world, it is evident that the ingredients themselves are not completely separable. We cannot so much as *think* them in complete disunion from one another. Let us notice a few examples of this.

Space and time constitute some kind of working pair. It may be possible to think of time without space. (Try, for example, to think of a flute solo heard in the dark; of course, space-ideas intrude themselves, simply because we cannot halt the imagery that runs along with all mental activity; but our question is whether they necessarily belong there.) But it seems impossible to think of space without time. Because if anything exists, it must last for at least a minimum of time: if its duration runs to the limit of zero, it vanishes. To last for no time at all is the same as not to exist. Hence any spatial world must also be a space-time world.

Whether matter and motion (or change of any kind) can be thought of separately is again highly doubtful. It seems at first easy to think of matter (or things) without motion: rest seems to be their normal state, and motion something which must be added to them by outside impulsion. But unless you can find a position of absolute fixity somewhere, it will prove hard to distinguish rest from motion; every body in the universe is in motion with reference to most other bodies, though it may have a local setting of repose as eternal as that of the Sphinx.

But can we think of motion (or change) apart from matter? Here, I suspect, we enter a world of trouble. Personally, when I think of motion, I think of something which moves. I cannot

[1] See BR. No. 93, E. S. Brightman, "Categories: The Structure of Reality."

any more think of change apart from *that which* changes, than I can think of the grin of the Cheshire cat without the face. But we are told by the French philosopher Bergson that this is a matter of habit, and of misleading habit at that. Change is the fundamental fact of the world: what we call "material things" are but geometrical patterns which throw a temporary and illusory fixity over a scene of infinite inner motion. We do not first have things and then the motion-of-things: we first have impulse-and-change and then the congealing of some of the more stable whirlpools of change into forms which dissolve more or less slowly, but none the less dissolve. The obelisks of Egypt have lasted long; but their molecules are in incessant motion, and within those molecules there are no fixed and eternal pellets of impenetrable atomic "substance," but atoms, which are themselves worlds of intricately interlocked energies.

Asking us to believe that things are derived from energies, instead of energies from things-in-motion, is asking us to give up using our imaginations as measures of what is "real." I cannot imagine an energy by itself; I cannot imagine a "quantum": I cannot imagine an electron as a center of an electric field; I can make no mental picture of electricity, still less of a unit of electricity. But this incompetence gives me no privilege of refusing to believe in them, if mathematical equations, into which they enter as "terms," actually predict how the physical world behaves. This is another way of saying that what is "real" may be, and very probably is, beyond the reach of imagination, though not necessarily beyond the reach of thought.

Fortunately for us, what our imaginations put inseparably together, as space-with-time, reality also for the most part puts together. And without pursuing this interconnection of the world ingredients further for the present, what we have so far discovered is that there is probably a very intimate union among them all, so that while we can name them in complete separation, and perhaps define them without much reference to each other, they are really closely dependent on one another.

323. Meaning of the Terms "Real, Reality"

Pause at this point to consider a word which we have now used several times, the word "real." It is a word which implies a distinction. The distinction is between that which is real and that which is apparent or seeming to be so. Sometimes this is expressed as the distinction of *the real* and *the illusory*. It is a distinction we all make as we recover from our many false first impressions: "I was completely taken in by it; his apparently sincere interest was a pure sham; in reality he doesn't care a fig for painting." The "real" in such cases is the judgment which displaces our quick and superficial judgments and which holds its own because we have now got the truth of the case. Any learning from experience, any growth in sagacity or sophistication or wisdom, is a process of discarding the relatively illusory for the relatively real. I dwell on this because one way of defining our present philosophical task is that we are *seeking the real* or, as we sometimes say, the *reality* — meaning thereby the more or less hidden truth about the inner connections and working of the world.[1]

For example, if Bergson is right — and his view has strong support from the scientific quarter, as well as elsewhere — the reality of our world is some kind of *activity*, rather than some kind of inert "substance." It is more like energy than it is like the old pellet-atom.[2] He declares in *Creative Evolution* that "reality appears as a ceaseless upspringing of something new."

324. Three Types of Order

If now we can discover some types of order or of connection which run through all of the things and events of the world, or through large groups of them, we shall be coming nearer to the true account of the world, nearer to the "reality," than in our loose list of ingredients.

There are three such pervasive types of order. We have already caught glimpses of them in piecemeal.

First, the order of *classes*, which we met in observing that all things come in kinds.

Second, the order of *causality*, which we noticed in the form of force and law as factors of change.

Third, the order of *purpose*, which is always present in the activity of the mind.

---

[1] See BR, No. 90, Thoreau, "Awake and Live."
[2] See BR, No. 101, Henri Bergson, "Creation, the Goal of Life."

325. (a) The Order of Classes

As we find things in the world which strike our interest, we give them names, or rather, we name their kinds. We do not pretend to name everything — there remains a large "miscellaneous" group. But we recognize that this is due to the limitation of our knowledge, not to any lack of character in the unnamed objects.

And in our thought, we provide *places* for this unexplored region. We do this by a scheme of higher (or more general) kinds which include the narrower kinds. Thus the term "animal" is a higher genus which includes the lower genera of protozoa, mollusca, vertebrates, and so forth, and the term "organism" includes animals and vegetables alike. The term animal is broad enough to cover all undiscovered or unnamed species; the term organism may cover any living things of which we are doubtful whether they are animal or vegetable.

By including all classes under higher classes, we come at last to a most inclusive class (*summum genus*), for which perhaps the word "thing" or "object" or "being" is a sufficient name. It must be broad enough to include qualities, quantities, relations, actions, etc., as well as "things" in the more physical sense. Thus the order of classes provides (mentally) for the entire world.

In the main the class-belongings of things have to be discovered, of animals and plants, of lightning and electricity, of cloud and sea. This is a part of the work of science; and the *logical* order of "kinds" which we have been tracing is, in part at least, a kinship of the things themselves and not merely a mental grouping. Science slowly brings its mental classes into agreement with the natural classes.

326. (b) The Order of Causes

The order of causes is the primary care of science, together with that of the practical sense of every man and animal; for survival depends on knowing how things may be expected to behave or "react." The order of classes and of causes together is sometimes called the "order of nature." In the case of causes, the "real" order is far more hidden than is the order of classes.

The illusion that has to be overcome is *the illusion of separateness* among the events. A few connections are fairly obvious and early made by every tribe of men — that between sun-and-star movements and the seasons, the round of the year, for example. But these are at first isolated instances in a sea of experiences which are running along together in time but seemingly independently in their careers. A flood in Mississippi, a bridge falling in Oregon, an avalanche on the Jungfrau have no perceptible repercussions in New York.

As a result of this independence between contemporary strands of happening, we think of cause-and-effect series as *chains*, link causing link, and this in turn another link, in linear order. For practical purposes we need to consider them that way; how else could we *direct* a cause to produce just the effect we desire and no other? There are always sidelong incidental effects; but we minimize them. The automobile is to push itself from A to B and us with it; if it wears out itself and the road in doing so, we improve construction at both ends till the side-effects are almost nil. If a sulfa drug cures pneumonia, and at the same time kills off some white corpuscles, we work on the sulfa series until we find a variant that does the one and not the other.

But this necessity is itself a confession that in the natural setting the causal order is not a set of parallel chains but a spreading meshwork. Every event, the closer we examine it, produces many effects. And equally, every event has many contributory causes. There is no "the cause" of anything. What caused the landslide? A series of heavy rains, a gradual increase of the weight of vegetation on the slope, a bit of an earth tremor, frost on the slanting surface of underlying rock; omit any one of these factors and it would not have occurred; which then was "the cause"? Evidently the causal context splays out from any event in both directions: the descendants multiply and so do the ancestors, the more deeply we look. But how far?

Newton's answer carries one causal context to the extreme limit: "Every particle attracts every other particle. . . ." If space is a "field of force," whether gravitational or electric or what not, and if the intensity of this force diminishes in some ratio to the distance, it will never become zero. And for the whole group of such forces, we may generalize Newton's formula: "Every event in the universe is affected by every preceding event, and affects every succeeding event." For practical purposes, we shall always quite reasonably neglect the great majority of these effects as insignificant. But for getting at the "reality" and overcoming the illusion of separateness, we should have to say that the universe is a *single system of causality*. The togetherness of things and events is not merely a time-space togetherness; it is a dynamic togetherness, unlimited in scope and perfect in its mathematical precision.

327. The Single Causal System

The idea of a seamless system of nature, into which nothing can come from outside and from which no wisp of mass-energy can ever disappear, has a fascination of its own, especially when it is coupled with the idea of unlimited extent. It has its disconcerting aspects; for no part can escape from the influence of all the rest. What we have to deal with, at every moment, is literally the whole universe. It has its converse exhilarating aspects: stamp your foot here and you shake India! True, India remains serene as before; is bound to ignore the great majority of universal foot-stampers elsewhere. Also for us it is as well that we do not have to consider legally the consequences of the universal spread of effects: philosophy is not committed to the loss of all sense of proportion! But the *fact* of the continuity of influence is what here interests us, not its quantity nor its practical utility. Given the fact, it can be built on when it is needed, as radio transmission builds on it. The cause-and-effect relationship ties the time-procession of events in the entire universe into a single mesh.

Within this infinite mesh there is no center and no periphery; for infinitude can have neither the one nor the other. Every place in such a system may be said to be *lost;* for the chances of finding it from any other place taken at random are nil. It cannot be located; its spatial significance is zero. This is the reason that Bruno's world-view, which gladly embraced both the causality and the infinity of the world, was looked on with horror by orthodox, and many unorthodox, contemporaries. The old picture could have domesticity; there were fixed points of reference; there was a special place for God, for man, for the Devil; the planet Earth was a perfectly appropriate place for the sacred drama and for the special interest of God. In an infinite and centerless system, all this is destroyed.

But the lost locality has its revenge. Where there is no center, each place (by the right of relativity) may regard itself as the center with as good claim as any other. By the nature of the system, all the infinitudes around each locality are reporting to that place, registering their effect there silently and automatically. Build a campfire at night in the Michigan woods and, no matter how deep the forest or how distant the view of space, the center of the universe is by that fire. The mind is itself a perspective effect and cannot get away from its own center of regard: so does it spontaneously establish a psychological at-home-ness wherever it is, within the infinite causal system.

But with this, of course, we are introducing elements not causal. The measurable causal context has no place for mentality nor for preference, which is an element in purpose. It therefore cannot include a feeling of at-homeness, which expresses a preference. The more perfect we have considered our causal system to be, the more difficult it is to see how a purposive order can get foothold within it. And yet *there is also a purposive order*.

328. (c) The Order of Purposes

The causal order is uni-directional; it runs from past to present. The purposive order is likewise uni-directional; it runs from the future to the present. The conceived future goal of action is what shapes the action. It is the end that lures us on, not the beginning which pushes us forward.

And since we cannot deny the presence of the purposive order in the world any more than of the causal order, our question about the types of order must certainly give it a place and also show its relation to causality. Here, I suspect, we can gain a certain amount of instruction, as well as relief, by returning for a moment to older and simpler conceptions of the world, unspoiled by scientific sophistication. In the traditional story of world beginnings, the several ingredients find their places easily and without argument. And especially, there is no difficulty about consciousness or mentality, that interloper whose presence is a standing puzzle to scientists and philosophers.

Herbert Spencer wrestled with the problem of consciousness manfully. He first took mind to be a form of energy, like light or heat, and supposed that in the brain a certain amount of energy went into consciousness and then came back again into the nerve-system when the mind through the motor nerves worked the muscles. This made mind a part of the physical-causal context. Then he saw that this would not do because no brain physiologist ever detected any energy running away from the brain into the mind nor returning therefrom and in the nature of the case never could concede such an occurrence to take place. Spencer in effect gave the problem up.

Not so the author of Genesis. For him, mentality is aboriginal. It does not enter a physical world already running along on its own. On the contrary, it is the physical world which enters the realm of mind. It is the Eternal Mind who in the beginning created the raw materials of the world, and whose word evoked order from chaos. He begins this labor, not as we did with systems and laws, but with the light-and-darkness contrast; this is, of course, a contrast of quality, a purely mental interest. And as the labor runs through its several days or stages, man appears as the crowning achievement and is set in a position of mastery over the rest. But mastery is not a causal relationship at all. It is a purposive relation. And I believe there was a garden in the story; a garden being something which never occurs in nature, and which implies purposive interference with the causal system. Does this story afford any suggestions we can use?

In my judgment, it does. It suggests that if we begin our world with a closed causal system, the entrance of purpose will be inexplicable. It suggests, then, the question whether this perfect and finished causal system is known to be the "real," or whether it is only supposed to be on the basis of incomplete evidence. When we raise that question, we see at once that the idea of an infinite system in which everything affects everything else can never be the result of experience; it is a mathematical ideal. It suggests that purposes and causes must have some natural way of fitting together, and that it would be well to inquire how, in fact, they cooperate.

329. Relations between Causal and Purposive Orders

Note, in the first place, that there are strong resemblances between a causal sequence and a purposive sequence. Compare a man hammering a stake into the ground and a steam pile-driver. You cannot see the purpose of the man, nor can you see the cause passing over into the effect when the weight hits the pile. You cannot prove that either one is actually present. All you see in either case is (a) the fall of a weight and (b) a lowering of the top of the stake or of the pile. You have to impute the causation, and you have to impute the purpose. Both processes use cause-and-effect; both take time.

In the purposive process, however, the several blows of the sledge are not merely causes, they are "means-to-an-end." And the difference appears precisely at the end. The man knows when to stop. The pile driver does not: somebody has to stop it.

Purposes and causes are, therefore, not incompatible; purposive processes usually *are* causal. But purposes *include* causes, whereas causes do not, and cannot, include purposes. The natural relation of purposive and causal order, then, appears to be that of the inclusion of cause within purpose, which is "mastery" or "control."

But there is this further difference between causal order and purposive order: that purpose appears to be *local, sporadic, and discontinuous*, not to say short-winded. Human purpose, at any rate, has to arrive at its end, and then, formulating new projects, make new starts. The causal scheme, having no terminus, has also no need to begin again; in fact, it cannot stop except by running to an equilibrium; and if it thus reaches quiescence, there is no possibility of a new start except by an impulse from outside. It looks as if the causal order were well fitted to be the main scheme for nature as a whole, with purposive enterprises as spot-wise and occasional riders, wherever minds happen to be stirring about. This leaves the problem as before — how the minds happened to be there; and how they are in a position to interfere with an otherwise undisturbed causal flow, channeling and shaping the causal processes to attain their "ends."

There is, however, this possibility for a wider role for purposive order. Notice that whenever causal processes run to purposed goal, *all the causes* leading to that goal take on the character of means-to-the-end. They do not drop out of their place in the causal order to do this, nor do they abandon the strict mathematics of their own behavior; it is the whole causal sequence, intact, which is rechristened "purposive" when it is aimed at a goal. A printing press does not cease to be a machine when it is set up for the purpose of turning out papers: the better a machine, the better it serves the purpose, and every pin and bolt in it acquires a "meaning." The same would be true of a machine of nature, if nature achieved an end. Now why is not the production of living beings, and of men, such an end? That is, might it be a purpose, which all nature serves, *to produce purposing beings?*

If so, these purposive beings, being "ends," would throw the whole of infinite preceding nature into the position of a huge "means." And further, since there is no physical center to the infinite causal universe, they would have a good reason for regarding the region of their appearance as a *purposive-center*. This would not be anthropomorphic conceit; it would correspond to the literal facts of the situation.

I am not saying that we, as philosophers, are justified by any evidence yet considered by us in asserting that there is any such universal purpose in addition to the minor, local, and fitful purposes displayed by ourselves. All I say is that it might be so. And that if it were so, the whole causal order at once becomes a total purposive order, *without any interference with its causality* other than what interference we animals carry out.

And, in that case, the seventeenth-century scientists who set up the principles of scientific method may have been too hasty in assuming that they had to expel "final causes" from the world in order to keep a clean slate for their mathematics. For if we are right, a total purpose could give them complete causal free-play in all of the universe leading up to the animals and man. To put purposes out of the laboratory is not to put them out of the universe.

We agree with them on this point, that the purpose *would have to be total* in order not to interfere. If such a total purpose exists, we may say that the world as a whole is at once a purposive order and a causal order in its main outlines, with the causal order *inside* of the purpose, not the fragments of purpose inside the total realm of cause. Two circles, one within the other, might symbolize the orders of cause and purpose.

330. The Ideal of Unity

We have now to notice how, in all this discussion about order and classification, the human mind is working toward discovering a *unity* in things. It acts as though the notion that there are many separate parts among the ingredients is an *illusion* — as if the reality were one, and not many.

Within science, we need but mention the great strides made in recent years to get a unitary picture of the physical world and of the biological world. Not a hundred years ago we had separate chapters in physics on heat, light, magnetism, electricity, sound, dynamics, gravitation, although it was already well established that heat is a mode of motion, and Joule in 1843 had demonstrated the "mechanical equivalent of heat." The general principle was fairly well accepted that while the several "forces" could be transformed into one another, there could be neither gain nor loss in the transformations: there was a "conservation of energy" in any closed physical system.

But it is only in the present century, with the development of the relativity theory, that a single set of formulae has begun to emerge, valid for light, gravitation, electro-magnetism. Einstein's ambition has been to show all these separate chapters as derivatives of a single law, which would then justly be called *the* law of nature. This has not yet been achieved, and new gaps threaten to appear as knowledge of the complex inwardness of atomic life grows. The unity of nature remains a "postulate" — that is, a demand that the mind makes in advance of proof — not a demonstration.

But this general postulate that "the real is one" is no modern conception. It has blossomed out in every great civilization of the past, sometimes as a product of religious thought and sometimes as a product of purely secular philosophizing. On the religious side, it cropped out in ancient Egypt, India, and, it is said, in Peru. Wherever there have been polytheisms, men have become uneasy under their numerous inconsistent authorities. In Greece and Rome, it was felt that there must be some power, call it Fate, Destiny, or what not, behind all the gods. In early India they called this power Rita, which comes as near as we can say it in English to the notion of just-law-in-cosmic-happening. In Peru, the story goes that a young Inca addressed his people with an argument: "We worship the sun. But the sun follows a regular course in the sky. There must be some rule which the sun obeys. We ought to worship that rule and not the sun itself." The Egyptian leap to the idea of one god is connected with the name of Amenophis IV, who tried in vain to bring about a religious revolution by making the sun-disc the symbol for all deity.

On the philosophical side, we have the profound later speculation of India which resulted in the Vedanta system, teaching the extraordinary paradox that everything is one being, and I, each human soul, *am that being:* "I am Brahm." [1] But there was much cruder speculation running to a similar conclusion in old Greece. The earliest philosopher, so-reckoned, Thales (about 600 B.C.), taught that the four elements — earth, air, water, fire, and therefore all things — are transformations of water. Since all life comes from fluid plasma, this must also hold good for the mental element, which Thales thought of as being everywhere: "All things are full of gods." The Stoics improved on this by considering *fire* to be the primeval element. For what is more like thought than fire; what more fit than fire, which passes from visible to invisible and runs towards Heaven, to embrace both the physical and the mental in one nature; and what more suitable name for the soul than a "spark of Zeus"?

Such notions as these are worth recalling if only to show that, long before it had adequate mental tools for critical thought on the subject, the mind of man reached out for a conception of a hidden unity in the real. It tried for a "monism" in place of its "dualism" or "pluralisms." Most of the early monisms were so far from grasping the difficulty of the problem that they have little instruction for us today. There are two great exceptions: the classical Taoism of China and the Vedanta of India. The Vedantists taught that there is one ultimate reality, and no other, Brahm, the eternal source of everything, a systematic unity embracing all individuals and absorbing all distinctions. But we shall look at the matter for ourselves and examine it with the tools of today.

[1] Cf. BR, No. 73 C, Hinduism: "The Indwelling Presence of the Supreme Being."

D. ENDEAVORS TO REACH A UNIFIED VIEW

331. (1) Is There One Primary Reality, or More than One?

So long as we are simply *describing* the world, we are not especially interested in getting rid of variety: we like it. A world that appeared to us an eternal repetition of one kind of thing would be appallingly monotonous. If the world is indeed composed of one kind of original stuff, say electrons, it is fortunate for our enjoyment of the physical scene that nobody can perceive the electron: our organs of sense are set at the level of its endlessly different combinations.

But when we go beyond description and undertake to understand the world, to *explain* it, there is a different interest. The impulse to explain drives us toward unity. When it is confronted by a multitude of things, it inquires whether they are different arrangements of the same building material. If it could reduce the multiplicity to a few different kinds, it would still ask, Why so many? How do they happen to be together? How do they cooperate to make a single world? Is there a thread conjoining the beads of things? Is there not some single source, or "real," from which they are all derived?

The early efforts in this direction which we have just been noticing followed a plan which was very natural, but which had a danger we can readily see. They picked out some one ingredient of the world, like matter, and tried to explain all the rest as arising from that. The danger is that, after the explanation has gone along merrily for quite a distance, *something will be left over* which refuses to be explained. What is more promising as a unit of explanation than a material particle, an "atom," indivisible and therefore everlasting, moving through space and generating all the various things by its combinations? Thinkers who follow this line have been called "atomists." But if the material atom is your original world-stuff, your "real," how do you explain mind or consciousness from that?

Would you regard it as an answer to the question to say, as these pioneers said, that the atoms themselves are very fine and subtle, and that some of them could be sufficiently active

and alert to explain consciousness? This is surely an evasion
rather than an answer: for consciousness is not the activity of a
swarm of swift atoms, however gaseous or ethereal. The refinement and distillation of matter does not carry us in the direction
of the mind; hence this kind of unification simply leaves the
mind out.

Seeing this, some later atomists adopted the idea that every
atom is conscious in some degree; and others have gone the
whole way across and have made their atoms *wholly mental*.
The world is composed, Leibniz believed, of unit-beings each
of which is a complete mental world, a "mirror of the universe."
He called them "monads." This is an exceedingly compact
account of the mental side of the universe: for each mind does
create for itself an image of the whole. But if we begin with a
purely mental atom, how are we to explain the physical world
from that? I will not say it cannot be done; I will say that it is
difficult. Our monism runs the risk of omitting an important
part of the universe.

But suppose it were successful; we have reduced the many *kinds*
of thing to one kind, but the things themselves are still many.
There are many monads, and we have not found a single explanation of our world until we can answer the question, Why are
there just so many of these units? The very fact that they are
all alike in kind suggests that they are the output of a single
creative or fabricating process, just as the presence of a group
of like coins suggests a single mint. But if there were such a
process, or creative power, it would be something else than its
products, the monads. Our monads, then, would cease to be
the final units of explanation; we fall back on this generating
process or power as the One we are seeking.

One of the most ambitious efforts the human mind has ever
made to conceive such a single being from which all things come
is the "Vedanta" philosophy of India, a still living and spreading
system of thought. Its central idea is that all the personal selves
of the world, all the "monads," *are in reality one Self*, somewhat
as the many flashes of light on a million ripples are in reality
images of the one sun. This one is Brahm, the indescribable;
but its essence is the same as the essence of each one of us. The
deepest truth, for each person, is "I am Brahm." The illusion

of the world is that we are distinct from Brahm and separate from each other; all the world of experience, plurality, material things, egoism, is an illusory veil which conceals from us the ultimate One, the alone Real.

Does this system succeed in unifying all things? Does it leave anything out? To say that the visible world is illusory still leaves the problem how that illusion arises; and why it is there. If Brahm is everything, and we are Brahm, why is there any illusion or any mystery?

There is a story of a Hindu guru, or teacher, who was seated under a mango tree, expounding this doctrine, when an elephant charged upon the assembly from the forest. They dispersed, and the guru betook himself to the tree. When the elephant had passed on, the group reassembled and recovered its poise; but one member put this question to the guru: "If the elephant was an illusion, why did you climb into the tree?" "It is true," answered the guru, "that the elephant was an illusion. But also, the forest is an illusion, the tree is an illusion, and *that I climbed into it was an illusion as well!*" The guru was correct to this extent: that a total illusion leaves all the parts in their normal order — no single appearance, such as the elephant, can be singled out as more illusory than anything else. But the questioner was also correct in doubting whether a theory of illusion which makes no difference in conduct is affording a genuine explanation of the world. That which is dismissed as "illusion," without any theory of the illusion, is simply not explained.[1] This monism, like the rest, *leaves something out.*

Is this a sort of nemesis, a punishment, which attends all our efforts to refer things to one source? Shall we always find that we have left something important out of account? This was the view of William James (1842–1910), who expressed the situation in the phrase, "Ever not quite!" Our monisms are always premature.

May it be that, after all, the universe is a two rather than a one? Is it an accident that so many efforts for unity end with *a pair* of contrasting ingredients, cause and purpose, mind and matter, ideas and facts, good and evil, permanence and change? It is at least worth considering that the universe is bi-polar, set

[1] Cf. BR, No. 91, Plato, "The Allegory of the Cave."

up around a double source, a twofold center of reality. We shall look at some of the major "dualisms."

332. The Great Dualisms: Explaining Things from Two Contrasting Facts: (a) Good and Evil

For human feeling, everything falls into contrasting qualities, such as pleasure and pain, comfort and discomfort, liking and disliking, approving and disapproving. The terms "good" and "evil" may be taken as general names, covering the positive and negative sides of all these contrasts and also the objects which excite these opposing feelings.

This contrast of good and evil is obviously the most fundamental one for the survival of living things, since they must at every moment distinguish the beneficial from the harmful, the friend from the enemy. Hence it is built into the organization of all of them. Animals and plants alike are set for expanding or contracting, for opening up or shrinking together. And animals, most of them, are organized in muscles and nerves for approaching an object or receding from it, according as they are moved by attraction or by repulsion or fear.

There is little wonder, therefore, that in their consideration of the universe men have been inclined to trace the good to a good principle or power and the evil to an evil source. Every one has plentiful experience with both good and evil arriving in such uneven mixtures that they seem to be apportioned, if not by chance, then as a result of a changing and unfinished struggle between the opposing powers.

Monism here seems peculiarly difficult: it is hard to refer the whole of experience to an evil power or to a good one. If every event is due to one power and that a good power, as the belief in an omnipotent God implies, the facts of evil are there to be dealt with: how can a good God be the source of *them?* Is it not more in accord with probabilities to regard the world as a sphere of action of two contending powers, one good and one evil?

In the most ancient philosophy of China, all the "ten thousand things" are referred to two principles, the Yang and the Yin, which in differing proportions enter as factors into the nature of all things. The Yang and the Yin, represented in the familiar symbol ☯, are a composite of all the quality-contrasts which can be thought of as better or worse, such as warm and cold, dry and wet, light and dark, active and passive, good and bad, male and female. The Yang is typified by the Sun, the Yin by the Moon; the Yang is dominant in the first, or ascending, half of the year; the Yin in the second, or recessive, half. No doubt this alignment tends to emphasize the superiority which the male chooses to assign to himself in the order of nature; but it is less harsh toward the female than it appears to be, since everything and every person is thought to have both principles in his makeup. And both are necessary, as negative and positive are necessary to each other; they constitute less a warfare than a cosmic rhythm, like the breathing-in and breathing-out of the year. The dualism of good and evil is thus mitigated by its associations.

But the fundamental conception is that the world is ruled by qualities, not by facts. Because of this, the chief wisdom for men is not (as with a primarily scientific civilization) the "objective" knowledge of a neutral physical fabric but the appreciation of values and value-contrasts which have to be recognized as the character-making constituents of all objects. It is perhaps this unique theory of the world which has given to Chinese civilization its strong aesthetic cast and has carried its art to so high a stage of perfection.

In ancient Persia, the contrast is more clearly moral. Zoroaster (or Zarathustra) taught that the history of the world is one of a warfare between two spiritual powers — that of Ahura Mazda, the power of goodness (symbolized by light), and that of Ahriman, the power of wickedness (symbolized by darkness). This warfare is carried on largely by the choices exercised by human beings, who can join either Ahura or Ahriman: when they try to do right, they enter the struggle on the side of the good power, who is worshipped under the symbol of fire. The physical world has been created by both, acting alternately — Ahura Mazda setting up the pleasant and propitious aspects of the earth, Ahriman adding the diseases, the noxious beasts, and the terrors of nature. Here again, the whole factual side of the world is subordinate to the qualitative side: the system of nature is derived from the system of purpose; nothing is indifferent; and the destiny of the soul in the afterworld is hung on the career of conscience in this world.

This conception is enjoying a certain modified reappearance in modern thought. The Jewish Satan and the Christian Devil, probably connected in history with the Persian Ahriman, have long been relegated to the symbolical aspects of faith for most modern believers. But quite recently (and here again William James has been a factor in the idea) the question has been seriously raised whether God is everything and therefore inclusive of the evil, or whether he is but a part of reality, namely, the good part, and therefore finite. And if he is finite, he has something outside of him, has something to work for and to fight against, calls for human participation in his world-purpose. He has to contend with powers of evil, which, having a certain corporate and persistent character, may be regarded as devilish or "demonic."

333. (b) Spirit and Matter

There is such a thing as a detached or disinterested look at the world, more or less free from our feelings of good and evil. In modern times, we have come to think it our intellectual duty to achieve this attitude of "objectivity" (for scientific purposes) or of "pure contemplation" (for philosophical purposes). Whether we get the best truth by ridding our intellects of all preference, we may leave an open question for the moment. In any case, it is a mark of mental progress to be able to look at the world purely as an object to be explained, in at least tentative freedom from our human contrasts of better and worse.

To take the contrast of Spirit and Matter as a basis of explanation is a long step in this direction. In a sense, this is the natural dualism; it fits closely the reports of experience. It corresponds fairly well to what we were calling the causal and the purposive orders. Whatever we mean by Matter, the network of physical fact on which the fabric of nature is stretched, we must use this material factor and its laws to explain things as far as it will go. And what is left over we may call "Spirit," as a general name for reality that is "immaterial," akin to consciousness and thought. To regard the world as a working-together of these two realities should give us a fairly complete account.[1]

---

[1] See BR, No. 98, Earl of Balfour, "Dualism: Reality Both Material and Spiritual."

In such a view, how are we to think of the realm of Spirit, and how is it related to the realm of Matter?

On this point, there are important suggestions, not at all outdated, which come to us from the great Greek thinkers. Let us look for a moment at the world through the eyes of Plato.

For Plato, the world might be summarily described as the material setting for a spiritual process. This process is a sort of long-range education in which souls, indestructible and therefore immortal, work their way through a series of lives to a clear grasp of truth. In this, they are hampered by their entanglement with the material principle in the shape of the body. The truth they have to reach is a clear vision of certain eternal "Ideas," as Plato calls them, ideas of the True, the Beautiful, the Good.

The souls are the restless and striving element of the realm of Spirit; the Ideas are its stable and changeless goal. As we use the word "idea," we commonly mean a conception which our minds have formed: Plato meant by it a conception which our minds *discover*. For the Ideas — as he thought of them — are independent of our thinking. The truths of geometry are discovered, not devised by our thought: they did not begin to be true when they dawned on our minds; they have always been true, and we cannot wish them away. They are eternal and unchanging. And when we first perceive them, it is as if we were recollecting something we had once known — we are coming to ourselves!

Having taken its abode in the body, the soul is misled by its bodily appetites and perceptions; but it remains, as we should say, subconsciously discontented with these substitutes for the Ideas. Instinctively, when we want to think things as they are, we shut our eyes and stop our ears to shut out the din of sensation; this discontent is the true love, the Eros, of the soul, which weans us away from the image of beauty disfigured by Matter to the Idea in its incomparable and unfading purity.

In a view like this, we feel that justice is being done to the independent importance of the spiritual reality in the world and to a certain genuine superiority which it has over whatever is subject to the ravages of time and is mixed with clay. At the same time, the material element, which for Plato plays the part of a drag on the soul's aspiration, seems unduly disparaged. Without matter there would be no life, no movement, no experience in time at all, and therefore no process of learning and growth.

We may well take a further step in separating the factors of the world from the contrast of our preferences. And this may be done if we follow the dualism of Spirit and Matter as it appears in the compass of the human self, in the contrast of Mind and Body.

334. (c) Mind and Body; Do They Interact?

Man has often been called a "microcosm," a small universe. If the great world is a duality of reals, man's nature will reflect that doubleness.

We have already encountered this contrast. At the outset of our study, we concluded that mind and body, though they are intimately conjoined, do not mean the same thing.[1] The time has now come to examine the nature of the association between them in the hope that light will thereby be thrown on the nature of the world.

For ordinary purposes, we can identify mind and body: we usually find a man's mind where his body is, though there are such things as "absent-minded" people. Throughout the past, the usual belief has been that mind and body are *separable*. Though the primitive belief that the soul could go off on an independent journey during sleep has had no following in modern times, the still more radical belief that the soul can begin an independent career at death continues to be widely held. And for Plato, as for other believers in transmigration, there seemed to be no difficulty in the thought that the soul, after existing in the underworld for some time without any body, could return to earth to take up a new career in an entirely different body than before. In the Indian view and also in that of Pythagoras, it might be the body of an animal.[2] But the soberer opinion of Aristotle is nearer the modern feeling, that to whatever degree the mind may be separable from the body, the mind of Peter will not fit the body of Paul nor the mind of either of them the body of any animal. The soul of a man cannot live in the body

[1] See Part I, sections 1, 3, 6.
[2] See BR, No. 73 E, "Reincarnation in Hinduism."

of a tiger nor vice versa. For, as Schopenhauer (1788–1860) later pointed out, the body very accurately expresses the instinct-chart of the animal's mind: the tusk teeth and claws of the tiger correspond precisely to its will-to-live-by-stalking-and-killing prey. There is what the mathematicians call a one-to-one-correspondence between the animal anatomy and the form of the animal will-to-live.

Now the simplest view of the relation between mind and body is that the mind, as a center of consciousness, reason, and purpose, *resides in* the body, having its seat in the brain, and there receives influence from the body via the sensory nerves and gives impulses to the body via the motor nerves and muscles. This is the theory of "interaction": the body affects the mind causally; the mind affects the body causally. And yet there is sufficient independence between them so that neither is wholly governed by the career and fate of the other.

It will be hard to convince anyone who is weakened by hunger and restored to good spirits by a square meal that the body has no effect on the mind. It will be equally hard to convince a man who has held himself to cutting a cord of wood in a day's time that the mind has no effect on the body. In fact, every act of will, such as deciding to stand up or sit down, is a sufficient illustration of the general and normal state of things — that the muscles are under the direct control of the will. A man whose muscles will not obey him, the purposer, is suffering from palsy or paralysis.

The difficulties with this view come, not from common sense, but from scientific theory. *The scientist can find no trace of a physical cause running over into a mental effect; nor can he find any place where such an event could occur.* Nor can he find any place for the reverse transaction. The motor nerves spread out into central connections with the brain; but there is no organ of any sort for the reception of influences from the mind. And no evidence that there is any exception to the steady flow of physical causes-and-effects right through the brain area. It is impossible for the laboratory to make any allowances whatever for exchanges of energy with an invisible entity called the "mind." In fact, the brain physiologist would get on with his work much better if the mind were left totally out of account.

Not only can he find no such interaction. He cannot *imagine* it. Try the experiment. Just what can we imagine taking place when a nerve impulse, or let us say an electrical disturbance in the brain-region, "causes" a sensation? The impulse comes in, for example, from the optic nerve: there is an image on the retina and the optic nerve is reporting at the base of the brain; some sort of complex oscillation is taking place. But an oscillation is not a sensation of light or color or shape. How does the unlighted, uncolored, unshaped oscillation "produce" a sensation of light, color, and shape? The nearer we get to the alleged interaction, the more incredible it appears.

The interesting thing about the interaction theory is that *nobody can get the mind and the brain into view at the same moment;* we do not observe them with the same instruments! In every other case of interaction, as of hammer and iron being both warmed by striking the iron, we get both objects before us at once: they are in the same visual field. But mind, being itself purposive, does not get into the causal system at all, so far as we can observe. And the first principle of scientific method, which we stated in Part I,[1] that physical causes have physical effects and vice versa, seems to exclude the theory of interaction.

All that we seem able to say with any assurance is that *when* the brain disturbance occurs, then, at that precise moment, a sensation also occurs. And again, when we decide to move our arm, then, at that precise moment, a brain disturbance actuates the motor nerve, which then operates on the appropriate muscles.

Let us hold to this fact of *simultaneity.*

We cannot observe it directly because we are still in the predicament that we do not observe brain-event and mind-event together. But we can infer that they are simultaneous because both can be inserted between a sense-stimulus and a muscular movement coming as nearly immediately afterward as possible. A man at bat follows with his eye the pitched ball; he must decide in a split second whether to strike. Between the stimulus (oncoming ball) and the muscular action (strike) must lie both the brain-event and the mental-event. They must be very close to simultaneous.

[1] See Part I, sec. 31.

335. The Theory of Parallelism between Mind and Body

May we perhaps generalize this situation and say that for every brain-event of a certain kind and intensity there is a simultaneous mental-event; and for every mental-event there is a simultaneous brain-event? If this were the case, the brain procedure would be simply mirrored in the mind without interaction. The two series of events would run along parallel timelines. This is the theory of mind-body relations known as *"parallelism."*

This theory leaves the causal order, in which the brain physiologist is interested, clean of all intrusion. It keeps our first principle of scientific method unsullied. After all, interaction calls for a sort of incessant miracle, the purposive order constantly interfering with the causal order in every act of will. It is highly satisfactory for science to be rid of miracles, even of the everyday variety. Parallelism meets the requirement.

The theory is less satisfactory from the point of view of our own sense of efficiency. *All the real work is done by the bodily network:* there alone does cause operate. The simultaneous mental events are entirely passive. They reflect what goes on in the body without really having any part in it. One begins to wonder why they exist. They can have no biological function for, by hypothesis, the nervous connections in the body carry out all the processes which control conduct. They do not remember anything; but they have that capacity to retain the traces of experience which is the brain-equivalent of memory. They do not plan anything; but they relate these same brain-traces to that modification of reactions which is the brain-equivalent of profiting by experience. In brief, nerves and brain run the man-body as an intricate and wonderful causal-organism: the consciousness which accompanies this management and seems to itself so purposive and efficient is really a sort of luminous shadow, which, like a ghostly companion of a galloping horse, might fancy itself to be producing both the speed and the thunder!

If this is a true theory, we are subject to one illusion about our position in the world, profounder and more pervasive than any other illusion — *the illusion that we can act.* Not only are we not free; we do not even do the things that we seem to ourselves to be doing. It is the body which carries the whole load. It becomes more and more mysterious why the mind, ou Darwinian principles, ever found its way into the biological totality of human nature; and how, once it is there, it maintains this perfect parallelism. For even a shadow is an effect; and on this hypothesis the mind is not, and cannot be, an effect of any kind or degree. And as a matter of interest, this theory is the working hypothesis of a good part of the scientific psychology of today, and not alone of the brain physiologists.

336. The Dilemma of Mind and Body

We thus reach a curious dilemma. If the mind and the body are different things and are yet concerned in the same actions, they must either interact or not interact — that is inescapable logic. And if they do not interact, they must be parallel. We have only the two alternatives. And neither of the two is satisfactory. Interaction commits us to an inconceivable and undiscoverable give-and-take between the purposive system of the mind and the causal system of the body. Parallelism commits us to an illusion in regard to our whole insertion in nature, and turns us, even in our most seemingly active moments, into helpless automata. The football game is indeed nothing that we do; it is something which happens to us.

Now dilemmas of this kind, which lead some of the weaker spirits to throw up the sponge and say: "It is too much for reason; we are not made to understand the mysteries of nature and the world," are as a rule a sign that our question is making some false assumption. I believe that is the case here. *Perhaps the false assumption is that mind and body are two independent things.*

Different they certainly are. *But may they be two different views of the same underlying being,* like the two sides of the same shield? If so, we can understand why it is that we cannot observe both of them at the same time. If we look with the eye which can see the causal system, we do not see the mind. If we look with that mental self-awareness which understands purpose, we do not perceive our brain at all. No one directly observes the operations of his own brain; for he cannot leave the directing center of his own system of purposes.

We have then to change our hypothesis and see, if mind and

body are two aspects of the same fact, what that fact can be. Is it identical with the body (which would then absorb the mind) or identical with the mind (which would then absorb the body) or with some third being which is neither mind nor body?

337. Is There a Unity behind These Dualisms?

Before launching on this new inquiry, let us look back over our several dualisms, and note that they all leave similar questions on our hands: (a) How do the two factors happen to be together and to work together? (b) How can we understand their resemblance to each other?

To begin with the second question: The contrast of light and darkness is one of the most ancient symbols of the universal dualism. We found it in China, in Persia, in the story of Genesis; but obviously light and darkness are alike as being in the field of vision. Good and evil are in the field of moral value; and if they are characters of opposing deities, then the devil, in order to be a good antagonist of the good God, must have good qualities of his own. Whatever it takes to make a good fighter would be necessary to maintain a struggle in the cosmos throughout the length of time. Milton had to make an heroic figure of Satan in order to work out his *Paradise Lost* with any plausibility. So of the purposive and the causal order: they are, at any rate, both "orders," i.e., forms of interpreting the arrangement of things and events in time; and both can make use of the same series of events, as every machine shows. And the fact that body and mind co-exist in the same person indicates that they must have much in common.

This leads us back to the first question: how do these contrasting and resembling factors come to be together? The only reasonable answer seems to be that there is some agency able to unite them in a working partnership, though we have no clue in experience to its nature. *There must be a unity behind the duality, whether we can define it or not.*

Now this vague indication of an unknown might be taken as the conclusion of the matter. Many have left it there. Indeed, if we look carefully into the dualistic world views, we shall almost always find, in the background of the two, a third and vaguer being who is the supposed source of the opposing principles.

For the Chinese, the Yang and the Yin are supposed to be differences within the *Tao*, *Tao* being an untranslatable term which (with the persistence of translators) some have rendered "reason" and some "the ultimate mystery"! In Persia, as also in Greece, there is a suggestion that Time (Chronos) may be the deepest reality in the universe, deeper than the contrasts in the world of the gods. The modern philosopher, Spinoza (1632–1677), not only taught but attempted to prove by strict argument that there must be a One behind the many, a One being which we perceive in two equivalent forms, Thought and Extension. But to the question, What is that One? Spinoza has only to say that we may call it God or Nature or Substance, but its nature is indescribable. Herbert Spencer found it as the most certain of all truths that there is an Unknowable which manifests itself both in consciousness and in the world of objects.

All of this evidence points the same way. Dualism is everywhere recognized as a preliminary and unfinished world-view. It gives us a rough approximation to truth. But it always points beyond itself to a unity which is deeper and more difficult to grasp. We are surer that there *is* such a unity than we are *what* it is. Nevertheless we would not be satisfied to leave our world-view at this tentative stage without a renewed and serious effort to discover the final ground of unity.

E. RENEWED ATTEMPT TO FIND A SINGLE PRINCIPLE OF EXPLANATION: THE GREAT MONISMS

338. The Formidable Problem of Defining World Unity

We do not conceal from ourselves the difficulty of the task we are now to undertake, that of *thinking out* the unity of the world. We might let it go with the conviction that there is such a unity, without trying to define what sort of unity it is, and how the many things come from it. It is something to agree that the world is one — "somehow."

But neither imagination nor science are content to stop with this vague conclusion. Poets and prophets, assuring us on the basis of their intuitions that the world is one, have usually given that unity a definite character: they have given it a personal name, God, or an impersonal name, Brahman, Tao, Reason, Law, the Alone, the Absolute. Philosophy is bound to examine these proposals with the scrupulousness of argument we associate with science.

And science itself presses the question. For while science moves steadily toward bringing its own vast domain into a systematic unity, and has gone far toward bringing the many laws of physics, chemistry, and astronomy within one law, there remains a difficulty in bringing the sciences of living things — biology, psychology, sociology — into that scheme. New attempts are being made today to provide a single set of terms, a single language, for all the sciences, so that this ancient gap between the nonliving and the living can be bridged over: science cannot give up the search for its own unity. But science can hardly be unified unless the world it describes is unified. Hence, philosophy must continue its effort to think out the unity of things, learning from the sciences and also aiding them.

Let us recall that, at the close of our discussion of the body-mind dualism, there appeared to be three possibilities of advancing toward unity. We had agreed that mind and body must be two aspects of one real being, two faces of the shield. Then this real being must be either (1) physical in nature, like the body, or (2) mental in nature, like the conscious self, or (3) some third kind of being which is neither physical nor mental, holding a sort of neutrality between mind and body (as "energy" has sometimes been considered a sort of middle term between the two, certainly not material in character, nor yet mental, but capable of showing itself in either physical or mental activities).

And let us further bear in mind that whatever we find to be "real" must be able to explain *both sides* of the duality, since we mean by "the real" that from which all other things are derived. If we judge the real to be physical, we must see our way to derive from it not alone the world of nature but also the world of mind. If we judge it to be mental, we have the responsibility of deriving from that source the world of nature. If we judge it to be a neutral being, we have the double responsibility of deriving from it both the mental and the physical phases of experience.

339. (a) Physical Nature as the Real

The attempt to read everything as an outgrowth of physical nature is not something which human thought outgrows.[1] We have indeed outgrown "materialism," which proposed to derive everything, including thought and feeling, from matter in motion; this we now see to be insufficient to explain physical nature itself. But as we see deeper into nature, the question recurs whether the new physical conceptions may not be more adequate as an explanation of the mind: perhaps the electron, and the developments in field-theory, may approach the notion of consciousness? And further, as we see more clearly year by year the intricate mechanisms of growth and development, of genetics and evolution, the hope revives of catching some hint of how living and thinking things can be derived from the physical universe.

In any event, the broad fact seems ever more impressive to us *that they are so derived.* The immediate source of living things, so far as known to us, is the earth: for speculative biology, as for the everyday work of the farmer, she is still Mother Earth. If the real is, by definition, that from which we come and that into which we go, there seems no escape from the inference that physical nature is the real: it was before us; it will be there after all trace of human life is obliterated from the solar system. The earth, as the product of millions of light-years of travail among nebulae and suns, arises out of a condition in which no kind of life could exist. Hence it appears that the nature which originally begets the whole panorama of life and mind is *inanimate nature.* If we seek the real through that kind of speculative history which uses the known laws of cosmic happening to work backward in time to *origins*, we shall have to find the real on the plane of the lifeless; such is the hypothesis we are continually led to reconsider.

Our present task, then, is to make a more intense effort than we have yet made to derive the living from the nonliving.

340. The Organism: Its Peculiarities

Now life appears always in connection with an arrangement of matter which we call an *organism*. An organism is an outlinable assemblage of material which maintains itself as an

---

[1] Cf. BR, No. 97, Lucretius, "Atomic Materialism."

assemblage, while constantly losing and taking in both matter and energy. It is in reality a stream whose stuff is continually being lost and replaced while putting up an appearance of stability which enables us to identify it. The human body appears solid, yet it is chiefly fluid and quite literally a stream of materials. It is this perpetual process, this metabolism, which marks it as "living." But the activity is achieving something, *as if it were purposive:* it is achieving (1) the building up of the organism, its growth; (2) the replenishing of the energy available for action, its nourishment; (3) the repair of the organism; (4) the protection of the organism; (5) its reproduction. The first four of the activities result in self-preservation; the fifth in the preservation of the species. In brief, what the organism shows is an extraordinary self-preservation of the individual and type, through processes which destroy structures and consume energy.

Now there are other processes in nature which are self-preserving up to a certain point. Any stable equilibrium will tend to restore itself when disturbed. A gyroscope will hold to its own plane of rotation. But there is no process outside the organism which builds itself by making outside matter over into *its own kind* of stuff. A squash and a pumpkin, growing side by side in the same garden, will make no mistakes of this kind: the squash will never accidentally build a pumpkin cell into its pulp. And there is no inorganic process which knows, as it were, when to stop: the push-out of a limb, a wing, a tail from the mass of the embryo goes a certain distance and then trims off the member with the proper terminus, hand, or feather. It builds as if to a plan which had its own inner balance to maintain. The limbs of the giant sequoia jut out almost at right angles from the trunk; but having reached a certain length, turn abruptly upward, as if aware that further extension would imperil their hold on the tree. More particularly, there is no inorganic substance which reproduces itself and in so doing reproduces a reproducing self, and so on ad infinitum. In all of these ways, the organism is unique in the physical world, and we are bound to use the phrase "as if," in describing it: it behaves *as if* it were following a plan and a purpose. It behaves *as if* an idea of the whole mature being were guiding the development of the parts.

And every mature organism behaves *as if* the whole were being served by each of the parts, as an end is served by the means.

Our question is whether this behaving-as-if-purposive can be regarded as a product of processes which are not living nor purposive, but purely causal.

341. Could Physical Nature Produce an Organism?

Now the imitation on a simple scale of some of the self-preserving and self-reproducing functions of the organism is among the possibilities of chemical synthesis. There is no chemical element found in organic matter that is not found outside: most organic tissues are built of oxygen, hydrogen, nitrogen, carbon, sulphur, with other elements in smaller proportions. The highly complex molecule of protoplasm has not been put together in the laboratory; but certain products of living organisms can be constructed, such as grape sugar, indigo, oxalic acid, urea. It is necessary to get the right elements in the right number into the right pattern. The practical difficulty of the problem does not prove its impossibility in principle.

The formal pattern of a self-reproducing process is already laid down in mathematics; you have only to divide ten by seven, and after each six decimals you reproduce the original problem. Mathematics, as the basis of all physical law, indicates the shape of physical events. I do not, therefore, see how it can be proved that something like an organic molecule *cannot* be produced from inorganic materials.

It is true that under present terrestrial conditions the rule holds, "Life comes only from life": there is no "spontaneous generation" that we know of. But it was not under such conditions as the earth shows at present that life took its beginning. On the bare question of possibility, we must, I think, give Nature the benefit of the doubt: in some past time, she might have produced an organic molecule.

But there are two questions which we have immediately to put. (1) What are the chances that such a molecule would continue to reproduce itself? (2) Would it be alive?

(1) The mathematical chance that any particular pattern of atoms will be struck out in the swirl of physical change, following specific laws, depends on the complexity of the pattern. To

make a going molecule of protoplasm, the adjustment of its many elements to each other would need to be fairly exact: it could be spoiled or just missed in an infinitude of ways. The antecedent probability of its occurring is equal to zero. But equally minute is the probability of everything that actually happens in a world containing a very large number of particles. The molecule of protoplasm is only a few degrees of infinitude more improbable than many other things which do occur. But the chance that the molecule thus struck out would produce livable variations destined to climb the whole organic ascent is a far more intense potency of zero! In other words, if, in the course of happening, an organic molecule should arrive, there would be nothing in its physical antecedents necessarily favoring its immortality, its posterity, or the upward organic march of that posterity.

(2) Would it be alive? This is not a verbal quibble, though it could be made such by defining "life" as meaning "organism." We mean to ask whether such a pattern of atoms, actually preserving itself, as a vortex puff from a chugging engine, would at the same time have an *inner feeling* of existence and an *inner urge* to preserve itself. My answer is No. A simulation of the behavior of life is not life, any more than the mechanical robot is a man. The characteristic thing about life is an inner center of direction, a spark, however dim, of the drive which in man becomes purpose.

342. Would the Living and the Nonliving Organism Behave Alike?

And without such inner drive or directivity, the imitation would sometime or other *give out*. For since a mechanism has no sense of the goal toward which it works (the locomotive is unaware that it approaches the station) it has no capacity to stop itself when the goal is reached nor to devise new procedures along the way which may better reach its object. The robot planes cannot alter their own line of flight to reach their target; of themselves they have no target. However exact the resemblance between two objects — one whose drive is from behind and one whose drive is from the goal ahead — however completely their behavior agrees for a considerable stretch, the purely causal affair cannot adjust itself to the unforeseen situation. The two careers diverge.

Biology is inclined today to recognize this difference. Darwin provided for the origin of new species by much relatively random variation, and the killing off of variations which were unfit. As variations in a purely mechanical organism would be wholly accidental so far as the purposes of survival are concerned, a large amount of killing-off would be required to secure a single advance. But a living organism has a certain power to vary its own behavior. Instead of moving mechanically onward and suffering elimination, it has some sense, however dim, of the difference between the response which will bring it into danger and the response which will favor its survival. It may make a new idea serve as well as a new species! This process is what Henry Fairfield Osborn has called "organic selection." It becomes more marked as life becomes more consciously self-directive. And in proportion as it occurs, Nature is spared a vast amount of the slaughter of the unfit which purely "chance variation" would require.

I conclude that the world of Nature, taken as purely physical and presumably inanimate, is not adequate to explain the actual phenomena of life and mind. Allowing that physical chances might produce organic molecules, those molecules would be "alive" only by introducing a germ of purpose which the causal system cannot beget. The recent variant of the theory of evolution, calling itself "emergent evolution," acknowledges this difficulty of principle and seeks to overcome it by the word "emergent," on the general theory that with new arrangements of elements new and unforeseen properties "emerge"; why not life and mind? This is to make a virtue not merely of an absence of insight but of an insight into impossibility. To say that something emerges whose relations to the antecedents one does not understand is no better than to say that something "evolves," whether gradually or by jumps. These are all ways of acknowledging that life and mind are not to be explained from physical nature taken as mindless; hence, physical nature is not the Real that we seek.

The more recent philosophers who have taken Nature as their best name for the one-and-real have been inclined to give Nature the character of a living being: life is not derived from the lifeless because Nature has always been in some sense alive. Professor A. N. Whitehead believes that every event in all the duration of the cosmos has its mental as well as its physical pole: *there is no purely inanimate fact*. Does this bring us back to a kind of dualism? I believe so, and for this reason we cannot linger with this enticing theory. It drives us on to examine our second type of monism, the view that the one reality is mental in character.

343. (b) Mind as the Real: Initial Difficulties of the View

Could anything mental in character be the source of all things? To make this hypothesis requires an abrupt reversal of our previous picture of mind as a product of nature: it asks us to consider nature as a product of mind. There is something startling in this proposal. However clearly we see that causality cannot produce purpose, the essential quality of all mind, and however ready we are to leave mentality as an unexplained arrival in the world of nature, we are less ready to promote mind at once to the position of the source-reality.

For one thing, we cannot reverse the astronomical picture. The physical universe remains the frame of life; it is that out of which mind appears to come, and that into which it appears to vanish. There is no scientific support for the supposition that this physical universe itself comes out of a preceding Mind (of a higher order than ours), or that it is eventually to vanish into Mind again: we are not quite sure that we can understand such a process.

Until recently, science has been inclined to take it for granted that the physical universe has no beginning or end. The chain of causes was assumed to run backward in time ad infinitum, reaching no beginning, and forward in time, also ad infinitum. There have been some recent speculations regarding one-way processes which seem to imply a terminus in one direction or the other or both. If our universe is, as some maintain, an "expanding universe," and if the rate of expansion is constant or linear, then at some past moment the universe must have had a minimum extent, therefore, a beginning. Even so, there is no scientific answer to the awkward question, "What preceded it?" and no suggestion that this something might be Mind.

Imagination, to be sure, seems to have less difficulty than sober reflection in giving mind the dominating position of source-reality. This may be because of the familiar traditional idea of Creation, according to which the one eternal being is not matter but the everlasting Mind; and this Mind "in the beginning created" the physical universe and all the subordinate mental beings. This creative Mind is considered as free from limitations of which, in our own finite minds, we are keenly aware. No doubt this idealizing of mind helps the hypothesis; but the question remains, can we understand it? Has it any philosophical support? In brief, can anything mental be considered the source-reality, even in principle?

Mind, as we know it, is insubstantial: it is in direct contrast to the firm reliability of nature. In ourselves it is a dependent and variable thing, a flame which fluctuates with its fuel and with every physical wind. To derive the solid world from anything mental seems like deriving the enduring from the temporary, the substantial from the fragile, the steady from the flickering and inconstant.

Nevertheless, it is just this hypothesis which is before us; and it has so much philosophical support that, until we have fairly considered it and thought it through, we are not initiated into the deepest philosophical conceptions, whether of ancient or of modern times. Many of the great thinkers have come to the conclusion that Mind is the only reality. Whether or not we accept this conclusion, we must undertake to see what it means.

As an aid to this, consider three things:

(1) That if nature has any source outside of itself, it will not be another nature but something quite different from nature;

(2) That the most certain thing in the world is not nature, but mind;

(3) That while the physical world can carry on a series of causes, mind is the only being that is known to create.

344. Aids to Understanding the Real as Mind: (1) The Sources of Nature Must Be Quite Different from Nature

So long as we explain events by causes, we remain within the mesh of nature: we do not explain nature itself. Since nature includes events *and their causes*, an explanation of nature would have to include an explanation of causes. But what is meant by explaining causes? We explain the fall of the apple by "gravity," but how shall we explain gravity? We need a cause for the event; but do we need a cause for the cause? The idea of finding a cause for causation hardly makes sense. To explain nature, then, would be to find something different from *causal* explanation. Power to create would be power of an entirely different order from the powers-to-cause which show themselves in nature. This is simple logic.

And it is clearly recognized in all serious human thinking that the ultimate power will not be one of the blustering and competing powers of the visible arena. Whoever wrestles with the champion wrestler may prove himself the greater; but it is always possible for a greater to challenge *him*. The supreme power cannot be in that position: its mastery is silent and inevitable. This is the paradox of power — that the mightiest acts without effort; it is the child that cannot be overcome! As Lao Tze puts it, *Tao*, the indescribable One, is "non-assertive": it is like water, "the weakest of all the elements, yet it wears away the strongest rocks." Whatever has to strive for mastery shows its weakness by its very effort: "When beauty makes a show of beauty, it is ugliness; when goodness makes a show of goodness, it is badness; *Tao* acts without pretense and without exertion." The Almighty is necessarily inconspicuous.

Indeed, the very necessity we are under of having to search for the real implies that it is not a self-announcing being. The patent fragility of mind will, therefore, not in advance exclude it from that role.

345. (2) We Are Most Certain of the Mind's Existence

Suppose the question were put to you, What is the item of your knowledge of which you are most assured: sun-moon-and-stars, the everlasting hills, or yourself? We are sufficiently sure of all of them. The point of the question is not to elicit a display of skepticism which no one feels: it is to bring about an analysis of the grounds of our knowledge. In this interest, we admit the theoretical possibility that sun-moon-and-stars may have been obliterated a moment ago, while their light continues to travel to the eye. Our knowledge is indirect and possibly belated, i.e., a shade less than complete certainty. The same is true of any sense-impression which I have to *interpret*, as when I call this faint bluish contour far out ahead of me the White Mountains. What I have in hand, so to speak, is not the mountains but the *present experience* of the blue outline, a mental fact. My knowledge of this experience, and thus of my own mind, is direct, inescapable, and certain.

All that we call "the outer world" is a spatial receptacle in which our thought places the various reports of our organs of sense. Our most useful and constant impression of this "outer world" is by way of our eyes: it is a visual image. Images of this kind can be produced in us by other things than the "real object." There are mirages; there are hallucinations; there are moving pictures — systematic optical illusions to which we willingly lend ourselves; there are dreams. And what is a dream if not a world-picture which we are subconsciously producing for ourselves and momentarily accept as the "real object"? How much subjective activity, then, may be involved in what we call our waking vision? Certainly very much. For, if the physiological account of visual sensation is correct, the colors are not *there* in the "real object." What is *there* is a set of light waves and quanta; the colors are contributed to the scene by the seer. The "real object," as physics describes it, is not the object we see clothed by our minds with sensory qualities.

We do not *believe* this experience of ours to be substantially deceptive. That is not the question now before us. The question is whether we can *conceive* this whole panorama of nature as just that — a panorama, a consistent and well-sustained dream from which we might imagine ourselves to wake up (and from which it has sometimes been supposed death does wake us up). In other words, what rigorous certainty have we, when we examine the case with the most careful analysis, that our visual image is not just exactly that and no more — a visual image?

346. The Analysis of Descartes

The above is substantially the course of reflection which the French thinker Descartes (1596–1650) followed out in one of the most famous passages of modern philosophy.[1] He was trying

[1] See BR, No. 92, René Descartes, "From Doubt to Certainty."

to see how much of what we are all habitually taking for granted it was possible for him to doubt. The existence of a physical world independent of his thought was one of these things: the vision might be conceived to be conjured up in him by a malicious spirit. He tried this same process of doubt on himself: perhaps I, too, he thought, am an illusion. But then, in order to entertain this fancy, I must be alive and doubting; he who doubts, is thinking; and he who thinks, exists. *"Cogito, ergo sum."* (I think, therefore, I am.) Here, Descartes concluded, I find that which it is impossible to doubt, the center of all other certitude, my own existence. From this certainty, I can reinstate most of my habitual beliefs, including the belief in an external world. But this outer world remains an object of belief rather than of certainty; the mind first knows itself.

This simple course of reflection so impressed the Europe of Descartes' day that it became the characteristic way of looking at things for the modern period. To the direct, natural, outward glance of the mind, the story is, "The world is there." The more complete story is, "*I see* the world as there; *I think* the world as there." And by this completion of the story, we are hanging our experience from a new peg, the peg of the mind, *without changing its contents*. We are simply recognizing the completer truth, "The world is something which I see-and-think." Or, as Schopenhauer later put it, rather radically, "The world is my idea."

At this point in the study of philosophy we must move forward with the utmost care. We are engaged in a work of analysis, not of skepticism. We are not questioning that the biological environment is the biological environment, and that if we are held under water, we shall drown. We are asking what we mean by these things, and what is the source of our firm belief in them. Drowning is an "experience." Eating food is an "experience"; feeling better on account of it is another "experience." What we directly know about it is the "I see," "I handle," "I taste," "I swallow," "I feel satisfied." How these experiences are connected, I try to learn by the type of thinking we call science. Science unravels for me the processes of nutrition, throws a theoretical bridge between the experiences of eating and being satisfied. But this theory is, after all, a matter of *thought:* and thought is certainly mental! To understand what my scientific authorities tell me, must I not reconstruct it in my own thought?

Thus we analyze our whole experience of the "outer world" into sensation and thought, both forms of mental activity. Is there anything else in it except this mental tissue?

347. (3) Mind Is the Only Being That Is Known to Create

In becoming acquainted with our own minds as centers of certainty, we are also becoming acquainted with them as centers of creative action. The physiology of sensation gives the mind credit for producing what physical causation cannot produce — the whole array of sense-qualities. The activities of thinking, dreaming, imagining, are capable of adding other elements of the physical picture, including what we think of as the rigid frame of the "outer world." No other agency in nature has this creative capacity, one which wins it complete freedom in the world of fine art, in which out of its own resources the mind projects other worlds than this.

With these things in view, the hypothesis that the physical world could be in some way derived from mind, our own or some higher mind, loses much of its original paradox.

We are now prepared to follow the reflection of a modern thinker who was disposed to indicate how this is actually the case, — the Irish philosopher, George Berkeley (1685–1753).

348. Berkeley's Analysis

Berkeley had the courage of his convictions: he saw things as "my experience" with an uncannily clear and forthright steadiness. He was ready to call all three of the above elements — sensations, thoughts, feelings of action — by one name which signalized their belonging to the mind: they were all "ideas." And because of this, he was able to take a step which Descartes had balked at. Descartes, having found the outer world in his sphere of "thought," wanted to restore his belief in its being *also out there in its own right*. For was it not *in space?* And is not space external to the mind?

Incomplete analysis! said Berkeley. Nothing is really more mental than space. Any photograph (or a pair of stereoscopic photographs) will put down faithfully everything you can see at one time in a two-dimensional surface. Yet you see things *in depth;* you contribute the third dimension from your own mental resources. Color is admitted to be mental: then follow the logic — color cannot be mental and the space in which it is spread out nonmental! The thing is absurd.

Hence, Berkeley boldly went ahead: The world-there-in-space is just what it appears to be; and "there-in-space" means "there-in-my-mind." To argue, as Descartes did, that there must be another and "real" external world is to try to duplicate the facts. There is only one "Nature," the one I perceive. And the guarantee that it is "real" is simply that the "ideas" I have of it follow one another with perfect reliability and consistency, according to the laws of nature. They do so because they are produced in my mind not by an additional physical fact (which would be to say that an idea causes an idea, or else that an unknown "substance" causes it, which involves us in all the puzzles of dualism and interaction) but by the one really active type of being we know, spirit. My experienced world is a system of ideas induced in me by the activity of God. Such is Berkeley's world-view.[1]

349. Merits of Berkeley's View

It is less important that you be convinced by Berkeley than that you be able to see things as he saw them. To do so is an achievement which unlocks many doors in all subsequent thought. The view itself in Berkeley's day was called "immaterialism," because Berkeley was unifying his world by dismissing material substance as an unthinkable superfluity — material substance, which for most people was the very basis of all certainty. Not being able to find a flaw in Berkeley's analysis, his sturdy critics called it an "irrefutable absurdity," and Dr. Johnson, bringing his foot down

[1] See BR, No. 99, George Berkeley, "The Universe as Fundamentally Spiritual." Berkeley's view of the world has much in common with that of the Vedanta (see sec. 330 above). Both views would assert that there is nothing real which is not spiritual or mental in nature; both would say that the apparent independence of the physical world is illusory — that world is an "appearance" to our consciousness, it has no substantial being of its own. The Vedanta philosophy, however, gives no very good reason for the existence of the illusion; it is the business of life to escape its seduction and, winning the realization that "I am identical with Brahman," lose one's personal being in the One. For Berkeley, the whole panorama of nature, being produced in us by the activity of God, has a purpose; and because of this, nature has far greater importance and dignity than it could have either for Vedanta or for any system which made it a simple, final, unexplained, and unmeaning fact.

on a boulder, said, "I refute him thus!" This kind of argument played directly into Berkeley's logic; for all the good Doctor could prove by his deed was that the "idea" of kicking a rock was a reliable way of getting an "idea" of resistance and, very likely, another "idea" of pain.

Indeed, one of the great advances which Berkeley's view makes over that of the physical world-view above considered (we may call it "physicalism") is that our experiences of quality, such as pain and pleasure, color and sound, taste and smell, remain in their places as *properties of the natural objects*, just as they seem to be. For physicalism, the real is the ultimate unit, electron, proton, or what not, with all its measurable aspects; but the sense-qualities are solely subjective. This splits nature into two phases — the quantities in the outer fact and the qualities in the mind; it is this "bifurcation of nature" against which Whitehead's thought today rebels. But this bifurcation is mended completely in the mental world-view; our ideas possess all the facts, all the quantities, all the "primary qualities" of position, size, number, motion, etc.; but they possess also the properties which arouse our feelings and make nature a region of enjoyment, danger, wonder, and hope.

On this score we should say, I think, that Berkeley's view of the real *contains more truth than the physicalist view*. It is more "concrete" as packing into itself a more complete report of what nature contains. The intensities of feeling and of the inner tension of living are real ingredients of the world; the subjective depth of modern spirit, as mirrored in the mental view of reality, can alone do justice to them. Reality must be centered there where the concerns, anxieties, strains, and passions of conscious life come to their birth, not in a region of dispassionate fact from which they are excluded.

350. Difficulties of Berkeley's View

If we ask whether a view like that of Berkeley does successfully account for physical nature as something derived from mind, the answer has to be that if you grant God the power of producing in us the panorama of experience we call physical nature, this view accounts for all we perceive and think of nature. It does not account for "physical substance," such as might be thought to exist prior to the advent of mind in the universe; for such a substance is simply rejected by Berkeley as a nonbeing which no one ever thought, though many think they think it. If Berkeley is asked about the world before life came into it, his answer would be that there never was a world before God came into it; the world has no existence at all except as a thought of God and other conscious beings. On Berkeley's premises, his world-picture certainly does not lack the whole physical scene: all of space is there and all its contents, just as we perceive them. But if you mean by nature something unperceived and unknown by any mind, Berkeley not only does not account for it, he defies you to say what you mean by it.

The theoretical difficulty with Berkeley's view is that the hypothesis of a God able to excite in our minds this vivid and dependable image is an hypothesis which goes beyond experience. We have no example of that kind of process. It means something like direct telepathy: God thinks the world, and his thinking results in our thinking. When *we* want to induce ideas in others, we have to do it by way of language, i.e., by sound or sight. And when we want to propose fancies of an imaginary world, we have not alone to make physical pictures, but we have to rely on a previous experience of the physical to set our imaginations working. Berkeley's God would have to be an original creative imagination working without previous materials. This is not to say that Berkeley's hypothesis is illegitimate; it is only to point out that he has made it to meet his difficulties, and that he has done so rather on faith than on hints given in experience.

If we were to question Berkeley how he knows about God, he would on his own theory have to say that God is a thought or notion in his mind, and he would have to give some reason for projecting the being of God beyond his mind. In the same way, if we ask him how he knows of the existence of any other person than himself, he would have to begin with his own notions. And if you insist that he deal with these notions of other persons as he deals with his notions of physical things, calling them his ideas, you begin to confine Berkeley into a rather solitary world, a world of himself alone, the position known as "solipsism" or "subjectivism."

What we miss from the world-picture drawn by the subjectivist is not "physical substance" — an undiscovered thing for which the physicist today has no more use than had Berkeley; it is the *"objectivity" of the world*. We mean by this that each mind, viewing its own image of the world, regards that image as there for other minds as well as for his own mind. Space may be one of my ideas, but, if so, it is an idea which each one has in common with all other minds in the world-community; and the puzzle is how can many minds have the same idea at once?

Subjectivism would give each mind a complete world-panorama to itself. This is not impossible. It was proposed in all literalness by the philosopher and mathematician Leibniz (1646–1716), co-inventor with Newton of the infinitesimal calculus. There is no more theoretical difficulty in supposing the visual panoramas of the world to be multiplied in this way than in supposing the same film-story to be run off simultaneously in a thousand different theaters. Indeed, if physical nature is the real, this is precisely what happens; for each brain would have to translate the impulses reaching it from the sensory nerves into its own private world-picture; there would be as many such pictures as there are living brains.

But this simply means that both physicalism and subjectivism run afoul of one deep-seated conviction we all have: that there is *but one space* for all of us, and *one physical world*, not many. Of all our physical objects, and of space itself, we believe we can say not alone "I see," "I think," but also "*we* see" and "*we* think": the world is "my idea," but it is also "ours." Subjectivism does not allow us to believe this to be true or even possible. Nor does physicalism allow it. Nor can any view which supposes thought to be a product of the physical brain.

351. (c) The Real as a Third Being, Neither Mind nor Body

Of the two hypotheses now reviewed, we may say that the first, Nature as the Real, fails in its responsibility of explaining the world of mind. The second, Mind as the Real, shows in principle how mind could give rise to an experience of physical nature. It has left us, however, incompletely satisfied that such an experience would have the objectivity and singleness which we find in the hard integrity of natural fact, in which the truth as brought to light by the sharpest focus of the individual scientist's thought becomes at once the universal truth for all inhabitants of the world.

Is it possible to combine in any one view the advantages both of the physicalist and of the mentalist world-views without running back into dualism?

Would it be possible to do this by resorting to a Neutral Being as a principle of explanation, and deriving both mind and body from that Neutral? Various such proposals have been made, most of which amount to incorporating one's sense of the mystery of the universe in a single symbol — the One, the Absolute, the Dialectic Process, Energy, the Unknowable. This is somewhat as if the mathematician should offer the letter x, not as the symbol of the unknown quantity to be found, but as the answer itself. Neutrality itself has no properties on which derivation can take hold; it is completely inferential and negative. It has one virtue: it registers the continued belief that there is one real being, and that this being will be different in character from either the physical object or the private human self.

It must be different, not by omission but by inclusion. We cannot derive mentality from anything less than mentality, nor objective fact from anything less than objective fact. The One we seek must combine the quality of consciousness and selfhood with the quality of being beyond-self or other-than-self which science and common judgment alike attribute to the world of nature. Our analysis has brought us very near to the discovery of such a being.

Let us go back for a moment to Descartes' discovery of the "I think" as the center of all certainty. He meant this "I think" to cover all mental activity, including sensing, feeling, remembering, deciding, imagining. He meant, as Berkeley did, to consider this activity as real, in the sense of its being productive of some part of the experience of nature. But both Descartes and Berkeley regarded this creative activity of our private minds as *instigated by some outside stimulus*. When we see the moon, we are indeed actively creating a visual image of the moon; but we do not invent the moon — this activity is excited from beyond ourselves. What is this outer stimulation? Descartes would say it is motion, motion of light communicated to the nerves, disturbing the finely balanced pituitary body in the midst of the brain, whose stirring is directly transferred to the mind as sensation. Berkeley would say it is God's direct suggestion of ideas to the mind. Descartes' proposal was a complete failure; physical motion cannot cause sensation. Berkeley's suggestion was a pious wish, not thought through. On his own theory, he might have found it hard to explain why he should regard God as anything more than one of his ideas, a private notion of his own mind and therefore wholly incapable of acting on him from outside.

But the failure of Descartes gives us a clue to remedy the failure of Berkeley. Sensation is a phase of experience in which we are certainly active and also certainly being acted upon. From the biological point of view, we are at once being "stimulated" and "responding" to stimulation. Descartes' failure consisted in taking the biological picture as the final analysis and therefore assuming that a physical motion could act upon a mind, which is impossible. But what is the alternative? If motion produces motion and nothing else, if physical change produces physical change and nothing else, then mental change must be referred to mind: nothing can act on a mind but a mind. Then, so far as sensation is a receiving-of-outer-action, it is a *direct experience of the action of another mind*. Insofar as, when I have a sensation, I know that it is something I do not wholly produce, something toward which I am passive or receptive, I am directly aware of another mind. As I cannot experience concave without experiencing convex, so I cannot experience passivity without, in the same moment, experiencing the activity of another; the two experiences are inseparable.

Berkeley was quite right, then, in regarding sensation as a *communicated experience*, not an experience caused by a mechanical agent. But he was wrong in regarding God as an object of theory or faith, an idea brought in to account for the sensation. *God is himself experienced*, the one experience which is *not* mere idea, not possibly subjective, the inescapable factor of outer action present in all sensation.

Descartes likewise was partly right and partly wrong. He was right in holding that each of us can be sure of his own experience: when we think, we act; and when we act, we exist. But he was wrong in supposing that this certitude is limited to our

own existence. For when we think, we are *both active and passive*.
The "I think" of Descartes includes the "I hear," "I feel," "I see"
of sensation; and in this form of "thinking," I am just as much
aware of being receptive toward outer activity as I am of my
own activity. I am just as sure of dependence-on-another as
I am of existence-by-myself. I can quite as well argue,

I think; I am acted upon; *Some other being exists;*
as
I think; I act; *I exist.*

The two arguments are inseparable. Hence it is an error to
suppose that I am first conscious of my own existence, and from
this primary certitude argue for the existence of God and of
nature. I am sure of myself and of God in the same breath —
and of nature as a region of shared experience, between us —
and therefore I require no speculative proofs or reasonings for
any one of these three beings.[1]

It is for this reason that sensation (and the physical frame of
space and time in which we place sensation) never strikes even
the infant as a private or subjective experience: it is referred
instinctively *beyond one's self.* It is "objectified." Its "objectivity"
consists in the fact that this physical scene is *not my world alone*,
but a world shared with at least one other mind, that of the giver;
and hence in principle shareable with all other minds to whom
this creative Mind may address itself. Nature cannot be a solitary panorama for any mind because the relation also-for-others
is built into its constitution: to be "alone with Nature" often
brings the sharpest awareness that one cannot be radically and
completely alone anywhere. And for the same reason, Nature
is one and not many: it is the same for all the recipients of that
system of sensations.

Seeing things in this way, we are free from both physicalism
and from subjectivism; we are also free from neutralism. The

[1] To regard nature as having a separate existence, in addition to the common
awareness-of-nature in the mind of God and the minds of men, would be to give
it a duplicate reality, one in our minds and one outside of all minds. Descartes
attempted to maintain this double life for nature, but without success. Our common perception of nature *is* the existence of nature. In communicating to me the
stuff of sensation, God sustains from moment to moment my conscious life and
thus nature itself; he creates the world anew at each moment. We revise Descartes'
formula thus: I think, therefore, God and I exist, and nature between us.

source-reality is neither physical nature nor the finite mind; but still it is mind — the eternal Mind. From it come the finite minds; and nature is for them, not for itself. In this way our world-view achieves its unity.

F. THE PLACE OF VALUES IN THE WORLD

352. The Purposive Order Includes the Causal Order

If the world is derived from one primary source and that source is not material but mental, one of our earlier questions is settled. We were asking how the purposive order is connected with the causal order. The answer is that, since mind is purposive, everything that is derived from it must have a purpose, including nature itself and the causal order of nature. The most fundamental explanation of anything will be the purpose it serves.

This seems on the face of it to undo the great accomplishment of the young science of the seventeenth century, which succeeded with great pains in expelling "final causes" from all explanations of natural phenomena. But this is not the case. There is no question of bringing back the piecemeal purposiveness which would explain the existence of bees by the pleasure their honey gives to man, forgetting the displeasure which is given by other features of the bee. The question is *whether causality itself has a purpose*.

A world which is a causal system is one which goes its own way regardless of our wishes. When we indulge in fairy tales, which presumably bring us nearer the ideal state of things, we introduce the element of magic, which has the function of unbinding the chains of causality, and effecting the changes we desire without the slow process of working through nature's laws. Aladdin with his lamp can have a banquet at the cost of a wish, and a free ride to any desired destination. Nevertheless, if the purpose of the world is not the satisfaction of human wishes as they arise, but the development of an intelligent animal — preferring to meet fair conditions for what he gets rather than to have satisfaction for nothing, finding a secondary satisfaction ın guessing the riddles which a secretive nature sets for his rewards — there is something to be said for a causal order.

Causality implies delay in getting one's goods; it implies a strict, uniform, reliable, and even-handed conditionality of every success; it implies that *means* have to be inserted between the desire and the end; it implies work and all that work has developed of the "economic virtues." [1] If we were making a world, and if the main object were not the maximum of pleasure but the development of the capacities of the man, we would want something of the nature of a causal system.

There was an instructive moment in the history of modern science when Galileo was experimenting with falling bodies and trying to determine how their velocity changed during the fall. Having no such timepiece as ours, he felt obliged to study a retarded fall. He rolled balls down an inclined plane instead of letting them drop straight. But the question came to him. What effect does the slope of the plane have on the speed of the ball at the bottom? Will the ball acquire a greater velocity on the steep slope or on the gradual slope? Of course, on the gradual slope it will start more slowly; but then it will have more time to get up speed. Galileo came to the interesting conclusion that the final speed would be independent of the angle of the slope.

His reason for this is the point that concerns us here. If there were any difference, we could choose two slopes so that the ball would run down the one giving the greatest terminal speed and then run up the one giving the slowest terminal speed, in which case it would rise higher than the level at which it started. This, Galileo felt, would not do. But why not? Galileo never developed his objection into a principle; if he had done so, he would have announced something like the conservation of energy. But with him it appears to have been something more like a *moral prejudice* read into the workings of nature; it ought not to be possible for us to get something for nothing! I know of no event in the growth of that modern scientific method, bent on getting rid of intrusive purposes in nature, which shows so clearly that the builders of that science felt a definite value in the unbribable mathematical integrity of the unpurposing system of causes: there was a purpose in getting rid of purpose.

[1] See Part I of this book, sections 50, 51, 137.

This means that a purposive order would include (and require) a causal order, as a causal order would not include a purposive order. It is a more concrete principle of explanation.

353. The Meaning of the Physical World and of the Human Body

This, of course, is very far from explaining the particular causal order we have: it simply shows one of the values involved in having any causal system at all. It is still farther from deriving the physical features of the world; and some have maintained that a philosophy in which mind is the real is bound to do that. I agree that this should be the goal at which explanation of the world must aim; but I do not believe we have reason to ask more than a very general insight at this stage of our knowledge.

We ought to be able to say, in some substantial fashion, why there should be a physical world at all, and why the mind has a body. We should also be able to indicate that the mind is a genuinely creative affair, as matter is not; so that the hypothesis of a creative mind is not pure mythology. This we can do.[1] But to show in detail how electrons, spiral nebulae, protozoa, and ourselves are produced is something we cannot do, nor can any known hypothesis. The major principle to which we have been driven, that the world is a work of living purpose, not living purpose a late product of inanimate necessity, simply justifies us in looking for *signs of meaning* in the arrangement of nature, on the general principle that in such a world *nothing is meaningless*, whether or not we can yet see how that is the case. And from this it follows that whatever comes out of the causal machinery is implanted by intention in the original set-up of things and does not arrive by chance.[2]

For example, what can we say to Plato when he suggests that the mind would be better off without a body? We are not allowed by our belief in unity to accept the charge, referring the misfortune to an independent principle of "matter" which entangles and confuses the soul. We should have to consider whether in some way a body is not an advantage, or a necessity, to the mind. That this must be the case is strongly hinted by the fact that those traditions which propose a disembodied spirit

---

[1] W. E. Hocking, *Types of Philosophy*, 2nd Ed., Chap. XXV and paragraphs 165, 166.

[2] Cf. BR, No. 101, Henri Bergson, "Creation, the Goal of Life."

as roving about in a dream or going to another world usually reject their own premises by providing the soul with an evanescent body, a ghostly but still physical shape, strongly resembling the outfit of limbs and organs possessed by the earthly self. For spirits must be able to be "apparitions," and to appear they must have a position in space, form and motion, and at least a limited capacity to speak. The Christian tradition speaks of a "resurrection of the body," implying that without its body the soul is incomplete. And if we may consult our own dreams for hints as to the way we think of ourselves when our bodily self-awareness is more or less out of circuit, we seem to be provided with facilities for observation, as if by eye and ear, and for locomotion in a physical setting. A mind without (a) the capacity to observe and have sensation, (b) the capacity to appear to others, and (c) the capacity to decide and act, would not be much like the human self. And each of these functions seems to require a body.

Put the matter on the simple ground of communication. What language means to the mind, we have considered in Part I, sections 7–10. But language between human beings requires physical signals plus a physical symbol for the speaker and another for the addressee. It is hard to talk to vacancy devoid of physical response. If the mind were devoid of body, it would desire one to make itself visible; it would equally desire the other person to have one. Hence, though we complain of the indirectness of verbal communication and the mutilations of our thought which occur in its passage through words, and fancy that a direct telepathy from mind to mind would be better, the real test would come if we were in doubt, in a telepathic communication, about who is speaking to us and just what is meant. In such a case, we would like to check up by a face-to-face verification or having it "in black and white."

We are carefully avoiding saying that there is first a mind, and then, since it would be a convenience in communication, a body is kindly provided by nature, as the agency through which God acts. The self requires the body *to be itself:* the visible body is the mind *made visible to others.* The visible musculature of the body is the mind's capacity of going across from deliberating to acting, made visible to others. Hence, in decision, the mind does not "act upon the body," as though the body were something else; the action of the bodily muscles *is* the mind's act of will, the same identical thing — only not as it feels to the mind acting, but as it looks to the outside observer. To put the matter in a nutshell: it is true, as we said a while ago, that we cannot set up a dualism between them, so that we land in the dilemma of interaction versus parallelism. The answer is that the body is a visible and tangible *symbol of the mind*. It is the report, so to speak, which the mind gives to other minds of its presence and interplay with them, in this present context of the physical world, which is common to all of them.

On the same ground, the physical world may be regarded as the symbol of the presence of God to all these minds at once. Like languages, this physical medium seems to put us off from God's direct presence; but again, like language, we should revert to it to check up and make definite the more intangible intuitions of the inner self.

354. The Source or Ground of Values in the World

We have need, therefore, for the body and for nature. We have need, as Fichte pointed out, for the *resistance* which nature offers to our impulses; for this resistance is a condition for the development of character. As he put it, "The world of nature is the material of our duty, made present to sense." But this idea of duty reminds us that there is much in the mind which the body and nature cannot express. The being who sustains us through sensation must indeed be the Other Mind; but what right have we to call it God? None whatever, unless we read into that relationship an element of *care*, i.e., that our existence is a part of the total purpose of things. If that is the case, it ceases to be a mere fact and begins to be attended with *obligations*. To an unconscious universe, we owe no debt and have no obligation; we have nothing to carry out with which that universe is in the slightest degree concerned. There is no total obligation on human life, unless the real and one is purposive; and, conversely, if there is such a purpose, an obligation is at once created. The general form of that obligation is that each one has a reason for his existence, that it is his business to find it out and to make good with it.

This is one of the great points in the world-view of Confucius, extremely reticent as he was on all matters outside of human nature and society. He believed that T'ien (heaven) had a mission for every man; that was about the sum and substance of his religious philosophy.[1] There is a story that on one occasion he was attacked by a mob and extricated with difficulty by his friends, who remonstrated with him for exposing himself to the anger of the crowd. His reply was the proud one: "T'ien has appointed me to teach this doctrine; and until I have done so, what can the inhabitants of Kwang do to me?"

Two corollaries of this position may be drawn.

First, no one's purpose has any bearing on any other one's purpose unless they have the same ultimate standards of value. This we have seen holding good of human societies. It also holds good as between man and the One. There is no obligation to a God for whom human truth is not truth, human goodness not goodness, human beauty not beauty. There must be a vast difference between what clarity we can achieve about goodness or beauty and the absolute truth about them. But if we are clear off the target, so to speak, then we might just as well stop trying for these objectives, lest we keep getting deeper into a false path. Plato had the right view of this matter; the Ideas are goals of which we already have an inkling, and the business of philosophy is to bring those latent perceptions to birth, which is recalling us to our true nature. But we can add this to Plato's view — that these same Ideas do not live by themselves in an abstract eternity; their place of being is in the purpose of the eternal Mind. And our share in those Ideas is the condition of our obligation to the world we live in.

355. May the Mind Survive a Particular Body?

Second, since the body and physical nature are dependencies of the mind and not vice versa, the break-up of the physical body need not destroy the mind.

Our argument shows that the mind requires a body. It does not show that it requires this particular body. This particular body is a symbol, if we are right, of our connection with this community of minds, engaged in working out their destinies in this particular space-time region. As long as we are with them,

[1] See BR, No. 76 B, Confucianism: "The Foundations of the Moral Law."

we require this body; and as long as we are using this body, we are with them. And for physical science, there is no other space-time universe than this one. But as to whether there are other space-time realms, science has no opinion and can have none. A century ago, it might have held that the conception of another space-time world is meaningless. Today, with the advent of newer conceptions in geometry, the notion of a plurality of spaces has become familiar to mathematicians, though it has not yet made its impression on physics or philosophy. Suffice it to say that science cannot rule out the possibility of other groups of minds in the total scheme of things, related to one another by way of other physical systems. Death is the severance of the mind's connection with this given space-time system and with its community of minds. But this need not obliterate its capacity to enter relationship with other such groups, and in that connection to express itself by way of another body.

The chief sign that this is a possibility lies in the fact that the human will is "free," in the sense that its decisions are not dictated by those laws of physical causation which are seen in the physics and chemistry of the body. The operations of the will do not violate these laws but go beyond them. For a causal sequence, as it moves into the future, there are no alternatives; there is but one necessary course. But as the mind meditates future courses of action, it devises alternatives; these are genuine possibilities, wholly additional to the one-track line of a purely physical order. In carrying out any such alternative, we assert that we control nature at this point; nature does not there control us. Human nature is there, no doubt; every impulse of heredity, every subconscious drive, every impression made by environment and training has its voice in the court of our judgment; but we know that they are *there to be mastered*, to become parts of a pattern of behavior which is our own. That is what it means to be free.

And if we can thus, as a part of everyday living, show ourselves masters or controllers of the stream of natural causes running through us, controlling them as from a position outside of nature, we are, by that same sign, outside the context of death. Death is an occurrence within physical nature; it reaches and breaks through all the connections which require this physical body; it cannot reach what is free.

G. THE RISKS OF EXISTENCE

356. Objections to Monism

We have followed the clue of the argument to the conclusion
that the real is one, and that this one is not material but mental
and purposive. In pressing beyond the "Ever not quite" of the
premature monisms into the apparent contrasts and dualities
of the world, and beyond these again into a final attempt to
unify our dualities, we knew that we were undertaking a task
both of difficulty and of peril. We have given reasons for our
belief that in *mind*, carried to its highest power, we have a principle from which the causal order and the physical world can
be understood.

The great obstacle to any such conclusion is not the inner
regularity of nature. The causal laws, requiring such high intelligence to decipher, suggest the work of a higher intelligence to
establish them. Each newly established scientific law corrobo-
rates the reality of such a cosmic Mind. Sir James Jeans has
recently proposed that the entire physical world could be regarded as a mighty thought-process in operation. And Kepler
considered that he was "thinking the thoughts of God after him."
The great obstacle is not the order in terms of law but the disorder in terms of fact: neither has the physical world as a whole
any sign of symmetry, nor does the social world show any sign
of a colony planted by divine purpose. One of the classical
arguments for the existence of God, the so-called argument from
design,[1] has been objected to because, in its attention to the
evidences for a friendly will, it overlooks the contrary evidences
of cruelty in nature, the deadly struggle and untold suffering
which must be involved in the blind efforts of animals to find
and keep an uncertain foothold among forces of which they
cannot hope to have any understanding

Based solely on the facts of quality, as we find them, there are
possible two quite opposite judgments: "The world is so good
that we must attribute it, not to chance, but to a divine maker";
"The world is so bad that we must either attribute it to uncon-

[1] See BR, No. 86, Georgia Harkness, "Evidence for Belief in God," section d.

scious forces, or else find some way to let God off from complete responsibility." This second judgment, as we have seen,[1] has led many in our time to favor the conception of a God who is finite, in the sense that there is an evil-working power or an unfeeling obstacle over against him; and that he could well use our aid in overcoming it. Zoroaster emphasized Ahura Mazda's need of man's help in winning the battle against evil.

There is, in our time, a widespread revolt from monism of any kind, resulting very largely from the increasingly serious attention which our time is giving to the facts of quality in the world. Nineteenth-century philosophy was so occupied with the impressive victories of the scientific conception of things that its philosophical activities were absorbed in the factual side of the universe. Our own century has rediscovered the deeper reality of feeling and will. And bringing its factually experienced eye to bear on the total emotional experience of men and beasts, its verdict is disharmony, irrationality, the work of the subconscious drives and of the conscious passions. There have been speculations whether the existing balances, even in the physical world, are not partial and temporary, a result of the mutual destruction of wilder cosmic ingredients, so that this phase of the universe is a relatively restful lull between periods of upheaval and nonsystem. Charles Peirce, an unconventional American mathematician and philosopher, believed that such order as the physical world now shows is not inherent, but a drastic self-reduction from primitive incoherence.

Now, strangely enough, this recognition of disharmony, which has been taken as a cosmic defect by some, has been demanded as a cosmic luxury by others.

For some of the revolters are denouncing the unity of the real because they feel it threatens human freedom and the reality of adventure. If there were one purpose in the universe, we should be too safe; there would be no real risk, no real novelty. There would be no real scope for the individual. They demand an "open universe," with unlimited possibility for human powers. We should have to summarize the indictment of monism under two heads:

[1] See Section 332 above, "The Great Dualisms: Good and Evil."

(1) Complaints: Evil is real; frayed ends and pluralism are real.
(2) Demands: Freedom must be real;
     Risk and adventure must be real;
     Novelty must be real;
     The individual must be real.

William James is on both sides; the universe is too bad to be a monism, and he wants it freer! [1] Anything to do away with the stifling oppression of unity! And Henri Bergson lends support to a part of this program by a third proposal, which has wide acceptance:

(3) Time and change are real — more real than stability; and intuition is deeper than intellect.

Let us give attention to the demands and the complaints separately.

357. The Demands for Risk, Adventure, and Freedom

In my judgment, the demands are all valid, and none of them is incompatible with the sort of monism we have found.

They would be incompatible with a monism of physical or causal order. For a strict causality, running through the human organism and determining behavior, shuts out (as we have just seen in sections 327–28 above) any concrete freedom. This is the point of William James' original revolt against the science-dictated philosophy of his student days; he stood out for indeterminism (or free will) when determinism had the value of an axiom. Further a strictly causal scheme of things excludes the arrival of any novelty in the course of nature: all the future is contained in the present. A law of nature is a law of recurrence: "When A occurs, B follows." A comprehensive law would describe in advance all the possible happenings; and if we could carry out the deductions, all the future would be known. A universe which can only repeat the same forever is indeed a horrible mill to be caught in.

Bergson's philosophy, like James', was groping its way out of mechanism toward freedom and novelty. Bergson pointed out that mental life could not be brought into a causal system;

---

[1] That is, he wants to be rid of the control implied by monism in order to have the full draught of the sense of individual power and risk-taking. See BR, No. 100, William James, "Pragmatism."

because cause and effect must be cleanly separate, whereas
mental states are never cleanly separate — they "interpene-
trate," as the first word of a sentence must be kept with all the
others in order that the sentence make sense. He also showed
that mental life could not be devoid of novelty. For if you set
up the most monotonous repetition you can think of, say the
strokes of a bell, the second stroke as heard cannot be identical
with the first, simply because it will have had one before it and
will be counted as number two. In brief, the cumulative character of life, endowed with memory, gives it a perpetual movement into novelty.

Now these are important insights, but they do not go to the
root of the matter. The kind of freedom we want is not simply
the complex forward movement of mental states which cannot
help interpenetrating. We want the freedom of being able to
change the course which nature would otherwise follow or to
give shape to a course which nature leaves shapeless. We want
the freedom to *create a part of the future*.[1] And this is the situation
when we deliberate between several courses of action. The
more concerned we are about the decision, the more vividly we
present to ourselves the alternatives X, Y, Z. We do not dwell
upon over-foolish and impossible alternatives; we consider only
courses any one of which, if we take it, we shall be able to defend
as "reasonable"; and any one of which will fit into the present
physical situation. X may take me to Kamchatka, Y to Pat-
agonia, and Z to Timbuctoo; and my body will go one of
those three ways. Now the physical world does not present to
any of its particles any such alternative, for it is confined within
a causal system. My freedom consists in the fact that I can
require the physical world to take any one of those three body-
movements as the follow-up of its own present state of things.
I do that because of my ideas, not because of arbitrary choice:
my picture of the possible future is *my creation* while in the process
of deliberating. Wilfred Grenfell requires his body to take him
to Labrador because he has built an idea of himself as surgeon
to a stranded community there. The future that exists will
exist solely because of the concrete picture which my imagination
has devised, and which, apart from that imagination, would

[1] BR, No. 105, William Yerington, "The Open Future."

not have been possible. Freedom *is the creation and execution of novelty.* And there is no need of killing off the world's unity to make room for it: freedom adds to what already exists, but without breaking its structure.

Risk and adventure, too, must be real. But how much risk do you want? Something short of complete risk, I suspect. Even in a cause-tight universe, human beings would face risks because of their ignorance of what is going to happen, and especially because of the unexpectedness of human behavior. They do not need to consider the universe loosened up in order to have plenty of uncertainty. (The business communities of America seem to assume, via the institution of insurance, that individual business risks are more than they want.) Complete risk is an indefinable situation in which "anything may happen"; and this, it may be safely said, is not the degree of risk that is demanded.

Significant risk is risk of a minor good for the sake of a major good. Prospecting for gold is a highly uncertain occupation at best; what saves it from pure folly is the certainty of the value of gold. If gold might easily become worthless tomorrow, few men would risk their lives for it. All significant risk is thus based on some certainty; and is therefore limited. But if risk is limited at all, it is because the frame of things is under control. Hence all significant risk, and adventure with it, not only is consistent with, but requires, a unitary reality. Indeed, the lure of adventure would vanish if nature did not preserve for the hardy sportsman the possibility of eventual success.

The great risk-takers of history have been the men who had great inner certainty. The distinction between a noble risk-taking and a great gamble lies in the justification of the certainty. Napoleon and Hitler incorporate the notion of a great gamble; and an interesting trait these men have in common is a belief, not in a pluralistic universe, but in a secret "destiny," which implies a controlled universe. Among the noble risk-takers are some that have lost, like Wallenstein or Julius Caesar, and some that have won, like Columbus or Pasteur. But the ones and the others had a good adventure through their risk because they were living in a universe which, not spoiling their risk by guaranteeing its outcome, did guarantee the validity of the sort of thing they were working for. Without this consciousness of secure worth in one's aim, the call for more and bigger risks is simply a version in English of Nietzsche's maxim, "Live dangerously," which can always be achieved simply by going out for trouble on a grand scale without regard for the nature of your objective. Whoever in the world at any time is public enemy number one is meeting all the requirements for dangerous living. The love of adventure, which is one of the best measures of the magnitude of a man, becomes praiseworthy only when its risk is the risk attending all efforts to make men more intelligent and humane. It is hard to see how such adventure would be promoted by dividing the ultimate responsibility for the world's goals.

We turn from the demands of the revolters to their complaints.

H. THE PROBLEM OF EVIL

358. Is the Existence of Evil Consistent with the Character of God?

The heaviest score made by the revolters against monism is also the most ancient protest: there is so much suffering, thwarting, indifference, misery, tragedy, so much of what we collectively call "evil" in the total inventory of life on this planet, that we cannot reasonably attribute the whole affair to a single purpose, still less to a single righteous purpose. If there is any purpose behind things, they argue, it cannot be at the same time all-good and all-powerful.[1] For such a being would not, in the first place, have created a world so heavily mixed with pain and strife; nor would he remain inactive in view of human catastrophe. To believe in his goodness, therefore, we must believe that his power is limited, i.e., that there is something else, some opposition: our monism must be abandoned.

If our monism were of the physical variety, referring all things to an unconscious source, this difficulty would not arise. From such a source, necessarily indifferent to human welfare, we should expect nothing better than the mixture of black and white which we have. Man would simply be an incompletely

[1] See BR, No. 103, Harry Emerson Fosdick, "What About Evil?"

adjusted animal, with hope of overcoming some part of his troubles by the aid of science. The existence of evil would not be a "problem." But once we attribute the world to a single responsible source, there is a "problem of evil," for then the question will not down: "How is this evil consistent with the alleged goodness of God?"

359. A Classification of Evils

It will help the clarity of our thinking if we take a look at the kinds of evil we have to reckon with, and their amount. The pessimist's stock list — death, disease, desire, and disappointment — hardly helps our sense of proportion; for this reason, among others: that if death is an evil, then life on the whole must be good. I suggest that we make a rough grouping of our major sources of suffering, without pretending to anything like logical exactitude, as follows:

(1) Evils of our physical situation:
>   The resistance of nature, necessity of work, poverty
>   Defects of our bodily machine, liability to breakdown, inadequacy, collapse, age

(2) Evils of finitude:
>   Ignorance, limited foresight, limited power
>   Limited time

(3) Evils of mischance:
>   Pain and other physical suffering
>   Failure, defeat, disappointment, futility
>   Loss of health, position, reputation
>   Loss of friends, bereavement
>   Loss of sanity

(4) Evils of social history:
>   Injustice, hatred, the ravages of prejudice and cruelty, war, frustration in the attempt to do good, loss of hope
>   Preponderance of indifference, venality, material ambition in the environment
>   Historical triumph of force, greed, and cunning

(5) Evils of our cosmic situation and of thought:
>   The muteness of the universe, silence of God
>   The law of increase of suffering with increase of sensitivity and of sympathy
>   The curse of tedium and of commonplaceness

(6) Moral evil:
>   Vice and crime in general, my own share in the general moral status, and my own defect of duty.

360. The Utility of Three Kinds of Evil

Of these six types of evil, three can be crossed off as possible criticisms of the One. By definition, the moral evil is not his responsibility but our own. It may be questioned whether God should have produced free agents. Huxley once said, "I believe that if some power would substitute for his power of choice a mechanism which would carry him automatically into right behavior, he would willingly surrender what freedom he had." One has to reserve the right to doubt Mr. Huxley's psychology at that point. For if the highest achievement of the universe is an honest man, and if the will to be honest implies the possibility of being dishonest, then Huxley's notable honesty is worth more to the world than any mechanism which could have saved him from moral lapse (not that I know of any such on his part). The only logical condition under which a moral creature could arise is the possibility of immorality. No one can be courageous unless he feels fear, and fear contains the possibility of cowardly action. If it is worth while producing a creature who can freely decide to do right, it is necessary to produce one who can freely decide to do wrong.

The evils of finitude are in a somewhat similar case. They could only be escaped by putting us at the end of our journey at the start. It is hard to be ignorant; but there is no greater joy than the pleasure of discovery. We should be deprived of it if we were born with all knowledge. And the history of growth of all kinds adds to the value of what is achieved.

As to the evils of the physical situation, we have already shown how the fact of resistance is involved in the development of character.[1] It is not this fact which can be objected to, but the irregularity of its distribution, whereby some have "the breaks" and others have none. The trouble is not in the constitution of the world, but in the chances of fortune and social history.

361. The Evils of Social History and Their Meaning

It is these which usually come to mind when we draw up a bill of indictment against the world. Buddha's four cases of suffering were from this group: bereavement, beggary, disease, old age. The deep voices of compassion which in all civilizations

[1] See BR, No. 9, L. P. Jacks, "Life Functions in a Resisting Medium."

have undertaken to take the measure of the world's tragedy have taken their themes from these phases of experience, adding to them only two notes: that nobody escapes them, and that the higher a man's aspiration, the more poignant is the pain life can bring him. Buddha and Schopenhauer, looking beneath the surface of accidental misfortune, undertook to show that the very processes of life involve suffering, especially those connected with desire and hope. For desire, which is a sweetened pain so long as it lives in hope, is at its root painful, as confessing an absence of the thing desired; whereas its satisfaction, which we foolishly promise ourselves will be our happiness, is but the beginning of a new and sharpened period of longing. One satisfies his hunger and grows by eating: and the larger body becomes more hungry. Both Buddha and Schopenhauer therefore propose that the course of wisdom is to cut the root of desire and attempt to overcome that central illusion of all conscious being, the belief that life is good because it contains the gratification of desire.[1]

In the psychological picture of the human will, these shadows are present. The more we concentrate attention upon the day-to-day processes of conscious feeling and subconscious conflict, the more we agree with the Indian sage that "life is a burning." It may indeed be said that it is not normal for life to bend inward and concentrate on its own physiology; and when it directs itself outward, the draft of the will brings the flame of that burning into the promising channels of available power. Nobody really wants to get rid of the pain always incident to healthy action; we cannot act without destroying tissue, but when the organism is set up for the special purpose of replacing destroyed tissue with new, why dwell on the destruction rather than on the replacement and the end for which the destruction takes place? It is, in a sense, the glory of life that it incorporates death into its natural circuits: the constant surmounting of this inner destruction and burning is the essence of pleasure and zest. It is the pride of any sportsman that he can use up so much energy and yet be ready for the next contest. This is true; but it also remains true that, with the widened comprehension of life, there is a steadily stronger undertone of sadness; and it is

[1] See BR, No. 75 B, "Buddha's First Sermon."

not accidental that, both for the seer of India and the seer of Nazareth, the dominant note of their contemplation of the human lot is described in the same word, "compassion."

Granting this, we have to notice another fact. The compassionate *recognition* of the universal strand of suffering does something to the one who recognizes it. It reduces his preoccupation with his own share in the common lot. And it renders him far less concerned to be one of the lucky ones who escape the evils of fortune. So much of misery is due to the ruthlessness of competitive relationships and the sharpened resolve which they excite not to be among the losers that the only state of mind in which one can go in for this fight-to-win with a single mind is one of a hardening and narrowing range of human interest. There are some who become cynical because of the selfishness of others; there are still more who become cynical in order to tolerate their own selfishness. The natural impact of a broadening human understanding is a certain detachment from the necessity of personal possession and position. And in many of the greatest minds there is an impulse to renounce all that can be attributed to accident or even the reward of personal power, a strong wish *not to be separated from others* by the barrier of fortune and success. Such a one finds a compensating happiness in the unhindered leap of his sympathy — unhindered by the self-saving reflection, "I must keep what I have."

There are aspects of a community of human suffering which do something to relieve that suffering. One is the strengthening of human solidarity when the suffering does thus excite compassion rather than the *sauve qui peut* (every man for himself) impulse of escape. The other is an inner superiority to the domination of life by those goods which are most the sport of chance — the development of dignity of spirit. This is why dignity is more often found among people whose lives are hard than among those whose ease has come to them easily. It is perhaps why Buddhism, which at its best has given to so many millions in Asia a sense of cosmic care and with it a feeling of fraternity across all national borders, has lent a certain distinction to the carriage of many of the most poverty-ridden of all civilized peoples, in China, Burma, Tibet, and to some extent in India. Asia has too feebly fought her poverty. The stimulus of the

West is making her conscious that man must take into his own hand *the remediable evils;* that part of the meaning of evil is the eliciting of human self-reliance. But we of the West, in our own contest with poverty, have habitually assumed that economic good fortune is the essence of human welfare and poverty the essence of human tragedy. This means that we have lost something of the perspective of values which the East can still teach us. The type of man whom poverty can degrade is morally weaker than the type of man whom poverty cannot degrade.

362. Evil Always Has a Sequel, the Quality of which Depends on Us

With this in mind, we can say (a) that the evils of fortune are not the worst of evils — the worst is, to be beaten by them; and (b) that whether they are total and final evils or not depends on what we do about them. Evil always has a sequel. Its quality, taken by itself, is "bad," but its quality is never by itself: each evil has its mental environment and its history. If it is surrounded by companionship, it is lessened, and the companionship is heightened. If it is surrounded by the regimentation of scientific attack, as in the evils of disease, it adds to the meaning of human self-help and the international community of scientific effort. If it is surrounded by the spirit of adventure, win or lose, it may be the essence of a story men will not willingly forget. *It is the last reflection that gives the evil its quality;* and in the transmutations of memory, many a painful and even shameful past, intolerable at the moment, has become precious as an ingredient of a growing life.[1]

Everyone has his memories of hardship or humiliation which have changed their quality with time. Of those experiences he would answer as two men of my acquaintance answered who, one day at nightfall, stumbled exhausted into our camp in the Giant Forest in the upper Kaweah. They had taken their trail too early in the season and for two days had been near death as they inched their way around an ice-bound shoulder of one of the high Sierras. A day or two later I asked them, "Would you go through that again?" "Never." "Would you want to leave it out of your life?" "Not a bit of it!"

[1] See BR, No. 104, Rabindranath Tagore, "The Problem of Evil."

No one, therefore, can pretend to take the balance sheet of good and evil in human life unless he can estimate, not alone the local color of pleasure and pain as the moment turns them up, but also the gathering effect of their sequels and transformations up to and including the last reflection. But *what is that last reflection?* Unless you are dogmatically sure that the last moment of a man's life contains his last reflection upon that life, you are in no position to estimate the net worth of that life in terms of good and evil; and you are in no position to judge whether a creative purpose is or is not condemned by his works.

And let us add this remark: that those who are angry with the One because of the evil that is here are angry with their only hope of a radical solution of it. In a mechanical universe, we said, the same evils would be present; and we should fight them as we do now; and we should, as now, die and be mutilated in the fight. In such a universe, that *would* be the end of the story for those who die — a mingling of glory and wretchedness. It would be a glory insofar as one already sees a future achievement coming out of the inhuman strain and wreck. It would be wretchedness insofar as one feels caught in a mill of horror which no human mind is great enough to defeat and banish, the ever recurrent outpouring of treasure and genius for the ruin of what treasure and genius have created and for the crushing of the spirit that made them. The one hope that this confusion, protest, demand, shall have some response to those who thus perish is that the universe is itself not dead and callous but is living, remembering, and responsible to the questioning spirits whom it has brought to birth. Those who denounce the One because of evil denounce the only possible cure of evil for those who fall in the midst of it.

363. Ways of Taking Evil: (a) Renunciation

We have been thinking about evil with only one question in mind: Does it discredit the world-view which refers things to a single purpose? Our conclusion is that it does not. But we have other questions to put. Evil is not a generality; it is a fact of experience which each individual has to meet for himself. Its distribution is without regularity and without pretense of justice.

It strikes for the most part unexpectedly, and the first question is, "Why should this thing light on me?" And the second, "How am I to take it?"

There are plenty of troubles we bring on ourselves by our own folly; and in their case the answers are simply: these evils may very well be nature's punishment or her way of trying to teach us something. But the evils we are now concerned with are the mischances which can be referred to no obvious fault of our own — catastrophe, undeserved malice, the inherited consequences of the wicked policies of a prior generation, or plain bad luck. Somebody said, "After us, the deluge," and we are in the deluge. Even for these evils, the formula "Nature's punishment" is still invoked by some traditions: my trouble is my Karma — I am paying for my sins in a previous life; [1] or, I am meeting God's rebuke for some earlier guilt or for present pride; or, God is trying me out, or is trying to teach me patience. All these theories close their eyes to an obvious feature of the world — that men can inflict harm on one another. The suffering they can inflict has no necessary relation to the moral history of the individual so injured. And the attempt to find some guilt in order that the suffering may be explained as just is likely to add a new injury to the lot of the sufferer.

We shall assume, then, that undeserved suffering can occur, frequently does occur, and in a greater or lesser degree occurs to everybody. Where the causes are not human, *the question of justice is irrelevant*. Fuming about justice or injustice is quite clearly not the way to take it. Human nature has a great capacity to recover its emotional balance after a radical misfortune. The refugee camps after the San Francisco earthquake and fire in 1906 were places of remarkably good spirits and friendliness; they only became soured in spots when relief agents were suspected of partiality!

Now one way of taking such events is to tune down one's wishes. Obviously, if it were not for my desires, hopes, and claims, I should not be pained by any disappointments. I am always a party to any of my disappointments, for I can only be disappointed by failing in something I have promised *myself*. Why not adopt the policy of *making myself no promises where I*

[1] Cf. BR, No. 73 E, "Compensation (Karma) and Reincarnation in Hinduism."

cannot control the outcome. To do this thoroughly, I shall have to modify my ambitions and even curb my natural desires. This is, in fact, the systematic recommendation of many a philosophy and religion. It is at the heart of Buddhism and Hinduism; it is strong in Christianity and in Stoicism. "Set your affections . . . where moth and rust do not corrupt, and where thieves do not break through and steal"; i.e. deliberately change the course of your demand on the world, and then accidental changes in supply will leave you undisturbed. The Stoic advice was to enter no race in which you did not know that you could win. The Bhagavad Gita, seeing that men were bound to be involved in races and battles of uncertain outcome, gave a different counsel: "Fight your battle, but do so with a mind unmoved by victory or defeat." [1] The great Stoic Epictetus most systematically divided all the objects of human pursuit into two classes, those within our power and those not within our power; all the latter, such as health, property, position, reputation, success, even friendship, we must hold ourselves at heart free from — enjoy them if they come our way but so steel ourselves that they cannot make or unmake our happiness. We must bring ourselves to the point at which "Nothing can harm us but ourselves," for the gods have placed in our control the one great and sufficient good of self-respect, self-control, and the perception of the degrees of worth in men and things, the power of judgment. This attitude gave the Stoic his memorable courage in a decadent Rome: "The Emperor may take my head; but he cannot compel my good opinion." [2]

Modernity has come to think this attitude, the way of detachment and renunciation, unnatural and overstrained, and so, taken alone, it is. But something of it belongs to every character worth the name: the Stoic principle that desire *can be modified*, instead of being taken as a fixed deposit of nature, and that my serenity in the world will be assured in proportion as I temper the demands I make on external fortune. Not every man is called on to be an ascetic; but the existence of the man who has renounced "the world," or has vowed himself to "poverty, chastity, and obedience," is an evidence of the capacity of a

[1] Bhagavad Gita, chap. iii, p. 19; chap. xviii, p. 26.
[2] See BR, No. 25, Epictetus, "Stoicism: Virtue, the Highest Good."

sound and healthy human nature to simplify and concentrate the claims of the will.

364. Ways of Taking Evil: (b) Altruism

A second way of taking the evils of fortune is in contrast with the Stoic way. It is the way of Altruism, or service to others at the cost of one's own external welfare. The idea of the altruist is that it does not matter what happens to him personally if his cause is promoted. Instead of trying to build up an inner self-sufficiency and pride, the altruist aims to be as nearly as possible selfless; he is willing to be ignored, over-ridden, forgotten, for the sake of the thing he believes in. He merges his happiness with the happiness of his larger self, be that a person, a family, a nation, or an abstract object of loyalty such as science or art. The way of altruism, like that of the Stoic, involves a discipline and repression of personal desire and claim. But it makes the individual a social being rather than, like the Stoic, a solitaire, strong and lonely in his citadel of self-respect.

Modernity looks with greater favor on this attitude and pays it honor in friend or enemy. In doing so, it pays honor to the principle expressed in the paradox, "He that saveth his life shall lose it, and he that loseth his life for my sake, the same shall find it." This maxim the German philosopher, Hegel, concentrated in the formula, "Die to live," and regarded it as the rule of the universe as well as of the human individual. For he felt that God had performed an act of self-renunciation in merging his own action in the world with the action of nature.

But while the capacity for altruism, like that for Stoicism, is a necessary element of character, it is not enough, nor is it a satisfactory attitude toward the evils of circumstance. Nobody quite wants the completely selfless follower and servant, if such a state of mind could actually be achieved. For the man who has had no practice in the successful administration of his own affairs is not likely to be a good trustee of the affairs of others. The strong man who insists on having selfless followers and surrounds himself with yes-men is inviting not the prosperity but the collapse of his cause. Aristotle long ago exposed the weakness of this kind of power: "The best rule," he said, "is *rule over the best.*"

Altruism as a rule of life so evidently lacks some element of virility that it has provoked reaction, not in the name of the reassertion of natural enjoyment (as in the Renaissance) but in the name of the natural "will to power." In Nietzsche's ideal, the life of man on the earth is no release from suffering; here he and Christianity agree. For Christianity, in contrast with Buddhism, promises its followers not less trouble in this world, but more; and it asks them to consider themselves blessed when they are persecuted. Nietzsche, likewise, defines the life of the spirit as the life that "does surgery on itself," and involves itself deliberately in greater pain rather than less. But the pain which Nietzsche's disciple invites is not the pain of sympathy or help for the afflicted and the weak; it is the pain of creation, of bringing to birth a better race, even at the cost of hardness to others and to oneself.[1] His Zarathustra speaks as follows:

> To myself I offer my love, and to my neighbor as myself.
> But the will of all great love is,
>   the beloved one to *create;*
> And *all creators are hard.*

Now Nietzsche has something to say to a one-sided Altruism and a one-sided Stoicism; but his will to power is too much a solitary feat of strength. It is a dramatic protest, right in its criticism but headed for futility, the one thing it tries to escape. We require a third attitude toward evil, beyond Stoicism, beyond Altruism and Nietzsche. It has no name, but we may refer to it as the way of *aggressive transformation.*

365. Ways of Taking Evil: (c) Aggressive Transformation

It goes without saying that activity meets a different kind of evil than does quiescence. A ship staying permanently in harbor meets the evil of rot; the same ship at sea meets the danger of storm. Most men are willing for the active sort of encounter with evil, if they have an errand which takes them into it and which is *their errand.* If their errand brings them opposition, then what they actively suffer becomes significant, as the rot-in-port suffering is not significant. The defect of the altruistic sort of acceptance of evil is that the objective is not enough *one's own task* in the world; it leaves it an open question why one exists.

---

[1] See BR, No. 31, Nietzsche, "The Origin of Morals."

But a task which is *only* one's own can be served only by self-assertion. What we require is a task which is one's own, *as a part of something necessary and eternal:* to fight for this sort of thing is to have an assurance of success, even if one seems to fail. As Socrates once put it when someone said it was hard to argue against Socrates: "It is not hard to argue against Socrates, but it is hard to argue against the truth." This is perhaps Nietzsche's chief difficulty: he has omitted the third partner. In declaring that God is dead, he has set aside the only element that could assure the success of his will to power, because he refuses to be working with the All-powerful.

No man ought to be content to be superfluous in the world. He ought to demand of his life that he count for something; that he attain a success which is not accidental but necessary, and that he have in it the inner persuasion of achievement. It is this which the Stoic and Altruist appear to abandon as impossible; and yet it is that which, without quite seeing it, they are trying to secure by a *transformation of ambition.* Now the transformation is necessary; but not the transformation of retreat nor that of self-abandonment. It is the transformation of finding one's specific task and limiting oneself to that. One cannot succeed in everything; one can only surely succeed in contributing to the world that idea which is one's own unique sight of things.

The point is that history, in spite of all appearances, is a tissue of ideas. An idea is the one thing to which all history is vulnerable, the one thing men in turmoil hope for, the one thing of which human evil is afraid. It was said savagely of Rousseau, "He wrote a book consisting of nothing but ideas; the skins of those who scoffed at him went to bind the second edition." No man is irresistible by himself; as a partner with a necessary step of thought, crucifixion itself cannot cancel his impression. For the universe, being alive and itself a truth-force, is with him. A man must find his own place in the idea-movement; he has something no one else has; without haste, self-conceit, anxiety, noise, he must do what that task demands. He will find his own share of pain; humanity still punishes those who try honestly to serve it. But this will be the aggressive transformation of suffering. And it will be for him the positive, rather than the negative, answer to the problem of evil.

I. SUMMARY OF WORLD–VIEW

366. The Wonder of Existence as a Stimulus to Philosophy

Philosophy, it is said, begins in wonder. Where does it end? Surely, not with the banishment of wonder.

The banishment of wonder would be a loss, not a gain. For wonder is not mystification nor inquisitiveness. Wonder is the opening of the eyes to an unexpected majesty, which is also an invitation to enter on what is our own. The world is infinite, and it does not repel us; it does not wholly rebuke the perspective of the minute human observer as out of place. It is our world.

The wonder that persists, and has grown, is not without its mystery. Herbert Spencer was not far wrong when he said that the one most certain truth, the one in which religion and science come to complete agreement, is that of the ultimate mystery of things. A Japanese student who came to America to study theology complained because "everything was made too clear." He missed the sense of vastness and unexplored wealth opened to him in the meditation halls of the Buddhist temples in his high northern hills. Mystery, too, if it means depth and the endless unfinishedness of the work of thought, is a part of the truth.

367. Some Certainties of Science, and of Philosophy: The World Has a Meaning

But what we have gained is a line or two of definition within the frame of the whole. There are certitudes of science: they have their place. There are also certitudes of philosophy.

Science avoids hastening to totalities in its assertions and prefers to regard its hypotheses as merely probable. But it achieves reliable and usable knowledge, and its projections of past and future have the corroboration of carefully tested predictions. Science gives us the foreground of every future world-view, so far as the world is measurable and socially observable. The causal order has become the ballast of every world-scheme. It is not an object of dispute. It only becomes such if it attempts, unscientifically, to exclude the purposive order with which it is everywhere tangent and to which, at one point, it becomes subordinate, that of the human will.

But what are the certitudes which belong especially to philosophy? They are not many. And not many are wanted. Not many stars are necessary to give a ship its bearings; sometimes one is sufficient. That one makes all the difference between having a direction and having a dead-reckoning guess. So it is with man in the world; if he has one point of certitude, he can navigate; if he has none, he is adrift.

One point of philosophic certitude is that the world has a meaning. It is not just an assemblage of interesting facts, with the fascination which lures the mind into the immensities of astronomical thought-journeyings. It exists *for* something. For what? We have only an inkling, namely, that we are a part of it. It is not necessary to know the "what" in any detail; it is necessary to know the "that." I must be sure that the thing is not meaningless, that is, pointless and purposeless, in its whole being. The "that" is more important than the "what."

To know "that" the world has a meaning, we shall call the philosophic minimum. It is the position of one philosophical school, which might be called the school of reticence though it is usually called the school of mysticism, that this is as far as we can go and as far as we need to go. The position may be illustrated by an episode in a recent novel in which two characters, Fergus and Saber, are engaged in solving problems at chess. Fergus has a belief which Saber regards as at least semi-superstitious — that every man has a mission marked out for him in the destiny of things, and that he must prepare himself to carry it out, though he must first find out what it is. Saber puts to him the skeptical question:

"How can you work toward a purpose, if you don't know what it is?"
"How can you work toward a [chess] solution, if you don't know what it is?"
"Yes, but you know that there *is* a solution."
"Well, there you are. And you know that there *is* a purpose."

That knowledge is all that is necessary to sustain the long labor of discovering and carrying out the mission. Without that minimal knowledge, there is no assurance that all the effort is not labor lost.

368. The Source of the World's Meaning Is One Mind

But this minimum carries with it certain other matters. If the world has a meaning, there is a "meaner," a Being whose nature is like the human self. Meanings cannot exist in detachment, as a realm of ideas in abstraction from any thought which thinks them. To say that meanings are meant is to say that the source of things is mind, not matter.

And if there is a meaning, there must be unity in that mind; for a clash of meanings would give not a meaning, but a confusion, a discord, or perhaps a neutralization. Since the meaning of things is plotted on the trend of the physical world, and since that trend is single (except for the shaping due to the inventions and decisions of free agents, such as human wills), the world is to be referred to a single purpose, which is what men have called God.

From the meaning of the whole, there follows also the meaning of the parts. This means all the parts, including the vast emptinesses, the wastes, and all the evils inherent in the physical arrangements of the world and the finitude of the human beings that emerge. Just as à park, planned as a whole, may include a planned area of wild growth, so a universe, purposed as a whole, may include a purposed factor of the empty, the waste, the arbitrary, as significant elements in the environment of conscious beings. To the human eye, the waste of worlds untenanted and the unimaginable intervals of space which separate the careers of the galaxies become items of value in the perspective of the universe.

369. The Uniqueness, Greatness, and Happiness of Man

And especially there follows the significance of man, whose self-estimate is not contradicted by the astro-physical picture of his petty corner of immensity, and is supported by the biological supremacy of man among the animals. All other living creatures are also "outcomes" and are equally with him the surviving products of a long biological ancestry. But the uniquenesses of the position of man which we have indicated justify his sense that his presence is at least one of the objects of the total cosmic history, so far as it is purposive.

Man is a creature having purpose. In man, purpose has produced purpose, freedom has produced freedom, creative power has produced creative power. He who entertains the eternal Ideas has produced a finite being who can participate in the appreciation of those same standards of truth, of goodness, and of beauty. This is what is meant by the saying, found in many of the great traditions of religion and philosophy, that man is "made in the image of God," [1] or that he "shares in the divine nature," that he is a "spark of Zeus," that he "has the Buddha nature in him," that he is "a little spark of God" (Meister Eckhart, "Fünklein Gottes").

This power of man to share, however dimly, in the perception of the true nature of standards is the source of his dignity, and at the same time of a momentous distinction: he is the only creature who can conceive his life as a whole as having something to carry out. His life is haunted — and in a way complicated — by a feeling of total duty or mission which he cannot shake off, although he sometimes tries to displace it by angry and ear-filling diversions.

At the same time, this responsibility to a purpose beyond his own contains his greatest possibility of happiness. For, while all the instincts offer their own promises of satisfaction, there is one instinct which requires to be satisfied — one only. It is the will to power, understood not as power over others, but as power for them, the power to serve and enrich the world by building into human history those feelings and ideas which are, at first, nothing but private states of mind. Power of this sort begins with seeing something wrong in the world or something needed — the capacity to criticize is universal! But among many objects of criticism some one may be joined with a second thought: "This is where my special ability has work to do"; the will to power is beginning to stir. What a man cannot endure is to count for nothing in the world's business; if he counts, he can stand the loss of most other things. There is his happiness. Such happiness promises no escape from suffering. It promises only a share in the necessary advance of man.

What one thus does *lasts*, because it makes connection with the ultimate purpose, which is irresistible. As an ancient Chinese saying has it, "The good man is a third partner with Heaven and Earth."

[1] See BR, No. 77 F, Judaism, "What Is Man?"

370. The World's Resources for Human Satisfaction

Thus, from the minimum certitude of philosophy, the simple affirmation that the world has a meaning, many things follow. But we may add to those one further trait of our world-view which comes rather from experience than from philosophical deduction; namely, the extent of the world's resources for human satisfaction.

The unity and regularity of the world is a sort of ground plan: it is like the bare and uncolored fabric into which the pattern of a tapestry is to be embroidered. It outlines the frame in which living is set; it has nothing to say of the discovery, the imagination, the adventure which will provide the design. In respect to this filling, the world is no monism; it is open at both ends. The past is not all carried along in memory; much of its rubbish, its nonsense, its error, having yielded its lesson, is forgotten. Forgiveness and new beginnings are cosmic facts as well as human facts. And toward the future, the task is not the carrying out of a preordained plan. Cooperation with the eternal leaves the human will its widest freedom to create novelty, to shape ways which were never in any mind, not even the mind of God.[1]

It is because of this, that every source of enjoyment comes for the first time with the character of a discovery. What color is, the blind can hear described but cannot imagine. What music is, no one can predict until music is made and heard; what Bach's music is, though it verges near to the realm of pure thought, no one could deduce from the general idea of music. And until Bach has written down his prelude (though it has lain all the time in the list of the mechanical possibilities of tone), that conception is, in the entire universe, strictly nonexistent. It is a pure addition to the wealth of the spirit.

All such discovery has a strange power. The opening of the eyes to beauty, like the opening of the mind to love, is itself an experience of such intrinsic happiness that it not alone cancels the memory of pain; it demands pain, as it were, to express its recognition. When one has felt it, one craves the privilege of serving and suffering for that exalted thing. With a universe whose wine vat is forever filling up with these creations, the problem of evil falls away.

[1] See BR, No. 105, William Yerington, "The Open Future."

371. Twelve Propositions by Way of Conclusion

In conclusion, let us resume in a number of propositions the main results at which our discussion has arrived. (We shall state them, for the sake of brevity, without the modifications which they need to be altogether exact; but these the reader of this text will be able to supply for himself.)

(1) There are two main kinds of order in the world, an order of classes (for things existing at the same time) and an order of events. The order of classes runs up to a unity chiefly because the mind works that way: it classifies its classes into higher classes, until it reaches the all-inclusive class, "being." This leaves open the question whether there is or is not any inclusive unity in the objects themselves.

(2) Of the events in time-sequence, there are two orders, a causal order and a purposive order. The fact that the causal order applies to all events, on the principle that every event has a cause, cannot exclude the actual existence of a purposive order, of which we are aware in ourselves, nor the possibility of a corresponding principle that every event has a purpose.

(3) These two orders are not independent; they constitute, not a dualism, but a single system of events.

(4) The purposive system can explain and include the causal system. The causal system cannot explain nor include the purposive system. Thus the purposive system must be the beginning of any explanation of the world. The physical must be understood from the mental, not the mental from the physical.

(5) This means that the event-structure of the world has its unity in purpose. And this purpose must be one and not many. The singleness of the causal order implies a corresponding singleness of the purposive order.

(6) This single purpose corresponds with the unity in the order of classes. The unity of purpose is the unity of being. This is the result which, in religious terms, is called the existence of God, as the one real from which all other things are derived.

(7) This proposition implies the following propositions: (a) the world has a meaning; (b) nothing in the world is meaningless, not even its wastes and its evils; (c) the existence of mankind has a meaning; (d) the existence of individual men has a meaning.

(8) Proposition 6 does not imply: (a) that the world has, or has not, a beginning in time; (b) that nothing is added to the world since the original deposit or creation of the physical order; (c) that there is no other space-time order than the one present to scientific inquiry; (d) that the human self is destroyed with the death of the body.

(9) In bringing forth man, the universe has brought forth a mind which is free and creative. Its freedom implies its power to determine the future from conceived alternatives; also its power to err, to reject duty, and to injure. Its creativity implies its capacity to add to creation and to cooperate with the original purpose in the finishing of the world.

(10) If man can cooperate with God, man must be able to grasp in substance, though not in plan, the nature of God's purpose: goodness and right must be the same for man and God, not different; truth must be the same; beauty must be the same. This is what is meant by the proposition, found in Buddhism, in Vedanta, in Stoicism, in Christianity, and in other traditions, that man "shares in the nature of God."

(11) This constitutes the dignity of human nature and, at the same time, the obligation of human beings.[1] Life is an occasion in which obligation, opportunity, and happiness normally coincide.

(12) Life is also an occasion in which the fulfillment of one's task is likely to be attended with suffering. But the suffering which is a consequence of the aggressive fulfillment of duty is significant suffering and loses the sting of pure accident or pure loss. And in it there need be no defeat; but rather the assured fulfillment of the deepest will of the individual.

[1] See BR, No. 106, Walt Whitman, "The Base of All Metaphysics."

INDEX